ELECTIONS AND DEMOCRATIC THEORY

Election Law, Politics, and Theory

Series Editor: David Schultz

Election Law, Politics, and Theory broadly examines election law at the national, subnational, and international or comparative levels. Titles in the series provide both empirical and theoretical analysis of topics and issues that affect voting, campaigns, and elections, and as such offer coverage of political as well as legal concerns and controversies. Useful for scholars, researchers, and practitioners in the field, volumes address such subjects as voting rights, reapportionment, ballot access, campaign finance reform, the courts and election regulation, and the role of actors including political parties and the media. The series' ultimate goal is to build scholarship in this key area by seeking to understand how elections function in an increasingly complex, technological, and global community, and the ways in which election law impacts outcomes, disputes, and eventually governance in particular nations and societies.

Other titles in this series

Group Representation, Feminist Theory, and the Promise of Justice
Angela D. Ledford
ISBN 978 1 4094 1843 6

**Political Parties and Elections
Legislating for Representative Democracy**
Anika Gauja
ISBN 978 0 7546 7704 8

**Electoral College Reform
Challenges and Possibilities**
Edited by Gary Bugh
ISBN 978 0 7546 7751 2

**State Secretaries of State
Guardians of the Democratic Process**
Jocelyn F. Benson
ISBN 978 0 7546 7745 1

For more information, visit www.ashgate.com

Election Law and Democratic Theory

DAVID SCHULTZ
Hamline University and University of Minnesota Law School, USA

LONDON AND NEW YORK

First published 2014 by Ashgate Publishing

Published 2016 by Routledge
2 Park Square, Milton Park, Abingdon, Oxfordshire OX14 4RN
711 Third Avenue, New York, NY 10017, USA

First issued in paperback 2016

Routledge is an imprint of the Taylor & Francis Group, an informa business

Copyright © 2014 David Schultz

David Schultz has asserted his right under the Copyright, Designs and Patents Act, 1988, to be identified as the author of this work.

All rights reserved. No part of this book may be reprinted or reproduced or utilised in any form or by any electronic, mechanical, or other means, now known or hereafter invented, including photocopying and recording, or in any information storage or retrieval system, without permission in writing from the publishers.

Notices:

Product or corporate names may be trademarks or registered trademarks, and are used only for identification and explanation without intent to infringe.

British Library Cataloguing in Publication Data
A catalogue record for this book is available from the British Library

The Library of Congress has cataloged the printed edition as follows:
Schultz, David A. (David Andrew), 1958– author.
  Election law and democratic theory : by David Schultz.
      pages cm.—(Election law, politics, and theory)
  Includes an index.
  ISBN 978-0-7546-7543-3 (hardback)
  1. Election law—United States. 2. United States—Politics and government.
  3. Democracy—United States—Philosophy. I. Title.
  KF4886.S38 2013
  342.73'0701—dc23
                                                                            2013032373

ISBN 13: 978-1-138-24872-4 (pbk)
ISBN 13: 978-0-7546-7543-3 (hbk)

Contents

Acknowledgments		*vii*
Introduction: Why Theory?		1
1	Theory: The Missing Piece in Election Law Scholarship and Adjudication	13
2	Democratic Theory and American Politics	45
3	Voting Rights	83
4	Minority Rights and the Failure of Direct Democracy	119
5	Representation and Reapportionment	137
6	Political Parties	197
7	Money, Politics, and Campaign Financing	229
Conclusion: Toward a Democratic Theory of Election Law		269
Index		*275*
Table of Cases		*285*

To Dan Lowenstein—without whose influence this book would not have been possible.

Acknowledgments

Alfred North Whitehead once declared all of philosophy is a series of footnotes to Plato. In stating that, he pointed to the indebtedness that scholars have to others and to the fact that no book or article is truly original or produced in isolation. The same is the case with this book. In so many ways, *Democratic Theory and Election Law* is a product forged by many experiences. It is of course an outgrowth of teaching election law at Hamline University, the University of Minnesota, and the American University at Armenia for nearly 15 years. It is also a product of nearly 25 years of teaching in the United States and abroad, as well as talking to thousands of reporters, citizens, colleagues, and students. In so many ways, the ideas here on democracy have been tossed around since my days as an undergraduate student and they have been refined and retooled over the years. It is impossible to recount or remember everyone whom I have intellectually profited from, but I am clearly indebted to many and thank them for encouraging my interest in election law.

Throughout a career thinking about democracy and the law I have immensely benefitted from conversations with and from the scholarship of so many others. In particular, two individuals stand out. The first is Dan Lowenstein—really the inventor of the field of election law—and John Shockley, a colleague of mine at Gustavus Adolphus College when I first started teaching. Dan and I first met in the early 1990s when I was writing about Justice Scalia. Our paths crossed because of our mutual interests in law and politics and he was so kind as to send me a crate of handouts and materials that would eventually form the basis of the first edition of his *Election Law* casebook. John and I wrote what was to be my first article on election law. My experiences with both stimulated an interest in election law that has continued to this day. To a significant extent, this book builds upon past scholarship and development of ideas that owe their origins to my association with Dan and John.

This book hopefully represents a deepening of ideas previously articulated in writing. Specifically, Chapter 3 is adapted in part from "Is Voter Fraud Like Littering?: Empirical and Methodological Considerations," *American Review of Politics*, 231 (Fall 2012) and "Less than Fundamental: The Myth of Voter Fraud and the Coming of the Second Great Disenfranchisement," 34 *William Mitchell Law Review* 484 (2008).

Chapter 5 is adapted in part from "Regulating the Political Thicket: Congress, the Courts, and State Reapportionment Commissions," 3 *Charleston Law Review* 109 (2008) and "The Party's Over: Partisan Gerrymandering and the First Amendment," 36 *Capital Law Review* 1 (2007).

Chapter 7 is adapted in part from *"Buckley v. Valeo, Randall v. Sorrell,* and the Future of Campaign Financing on the Roberts Court," 12 *Nexus* 153 (2007), "Disclosure is not Enough: Empirical Lessons from State Experiences," 4 *Election Law Journal* 349 (2005), and "Revisiting *Buckley v. Valeo*: Eviscerating the Line Between Candidate Contributions and Independent Expenditures," 14 *Journal of Law & Politics* 33 (1998).

Finally, thanks go to Helene who has heard me talk about these ideas way too much. She is always there to support me.

Introduction
Why Theory?

Election law disputes are some of the most contentious issues in politics. Yet the answers provided by the Supreme and other courts often fail to resolve debates because they look as if their rulings are simply edicts. Perhaps that is because election law is an endeavor in search of a political theory.

In the United States, election law as a field of study is young. Daniel Lowenstein, emeritus professor at UCLA, perhaps pioneered the field and gave it legitimacy when he published the first election law casebook in 1995.[1] Prior to that his election law class at UCLA Law School was taught with handouts of cases and materials, none of which had been assembled into a book. But even in 1995, the number of academics who taught election law or identified themselves as scholars in this field was quite thin, perhaps constituting merely a handful or so of law professors across the country. But then Florida 2000 happened. Florida 2000 refers to the controversy surrounding the 2000 presidential election between Al Gore and George Bush.[2] The election unfolded without major controversy on election day and into the night. At one point the major network news channels, using exit polls, declared Al Gore the winner of the election in that state and therefore the next president of the United States. But then something funny happened, the major news services retracted their projections. What then unfolded over the next several weeks was a major news item across the state, nation, and perhaps even around the world.

Stories from the Sunshine State soon revealed that there were a host of problems with ballots and voting. On the one hand in places such as Palm Beach County a

---

1 DANIEL LOWENSTEIN, ELECTION LAW: CASES AND MATERIALS (1995).

2 Descriptions and critiques of what the entire Bush v. Gore Florida controversy are plentiful. *See:* VINCENT BUGLIOSI, THE BETRAYAL OF AMERICA : HOW THE SUPREME COURT UNDERMINED THE CONSTITUTION AND CHOSE OUR PRESIDENT (2001); JAMES W. CEASER AND ANDREW E. BUSCH, THE PERFECT TIE: THE TRUE STORY OF THE 2000 PRESIDENTIAL ELECTION (2001); ALAN M DERSHOWITZ, SUPREME INJUSTICE: HOW THE HIGH COURT HIJACKED ELECTION 2000 (2001); E.J. DIONNE, JR., AND WILLIAM KRISTOL, BUSH V. GORE: THE COURT CASES AND THE COMMENTARY (2001); HOWARD GILLMAN, THE VOTES THAT COUNTED: HOW THE COURT DECIDED THE 2000 PRESIDENTIAL ELECTION (2001); CASS R. SUNSTEIN AND RICHARD A. EPSTEIN, THE VOTE: BUSH, GORE, AND THE SUPREME COURT (2001); ABNER GREENE, UNDERSTANDING THE 2000 ELECTION: A GUIDE TO THE LEGAL BATTLES THAT DECIDED THE PRESIDENCY (2001); DOUGLAS KELLNER, GRAND THEFT 2000: MEDIA SPECTACLE AND A STOLEN ELECTION (2001); RICHARD A. POSNER, BREAKING THE DEADLOCK: THE 2000 ELECTION, THE CONSTITUTION, AND THE COURTS (2001); JACK N. RAKOVE, THE UNFINISHED ELECTION OF 2000: LEADING SCHOLARS EXAMINE AMERICA'S STRANGEST ELECTION (2001).

ballot design soon to become famously called the "butterfly ballot" revealed that many voters might have miscast their votes for Pat Buchanan and not Al Gore. Other accounts rumored of defective absentee ballots that could not be counted. Or that public officials were cooperating with Republicans in the processing and correcting of absentee ballots. Some contended that felon disenfranchisement laws—laws that barred individuals convicted of felonies from voting, often for life as in Florida—were being aggressively enforced by a Republican Secretary of State, Katherine Harris, to the detriment of the Democrats and the benefit of George Bush, for whom she was the state campaign manager. Still other stories told of voting locations mysteriously being closed or moved. Still others asserted voter fraud and that the dead, felons, immigrants, or others were forging themselves into the voting booths.

But on top of all of these stories, the American public was treated to a new vocabulary. The public learned that one type of voting technology to record votes—punch cards—was defective. When voters inserted the stylus to cast a vote often times the vote was not properly recorded since it did not completely cut out a hole in the paper. This piece of paper Americans came to learn was called a chad. Punch card voting mechanisms could produce several results including what came to be known as hanging chads, dimpled chads, and pregnant chads. All referred to various ways that a voter sought to mark the ballot. But the question emerged: What did the voter intend or seek to do? As would eventually be shown on television and in the media, election officials across several Florida counties would hold up ballots and try to make sense out of ballots, asking if a dimpled or hanging chad was indication of a particular voter's choice. This is where the real controversy occurred.

Republicans and Democrats fought over all of the above issues as calls for a recount mounted in an election where the number of votes separating the two was merely a few hundred out of millions cast. One issue was over how to count disputed ballots. This battle took place under the aegis of a clock. It was a clock to count the votes and decide a winner in time for the Electoral College to meet to decide how to cast Florida's votes for president. It also took place cognizant of the need to seat a new president by January 20, 2001, and it took place under the impatient eyes of the media and a public demanding quick resolution of the race and skeptical that some partisan shenanigans were afoot. But this controversy soon revealed how complex it would be to declare a winner quickly. Not only had the issue become a major political controversy but resolution involved difficult and overlapping issues involving constitutional, federal, and state law.

The Florida 2000 controversy resulted in several state and federal court decisions. There were two cases before the Florida Supreme Court, the first of which produced a unanimous decision favorable to Gore prompting calls that this was a Democratic Party leaning decision.[3] But soon that decision was overturned by

---

3 Palm Beach County Canvassing Bd. v. Harris, 772 So. 2d 1220 (Fla. 2000).

the United States Supreme Court[4] prompting additional litigation, another Florida Supreme Court decision—this time a split 4-3 one[5]—and then more recounts in several counties. All of this culminated in a surprising and controversial temporary restraining order by the US Supreme Court to halt the counting,[6] and then a decision by the Court in *Bush v. Gore* that ruled in favor of Bush, declared that there was no more time to do ballot counting, and that it was time to pronounce the election over.[7] The Supreme Court, and not the people, had effectively decided who would become president of the United States.

Bush v. Gore put election law on the map in the United States. *Bush v. Gore* represents more than a single simple court case. It symbolizes a constellation of election issues that came to light in the 2000 presidential race. Americans learned that millions of votes cast are often not counted because of defective voting technology. They learned about rules regulating who can vote, where, and how, and about complex laws on ballot access for minor parties, and how the appearance of third party candidates such as Ralph Nader might impact the way elections are run. *Bush v. Gore* simply highlighted the fact that American democracy and its electoral process are governed and structured by complex rules. But it did not stop with that decision.

Since Florida 2000 other disputes have brought focus to the ways that the law can determine the outcome of elections. In fact, since 1996 there has been a dramatic increase in election law challenges and litigation, not just after an election but before.[8] Such litigation is testimony to how important the laws are to determining how elections are run. Questions surrounded allegations of voter suppression and irregular voting patterns in several Ohio counties during the 2004 presidential election, again leading to allegations by some that Bush had yet again stolen the election.[9] Then in 2008 in Minnesota a hotly contested Senate race between incumbent Republican Norm Coleman (who won in a legally contested race in 2002 over Walter Mondale after he replaced Senator Paul Wellstone who died in a plane crash just days before the election and there were disputes over how to allocate absentee ballots for him)[10] and former *SNL* and Air America writer host Al Franken ended in a virtual tie with the former ahead by merely a few hundred votes. After nearly eight months of recounts, litigation, and a repeating

---

4   Bush v. Palm Beach County Canvassing Board, 531 U.S. 70 (2000).

5   Palm Beach County Canvassing Bd. v. Harris, 772 So. 2d 1273 (2000).

6   Palm Beach County Canvassing Bd. v. Harris, 531 U.S. 1036 (2000).

7   Bush v. Gore, 531 U.S. 98 (2000).

8   Richard L. Hasen, *Judges as Political Regulators: Evidence and Options for Institutional Change*, in GUY-URIEL E. CHARLES, HEATHER K. GERKEN, AND MICHAEL S. KANG, EDS., RACE, REFORM, AND REGULATION OF THE ELECTORAL PROCESS, 101 (2011).

9   ROBERT J. FITRAKIS, STEVEN ROSENFELD, AND HARVEY WASSERMAN, WHAT HAPPENED IN OHIO: A DOCUMENTARY RECORD OF THEFT AND FRAUD IN THE 2004 ELECTION (2006).

10   *See:* Erlandson v. Kiffmeyer, 659 N.W.2d 724 (2003), for a discussion of the legal issues surrounding the allocation of already cast absentee ballots for Senator Wellstone in the 2002 Minnesota Senate race.

of legal arguments reminiscent of those raised in *Bush v. Gore*, Franken emerged as the winner by a mere 312 votes when the Minnesota Supreme Court ruled in his favor.[11] Again allegations of a stolen election were shot across the country, as well as claims that yet again the courts and not the people had decided the outcome of an election.[12] Yet again in Minnesota, this time in 2010, a close governor's race between Mark Dayton and Tom Emmer yielded a vote total for the two that differed by barely 0.5 percent, triggering another recount, court litigation,[13] and again cries of fraud and theft.[14]

But beyond specific disputes over who won a race, election law has crept into the news repeatedly. In 2002 the McCain-Feingold Act was enacted to bring some order and limits to money in politics. While initially the Supreme Court in *McConnell v. Federal Election Commission* effectively upheld the entire act,[15] subsequent decisions by the Supreme Court under Chief Justice Roberts have rethought the role of money and politics and rejected many of its key provisions.[16] Perhaps among the most notable of recent Court decisions addressing money and politics has been its 2010 *Citizens United v. Federal Election Commission* decision where it ruled that the First Amendment protected the right of corporations to expend money for the purposes of opposing or endorsing candidates in federal elections. While the decisions also freed up labor unions to do the same, and the decision affected many state laws that had barred corporate expenditures, the real attention was on federal law and corporations, prompting many to worry about the impact of corporations on national races such as the presidency. The impact of the decision and then in *Speechnow.org v. Federal Election Commission*[17] in unleashing what have now come to be called Super-PACs was already felt in 2010 as corporate spending rose dramatically. The same was true in the early 2012 Republican Party primaries as unaffiliated Super-PACs unleashed a flood of money and attack advertisements. Election law yet again proved to be important.

Two other issues in the news demonstrate the increasing attention that election law now garners. The best social science research fails to detect in-person voter

---

11   Coleman v. Franken, 767 N.W.2d 453 (Minn. 2009).

12   *See:* Jay Weiner, This Is Not Florida: How Al Franken Won the Minnesota Senate Recount (2010), for a discussion of the history and controversy surrounding the Franken-Coleman race.

13   In re Petition regarding 2010 Gubernatorial Election, 790 N.W.2d 706 (Minn. 2010).

14   Baird Helgeson and Rachel Stassen-Berger, *Guv's Race: Long Ride, No End in Sight*, Minneapolis Star Tribune (November 4, 2010), at A1.

15   540 U.S. 93 (2003).

16   *See:* Federal Election Commission v. Wisconsin Right to Life, Inc., 551 U.S. 449 (2007); Davis v. Federal Election Commission, 554 U.S. 724 (2008); and Citizens United v. Federal Election Commission, 558 U.S. 50 (2010).

17   Speechnow.org. v. Federal Election Commission, 599 F.3d 686 (Ct. App. D.C., 2010).

fraud as a serious problem.[18] Despite this lack of evidence, polling data suggest that 75 percent of the American public support the showing of photo identification at the polls to detect fraud.[19] In 2011, bills in 34 states were introduced calling for photo identification for in-person voting.[20] In 12 states both houses of the legislature passed the bill, and after vetoes, a total of nine states now have photo identification requirements for voting. In 2012 more states attempted to pass similar legislation. Opponents have fought voter identification bills and the decision by the Justice Department, in March 2012, to use the Voting Right Act to refuse pre-clearance to the Texas law (and in April 2012 with South Carolina) guaranteed that these decisions would face further litigation.

The debate over voter fraud and identification is about election law. It is about the rules that govern who is entitled to vote and how. It is about—depending on whom you listen to—efforts to rig the electorate and determine the outcome of elections, versus the efforts to ensure that ballots are secure, votes are legal, and that there is no one voting in an election who should not. But however the debate is cast, it certainly is one that has major implications in terms of how elections are run.

Finally, turn to the 2012 elections and more specifically the Republican primaries to select a nominee. Getting on the ballot is never easy, and the state of Virginia required candidates to produce 10,000 signatures in order to qualify for the Republican primary. This necessitated candidates to circulate ballot petitions but Virginia made it illegal to employ or use non-residents to gather the signatures. Because of this requirement, Rick Perry, Newt Gingrich, and other Republican presidential candidates failed to produce the requisite number of signatures to qualify for the ballot. They challenged the law, eventually prevailing in their claim that the ban on out-of-state petition circulators violated the First Amendment, yet losing on other grounds.[21] Laws such as those in Virginia determine who gets on the ballot. Again, this is election law in action.

The point is that the once sleepy field of election law is now a center of news. From the time when Dan Lowenstein produced the first election law textbook and few taught the subject it has now changed with several competing texts and a dramatic growth in the number of people teaching the subject. It does not seem that a Supreme Court term goes by now without a major election law case docketed and decided. Questions over who can vote, who has access to the ballot, who can

---

18 David Schultz, *Less than Fundamental: The Myth of Voter Fraud and the Coming of the Second Great Disenfranchisement*, 34 WILLIAM MITCHELL L. REV. 484 (2008).

19 Rasmussen Reports, *75% Support Showing Photo ID At The Polls* (2011), available at http://www.rasmussenreports.com/public_content/politics/general_politics/june_2011/75_support_showing_photo_id_at_the_polls (site last visited on June 2, 2012).

20 WENDY R. WEISER AND LAWRENCE NORDEN, VOTING LAW CHANGES IN 2012 (2011), available at http://brennan.3cdn.net/9c0a034a4b3c68a2af_9hm6bj6d0.pdf (site last visited on June 2, 2012).

21 Perry v. Judd, 840 F.Supp.2d 945 (E.D.Va., 2012).

spend money and how, along with a host of similar questions, are recurrent topics in the media.

But the decisions are controversial. They are so because, as noted, they define who runs or who gets elected and how. But more so, they are controversial because election law is the wiring that gives life or meaning to a political system, such as a democracy. While some may say "show me the money" or the budget when seeking to see if someone is serious about supporting some program, one can really decide the character of a political system by asking to look at its election laws. In the American context, election law is the law of democracy—it is the set of laws that make our political system actually operate.

But the decisions are controversial also because they are about power. Political scientist David Easton once stated that politics is about the authoritative allocation of values.[22] It is about determining what political systems will do and how. Harold Laswell, another political scientist, declared politics as governmental determination of who gets what, when, and how.[23] Politics for these two is distributional, it is about who gets what and what values win or get implemented. The actual allocation of power and values falls to election law. Election law comprises the rules that determine the rules of the game. The rules of election law determine who can vote, run for office, give money, speak, or even how to count (ballots). The ability to decide winners and losers—to be a zero sum game—makes election law a controversial topic.

Yet election law is frequently controversial because often times the method of resolution seems arbitrary or unpersuasive. For many, the Supreme Court's *Bush v. Gore*, as discussed earlier, was so controversial not only because it looked like the judiciary and not the people were deciding who would become president, but also because of a partisan alignment that yielded mostly Republican appointees determining that a Republican would become the winner. This decision looked as partisan and as arbitrary as the 4-3 Florida Supreme Court decision that it overruled, which too seemed to break along party lines. Other decisions over the years, for example when it comes to ballot access or campaign finance reform, seem arbitrary on many levels. Debates at the legislative level, including in Congress, often seem to break along party lines. For years before McCain-Feingold passed, one saw Democrats favoring reform and Republicans opposing it. At the state level, incumbents seem bent on gerrymandering lines to favor themselves or their party over challengers. With the Supreme Court, the composition of the court seems to affect how they will rule on pressing issues. The Rehnquist Court affirms McCain-Feingold, the Roberts Court is gradually whittling away at it and many precedents regulating money in politics that have stood for 50 or more years. In 2013, the Supreme Court granted review to a case challenging overall contribution limits to federal candidates,[24] leading to speculation that the Roberts Court was

---

22 David Easton, A Framework for Political Analysis (1965).
23 Harold Laswell, Politics: Who Gets What, When, How (1961).
24 McCutcheon v. Federal Election Commission, 2013 WL 598469 (Mem) U.S., 2013.

now beginning a final assault on *Buckley v. Valeo*[25] and all contribution limits.[26] If this is accurate, it all looks arbitrary and the product of politics and not principle. This adds to the controversy.

The subject of election law is important because it defines how the political system should operate. In a democracy, election law should implement democratic values, but that is exactly the problem. What are democratic values and how is election law connected to this type of political system? This is the task of this book—to connect election law, at least in the United States, to a broader set of democratic values important to this country.

As one reads Supreme Court decisions that cover the panoply of subjects that election law covers, one is struck by how often they address or implicate democratic values yet fail to articulate a theory. Only on rare occasions does the judiciary seem to venture into the theory behind their decisions as they affect American democracy. Perhaps the most classic place where they did that was in *United States v. Carolene Products*,[27] a case nominally about the regulation of the interstate shipment of tainted milk. Few read the case for the decision but instead many do for what is arguably the most important footnote in legal history. In footnote 4 the Court states:

> There may be narrower scope for operation of the presumption of constitutionality when legislation appears on its face to be within a specific prohibition of the Constitution, such as those of the first ten Amendments, which are deemed equally specific when held to be embraced within the Fourteenth.
>
> It is unnecessary to consider now whether legislation which restricts those political processes which can ordinarily be expected to bring about repeal of undesirable legislation, is to be subjected to more exacting judicial scrutiny under the general prohibitions of the Fourteenth Amendment than are most other types of legislation.
>
> Nor need we enquire whether similar considerations enter into the review of statutes directed at particular religious, or national or racial minorities. [W]hether prejudice against discrete and insular minorities may be a special condition, which tends seriously to curtail the operation of those political processes ordinarily to be relied upon to protect minorities, and which may call for a correspondingly more searching judicial inquiry [citations omitted].[28]

Carolene Products seemed to articulate the beginnings of a theory of democracy with implications for election law. The second paragraph of the note, for example, describes those rights which are deserving of special protection or scrutiny

---

25   424 U.S. 1 (1976).
26   Adam Liptak, *Court Takes Case on Overall Limit in Election Cash*, N.Y. TIMES (February 20, 2013), at A1.
27   304 U.S. 144 (1938).
28   *Id.* at 153.

including the right to vote, interference with political organizations, and peaceful assembly, all core political rights associated with democratic engagement and participation. Finally, the third paragraph references protection of minorities who may be unable to defend themselves in a majoritarian political process because they are out-voted or otherwise potentially disenfranchised in some way.

There is no question that footnote 4 is a discussion of American democracy, but its focus was less on election law than on justifying the role of the federal courts to intervene in the political process. This at least is part of what John Hart Ely contends in his *Democracy and Distrust*.[29] To a large extent Ely develops a theory of judicial review under the Warren Court that argues for the judiciary serving as a counter-majoritarian or representation-reinforcing institution in American politics when the other branches of the government appear to have failed. Ely's gloss on footnote 4 is meant to defend the institutional role of the courts as they come to address, in part, election law issues, but the decision is not meant to provide a theory of discussion of democratic theory as it directly pertains to election law.

Conversely, now turn to *Citizens United v. F.E.C.* In that decision, at issue was whether Congress' enactment of a law (McCain-Feingold Act, 3 USC section 441B) that prohibits corporations from expending money directly from their treasuries to advocate for or against the election or defeat of political candidates for federal office violated the First Amendment. The Court struck down this ban and in the process overturned two federal precedents that had previously upheld this type of corporate political expenditure. In seeking to support its holding the Court should have weighed some competing democratic values. One is the importance of free speech and robust expression in politics. A second had to address the problem of who gets to speak in the political arena and whether it includes corporations. Third, the Court had to address the potential impact of additional money in politics and what consequences freeing up corporations (and labor unions) might have upon corrupting or distorting campaigns and elections. For the most part, the Court did little weighing and instead simply imposed its answer that McCain-Feingold was a form of censorship that trumped other concerns. However, the Court did not explicate these concerns or really address them in a way that placed its holding in *Citizens United* within a broader context of a democratic theory.

Simply asserting that free speech wins is not a theory about a democracy. There are many competing values in a democratic society that have to be reconciled. For example, in *Burson v. Freeman*,[30] at issue was a Tennessee law banning political advertising within 100 feet of a polling place. What makes this case so difficult is that it placed into conflict two important competing democratic values—the right to vote and the right to political speech to advertise a position or support a candidate for office.[31] Tennessee defended the law by asserting that it promoted integrity and reliability in elections and also it guaranteed that voters could exercise their

---

29 JOHN HART ELY, DEMOCRACY AND DISTRUST: A THEORY OF JUDICIAL REVIEW (1980).
30 504 U.S. 191 (1992).
31 *Id.* at 198-99.

Introduction: Why Theory?

franchise rights freely. Both are important values, but just as easily a candidate for office might assert that voting could be enhanced if voters received last minute information about issues and persons running for office just as they were entering the voting booth. There is no simple answer here to what is the correct answer and this is what the Supreme Court had to address—it had to weigh competing rights or values within a broader theory of democracy.

To resolve the controversy the Court looked at the history of voting in America from the days of colonial times, when voice voting was taken, to reforms to introduce the secret ballot and then to limit campaigning near voting sites.[32] The discussion provided in part an important discussion about why voting is so critical to a democracy and how the 100-foot restriction on advertising represented a minor infringement on another right in order to promote franchise. Even though the dicta in this case did not constitute a full-blown theory about democracy, it began a process of seeking to resolve election law issues by placing the discussion into a broader framework of democracy in general and American democratic theory in more specific detail. Still missing from the Court's decision here, as is true also for the major textbooks on election law, as well as for the major books on the subject, is a situation of election law within a democratic theory that suggests ways of defining, articulating, and resolving major election law controversies. This is the purpose of this book—to begin to bring some order to election law and its jurisprudence. It is the first step in a long road to creating a democratic theory of election law for the twenty-first century.

Chapter 1 will review many of the major election law cases such as *Buckley v. Valeo*, *Reynolds v. Sims*,[33] and *League of United Latin American Citizens v. Perry*,[34] as well as several of the leading books and articles in election law by Rick Hasen, Pamela Karlan, and others, The goal will be to show that, while these works often invoke questions of political and democratic theory, they are often deficient in their failure to explore adequately the values and norms they are invoking. Election law disputes are often hopelessly unresolved because of a failure of the courts or scholars to contextualize the disputes in a larger set of theoretical premises regarding how a democracy should operate.

Chapter 2 provides a twofold overview of democratic theory. First, drawing upon classic and contemporary theorists such as John Locke, James Madison, Robert Dahl, Carol Pateman, and others, the chapter will provide an examination of the basic principles of democratic theory and practice. The second half of the chapter draws specifically upon American political thought to elucidate the basic principles and premises located historically and in contemporary American theories of politics. In particular, it develops two lines of American democratic theory—Madisonian democracy and pluralism. In describing these two dominant theories of American democracy the goal is to begin explicating the major values

---

32 *Id.* at 200-204.
33 377 U.S. 533 (1964).
34 548 U.S. 399 (2006).

that are or should be at the core of American democratic theory. As will be clear, Madisonian and pluralist theories are not necessarily compatible and they often reach contrasting views about democracy. The chapter will seek to synthesize a theory about how American democratic theory is supposed to operate and it begins to bridge the gap from theory to law. It will develop an argument showing how to translate the political principles into a constitutional theory of election law. The goal will be to provide a constitutional foundation upon which the issues in the next several chapters shall be examined.

Beginning with Chapter 3, the book shifts from a more general discussion of election law and democratic theory to addressing specific subjects. Who is entitled to vote is the subject of this chapter. It will examine why voting is important in a democracy and will discuss several of the major disputes in this area such as felon disenfranchisement, voter identification laws, and the counting of ballots through alternative processes such as instant runoff voting.

Chapter 4 discusses the Progressive Era reforms to American democratic theory and practice, keying in especially on the use of initiative and referendum. The discussion will seek to explore the initial goals and promise of government by ballot initiative and then it argues that the use of direct democracy has largely failed to achieve its objectives. More troubling, if one of the primary goals of American constitutionalism and democracy is the protection of minority rights, then the Progressive Era embrace of initiative and referendum has largely failed. The chapter concludes by arguing that this form of democratic decision-making needs to be abandoned.

Chapter 5 examines reapportionment and districting issues. The drawing of district lines is a controversial topic that by default has fallen to the courts to police due to the failure of the political process to perform it adequately and fairly. This chapter examines the topics of racial and partisan gerrymandering, redistricting commissions, and the criteria and processes that should be employed when district lines are drawn. The chapter will also explore alternative theories of proportional representation and multi-member districting. The argument here will be that the current process of giving primary responsibility to elected officials such as state legislatures to draw district lines is a conflict of interest that has failed to further core democratic values. The chapter argues for alternative ways to redistrict, and also for the shifting away of the responsibility to perform this function to some other body.

Chapter 6 turns to the topic of political parties. Within a democracy and the field of election law there are many actors who wish to participate. These include real biological individuals as well as artificial entities such as corporations, non-profits, and political parties. The discussion in this chapter seeks to isolate a series of questions about the role of political parties. It will explore who is the party and what rights they have in a democratic process. This chapter discusses efforts to regulate parties to assure more competitive elections. Issues such as ballot access, third parties, discrimination, and regulation of primaries will be examined.

Chapter 7 turns to one of the pressing issues of the day in light of the 2010 *Citizens United* decision—money and politics. Is money speech and can it be regulated successfully to promote fairer and more competitive elections? This chapter explores the underlying disputes over the connection between market capitalism, constitutionalism, and the First Amendment when it comes to the financing of political campaigns and elections in America. Fundamentally, it rejects most of the contemporary jurisprudence and debates regarding money and politics that have dominated election law. Those debates seem to accept the fact that economic resources have a legitimate role in affecting the allocation of political influence in the United States. The chapter takes a contrary position, contending that money and economic resources are an illegitimate allocative mechanism in the political arena. While the free market and money may be a terrific way to allocate sail boats, neither should be used to affect political influence and power.

The book concludes with an argument that there needs to be a more comprehensive discussion and development of a democratic political theory to support and guide election law jurisprudence. It is not just a theory about the way American democracy has operated, but about how it should operate in light of evolving democratic values and institutions. Further, it is not just theory in the normative sense—it is also empirical. The field of election law, as this book will argue, has been captured by legal theory and it is often not well informed by empirical political science or evidence regarding what we know about how democracies do operate. This book thus brings together legal, normative, and empirical theory to make its arguments.

There is a need for a democratic theory of election law to address the world of an electronic commonwealth where governance takes place across institutions that blur the edges between government and non-governmental actors and institutions. Clearly, that task will not be completed here. There are many subjects that this book did not examine, or discussed only in passing and without elaboration. However, the chapters of this book take the first steps in proposing what such a theory should look like and what issues a broader American democratic theory of election law needs to address.

Chapter 1
Theory: The Missing Piece in Election Law Scholarship and Adjudication

The most curious feature about election law scholarship and adjudication is the degree to which it is theoretically rudderless. What is meant by rudderless? Simply put, it is the extent to which the critical debates and issues that are at the center of many election law disputes are often addressed in the most minimal of matter, generally without regard to any broader sense of a political theory which should guide decisions. In reaching decisions addressing political speech versus promoting the integrity of elections in the area of campaign financing, or ballot access versus electoral integrity, voting rights versus fraud prevention, or any other innumerable issues, election law scholars and judges seem to assume that the matters at stake are devoid from a broader political or democratic theory context. They essentially ignore how embedded election law actually is to politics and normative values about government.

But that should not be the case. Alexis de Tocqueville declared in a famous and often quoted passage in his *Democracy in America*: "There is hardly a political question in the United States which does not sooner or later turn into a judicial one. Consequently the language of everyday party-political controversy has to be borrowed from legal phraseology and conceptions."[1] How prescient. What de Tocqueville saw 170 years ago in America was the connection between politics and the law. He recognized that the critical political or policy issues of the day—then perhaps slavery—would soon turn into matter for the courts to decide, such as in *Dred Scott v. Sanford*.[2] The line between politics and law is always fine, with some controversial decisions demonstrating how eroded or absent it often is. When some accused the Supreme Court of deciding the outcome of the 2000 presidential election in *Bush v. Gore* one can almost hear the French writer saying "I told you so."[3] Contrary to Justice Frankfurter's admonition in *Colegrove v. Green* that "Courts ought not to enter this political thicket" when it comes to redistricting and reapportionment,[4] there was an

---

1 ALEXIS DE TOCQUEVILLE, DEMOCRACY IN AMERICA, ed. J.P. Mayer, trans. George Lawrence, 270 (1969).

2 60 U.S. 393 (1857).

3 Bush v. Gore was not the first time the Supreme Court ruled on the allocation of state electoral votes. *See:* McPherson v. Blacker, 146 U.S. 1 (1892). However, the McPherson decision was certainty less decisive to the final outcome than was Bush v. Gore.

4 328 U.S. 549 (1946).

inevitability to doing so (as later permitted by *Baker v. Carr*) for the reasons suggested by de Tocqueville.

It would be easy to argue that criticizing the Supreme Court and election law scholars for not discussing political theory is a cheap shot that is off the mark. After all, judges are generally not political theorists and election law scholars are lawyers and not philosophers. Paraphrasing Justice Robert Jackson, who once declared in *Brown v. Allen* "We are not final because we are infallible, but we are infallible only because we are final,"[5] the Supreme Court is not the final word on election law because they are theorists, they are theorists only to the extent they are final. But while the judiciary generally gets the final word in resolving election law issues, that does not mean that their answers are theoretically rich or that they have even really crafted decisions that are satisfactory.

Consider a parallel problem briefly noted in the introduction—the problem of judicial review. Judicial review may well be a necessary but contentious power within a democratic society such as the United States. The controversy begins in America with simply a textual issue—does the Constitution provide support for such a power. Alexander Hamilton in *Federalist* 78 hinted at the power of judicial review for the proposed new Supreme Court in the new constitution.

> The interpretation of the laws is the proper and peculiar province of the courts. A constitution is in fact, and must be regarded by the judges as, a fundamental law. It therefore belongs to them to ascertain its meaning as well as the meaning of any particular act proceeding from the legislative body. If there should happen to be an irreconcilable variance between the two, that which has the superior obligation and validity ought, of course; to be preferred; or, in other words, the Constitution ought to be preferred to the statute, the intention of the people to the intention of their agents.[6]

Yet, despite this power, Hamilton also sought to comfort those who feared the new court:

> The judiciary, on the contrary, has no influence over either the sword or the purse; no direction either of the strength or of the wealth of the society, and can take no active resolution whatever. It may truly be said to have neither FORCE nor WILL but merely judgment; and must ultimately depend upon the aid of the executive arm even for the efficacy of its judgments.[7]

Even though later, in *Marbury v. Madison*, Chief Justice John Marshall pronounced: "It is emphatically the province and duty of the judicial department to say what

---

5   344 U.S. 443 (1953).
6   ALEXANDER HAMILTON, JAMES MADISON, AND JOHN JAY, THE FEDERALIST, 506 (1937).
7   *Id.* at 504.

the law is,"[8] President Andrew Jackson may have captured the spirit of Hamilton's caution when he supposedly stated about one Supreme Court decision: "John Marshall has made his decision; now let him enforce it!"[9] The problem of judicial review then is one of textual support for the power and of balancing it with the authority of the other branches of government.

But at a second level the problem of judicial review is one of popular government. In *Federalist* 10 Madison sums up the central problem of government:

> When a majority is included in a faction, the form of popular government, on the other hand, enables it to sacrifice to its ruling passion or interest both the public good and the rights of other citizens. To secure the public good and private rights against the danger of such a faction, and at the same time to preserve the spirit and the form of popular government, is then the great object to which our inquiries are directed.[10]

For Madison, the problem is of checking majority faction while preserving liberty and popular government. Later the problem was restated by de Tocqueville as the problem of the tyranny of the majority,[11] or even later by James Bryce as the fatalism of the multitude.[12]

The simplest way of describing it is as balancing majority rule with minority rights. How far can a majority go in securing its will before it infringes on minority rights? A constitutional democracy is not a winner-take-all game, that is the purpose of the Bill of Rights. Again quoting Justice Jackson:

> The very purpose of a Bill of Rights was to withdraw certain subjects from the vicissitudes of political controversy, to place them beyond the reach of majorities and officials and to establish them as legal principles to be applied by the courts. One's right to ... freedom of worship ... and other fundamental rights may not be submitted to vote; they depend on the outcome of no elections.[13]

Balancing majority rule and minority rights is essentially the same problem with judicial review, only it is expressed in a different way. Alexander Bickel once wrote of judicial review facing the problem of countermajoritarianism.[14] By that, writing in the wake of *Brown v. Board of Education*,[15] the issue was how to reconcile the power of the courts effectively to resolve contentious social and

---

8   5 U.S. 137, 177 (1803).
9   Worcester v. Georgia, 31 U.S. (6 Pet.) 515 (1832).
10 Hamilton, Madison, and Jay at 57-58.
11 De Tocqueville at 250-53.
12 JAMES BRYCE, THE AMERICAN COMMONWEALTH, vol. 1, 297-307 (1891).
13 West Virginia v. Barnette, 319 U.S. 624, 638 (1943).
14 ALEXANDER BICKEL, THE LEAST DANGEROUS BRANCH (1962).
15 347 U.S. 483 (1954).

policy issues within the framework of a representative democracy that says that elected officials should be given the duty to do this. Should unelected, tenured for life judges be making decisions about integration, contraception, and abortion? What about issues of gay marriage, or about how much money can be spent in politics or who can give, appear on a ballot, or vote in an election? What is the line between appropriate authority of the courts versus Congress, the president, and the states? At what point can the courts thwart the will of the majority? This is the problem that Bickel raised, and over the last 60 or so years, has been revisited numerous times by critics of the Supreme Court as they assail it for legislating from the bench or judicial activism.[16]

One solution offered by Herbert Wechsler was to argue that what should guide the judiciary in its decision-making is that it has to be guided by neutral principles of law.[17] Robert Bork similarly asserted this point too.[18] But the core argument here is that what distinguished judicial from policy pronouncements is that the former were crafted on general principles that were politically neutral and which could guide resolution not simply of the case at hand but others too. Bork took this claim even further, declaring that not only should the Court decide based on neutral principles but that it was not the task of the judiciary to craft them. Thus, absent the ready availability of neutral principles, the judiciary should abstain from deciding cases.

The point of discussing judicial review here does get to the issue of the connection between election law and political theory. If one looks at Supreme Court judicial review over the last 30 or so years, one criticism of it has been its minimalist nature. By that, some have lauded or criticized the Court—in particular Justice O'Connor—for a minimalist approach to the law; decisions without a grand theory.[19] Decisions made on very narrow grounds that do not seem

---

16 *See:* Barry Friedman, *The Counter-Majoritarian Problem and the Pathology of Constitutional Scholarship*, 95 Nw. U. L. Rev. 933 (2001); Mark Graber, *The Nonmajoritarian Difficulty: Legislative Deference to the Judiciary*, 7 Studies in American Political Development 35 (1993); Miguel Schor, *The Strange Cases of Marbury and Lochner in the Constitutional Imagination*, 87 Tex. L. Rev. 1463, 1477-86 (2009); Ilya Somin, *Political Ignorance and the Countermajoritarian Difficulty: A New Perspective on the Central Obsession of Constitutional Theory*, 89 Iowa L. Rev. 1287 (2004); Nimer Sultany, *The State of Progressive Constitutional Theory: The Paradox of Constitutional Democracy and the Project of Political Justification*, 47 Harv. C.L.-C.R. L. Rev. 371 (2012); Mark Tushnet, *Policy Distortion and Democratic Debilitation: Comparative Illumination of the Countermajoritarian Difficulty*, 94 Mich. L. Rev. 245 (1995), for a review of this scholarship and criticism.

17 Herbert Wechsler, *Toward Neutral Principles of Constitutional Law*, 73 Harv. L. Rev. 1 (1959).

18 Robert H. Bork, *Neutral Principles and Some First Amendment Problems*, 47 Ind. L. J. 1 (1971).

19 *See:* Cass Sunstein, Radicals in Robes: Why Extreme Right-Wing Courts Are Wrong for America (2005) and One Case At A Time: Judicial Minimalism on the Supreme Court (1999).

grounded in a broader theory or perhaps set of neutral principles. While perhaps not an accurate summation of her decision in *Shaw v. Reno*,[20] in part O'Connor's decision was guided by her visual impression and looks of the redistricting maps in North Carolina that she described could only be explained by race. Similarly, look again at *Bush v. Gore*. The Court in seeking to resolve the controversy in that case pronounced the decision was "limited to the present circumstances,"[21] suggesting no intention to forge broader precedent. But that is the very criticism of the decision—it looked as ad hoc and political as many other decisions are criticized as being, coming down simply to the "rule of five" and not necessarily what is the correct answer.

This is the core criticism of election law scholarship. While the argument is not that political or democratic theory provides the neutral principles to guide resolution of disputes, there is no question that the disagreements and jurisprudence in this area of law could benefit from more contextualization and grounding in a political or democratic theory.

This chapter will review several of the major election law cases such as *Buckley v. Valeo*, *Reynolds v. Sims*, and *LULAC v. Perry*, as well as several of the leading books and articles in election law by Rick Hasen, Samuel Issacharoff, and others. The goal will be to show that, while their works often invoke questions of political and democratic theory, they are often deficient in their failure to explore adequately the values and norms they are invoking. Election law disputes are often hopelessly unresolved because of a failure of the courts or scholars to contextualize the disputes into a larger set of theoretical premises regarding how a democracy should operate.

The Supreme Court and Democratic Theory

While one can criticize the Supreme Court's decisions over the last generation or so as being minimalist, an argument can also be made that in general its jurisprudence has only occasionally addressed some of the more broad political theory questions when it has addressed major election law cases or disputes. A sampling of decisions supports this contention.

Right to Vote

Begin with the right to vote cases. Nowhere is there a textually explicit guarantee of the right to vote in the original Constitution. It was not until the 1940s that the Supreme Court affirmatively addressed the constitutional right to vote. In *United States v. Classic*,[22] a case arising out of vote fraud in a Louisiana federal election

---

20 509 U.S. 630 (1993).
21 531 U.S. at 109.
22 313 U.S. 299 (1941).

imary, the Court was faced with the issue of whether one has a right to vote as a primary question,[23] and then whether the depriving a person of that right came within the meaning of a federal criminal law that made it illegal to "injure a citizen in the exercise 'of any right or privilege secured to him by the Constitution' or laws of the United States."[24] The Court stated:

> We come then to the question whether that right is one secured by the Constitution. Section 2 of Article I commands that Congressmen shall be chosen by the people of the several states by electors, the qualifications of which it prescribes. The right of the people to choose, whatever its appropriate constitutional limitations, where in other respects it is defined, and the mode of its exercise is prescribed by state action in conformity to the Constitution, is a right established and guaranteed by the Constitution and hence is one secured by it to those citizens and inhabitants of the state entitled to exercise the right.[25]

In addition in *Reynolds v. Sims*[26] the Court embraced the principle of equal representation for equal numbers of people—one person, one vote—for the purposes of reapportionment.[27] More importantly, in *Reynolds* the Supreme Court again reaffirmed that the Constitution protects the right to vote in federal elections. Furthermore, in *Reynolds* the Court drew a parallel between the right to vote and right to procreate in *Skinner v. Oklahoma*,[28] declaring the right to vote as a fundamental.[29]

Locating a constitutional text to support the right to vote in state elections is more problematic. In *Harper v. Virginia State Board of Elections*,[30] in striking down the imposition of a poll tax in state elections, the Supreme Court ruled that the right to vote in state elections was located in the First Amendment by way of the Fourteenth Amendment's Due Process and Equal Protection Clauses.[31] Although the tax met traditional constitutional standards, being neither racially discriminatory nor indefensible as rational policy, yet the court found that it unconstitutionally singled out the poor.[32] More importantly, the Court once again affirmed the importance of voting, stating that: "Long ago, in *Yick Wo v. Hopkins*, the Court referred to 'the political franchise of voting' as a 'fundamental

---

23 *Id.* at 308.
24 *Id.* at 308, *quoting* then 18 U.S.C. 51 (1940).
25 *Id.* at 314-15.
26 377 U.S. 533 (1964).
27 *Id.* at 558.
28 *Id.* at 561-62, *citing* 316 U.S. 535 (1942)
29 377 U.S. at 561.
30 383 U.S. 663 (1966).
31 *Id.* at 664.
32 *Id.* at 666-67.

political right, because preservative of all rights.'"[33] Again, as in *Reynolds*, the Court drew a parallel between voting and the right of procreation found in *Skinner v. Oklahoma*,[34] ruling that where "fundamental rights and liberties are asserted under the Equal Protection Clause, classifications which might invade or restrain them must be closely scrutinized and carefully confined."[35] Specifically, the Court cites to language in *Skinner* that dictates that efforts to interfere with the right to procreation must be subject to strict scrutiny.[36]

The legacy of *Classic*, *Reynolds*, and *Harper* is that these three cases stand for the proposition that voting is a fundamental right that must be subject to strict scrutiny. In addition to these three cases, the Court has also reached a similar conclusion elsewhere.[37] But look at these opinions—the discussion of a right to vote is framed more in terms of singular declarations about franchise and less in terms of a broader political theory discussion of the topic.

In *Classic*, the majority opinion is devoid of a broader discussion of the importance of elections in a democratic society. The decision seems only to reference in a veiled way the intent of the Framers to grant a right to choose representatives, but for the most part the majority resolves the matter by borrowing tools of statutory construction to give meaning to Article I, Section 2. Not until one turns to Justice Douglas's dissent—"Free and honest elections are the very foundation of our republican form of government. Hence any attempt to defile the sanctity of the ballot cannot be viewed with equanimity"—does one find anything that even remotely approaches an effort to build a political theory around why a right to vote is important.[38]

Now turn to *Reynolds*. The case is incorrectly attributed to be the one where the Court articulates the "one person, one vote" standard for reapportionment. That is

---

33 *Id.* at 667.
34 *Id.* at 668, 670.
35 *Id.* at 670.
36 *Id.* at 670 (*citing* 316 U.S. at 542).
37 *See, e.g.*, Illinois Bd. of Elections v. Socialist Workers Party, 440 U.S. 173 (1979); Bush v. Gore, 531 U.S. 98, 104 (2000); Oregon v. Mitchell, 400 U.S. 112, 142 (1970); Rosario v. Rockefeller, 410 U.S. 752, 767-68 (1973); Dunn v. Blumstein, 405 U.S. 330, 336 (1972); Williams v. Rhodes, 393 U.S. 23, 38 (1968) (*declaring* "When 'fundamental rights and liberties' are at issue a State has less leeway in making classifications than when it deals with economic matters") (citations omitted); Cardona v. Power, 384 U.S. 672, 676 (1966) (*ruling* that "Where classifications might 'invade or restrain' fundamental rights and liberties, they must be 'closely scrutinized and carefully confined.'"); and Storer v. Brown, 415 U.S. 724, 756 (1974) ("when legislation burdens such a fundamental constitutional right, it is not enough that the legislative means rationally promote legitimate governmental ends. Rather, 'governmental action may withstand constitutional scrutiny only upon a clear showing that the burden imposed is necessary to protect a compelling and substantial governmental interest'").
38 313 U.S. at 329.

really *Wesberry v. Sanders*.[39] However, *Reynolds* does establish important precedent regarding reapportionment and the right to vote, ruling that the lines drawn in the apportionment of legislative seats in Alabama was so deficient and unreflective of the current population demographics that it violated the Equal Protection clause.[40] But *Reynolds* also offers some rudimentary thoughts connecting voting to apportionment that seem to suggest a broader theory about democracy. For example, the Court begins its analysis and drawing the connections by declaring: "Undeniably the Constitution of the United States protects the right of all qualified citizens to vote, in state as well as in federal elections."[41] The Court then states that right extends to the counting of votes and ballots.[42] Protection of this right is described by the Court as so important because it is "a fundamental political right, because preservative of all rights."[43] But then the Court makes its major argument drawing connections between voting, apportionment, majority rule, and democracy:

> State legislatures are, historically, the fountainhead of representative government in this country. A number of them have their roots in colonial times, and substantially antedate the creation of our Nation and our Federal Government. In fact, the first formal stirrings of American political independence are to be found, in large part, in the views and actions of several of the colonial legislative bodies. With the birth of our National Government, and the adoption and ratification of the Federal Constitution, state legislatures retained a most important place in our Nation's governmental structure. But representative government is in essence self-government through the medium of elected representatives of the people, and each and every citizen has an inalienable right to full and effective participation in the political processes of his State's legislative bodies. Most citizens can achieve this participation only as qualified voters through the election of legislators to represent them. Full and effective participation by all citizens in state government requires, therefore, that each citizen have an equally effective voice in the election of members of his state legislature. Modern and viable state government needs, and the Constitution demands, no less.
>
> Logically, in a society ostensibly grounded on representative government, it would seem reasonable that a majority of the people of a State could elect a majority of that State's legislators.[44]

What the *Reynolds* majority does is to begin to ground or sustain its constitutional argument within a political theory about democracy. It describes the importance of the Framers in wanting to produce a representative government founded upon a

---

39   376 U.S. 1 (1964).
40   *Id.* at 545.
41   *Id.* at 554.
42   *Id.*
43   377 U.S. at 562.
44   *Id.* at 564-65.

theory of majority rule. In order to effectuate majority rule the citizens have a right to vote and this vote includes a right to having their ballots counted and weighed equally. While not a full-blown theory, the Court nonetheless describes at least a crude version of a democratic theory that supports its constitutional arguments for its analysis on reapportionment.

Money and Politics

Now turn to the area of campaign financing for elections. If ever there has been a topic that has bedeviled the Court it has been over what constitutional protections should be extended to political contributions and donations. In everyday language or parlance, the question is posed whether "money is speech." This is a complex constitutional issue as well as a question from the point of a discussion about democracy. By that, there is no question that theories of democracy describe free speech as important.[45] Free speech and freedom of inquiry, as John Stuart Mill pointed out, make discovery of the truth possible. But free inquiry also makes it possible to criticize the government, to gather information necessary to make informed political choices, and also to be able to get information out about candidates. There are a host of arguments that can be made about how free speech facilitates democracy. Yet it is less clear how money is related to speech and this is where the Supreme Court is torn.

Debates over the role of money in politics potentially implicate a host of issues. The cornerstone for how the Supreme Court has framed such debate is in *Buckley v. Valeo* and legal challenges to the 1974 Federal Election Campaign Act amendments. These amendments arose as a result of the corruption surrounding the fundraising and campaign spending in the 1972 presidential election, generically referred to as Watergate.[46] In seeking reelection as president in 1972, Richard Nixon's fundraising organization, Committee for the Reelection of the President (CREEP), had raised well in excess of $50 million, often in illegal fashion or otherwise in ways meant to bypass the 1971 FECA disclosure requirements.[47] CREEP not only funneled money from corporations and political groups in ways to avert disclosure, but it used that money for many illegal purposes, including funding the break-in of the Democratic National Headquarters at the Watergate office building in Washington, D.C. on June 17, 1972. Public revulsion towards

---

45 *See, e.g.*, JOHN STUART MILL, ON LIBERTY (1978); ROBERT A. DAHL, DEMOCRACY AND ITS CRITICS (1989); Thomas Scanlon, *A Theory of Freedom of Expression*, 1 PHILOSOPHY AND PUBLIC AFFAIRS 204 (1972); FREDERICK SCHAUER, FREE SPEECH: A PHILOSOPHICAL ENQUIRY (1982).

46 Marlene Arnold Nicholson, *Buckley v. Valeo: The Constitutionality of the Federal Election Campaign Act Amendments of 1974*, 1973 WISC. L. REV. 323, 323 (1973); FRANK J. SORAUF, MONEY IN AMERICAN ELECTIONS, 36-37 (1987); HERBERT E. ALEXANDER, FINANCING POLITICS: MONEY, ELECTIONS, & POLITICAL REFORM, 32-38 (1992).

47 THEODORE H. WHITE, THE MAKING OF THE PRESIDENT: 1972, xxv, 370-80 (1973).

the Watergate fundraising, spending, and other illegal activity thus prompted Congress to reconsider the 1971 FECA and to place restrictions both upon political contributions and expenditures.[48]

In 1974, S. 3044[49] and H.R. 16090[50] were offered as amendments to FECA. In its report, the Senate Committee on Rules and Administration described the purpose of its proposed amendments as "providing complete control over and disclosure of campaign contributions and expenditures in campaigns for Federal elective office,"[51] while a House report prepared by the Committee on House Administration described the purpose, inter alia, "to place limitations on campaign contributions and expenditures"[52] because the "unchecked rise in campaign expenditures, coupled with the absence of limitations on contributions and expenditures, has increased the dependence of candidates on special interest groups and large contributors."[53] As a result, both the Senate and House bills sought to place restrictions not only on contributions to political candidates but also upon expenditures made by candidates and independent organizations.[54] Lacking restrictions upon expenditures, wealthy individuals would be able to subvert contribution limits, rendering the latter meaningless.[55] Exactly how important regulation of expenditures was deemed to be was aptly described by Senator Clark who stated:

> Perhaps the central lesson of Watergate is that we must carefully guard, not only the sources of campaign contributions, but their use. The Commission established in my amendment would police expenditures before they are made, rather than simply audit them after they are made—when it is too late either to prevent the harm or remedy its consequences. The threat of punishment alone is too weak a deterrent when so much political power is at stake.[56]

Simply put, Congress did not believe that mere disclosure of expenditures by candidates or political organizations was enough. Instead, legislation was necessary to place an absolute amount of money that could be expended by candidates, individuals, and political organizations, otherwise such expenditures would upset the contribution limits and regulatory framework to regulate political spending. As a result, several types of contribution and expenditure limits were added to FECA.

---

48   Herbert E. Alexander, Financing the 1972 Election, 591 (1976); Warren E. Miller and J. Merrill Shanks, The New American Voter, 29 (1996); Tom Rhodes, *Watergate's Poison of Mistrust Lingers On*, THE TIMES (June 17, 1997), at 12.
49   S. 3044, 93d Cong. 2d Sess. (1974); S. Report No. 93-689 (1974).
50   H.R. 16090, 93d Cong. 2d Sess. (1974); H.R. Report No. 93-1239 (1974).
51   S. Report No. 93-689 at 1.
52   H.R. Report No. 93-1239 at 1.
53   *Id.* at 3.
54   *Id.* at 6-7; S. Report No. 93-689 at 2, 18-19.
55   S. Report No. 93-689 at 18.
56   150 Cong. Rec. S.5338-39 (daily ed. April 5, 1974) (statement of Sen. Clark).

Theory: The Missing Piece in Election Law Scholarship and Adjudication

The 1974 FECA Amendments limited to $1,000 political contributions by individuals or groups, and $5,000 by political action committees (PACs) and party organizations to candidates for federal elective office per election cycle, with a cap of $25,000 by an individual per election cycle. In addition, individuals and groups were limited to $1,000 as the amount they could expend per election to a clearly identified candidate. Finally, other restrictions on how much of one's personal wealth could be spent on a campaign were also imposed, as were overall expenditure limits. All of these restrictions were deemed necessary by Congress as the "only way in which Congress can eliminate reliance on large private contributions and still ensure adequate representation to the electorate of opposing viewpoints of competing candidates,"[57] otherwise such a "loophole would render direct contribution limits virtually meaningless."[58]

The 1974 FECA amendments did not go unchallenged. Throughout the debates on the Senate and House bills, there were numerous concerns regarding the constitutionality of restrictions on independent expenditures. For example, Senator Buckley argued in the Senate that:

> most constitutional experts who have analyzed campaign reform proposals of the kind we are debating today have concluded that limits on total expenditures raise the most serious constitutional questions. It is their belief that such limits are necessarily violative of the first amendment and would be found unconstitutional if a proper case were brought before the Supreme Court.[59]

However, despite these concerns, Congress legislated to restrict expenditures, stating:

> If Congress may, consistent with the First Amendment, limit contributions to preserve the integrity of the electoral process, then it also can constitutionally limit independent expenditures in order to make the contribution limits effective.[60]

Hence, while Congress conceptually distinguished expenditures from contributions, it did not see any reason to treat them differently in terms of First Amendment analysis and constitutional protection.[61] However, in *Buckley v. Valeo*, the Supreme Court failed to agree with Congress' constitutional analysis.

---

57 S. Report No. 93-689 at 5.
58 *Id.* at 18.
59 Cong. Rec. S.5702 (daily ed. April 10, 1974) (statement of Sen. Buckley).
60 S. Report No. 93-689 at 19.
61 *See:* 18 U.S.C. 591(e)(1) and 18 U.S.C. 591(f)(1) where the FECA amendments defined contributions and expenditures in strikingly similar terms:
"'Contribution' means a gift, subscription, loan, advance, or deposit of money or anything of value (except a loan of money by a national or State bank made in accordance

In *Buckley*, at issue were several challenges to the 1997 FECA Amendments. Specifically, for our purposes, at issue were challenges to the expenditure and contribution limits that the Amendments imposed.[62] In examining limits on contributions and expenditures, a *per curiam* opinion the Court applied very different lines of constitutional analysis. First, the Court noted that Congress had broad power to regulate federal elections,[63] yet the question in this case was whether the contribution and expenditure limitations violated the First Amendment free speech clause.[64] The Court of Appeals, in upholding the FECA contribution and expenditure limitations,[65] ruled that the restrictions were directed towards conduct and not speech and that, accordingly, the frame of analysis as dictated by *United States v. O'Brien*[66] should apply.[67] The Court rejected the assertion that contribution and expenditure limits were conduct and not speech,[68] stating:

> We cannot share the view that the present Act's contribution and expenditure limitations are comparable to the restrictions on conduct upheld in *O'Brien*. The expenditure of money simply cannot be equated with such conduct as destruction of a draft card. Some forms of communication made possible by the giving and spending of money involve speech alone, some involve conduct primarily, and

---

with the applicable banking laws and regulations and in the ordinary course of business, which shall be considered a loan by each endorser or guarantor, in that proportion of the unpaid balance thereof that each endorser or guarantor bears to the total number of endorsers or guarantors), made for the purpose of influencing the nomination for election, or election, of any person to Federal office or for the purpose of influencing the results of a primary held for the selection of delegates to a national nominating convention of a political party or for the expression of a preference for the nomination of persons for election to the office of President of the United States."

"'Expenditure' means a purchase, payment, distribution, loan, advance, deposit, or gift of money or anything of value (except a loan of money by a national or State bank made in accordance with the applicable banking laws and regulations and in the ordinary course of business), made for the purpose of influencing the nomination for election, or election, of any person to Federal office or for the purpose of influencing the results of a primary held for the selection of delegates to a national nominating convention of a political party or for the expression of a preference for the nomination of persons for election to the office of President of the United States."

While Congress offered separate definitions to the terms contribution and expenditure, both were described with the essential purpose of influencing an election through some disbursement of money.

62   *See:* 18 U.S.C. 608 (a)-(e).
63   424 U.S. at 13.
64   *Id.* at 13-14.
65   Buckley v. Valeo, 519 F.2d 821, 840 (1975).
66   391 U.S. 367 (1968).
67   424 U.S. at 15-16. *See:* 391 U.S. at 377 (describing the basic substantial interest test the Court employs to examine regulation of conduct draped with speech).
68   424 U.S. at 16.

some involve a combination of the two. Yet this Court has never suggested that the dependence of a communication on the expenditure of money operates itself to introduce a nonspeech element or to reduce the exacting scrutiny required by the First Amendment.[69]

Hence, the Court seemed to regard the giving of money for political purposes as a form of protected speech. Specifically, in terms of the limits on independent expenditures, the Court saw the restrictions as a "substantial rather than merely theoretical restraints on the quantity and diversity of political speech."[70] In addition, the Court described contributions as a means of expressing support for a candidate or otherwise indicating one's preference for political candidates such that restricting political contributions also imposed First Amendment associational limitations upon political dialogue.[71] In short, both contributions and expenditures were protected speech, subject to First Amendment analysis. But how did the Court reach this conclusion that money given or expended for political purposes implicated the First Amendment? Perhaps it simply acknowledged the obvious—that talk is not cheap and that it takes money to speak. Or maybe it conceded that the United States was a market capitalist country which permits the conversion of economic resources into political influence. But in *Buckley* the Court drew on at least one odd analogy or metaphor. At one point in discussing expenditure limits the Court noted in footnote 18 that: "Being free to engage in unlimited political expression subject to a ceiling on expenditures is like being free to drive an automobile as far and as often as one desires on a single tank of gasoline."[72] Money is the fuel of speech and presumably of democracy too.

As one scans *Buckley* one searches in vain for a broader argument about money and its relationship to democracy. At least in the *per curiam* decision there is no argument from anything approaching a democratic theory—instead one finds something approaching bullet points about the important role of free speech. For example, at one point the Court declares: "The First Amendment affords the broadest protection to such political expression in order 'to assure (the) unfettered interchange of ideas for the bringing about of political and social changes desired by the people.'"[73] The Court continues by declaring:

> "[T]here is practically universal agreement that a major purpose of that Amendment was to protect the free discussion of governmental affairs. ... of course includ(ing) discussions of candidates ..." This no more than reflects our "profound national commitment to the principle that debate on public issues should be uninhibited, robust, and wide-open," In a republic where the people

---

69 *Id.* at 16.
70 *Id.* at 19.
71 *Id.* at 21, 24.
72 *Id.* at 19 n. 18.
73 *Id.* at 14, *quoting* Roth v. United States, 354 U.S. 476, 484 (1957).

are sovereign, the ability of the citizenry to make informed choices among candidates for office is essential, for the identities of those who are elected will inevitably shape the course that we follow as a nation.[74] (Citations omitted)

Here the *per curiam* opinion draws linkages among free speech, elections, voting, and citizens' accountability. This is an important elaboration of a political theory justifying the importance of protecting free speech and perhaps few would quibble with this argument. But the core of the debate in *Buckley* is over the role that political contributions and expenditures have in terms of furthering democratic functions. This is where the critical tradeoff is at issue, seeking to balance the use of money for political purposes with other goals in a democracy, perhaps such as fair elections, one person one vote, formal if not substantive equality, or perhaps other goals or values that one would want to promote. That discussion does not occur until the Court first establishes that money expended or contributed for political purposes raise First Amendment issues (again the Court does not say money is speech) and then it deploys the compelling government interest test to determine under what circumstances speech (money) may be regulated.

The Court rejects several governmental interests as less than compelling, including the assertion that regulation of money is necessary to equalize voices. The Court pronounces that equalizing voices was never the goal of the First Amendment. Instead, the Court finally locates a compelling governmental interest in preventing corruption or its appearance. It finds such interests to be compelling when it came to contribution limits, and in theory to expenditures, but not in that case and not subsequently except for in the case of *Austin v. Michigan Chamber of Commerce*.[75] Preventing political corruption—of the *quid pro quo* version (a bribery model)—is found to be compelling. Beyond that, the Court in *Buckley*, and in subsequent decisions, has been unsympathetic to other interests in regulating money in politics.

In addition to the *per curiam* discussion of contribution and expenditure limits, the Court also reviews the disclosure requirements under FECA. Here again the Court offers a thin defense of them, noting their importance in terms of how they provide information about the source of money, are important to detecting corruption, and are also critical to ensuring compliance with record keeping.[76] The Court finds that these justifications override a contrary argument—that some type of privacy might be essential to promoting group advocacy—yet the Court really does very little to explicate where disclosure fits into a grander scheme of democracy where issues such as privacy, transparency, and accountability must be balanced.[77] The point here is that perhaps the failure to provide a broader

---

74   424 U.S. at 14-15.
75   494 U.S. 652 (1990).
76   424 U.S. at 66-67.
77   *Id.* at 66.

grounding for disclosure within some theory of democracy points to how r 40 years after *Buckley* was decided disclosure is controversial and is under ¿ by some.

Finally, in addition to the *per curiam* opinion, various members of the Court also discuss the contribution and expenditure limits and the disclosure requirements. Justice White, for example, upheld most provisions of FECA, both by deferring to Congress' expertise and declaring:

> It is accepted that Congress has power under the Constitution to regulate the election of federal officers, including the President and the Vice President. This includes the authority to protect the elective processes against the "two great natural and historical enemies of all republics, open violence and insidious corruption,"; for "(i)f this government is anything more than a mere aggregation of delegated agents of other states and governments, each of which is superior to the general government, it must have the power to protect the elections on which its existence depends, from violence and corruption," the latter being the consequence of "the free use of money in elections, arising from the vast growth of recent wealth ..." [Citations omitted][78]

White begins to discuss how the use of money in a democracy must be balanced against other competing goals in society, such as promoting free elections. His comments about balancing wealth (free enterprise) with free elections (democracy), parallel concerns raised by Justice Rehnquist in *First National Bank of Boston v. Bellotti*:

> A State grants to a business corporation the blessings of potentially perpetual life and limited liability to enhance its efficiency as an economic entity. It might reasonably be concluded that those properties, so beneficial in the economic sphere, pose special dangers in the political sphere ... Indeed, the States might reasonably fear that the corporation would use its economic power to obtain further benefits beyond those already bestowed.[79]

Overall, *Buckley v. Valeo* is perhaps the most important Supreme Court precedent there is in terms of seeking to grapple with the role of money and speech in elections, yet the decision at best only offers fragmentary thoughts about how a democracy needs to balance them. Perhaps 40 years later the inability to reach consensus on the Court and in society over the wisdom and merits of campaign finance reform resides in the initial failure of the judiciary to offer anything more than simply a legalistic argument about this topic.

---

78   *Id.* at 257.
79   435 U.S. 765, 826 (1978).

Rights of Political Parties

Political scientists such as E.E. Schattschneider[80] and Gerald Pomper[81] have argued that political parties are a critical agent in a democracy, making governance possible. Parties perform a plethora of functions that include candidate recruitment, voter education, and coalition building.[82] Yet, while parties are important, who the party is from a legal point of view is more complicated. Is the political party its candidates, the officers, those who attend the conventions, caucuses, or primaries, or those who vote for their candidates in a general election? The reason why identifying who the party is is so important is because it has implications for decisions as diverse as deciding on the platform or deciding who can be admitted or excluded from participation in its events. In simple language, the party decides it orthodoxy and depending on who the party is, orthodoxy of the party may be decided or defined in very different ways.

If defining who the party is, is an important question, so is deciding what rights a party has. These rights may extend to ballot access, candidate recruitment, and who gets invited or excluded from its events. Supreme Court opinions seem confused on the topic. Again, consider just a couple of examples of how the Supreme Court has tried to address these questions. Begin with *Tashjian v. Republican Party of Connecticut.*[83]

In *Tashjian* the State of Connecticut had a closed primary law[84] requiring voters in a political primary to be members of that primary. The Republican Party in Connecticut, in an effort to broaden their political base, sought to open up their primary to independent voters who were not registered with any party. The majority of the Court voided the Connecticut law claiming that the law violated the freedom of association rights of the Republican party and its members. It rejected arguments by the State that the law was necessary to protect the Republican Party from undertaking actions destructive to its own interests.[85] Instead, they held that the "Party's determination of the boundaries of its own association, and of the structure which best allows it to pursue its political goals, is protected by the Constitution."[86]

The Court rejected the claims by the State of Connecticut that the law was necessary in order to further "the State's compelling interests by ensuring the administrability of the primary system, preventing raiding, avoiding voter

---

80 E.E. SCHATTSCHNEIDER, PARTY GOVERNMENT (1977).
81 GERALD POMPER, PASSIONS AND INTERESTS: POLITICAL PARTY CONCEPTS OF AMERICAN DEMOCRACY (1992).
82 MARTIN P. WATTENBERG, THE DECLINE OF AMERICAN POLITICS PARTIES: 1952-1984 (1986).
83 107 S.Ct. 544 (1986).
84 Conn.Gen.Stat. § 9-431 (1985).
85 *Id.* at 554.
86 *Id.* at 554.

confusion, and protecting the responsibility of party government."[87] Instead, the Court defended the right of the Republican Party to determine its own membership by declaring: "[T]he freedom to join together in furtherance of common political beliefs necessarily presupposes the freedom to identify the people who constitute the association."[88]

No one will deny that freedom of association is an important legal and political value. If parties are to be effective they must be able to govern themselves internally and determine their composition. Yet it is not so clear that the principle articulated in *Tashjian* really constituted a broader theory about how far, if at all, the government could go in seeking to regulate parties in order to promote a democracy. Does the logic of *Tashjian* suggest no regulation is at all permissible? Hardly. Could a political party refuse to admit someone who did not subscribe to that party's views on critical issues of the day such as gay marriage, abortion, civil rights, and religious freedom? It would seem that a party should be able to do that because it has a right to define its orthodoxy and views. But conversely, what if the party wished to exclude gays and lesbians, women who have had abortions or used birth control, people of color, and Muslims? Should it be allowed to do that? Decisions in the White Primary cases such as *Smith v. Allwright*[89] raise questions about the extent of a party's right to do that.

Now also place *Tashjian* alongside some other Supreme Court cases looking at the associational rights of parties. In *Smith v. Allwright* the Court ruled that a party primary is treated as state action for the purposes of ruling that banning African-Americans from their proceedings violated the Constitution. Associational rights of parties took a backseat to equal protection concerns and presumably associational rights of individuals. In *Eu v. San Francisco County Democratic Central Committee*[90] the Court strikes down state laws that limit the terms and composition of some party officer positions. In searching for some compelling state interest that would justify regulation of the party structure—*i.e.*, to preserve the integrity of primary elections or ensure fair and honest elections—Justice Marshall could find none and his majority opinion concluded instead that free association claims should be respected to allow the party to develop a "structure which best allows it to pursue its political goals."[91] It would appear in *Eu* then, that existing party organization did not appear to be factionalizing or thwarting the maintenance of party mobilization. Presumably the state law, by telling who could be officers and for how long, interfered with international mobilization of majorities that would be necessary to overcome internal organizational problems and sectarianism.

---

87   479 U.S. at 217.
88   *Id.* at 214.
89   321 U.S. 649 (1944).
90   489 U.S. 214 (1989).
91   *Id.* at 229.

California Democratic Party v. Jones,⁹² the Court struck down a state ballot ire creating a blanket primary system where voters, regardless of their party affiliation, could vote in primaries for candidates of any party affiliation. The Court ruled that such a measure violated the associational rights of the party (who is the party or who can speak for it is an interesting question here) not to affiliate with individuals with whom they do not wish to associate. The *Jones* opinion seems to stand in sharp contrast to *Allwright*, suggesting that parties are more private than public entities and therefore insulated from state regulation.

Finally, in *Washington State Grange v. Washington State Republican Party*,⁹³ the Supreme Court upheld a State of Washington law that identifies candidates by party affiliation on the primary ballot, lets voters select any candidate, and the two candidates who receive the most votes, regardless of affiliation, will proceed to have their names advanced to the general election. Political parties had objected to the law claiming that their First Amendment rights under *Jones* had been violated. The Court rejected this, claiming that party associational rights were not burdened.

Looking at all of these cases one is struck by two things. First, there appears to be no real consistent pattern defining the limits of party associational rights. Second, examination of these decisions reveals that the Court's discussion of party rights is almost rudderless. By that, except for some anecdotal comments, no broader principles or political theory about property rights has emerged. Legal minimalism and enough argument or reasoning to resolve the case at hand is provided, but certainly no broader or overarching argument is provided that explicates the tradeoffs between association rights of the party (or who is the party) versus equal protection concerns versus when the state can regulate internal affairs.

Partisan Gerrymandering

One last area of election law that demonstrates a lack of theorizing on the part of the Court addresses partisan gerrymandering. One-person, one-vote was a redistricting revolution launched from the equal protection clause. Using it as a basis of litigation may have made sense given the differential treatment alleged among voters, or the racial motives that often were at the root of much malapportionment, such as in *Gomillion v. Lightfoot*.⁹⁴ Thus, if violation of the one-person, one-vote mandate and racial gerrymandering could be actionable under the equal protection clause, why could not gerrymandering solely for the sake of partisan advantage not also be a constitutional violation? After all, was not the redrawing of lines to help incumbents or one particular party a practice that went all the way back to Ellbridge Gerry's day? Addressing partisan gerrymandering has been the object of three Supreme Court decisions that have done no more than

---

92   530 U.S. 567 (2000).
93   552 U.S. 442 (2008).
94   364 U.S. 339 (1960).

muddle the issues. In all three cases, the equal protection clause was the primary constitutional hook for the litigation, and perhaps for the confusion that resulted.

First, in *Davis v. Bandemer*[95] at issue was a suit brought by Indiana Democrats contesting the constitutionality of a 1981 state redistricting plan. The specific allegation was that the plan drew legislative lines and seats in such a way as to disadvantage Democrats. It did so by dividing up cities such as South Bend in arguably unusual ways.[96] The Democrats filed suit, contending that these districts violated their rights as Democrats, under the Fourteenth's equal protection clause.[97] The district court had ruled in favor of the Democrats, in part, because of evidence and testimony suggesting that the Republicans had in fact drawn the lines to favor their own party.[98] When the case reached the Supreme Court a central issue was whether this was a justiciable controversy under the equal protection clause.[99] The Court held that it was.[100]

To support its conclusion it returned to the discussion of the political question doctrine that it had in *Baker v. Carr.*[101] It quoted from *Baker* its famous formulation of its view on what a political question was,[102] noting that, unless a matter was textually committed to another branch, required a specific type of policy determination not appropriate for the Court, or there were missing manageable standards for resolving the controversy, the issue could be addressed by the federal judiciary. Finding that none of the characteristics outlined in *Baker* existed in the political gerrymandering case before it, it held that the matter was justiciable.[103] For the Court:

> Since the achieving of fair and effective representation for all citizens is concededly the basic aim of legislative apportionment, we conclude that the Equal Protection Clause guarantees the opportunity for equal participation by all voters in the election of State legislators. Diluting the weight of votes because of place of residence impairs basic constitutional rights under the Fourteenth Amendment just as much as invidious discriminations based upon factors such as race …[104]

Yet while the case was deemed justiciable, it did not uphold *in toto* the lower court's determination that there was an equal protection violation in *Bandemer.*

---

95 478 U.S. 109 (1986).
96 478 U.S. 109 at 115.
97 *Id.*
98 *Id.* at 117.
99 *Id.* at 117-18.
100 *Id.* at 113, 119, 124.
101 *Id.* at 121.
102 *Id.* at 121-22 (*quoting* Baker at 396 U.S. at 217).
103 478 U.S. 109 at 126-27.
104 *Id.* at 123-24.

[...]¹, the Court articulated several stipulations that had to be met to sustain [...]tical gerrymandering claim. First, there had to be proof of intentional [discri]mination against the one party, here, the Democrats.¹⁰⁵ Second, "a group's electoral power is not unconstitutionally diminished by the simple fact of an apportionment scheme that makes winning elections more difficult. A failure of proportional representation alone does not constitute impermissible discrimination under the equal protection clause."¹⁰⁶ Instead, the Court stated that the political process must frustrate political activity in a systematic fashion:

> As in individual district cases, an equal protection violation may be found only where the electoral system substantially disadvantages certain voters in their opportunity to influence the political process effectively. In this context, such a finding of unconstitutionality must be supported by evidence of continued frustration of the will of a majority of the voters or effective denial to a minority of voters of a fair chance to influence the political process.¹⁰⁷

Finally, the Court contended that showing frustration or dilution of political influence in one election was also insufficient.¹⁰⁸ Instead, it would need to be shown that this took place over several elections.¹⁰⁹ In sum, the *Bandemer* Court stated that, to support a constitutional claim for partisan gerrymandering, one would have to demonstrate intentional discrimination against a party that systematically frustrated and diluted their ability to influence the political process across several elections.¹¹⁰ What emerged from *Bandemer* was perhaps the manageable standards called for in *Baker* that would allow the federal judiciary to resolve a controversy. Yet the three conditions of the case proved to be anything but manageable, and the federal courts had never invalidated a redistricting plan as a partisan gerrymander.¹¹¹ This led to demands for the Court to rethink the question of the justiciability of partisan gerrymandering. It did that first in *Vieth v. Jubelirer*¹¹² and then again in *League of United Latin American Citizens v. Perry.*¹¹³

In *Vieth*, at issue was the constitutionality of a Pennsylvania districting plan that drew the seats for its congressional delegation after the 2000 census. Prior to the census the state had 21 representatives but after 2000 it was only entitled

---

105 *Id.* at 127-28.
106 *Id.* at 131.
107 *Id.* at 132.
108 *Id.* at 135.
109 *Id.*
110 Donald Grier Stephenson, Jr., The Right to Vote: Rights and Liberties Under the Law, 246 (2004).
111 *Id.* at 246-47.
112 541 U.S. 267 (2004).
113 548 U.S. 399 (2006).

to 19 seats.[114] Republicans controlled both houses of the Pennsylvania legislature as well as the governor's office.[115] State Democrats contended that the district lines drawn violated Article I, Sections 2 and 4, and the equal protection clause,[116] thereby constituting both a violation of the one-person, one-vote standard and, more importantly here, a partisan gerrymander.[117] The district court dismissed the partisan or political gerrymandering claim[118] (with some of the other issues addressed or resolved in other litigation in the case) and it was appealed to the Supreme Court.

In what could easily be considered a split decision if ever there was one, the Supreme Court ruled several things. First, a four-person plurality opinion written by Justice Scalia reviewed the history of partisan gerrymandering in the United States, concluding that such a practice went back to the early days of the republic.[119] Given this history, there had also been numerous efforts to address it, with the Court first in *Baker v. Carr* seeking to demonstrate why redistricting issues were justiciable.[120] The Court homed in on the *Baker* discussion that judicially manageable standards or a clear rule was needed for the judiciary to resolve this controversy.[121]

Scalia next argued that the standards for addressing partisan gerrymandering in *Bandemer* had proved unworkable.[122] For Scalia:

> Eighteen years of judicial effort with virtually nothing to show for it justify us in revisiting the question whether the standard promised by *Bandemer* exists. As the following discussion reveals, no judicially discernible and manageable standards for adjudicating political gerrymandering claims have emerged. Lacking them, we must conclude that political gerrymandering claims are nonjusticiable and that *Bandemer* was wrongly decided.[123]

Scalia begins his argument by examining Justice White's plurality opinion in *Bandemer*. He criticized the three-prong test enunciated there, contending that it was unmanageable, arbitrary, and that it would fall into a simple proportionality test between voting percentages and seats won by a particular party.[124] But more importantly, in examining the legacy of test in the lower courts, the *Bandemer* opinion provided no guidance to them.[125]

---

114 541 U.S. at 272.
115 *Id.*
116 *Id.*
117 541 U.S. at 272.
118 *Id.* at 273.
119 541 U.S. at 274.
120 *Id.* at 278.
121 *Id.* at 278.
122 *Id.* at 278.
123 *Id.* at 281.
124 *Id.* at 282.
125 *Id.* at 282.

ı criticizing the standards for adjudicating partisan gerrymandering the ality opinion characterizes them all as a variation of intent plus effects, with focus being upon the plaintiff's claim that predominant intent plus effect of the gerrymander is what should guide resolution of the case.[126] This predominant intent standard, as noted in the opinion, was borrowed from the racial gerrymandering litigation under the Voting Rights Act and the equal protection clause.[127] Yet the predominant intent standard is further qualified by the plaintiffs, stating that it must apply to the entire statewide redistricting plan, creating even more problems for Scalia:

> Vague as the "predominant motivation" test might be when used to evaluate single districts, it all but evaporates when applied statewide. Does it mean, for instance, that partisan intent must outweigh all other goals—contiguity, compactness, preservation of neighborhoods, etc.—*statewide?* And how is the statewide "outweighing" to be determined? If three-fifths of the map's districts forgo the pursuit of partisan ends in favor of strictly observing political-subdivision lines, and only two-fifths ignore those lines to disadvantage the plaintiffs, is the observance of political subdivisions the "predominant" goal between those two? We are sure appellants do not think so.[128]

If plaintiff's test for determining intent was not bad enough, Scalia also criticizes the borrowing of the effects test from the racial gerrymandering/equal protection jurisprudence. While race is immutable, one's politics is not, rendering it difficult to ascertain if people of a specific political affiliation or stripe have been packed or cracked into or among districts.[129] Moreover, the plurality also states that, even if the effects of a gerrymander could be ascertained and one accepted the fact that a majority has had their political will frustrated, the Court contended that there would be no constitutional violation because the equal protection clause does not provide for proportional representation.[130] What does the equal protection clause provide? "It guarantees equal protection of the law to persons, not equal representation in government to equivalently sized groups. It nowhere says that farmers or urban dwellers, Christian fundamentalists or Jews, Republicans or Democrats, must be accorded political strength proportionate to their numbers."[131] Finally, Scalia also questions how we measure the strength of a party. While one party may capture more votes in a federal race in a state, another may well capture more in a state race for governor. In addition, since legislative races are not at-large, aggregating votes in district contests may also not produce a sense of who or what constitutes

---

126 541 U.S. at 284.
127 *Id.* at 284.
128 541 U.S. at 285.
129 *Id.* at 287.
130 541 U.S. at 287-88.
131 *Id.* at 288.

a majority party.¹³² Thus, for all of these reasons, the intent plus effect standard is unmanageable.

The plurality opinion also criticized alternative standards proposed by the dissenters in the case, dismissing all of them as deficient. Of special interest here is the argument presented by Justice Stevens (as criticized and characterized by the plurality) who drew an analogy between First Amendment jurisprudence and the equal protection claims here:

> Justice Stevens relies on *First Amendment cases* to suggest that politically discriminatory gerrymanders are subject to strict scrutiny under the *Equal Protection Clause*. It is elementary that scrutiny levels are claim specific. An action that triggers a heightened level of scrutiny for one claim may receive a very different level of scrutiny for a different claim because the underlying rights, and consequently constitutional harms, are not comparable. To say that suppression of political speech (a claimed First Amendment violation) triggers strict scrutiny is not to say that failure to give political groups equal representation (a claimed equal protection violation) triggers strict scrutiny. Only an equal protection claim is before us in the present case—perhaps for the very good reason that a First Amendment claim, if it were sustained, would render unlawful *all* consideration of political affiliation in districting, just as it renders unlawful *all* consideration of political affiliation in hiring for non-policy-level government jobs. What cases such as *Elrod v. Burns*, 427 U.S. 347, 96 S.Ct. 2673, 49 L.Ed.2d 547 (1976), require is not merely that Republicans be given a decent share of the jobs in a Democratic administration, but that political affiliation *be disregarded.*¹³³

In part, the plurality's claim is that, were the tools for assessing First Amendment claims adopted to apply to political gerrymanders, then either the standards would still be unmanageable or all political considerations in redistricting would need to be banned.¹³⁴

Overall, a four-Justice plurality ruled that partisan gerrymanders were not justiciable and therefore in the case before them the claims of the Democrats should be rejected. However, only four Justices agreed that the Democrats had not proved that a partisan gerrymander existed in the case before and that this type of issue was not justiciable. Justice Kennedy concurred that there was no partisan gerrymander here, but he refused to go along with overruling *Bandemer*.¹³⁵ He agreed that neutral rules for resolving and adjudicating partisan gerrymanders were needed but he did not agree with the majority that it would never be possible

---

132   541 U.S. at 288-89.
133   541 U.S. at 294.
134   541 U.S. at 294.
135   541 U.S. at 306-7.

to find them.[136] This thus created a five Justice majority to reject the plaintiffs' claims. However, five Justices in several dissents, including Kennedy, refused to overrule *Bandemer*, continuing to make partisan gerrymanders justiciable issues. What the dissenters could not agree on were what constituted acceptable or manageable standards for adjudicating a partisan gerrymander dispute. The hope was that *League of United Latin American Citizens v. Perry* (*LULAC*) would do that, but it did not.

LULAC arouse out of a high-profile partisan battle in the Texas legislature that involved U.S. Representative Tom DeLay and a battle for the state legislature and its congressional delegation. The 2000 census indicated that the State of Texas should receive two additional seats in the House of Representatives beyond the current 30 that it had.[137] At the time of redistricting the Texas Republican Party controlled the State Senate and governor's office but the Democrats controlled the State House of Representatives.[138] Unable to agree to adopt a redistricting scheme, litigation eventually led to the creation of a court-ordered one.[139] This plan produced a 17-15 Democratic majority in the Texas congressional delegation.[140] But in 2003 state elections gave Republicans control of both houses of the state legislature as well as control of the governor's office.[141] With the encouragement of Tom DeLay, and after a long struggle, including Democrats in the legislature hiding out in Oklahoma to avoid a special session, the state passed a new redistricting plan in 2003.[142]

In 2004, elections using this new plan gave Republicans 58 percent of the statewide vote compared to 41 percent for Democrats. Republicans also captured 21 of the congressional seats to the 11 won by the Democrats.[143] The 2003 plan was challenged in court, claiming, *inter alia*, that it was a partisan gerrymander and that the state and federal constitutions barred a second redistricting scheme following a decennial census.[144] Judgement was for the appellees but in light of the *Vieth v. Jubelirer* decision, the Supreme Court vacated and remanded it to reconsider.[145] The district court then solely considered the political gerrymandering claim and again ruled in favor of the appellees.[146] Before the Supreme Court were arguments that the 2003 redistricting schema was a partisan or political gerrymander, that it violated the Voting Rights Act (VRA), and that the mid-decade redistricting

---

136 *Id.*
137 548 U.S. at 410-12.
138 *Id.*
139 *Id.*
140 548 U.S. at 412.
141 *Id.*
142 *Id.*
143 548 U.S. at 412.
144 *Id.*
145 *Id.*
146 *Id.*

violated the one-person, one-vote requirement under the Fourteenth Amendment.[147] While the Court did find that one of the districts did violate the VRA,[148] it rejected claims that the mid-decade redistricting violated the Constitution and it also ruled that the appellants had failed to state a claim upon which relief could be granted for the political gerrymander.

Justice Kennedy, writing for yet another divided Court when it came to the partisan gerrymander claim, specifically noted that the theory of the plaintiffs was that mid-decade redistricting when solely motivated by partisan objectives violated the Fourteenth Amendment.[149] A majority of the Court rejected this claim,[150] stating that not every line drawn was done based on partisan objectives.[151] Yet even if mixed motives were not present in this case, Kennedy asserted that one challenging a gerrymander as partisan would have to show how it burdened, according to a reliable standard, their representational rights.[152] The simple fact that a mid-decade redistricting schema took place is rejected as a per se standard to show burden.[153] Similarly, the claim that a mid-decade redistricting violates the one-person, one-vote requirement if done for partisan purposes is also rejected.[154] While Kennedy clearly stated that this decision did not revisit the justiciability of partisan gerrymandering, it rejected the tests offered in this case to define a standard for resolving disputes averring this as a claim.[155]

As with *Vieth*, *LULAC* produced a divided Court that failed to mend the split over partisan gerrymandering. Kennedy wrote the opinion for the Court with various Justices concurring with parts of the decision. The splits occurred over whether partisan gerrymanders are justiciable (five Justices agreed that they were), whether there was a VRA violation in the drawing of district 23 (five agreed there were), and over whether there was an agreement on what constituted manageable standards for resolving a political gerrymander (Kennedy rejects the plaintiff's proposed standard, four Justices reject all standards, and four other Justices splinter over various possible standards). *LULAC* left the Court no better off than before, despite a change in two Justices since the *Vieth* decision and with four Justices saying political gerrymanders are non-justiciable, four saying they are and proposing different standards, and Kennedy in the middle saying the issue is justiciable but still in search of a standard. Yet unlike in *Vieth* where the plurality opinion engaged in a discussion of the equal protection logic underlying the

---

147 548 U.S. at 412.
148 548 U.S. at 421-23 (*finding* that district 23 did violate the VRA). For our present purposes, the VRA claim shall not be discussed.
149 *Id.* at 416-17.
150 *Id.* at 418.
151 *Id.*
152 *Id.*
153 *Id.*
154 548 U.S. at 421.
155 *Id.* at 414.

claims, little of that took place here. Similarly, while in *Vieth* Justices Kennedy and Stevens raised the possibility that these types of claims might be better suited as First Amendment challenges (and Scalia responded to that), only Stevens ever so briefly references this line of debate.

Several points stand out when the partisan gerrymander cases are examined. First, the Justices are clearly divided over whether the courts have jurisdiction to hear these type of cases. All three cases are wrapped in discussions of justiciability and the political question doctrine. Second, all three cases are narrowly drawn to discuss the question of whether there are any Equal Protection violations. Third, the Court has failed to explain how or why partisan gerrymandering is a problem beyond addressing a constitutional issue. Missing from the three cases is any substantive discussion of representation, the reasons why gerrymandering is wrong, why it may be impermissible for one party to use its political power to entrench itself, or perhaps any other of a set of issues that may provide a foundation or clarification regarding how such a practice should be viewed within a theory of democracy. This failure, as with other areas of election law, of course speaks to significant dissensus on the Court, but the continuing disagreements also might be the product of a judiciary that has failed to provide a real grounding in democratic theory for its decisions. Thus, at least in the four areas of election law briefly surveyed here, the evidence seems to be that there is no clearly articulated theory of democracy grounding its decisions.

Election Law Scholarship

So Supreme Court Justices are not political theorists, what did you expect? No doubt this is a criticism or argument being raised by some. The Justices are lawyers and judges, not philosopher kings and queens and we should not expect them to be waxing about democratic theory in crafting their opinions. This is a fair criticism even though it misses the major point that this chapter is seeking to assert—that election law is so incoherent and rudderless because it has failed to recognize its connection to democratic theory. The fact that Justices are ruling on a case-by-case basis both regarding and without regard to a theory is the problem, and perhaps the reason why they are confused or so rudderless in their approach to the topic.

But what about the election law scholarship? Perhaps scholars in this field are better at addressing theory than is the judiciary. One way to assess this is by looking at how leading election law textbooks discuss or approach the topic of democratic theory. There are three major texts to examine.

The first and the oldest is *Election Law: Cases and Materials*, now in its fifth edition and edited by Daniel Lowenstein, Richard Hasen, and Daniel Tokaji. The original first edition was published in 1995 by Dan Lowenstein who probably invented the field of election law as a law school class and scholarly field. The original edition as well as through the fifth covered a range of topics including voting rights, representation, the Voting Rights Act, redistricting, political parties, campaigns, and money and politics. These would be staple topics for all of the three election law textbooks. But unique to the Lowenstein text is that its first chapter does introduce readers and the discipline of election law by discussing some political science and political theory readings. Chapter 1 contains James Madison's *Federalist* 10 which discusses the problem of factions and popular government in the view of the constitutional Framers. *Federalist* 10 is famous for defining what later in this present book will be referred to as the problem of politics and the solution to it. However, surprisingly, missing from this chapter is *Federalist* 51, also by James Madison, which is often read together with number 10. *Federalist* 51 elaborates in more detail upon the structure of government and theory of human nature embedded in the Framers' theory of government.

But, in addition, Lowenstein offers Edmund Burke's famous Bristol speech as a way to describe some points about representation. This speech contrasts theories of representation asking if the job of an elected official is to be simply a delegate or additionally exercise independent discretion in performing duties. Clearly these are important issues to representation but do not capture the total of the theoretical points implicated by representation. Finally, the fifth edition has excerpts by Richard Ellis and Irving Kristol as two efforts to begin to articulate pluralism and its critique. Both pieces are fine selections, but do not really delve into the full exposition of pluralism and its critique. Scholarly works, such as those by David Truman (*The Governmental Process*),[156] Robert Dahl (*Who Governs* or *A Preface to Democratic Theory*),[157] or Theodore Lowi (*The End of Liberalism*),[158] among many others, would again be considered by many political scientists to be the classics in seeking to articulate or describe some of the major theories that capture important aspects of American democratic theory.

The Lowenstein text thus begins an effort to describe the difference between Madisonian and pluralist theories of democracy. Yet it neither pushes very far into this discussion nor develops or connects these opening readings in sufficient detail to the topics found throughout the remainder of the text. Chapter 1 literally hangs out there as a preface to a text, divorcing political science and democratic theory from the law. Moreover, while there is some introductory material in each chapter or in the notes that raise some points about the literature on political science and political phenomena as they connect to some of the legal issues discussed in the book, for the most part there is very little attention given to connecting democratic theory and the field of political theory to election law. In short, little attention is given to overall descriptions and questions regarding what is a democracy, the specific of American democratic theory, and special issues that connect either to

---

156 DAVID TRUMAN, THE GOVERNMENTAL PROCESS (1951).
157 ROBERT A. DAHL, WHO GOVERNS? DEMOCRACY AND POWER IN AN AMERICAN CITY (1961); ROBERT A. DAHL, A PREFACE TO DEMOCRATIC THEORY (1956).
158 THEODORE LOWI, THE END OF LIBERALISM: THE SECOND REPUBLIC OF THE UNITED STATES (1979).

most of the topics in the book. The text is terrific on cases and commentary, but weak on democracy.

The second text is *The Law of Democracy* by Samuel Issacharoff, Pamela Karlan, and Richard Pildes.[159] Now in its fourth edition, this was first published in 1998. Given its title—especially with the reference to democracy—one would expect that the text would have significant references to political theory and political science in terms of how both impact election law. But that is not necessarily the case. Unlike the Lowenstein text, there is no chapter devoted to the basics of democratic theory. There is no subject heading for the *Federalist Papers*, there is no substantial discussion of pluralism, missing is any serious discussion of the goals and theories of representation, and absent from the chapters on voting, political parties, and money and politics are more than perfunctory discussions of some of the major political theoretical issues or controversies surrounding these topics.

Perhaps the most extended discussion of democracy occurs in the final chapter where the authors explore what they call alternative democratic structures. This chapter engages the topics of cumulative voting, single transferable voting (ranked choice voting), proportional voting, and other similar franchise options. The discussion here is case law driven, with no excerpts from works or theories on voting that explain that democratic theory basis or rationale for these procedures. Thus, even within the chapter that seems most conducive to bringing in democratic theory discussion, it does not occur.

Yet in all fairness, *The Law of Democracy* does not completely ignore democratic or political theory. In Chapter 3, on reapportionment, the authors do discuss republican theory and the concepts of representation that flow from it. Chapter 2, "The Right to Participate," has historical discussion on voting in the United States and it includes excerpts or references to social science works by Gordon Wood and Frances Fox Piven seeking to explain voting behavior in the United States. Chapter 5, "The Role of Political Parties," too has some discussion on party functions, voting, and ballot access, but the topic is not well developed and receives little attention. The point here is that one has to search hard to find much of discussion of democracy in this text.

The third leading election law textbook is *Voting Rights and Election Law* by Michael Dimino, Bradley Smith, and Michael Solimine.[160] Published in 2010 it covers essentially the same ground as *Election Law* and *The Law of Democracy*. The chapters are similarly organized, with almost identical cases covered in all three. But, like *The Law of Democracy*, *Voting Rights and Election Law* has no chapter devoted to democratic theory. Moreover, there is little discussion in the chapters devoted to what one might consider to be democratic theory or

---

159 Samuel Issacharoff, Pamela Karlan, and Richard Pildes. The Law of Democracy (2012).

160 Michael Dimino, Bradley Smith, and Michael Solimine, Voting Rights and Election Law (2010).

the political science literature that addresses the topics in the book. While case coverage here is perhaps the richest and most comprehensive of the three major texts, it too is generally devoid of a serious discussion of the underlying issues of democratic theory that are at the basis of disputes that range from voting rights to representation and campaign financing.

Finally, in late 2012 a fourth text by James Gardner and Guy-Uriel Charles made its appearance.[161] Their *Election Law in the American Political System* is definitely different from other leading texts. Chapters 1 and 2 actually do discuss many of the classics of political and democratic theory ranging from Plato to John Locke and Jean-Jacques Rousseau. It also covers many contemporary or recent democratic discussants that include Benjamin Barber, Judith Shklar, and Anthony Downs. It contrasts Madisonian democracy to pluralism, examines the problem of majority rule, and voting behavior. In contrast to its rivals, Gardner and Charles have produced the most political science- and theory-orientated book on election law to date. They have done the best job setting the context for the subsequent election law cases and topics to be discussed. Yet, strong as this book's aim is, it too fails to carry over the discussion of the first two chapters into the rest of the book in terms of seeking to offer a framework for how to think about the topics and cases discussed. Perhaps this is not the purpose of a teaching book, and that is a fair rejoinder. But this book definitely points to how most of the case law and scholarship on election law largely fails to integrate the field with democratic theory.

In sum, the leading election law books are all excellent in their coverage of the major cases and legal doctrines. This is not a surprise given that all the books were prepared by law school professors for law school instruction. Except perhaps for Gardner and Charles, they reflect and approach to the subject that has become the dominant paradigm for the field—examining election law issues devoid of a discussion of deeper normative issues embedded within contested theories of democracy that shape the debates over how questions of voting rights, reapportionment, ballot access, and party rights are divided.

But clearly the field of election law is broader than these texts. The *Election Law Journal* is the flagship publication in the field. Its editors and editorial board (which does include this author) include many if not most of the leading scholars and teachers in the field of election law. The articles definitely reflect the best scholarship in election law but again, a fair criticism of the journal is that it really is legalistic in most of its focus. Although most of the scholarship does a terrific job examining specific cases or topics, seldom is the focus of argument upon an integration of law back into democratic theory or the field of political science. Many pieces feel more like legal briefs for specific issues, and do not rise to theory.

The *Election Law Journal* (ELJ) began publication in 2002. In the course of a decade the word "democracy" has seldom appeared in the title of the main

---

161 JAMES GARDNER AND GUY-URIEL CHARLES, ELECTION LAW IN THE AMERICAN POLITICAL SYSTEM (2012).

articles, with one issue—June 2004—containing four articles with that word, two authored by politicians John McCain and John Anderson. While the pieces in the ELJ are intellectually astute, their focus as noted, has generally been on case law and doctrine, with only occasional reference to broader institutional forces and concerns about democracy.

Others too have noted that the narrow description of the field as limited to the study of cases and doctrine may fail to capture its broader significance. For example, Bruce Cain has noted how "democratic theory provides a normative framework for thinking about concepts such as equity, representation, and influence, which find their way into legal scholarship and judicial decisions."[162] Cain also notes that many other aspects of political science speak to or frame many issues found in the topic of election law. He concludes his critique or gloss on election law by arguing for more interdisciplinary work cooperation, suggesting that a more appropriate name for the field would be "political regulation."[163] Similarly, Rick Hasen noted in his overview of articles in the same law review issue that others too have objected to the narrowness of the term "election law" in capturing the field. He states for example:

> Samuel Issacharoff and Richard Pildes, co-authors—along with Pamela Karlan—of the other casebook in this field, object that the term "election law" may signal a "tedious focus on the narrow regulatory questions of most interest to political junkies." In their view, the field is about "taking democracy itself out of the background and placing it squarely at the center of our inquiries." Not coincidentally, their casebook is entitled "The Law of Democracy."

The critique here is that election law as it has evolved has been defined by law professors and the law, perhaps ignoring or taking democratic theory and larger institutional issue out of the debate. In effect, academic lawyers have narrowly defined the field and when they then litigate the cases or are called up as experts in disputes, this focus then translates into how judges and Justices approach the topic. Finally, this narrow focus by lawyers and judges is not because other parties have not tried to offer views, especially in terms of *amicus curiae* briefs. Occasionally, political scientists have submitted briefs on election law topics, such as in United States Supreme Court in *Colorado Republican Party v. Federal Election Commission*[164] and *McConnell v. Federal Election*

---

162 Bruce Cain, *Election Law as a Field: a Political Scientist's Perspective*, 32 LOY. L.A. L. REV. 1105, 1105 (1999).

163 *Id.* at 1119.

164 Federal Election Commission v. Colorado Republican Federal Campaign Committee 533 U.S. 431 (2001), "Brief of Paul Allen Beck, Janet M. Box-Steffensmeier, Leon D. Epstein, Anthony Gierzynski, Donald P. Green, Paul S. Herrnson, Ruth S. Jones, Ira Katznelson, Bruce Larson, David B. Magleby, Thomas E. Mann, David Schultz, Daniel M. Shea, and Frank J. Sorauf as Amici Curiae in Support of Petitioner."

Commission.[165] Given the lack of citation by the Supreme Court, it is unclear how much of an impact these briefs have had.

Conclusion

The field of election law has come to be defined as one narrowly focusing on case law and doctrine, with special emphasis directed at the primacy of the courts as the primary regulator and definer of the law affecting the political process. It is a field generally devoid of theory. But what is theory? Theory can be articulated at several levels, ranging from asking basic questions about "Why government?" to lower order questions about the specific roles of particular agents and institutions within a democracy.[166] The purpose of a theory is to define values, and to articulate a relationship among concepts and ideas. While the field of election law often invokes values and concepts, it has largely failed to reach a broader theory beyond perhaps at a lower level or order to define how many of its concept and ideas exist together. A discussion about money in politics, or voting, or representation cannot be undertaken in isolation of a broader reflection regarding how they fit together into a more coherent vision about how an American democracy should work.

The purpose of this chapter was to establish a simple concept—that the field of election law as it has evolved since *Bush v. Gore* is one that seems increasingly divorced from theories of democracy and empirical understandings of the political process. This legal formalism may be contributing to the problems that the courts have in articulating meaningful and effective solutions to the problems of democracy. Election lawyers have shaped a field in their research that generally is devoid of reaching out to broader considerations of how the laws need to connect to wider institutional concerns about democracy. The aim of the remainder of this book is to begin to rectify this parochialism.

---

165 McConnell v. Federal Election Commission, 540 U.S. 93 (2003), "Brief of Political Scientists Norman J. Ornstein, Ph.D., et al. as Amici Curiae Supporting the Constitutionality of Title 1 of the Bipartisan Campaign Reform Act of 2002."

166 David Schultz, *The Crisis of Public Administration Theory in a Post-global World*, in Don Menzel and Harvey White, eds., The State of Public Administration: Issues, Challenges, Opportunities, 453 (2011).

Chapter 2
Democratic Theory and American Politics

Election law is the jurisprudence that puts democracy into action. As Chapter 1 demonstrated, many of the critical Supreme Court decisions affecting issues such as ballot access, political parties, and voting rights all hinge on a theory of democracy or a democratic theory. The way critical tradeoffs are affected between determining how much money individuals should contribute versus policing for corruption, or decisions on promoting franchise versus increasing ballot security to prevent voter fraud, are, in part, not questions that are singularly empirical in nature. Instead, they are also questions about fundamental values. They are about the values important to how we think a democratic political regime such as the United States should operate. They define and describe what is important to our concept of a fair and democratic political system.

Another way to think about election law is to describe it as the rules of the game. As with all board games or any types of sports, there are rules regarding how to play the game. Rules determine what is considered a ball or strike in baseball or even what is considered a home run versus a foul ball. Football has rules regarding what counts as a fair catch or offsides or what is considered illegal use of hands. Generally one thinks of these rules as simply procedural or process-orientated. By that, the rules are thought of as not being outcome-determinative. The rules are considered neutral. They do not favor any one player but instead simply describe how to play the game and whoever best masters the rules, along with some skill and luck, generally can win.

But as we have come to learn, rules are not always neutral. For one, some may come to a game more skilled than others. Those more talented in hitting a baseball are generally better at playing the game than are those who are novices to the sport. Skill and experience matter. In addition, rules can affect outcomes because the rules affect or define critical tradeoffs in the sport. They define what constitutes as cheating or fair play, excluding some from winning because of certain tactics that are employed. Lance Armstrong for years was thought of as one of the greatest cyclists ever and he won numerous races, including repeated titles to the Tour de France. But allegations and then his admission of use of illegal steroids cost him his titles because the use of drugs to enhance performance constitutes cheating, thereby a violation of the rules.[1]

---

1 Greg Botelho and Josh Levs, *"Deeply Flawed" Lance Armstrong Admits Using Performance Enhancing Drugs*, CNN (January 18, 2013), http://edition.cnn.com/2013/01/17/sport/armstrong-doping/ (site last visited on February 27, 2013).

Beyond games and sports, many activities have rules that really are outcome determinative even though they are often thought of as neutral. The rules of the criminal justice process defining an adversarial process for finding truth and determining guilt or innocence is an example. Lawyers like to think the rules of evidence and trial processes are neutral, but they are not. Rules that determine what is evidence, what is a valid search and seizure, or what constitutes an acceptable interrogation of a witness reflect critical tradeoffs in values about privacy and police authority. Those who, over the years, have claimed that the law favors police or suspects understand how rules may favor one side over another. Additionally, feminists such as Catherine McKinnon have argued that the law reflects a male perspective, especially when it comes to rape and sexual harassment, thereby influencing the outcomes of cases involving these issues.[2]

The rules of democracy are similarly outcome determinative. John Hart Ely in *Democracy and Distrust* has argued that the Constitution is generally a process-orientated document but it too reflects at least one substantive value—individual freedom. The importance of his argument is that the process or rules of the Constitution, including clauses that refer to concepts such as due process or equal protection, both define a way for the government to act and also reflect specific substantive values about the relationship of the government to individual liberty. We are to read the Constitution as a process-orientated document, but one which defines fair play and the rules as those which encourage individual liberty.

One should think of election law as the rules of democracy that embody both the process of how democracy is played and the substantive values which the rules are meant to encourage. The rules of democracy are perhaps like Wittgensteinian language games. Words, for Ludwig Wittgenstein, derive their meaning, in part, from their use.[3] An entire language is defined by a collection of language games surrounding specific uses of words. Their meaning is determined by the games users play with them. Words derive their meaning from their context and their relationship to other words around them. What a democracy is, what it means, and what critical terms or values such as free and fair elections, free speech, and the right to vote mean are determined by their relationship to other concepts and by how all of them come together to be applied and implemented or put into use by election law and the application of a democracy. To paraphrase Justice Oliver Wendell Holmes, Jr., the life of democracy is experience and not logic.[4]

Once I had the privilege to talk to Archibald Cox. Although he was once the Solicitor General for the United States and argued many important cases for the federal government before the Supreme Court, he is most famous for having been the special prosecutor fired in the famous Saturday Night Massacre in 1973 after he was hired to investigate the Nixon administration for events surrounding the

---

2 CATHARINE A. MACKINNON, TOWARD A FEMINIST THEORY OF THE STATE (1991).
3 LUDWIG WITTGENSTEIN, PHILOSOPHICAL INVESTIGATIONS, paragraphs 432, 559 (1968). The standard citation to the Philosophical Investigations is to cite to paragraph numbers.
4 OLIVER WENDELL HOLMES, JR., THE COMMON LAW, 1 (1991).

Watergate break-in. Cox once stated to me that election laws were the "rules that determined the rules of game." By that he meant that the rules of election law, including how money could be spent for political purposes, determined how the game of politics and democracy would be played. Decide these prior rules and they determine the latter. His point is simple—there are important values that a democracy must articulate and enable. Democracies are distinguished from authoritarian governments because of the values they articulate. The question then becomes what are those values?

Defining Democracy

Democracies have their own unique values structure. According to Schultz:

> Democratic theories have ontologies. Each defines its object of inquiry, the critical components of what makes a political system work, and what forces, structures, and assumptions are core to its conception of governance. This ontology will not only include a discussion of human nature but also examination of concepts such as representation, consent, political parties, liberty, equality, and a host of other ideas and institutions that define what a democracy is and how it is supposed to operate.[5]

The ontology of a democracy is what distinguishes it from other types of political regimes. In Ancient Greek political thought Plato and Aristotle, for example, often distinguished types of political regimes from one another by the values they embodied.[6] For example, Plato saw monarchies as characterized by knowledge and wisdom. Aristocracies were characterized by courage, and democracies by passion.[7] Each regime had a different what we would call today political culture to distinguish it from other regimes. The same basic idea applies here. According to Robert Dahl, polyarchies—the term he prefers to use in lieu of democracy—are also characterized by a distinct set of values.[8] What are they?

Robert Dahl lists five of what he calls criteria or values for a democracy.[9] These five are voting equality, effective participation, enlightened understanding, control

---

5   David A Schultz, *The Phenomenology of Democracy: Putnam, Pluralism, and Voluntary Associations*, in. SCOTT L. MCLEAN, DAVID A. SCHULTZ, AND MANFRED B. STEGER, EDS., SOCIAL CAPITAL: CRITICAL PERSPECTIVES ON COMMUNITY AND "BOWLING ALONE," 74 (2002).

6   SIR ERNEST BARKER, THE POLITICAL THOUGHT OF PLATO AND ARISTOTLE, 172-76, 307-20 (1959).

7   PLATO, THE REPUBLIC, trans. Francis MacDonald Cornford, 145 (1945).

8   ROBERT A. DAHL, A PREFACE TO DEMOCRATIC THEORY (1956); ROBERT A. DAHL, POLYARCHY: PARTICIPATION AND OPPOSITION (1972).

9   ROBERT A. DAHL, DEMOCRACY AND ITS CRITICS, 222 (1989).

of the agenda, and inclusion. Dahl's criteria are similar to what other democratic theorists have described as the requisites or values central to describing what a democracy is.[10]

If democracy means anything it seems to include the idea of some sort of equality.[11] Now there are significant debates regarding what type of equality is demanded of a democratic society. Dahl himself argues for both a procedural or formal sense of equality before the law as well as sometime of substantive equality in terms of economic resources.[12] Others too have described various meanings of equality as essential to democracy.[13] Theorists such as John Rawls have rendered similar claims, contending that a liberal democracy adhering to his two principles of justice—equal liberty for all consistent with like liberty for others, and the structuring of economic inequalities so that they are of benefit to the least advantaged representative person in society—demand something approaching an equality both in terms of economic conditions and equality before the law.[14]

With Dahl, the concept of equality entails two important concepts. The first is the notion of individual moral autonomy.[15] For many democratic theorists, democracy begins with the idea of individual liberty or freedom. For John Locke, the idea that government derives its justification from a social contract and consent of the people is a powerful metaphor to enabling a theory about limited government. The government derives its just ends (as it states in the American Declaration of Independence) from the people. Other theorists, such as Jean-Jacques Rousseau and Immanuel Kant, echo similar thoughts. For Rousseau, the concept that freedom resides in conforming to the general will is an important one. It is here where the people get to make the laws that will govern them that one gets a sense of Rousseauian democracy. For Kant, the very notion of autonomy—living according to rules that one has legislated for herself[16]—is the purest notion of what a democracy is. It is self-rule. It is where the people, as French political

---

10 *See, e.g.*, J. ROLAND PENNOCK, DEMOCRATIC POLITICAL THEORY (1979); and GIOVANNI SARTORI, THE THEORY OF DEMOCRACY REVISITED, 2 vols. (1987), for general discussions of democratic theories and criteria used to evaluate regimes.

11 Pennock at 35; Sartori at 58-59, 342-44.

12 ROBERT A. DAHL, A PREFACE TO ECONOMIC DEMOCRACY (1986). *See also:* Dahl, Democracy and its Critics, 83.

13 JOHN LOCKE, TWO TREATISES OF GOVERNMENT, Second Treatise, ¶ 4, 54, 123 (1996); JEAN-JACQUES ROUSSEAU, THE SOCIAL CONTRACT, 96 (1977); JOHN STUART MILL, THE SUBJECTION OF WOMEN, 48-50 (1986); RONALD DWORKIN, TAKING RIGHTS SERIOUSLY (1978).

14 JOHN RAWLS, A THEORY OF JUSTICE (1971); JOHN RAWLS, POLITICAL LIBERALISM (1993). For a more general discussion of the role of equality in modern Western political thought, see JOHN RAWLS, LECTURES ON THE HISTORY OF POLITICAL PHILOSOPHY (2007).

15 Dahl, Democracy and its Critics, 97.

16 IMMANUEL KANT, FOUNDATION OF THE METAPHYSICS OF MORALS, ed. Robert Paul Wolff (1978); Rawls, Theory of Justice, 252-54.

theorist Jean Bodin stated, are sovereign.[17] Democracies are where the people hold political power, either directly or indirectly, and generally, at least in the United States, are viewed as the ultimate source of authority.

Thus, for a democracy, personal autonomy or liberty of some fashion is required. That autonomy is also one that is shared equally. As Jeremy Bentham and other nineteenth-century philosophers would declare, each person should count as one and no more than one.[18] Democracies mean that each person has an equal voice, and the equal freedom to act upon that voice. Thus Rawls may be correct in describing the first principle of justice as perhaps also the first rule of a democracy that each person is entitled to "the most extensive basic liberty compatible with similar liberty for others."[19] Later, in his 2005 book *Political Liberalism*, he refines this statement to declare that "each person has an equal claim to a fully adequate scheme of equal basic rights and liberties."[20] In reformulating the way he does in his latter book Rawls makes it clear that democracy embraces both concepts of equality or equal voice and the personal liberty to act on that voice.

But exactly what the liberty and equality extends to is a matter of contention. Moreover, how deep that equal voice is, is also a matter of dispute in a democracy. At the least it appears to extend to formal voting perhaps, with each person given the same opportunity to cast a vote for a candidate or issue of her choice. Yet even in declaring this proposition, many questions remain. Who is allowed to vote, over what matter, and when? Is voting for representatives the sum total of what equality is about, or is something else required? All of these are important questions, perhaps answered in part by the other criteria or values that Dahl describes.

The second criterion or value of a democracy is effective participation. What does effective participation mean? Here Dahl describes this requirement as giving citizens a way to express their views on the final outcome of a choice, and that includes time to place questions on the agenda and the chance to opt for one outcome over another. It also includes giving voters the choice at the decisive points in the decision-making process.[21] Of course it would be meaningless to say one has effective participation in making choices if the critical choices are already made before one gets to act. If the agenda has already been set for example, or if items are kept off the agenda, the range of potential choices is already narrowed.[22]

---

17 JEAN BODIN, ON SOVEREIGNTY: FOUR CHAPTERS FROM THE SIX BOOKS OF THE COMMONWEALTH, trans. Julian Franklin (2003).

18 JEREMY BENTHAM, THE PRINCIPLES OF MORALS AND LEGISLATION (1948); ELIE HALÉVY, THE GROWTH OF PHILOSOPHICAL RADICALISM, trans. Mary Morris, 139, 147 (1955).

19 Rawls, Theory of Justice, 60.

20 Rawls, Political Liberalism, 5.

21 Dahl, Democracy and its Critics, 109.

22 *See:* Peter Bachrach and Morton S. Baratz, *Two Faces of Power*, 56 AM. POL. SCI. REV. 947 (December, 1962), for a discussion of non decision-making and the ability of some groups to keep issues off the agenda. *See also:* E.E. SCHATTSCHNEIDER, THE

Effective participation means a voice both over a range of issues that are important as well as temporally early and late enough in the decision-making process to ensure that the choices are meaningful and can really affect outcomes.

In the field of election law one good example of this involves *Smith v. Allwright*.[23] *Smith* is part of a cluster of Supreme Court decisions referred to as the White primary cases. Back in the first half of the twentieth century the southern part of the United States was solidly Democratic when it came to the election of candidates of office. This was a legacy of the segregation, discrimination, and the Civil War. Places such as Texas and Louisiana were effectively one-party states. This meant that whoever won the Democratic primary would effectively be the winner in the general election because the Republican Party was so weak. Thus, primaries were where the action was at. An African-American individual wished to participate in the Democratic primary but the Party's rules barred individuals of this race from their primaries. The constitutional issue in this case was whether a party primary was a private affair that would allow for exclusion of individuals based on race or it was a form of state action and therefore the Constitution and Fourteenth Amendment protected a right to participate. The Court did eventually rule that the party primary was entwined with state action and therefore the discrimination was illegal. But the point in bringing up this case here is less about the constitutional issue than in making a point about effective participation. If the primaries are politically decisive, then excluding someone from participating in them is a denial of a right to effective participation. To say one has a right to vote, but not when it really matters, dilutes that right to vote.

A third value that Dahl describes as essential for a democracy is enlightened understanding.[24] It would be naïve to say that one has a right to vote or make choices but that one has no right to gather the information necessary to make informed choices. At some point along the way there is a belief or need for citizens to gather information, talk to others, share ideas, or even work together if the idea of effective participation is to mean anything. James Madison would claim in *Federalist* 47 and 49 that "all government rests on opinion."[25] The people have a right to form opinions about public matters. To do that requires that the people know something, that they gather information, and that they are informed. Thomas Jefferson's view of politics also emphasized the "Jeffersonian ideal" of an educated public. It is the concept that the people can rule but only if they have access to an education that makes it possible for them to be informed. John Stuart Mill too believed in the importance of education as critical to self-governance, with his *On Liberty* often seen as the classic defense of freedom of thought and expression in the pursuit of truth.

SEMI-SOVEREIGN PEOPLE: A REALIST'S VIEW OF DEMOCRACY IN AMERICA, 20-47 (1960), discussing how the group mobilization of bias and control over the scope of conflict can affect what issues are on the agenda.

23 321 U.S. 649 (1944).
24 Dahl, Democracy and Its Critics, 111-12.
25 Hamilton, Madison, and Jay, The Federalist, 329.

Enlightened understanding also refers to the idea that political choices are more than simply raw expressions of preferences. Yes political scientists will often describe voting choices as based on self-interest or pure economics—"Are you better off now than four years ago?" But even to be guided by self-interest requires knowledge of preferences and how different options better serve them. John Stuart Mill emphasized the role that political participation can play in educating people.[26] The process of being exposed to other people and ideas educates one, hopefully producing a more refined set of choices that may transcend raw self-interest. Civic engagement builds social capital and trust, facilitating cooperation.[27] Collective action or decision-making is educative. Alexis de Tocqueville, in *Democracy in America*, described the people of the United States as acting from self-interest rightly understood.[28] It was an enlightened self-interest that made America work because service on juries or participation in voluntary associations educated individuals as to how to make better choices.[29]

What the concept of enlightened understanding is about then on one level is education and information gathering. It is amassing the necessary information to make good political choices. But it is also about the marketplace of ideas. It is the concept that in a free society no one is the final arbiter of truth and that, as John Stuart Mill described it in *On Liberty*, the clash of competing ideas would test competing proposals, producing relevant and important information needed to make choices and yield the truth.[30] Democracy means then that no one is the final imprimatur of truth and that all opinions and diversity of thought should be tolerated.[31] Democracy is part of a process or a decision-making system to locate and define the truth.

The fourth requisite for a democracy, according to Dahl, is control of the agenda.[32] This value has already been spoken of above. Control of the agenda means the people get to decide what will be decided. They get to make the choices

---

26   JOHN STUART MILL, *Representative Government*, in UTILITARIANISM, LIBERTY, AND REPRESENTATIVE GOVERNMENT, 252-55 (1951); DENNIS F. THOMPSON, JOHN STUART MILL AND REPRESENTATIVE GOVERNMENT, 137-41 (1979); CAROLE PATEMAN, PARTICIPATION AND DEMOCRATIC THEORY, 28-35 (1970).

27   ROBERT PUTNAM, BOWLING ALONE: THE COLLAPSE AND REVIVAL OF AMERICAN COMMUNITY (2001).

28   ALEXIS DE TOCQUEVILLE, DEMOCRACY IN AMERICA, ed. J.P. Mayer, trans. George Lawrence, 525 (1969).

29   *Id.* at 189-95.

30   Mill, *On Liberty*, in UTILITARIANISM, LIBERTY, AND REPRESENTATIVE GOVERNMENT, 104-11.

31   *See:* JOHN LOCKE, A LETTER CONCERNING TOLERATION (1983); JOHN MARSHALL, JOHN LOCKE, TOLERATION AND EARLY ENLIGHTENMENT CULTURE (2006); and JÜRGEN HABERMAS, THE STRUCTURAL TRANSFORMATION OF THE PUBLIC SPHERE: AN INQUIRY INTO A CATEGORY OF BOURGEOIS SOCIETY (1991), for a general discussion on the importance of toleration and appeal to rationality and search for truth in free societies.

32   Dahl, Democracy and Its Critics, 112-14.

over who the elected leaders are and with that what are the major issues and perhaps ideas that they want pursued in furtherance of their concept of the good. The idea of "We the people" or popular sovereignty is the idea that power belongs to the people. Jefferson's and the Declaration of Independence's idea in the second paragraph that the people have a right to form and disband governments—"Governments are instituted among Men, deriving their just powers from the consent of the governed," which was appropriated from John Locke's theory of the social contract—captures this point. If the people have a right to create their own government based on consent, they too have the right to decide the direction of the government and where it is headed. They get to decide for themselves what the government will do.

Buried within this idea of control of the agenda is the concept of majority rule. Again this idea seems to come from John Locke.[33] But majority rule suggests that the decision-making system that defines what will be on the agenda is also determined by the majority. This speaks to the notion that there has to be some mechanism for deciding what to do when everyone does not agree. While in the initial forming of the social contract or political society Locke emphasizes unanimous consent as the precondition for membership, once it is in operation he relies upon both the concept of tacit consent and majority rule to continue to enforce the rules and laws.[34] Majority rule recognizes the realities that not everyone agrees and instead there will be disagreement. What does one do when disagreement exists? Lacking a better mechanism, whatever 50 percent +1 of the population wants seems to be the answer.

But even with Locke the majoritarian control of the agenda at all critical stages of the decision-making process does not mean that the majority gets its way over all matters. For Locke, political society is instituted to protect certain natural rights of life, liberty, and estate.[35] These natural rights serve as a limit on governmental power, along with the terms of the original contract. Thus, majority rule is tempered by respect for minority rights. Majority rule means they may not ever vote to limit the rights of the minority. This principle will be discussed later on as an important qualification upon the American conception of democracy.

Another qualification imposed upon the control of the agenda is the idea of a representative government. Dahl describes how the movement from a small face-to-face direct democracy to a representative democracy was the second transformation in democratic theory.[36] As communities grew it became no longer

---

33 Locke, *Second Treatise*, ¶ 140; WILLMOORE KENDALL, JOHN LOCKE AND THE DOCTRINE OF MAJORITY-RULE (1965).

34 However, as some note, the original social contract and unanimous consent comes at the expense of women and people of color being excluded from taking part in the making of decisions. *See:* CAROLE PATEMAN, THE SEXUAL CONTRACT (1988); and CHARLES W. MILLS, THE RACIAL CONTRACT (1999). The arguments of Pateman and Mills speak to the problem of exclusion of some from the demos.

35 Locke, *Second Treatise*, ¶ 87.

36 Dahl, Democracy and Its Critics, 28.

practical for everyone to huddle in the town square and deliberate upon the issues.[37] John Stuart Mill makes a similar argument in *Considerations On Representative Government*:

> From these accumulated considerations it is evident that the only government which can fully satisfy all the exigencies of the social state is one in which the whole people participate; that any participation, even in the smallest public function, is useful; that the participation should everywhere be as great as the general degree of improvement of the community will allow; and that nothing less can be ultimately desirable than the admission of all to a share in the sovereign power of the state. But since all cannot, in a community exceeding a single small town, participate personally in any but some very minor portions of the public business, it follows that the ideal type of a perfect government must be representative.[38]

The ideal of course would be a government where all of us participate. But for all practical purposes that is not possible. Time constraints alone prevent all from deliberating or speaking on the issues of the day. Instead, some type of mechanism is needed in larger communities to make decisions—thus elections for representatives. Joseph Schumpeter describes democracy as a process where elites compete for the votes of citizens, seeking the authority to make decisions for them.[39] Representative government alters the concept of control of the agenda to mean primarily the voting for individuals who will then make policy or choices for the people. Thus an important value of agenda control is enabling free and fair elections that make such a process possible. Of course, in some situations, such as with ballot propositions that include initiatives and referendums, direct democracy is possible. Conversely, in the age of the Internet, maybe an electronic commonwealth is also possible.[40] Many states and communities do allow the public directly to vote on matters ranging from taxes to the amending of a constitution. All of these types of votes are a form of direct democracy and in many cases, especially with initiatives that perhaps allow the people to place propositions on the ballot, this is clear control of the agenda. For reasons to be described in Chapter 4, ballot initiatives may only offer the illusion of direct democracy and majority control of the agenda.

---

37 *See:* ROBERT A. DAHL AND EDWARD R. TUFTE, SIZE AND DEMOCRACY (1973), for a discussion on how population affects democratic governance possibilities.

38 John Stuart Mill, *Representative Government*, in UTILITARIANISM, LIBERTY, AND REPRESENTATIVE GOVERNMENT, 291-92 (1951).

39 JOSEPH A. SCHUMPETER, CAPITALISM, SOCIALISM, AND DEMOCRACY, 269-73 (1975). *See also:* PETER BACHRACH, THE THEORY OF DEMOCRATIC ELITISM: A CRITIQUE (1967), for criticism of this democratic revisionism or elite driven model of politics.

40 JEFFREY B. ABRAMSON, F. CHRISTOPHER ARTERTON, AND GARY R. ORREN, THE ELECTRONIC COMMONWEALTH: THE IMPACT OF NEW MEDIA TECHNOLOGIES ON DEMOCRATIC POLITICS (1990).

A final value or criterion for a polyarchy according to Dahl is the principle of inclusion.[41] The principle of inclusion asks who gets to have a voice in the affairs of the government and what constitutes a voice. Begin first with who gets to speak. One answer is to say that the right to speak is limited to citizens of a country or of a specific jurisdiction. This seems to make sense. A privilege of citizenship is the right to participate and make decisions for the community. After all, we do not want perhaps foreigners or worse, enemies, making decisions for us. The parallel is to having a club. A club is a voluntary association and only those who are members should presumably be allowed to vote or make decisions for the club. A political society is similar to a large club and perhaps the same rule should apply. Thus perhaps only those who are citizens should be allowed to have a voice. Yet even this principle is highly contestable. In the case of *Minor v. Happersett*, the Supreme Court ruled that while women were citizens of the United States the evidence was that the constitutional Framers did not intend them to have the right to vote.[42] Citizenship and voting, concepts which many see as linked, the Court did not see as connected. Of course the Nineteenth Amendment changed this issue for women in 1919.

But arguing that all citizens should be allowed to speak perhaps is overbroad or overly inclusive. Children are citizens, do they get a right to speak? At one time voting was confined to those at least age 21 or older in the United States. But the draft and the Vietnam War led to pressures to let 18-year-olds vote. This happened first in 1970 in *Oregon v. Mitchell*[43] where the Supreme Court upheld a congressional law extending franchise in federal elections to 18-year-olds. Then the Twenty-Sixth Amendment did the same in state and local elections. But while 18-year-olds can vote, why not 16 or younger? They are citizens. Additionally, felons or ex-felons are citizens in many cases, but most states deny them the right to vote for some period of time after conviction, whether it be until out of prison, off probation, or perhaps even never. But then take it even further. Why just citizens? Why not permit individuals who are permanent resident aliens to vote in the United States? Why not permit individuals who are on the path to citizenship to vote? They have to pay taxes and comply with the laws, should they not be allowed to vote? At one time in Minnesota, in the nineteenth century, aliens expressing intent to become citizens were given the right to vote, and in New York City some resident aliens were allowed franchise rights in local elections.

Another way to approach the question of who is included in terms of being allowed a voice (besides voting) is to say that all persons are entitled to speak. Why is this a critical distinction? To say that only citizens get a voice may deny a role to critical speakers in a democracy. Do political parties get a voice? How about interest groups or unions or corporations? None of them are citizens but in some cases they are persons for the purpose of the US Constitution. But even

---

41 Dahl, Democracy and Its Critics, 119–21.
42 Minor v. Happersett, 88 U.S. 162 (1875).
43 400 U.S. 112 (1970).

if not persons, should they be allowed to speak? Moreover, one of my students one day argued that only "biological persons" should be allowed to speak. He wanted to exclude corporations from those who get to have a voice, referring to his disagreement with the *Citizens United v. Federal Election Commission* decision which ruled that corporations have the right in some instances to expend money for the purpose of influencing elections.[44] His argument was that, since corporations were composed of people, the people within one could speak but not the corporation itself. This may be true, but by limiting voice to only biological persons (of a certain age presumably) other groups that many think are important to a democracy are silenced.

But the other issue that complicates the matter on who gets to speak or who is included is to ask inclusion to do what or what does it mean to have a voice or speak. Voting is perhaps the most important or common answer when discussing what it means to have a voice. But it is not the only form of voice that exists. A voice might also include simply talking and urging others to vote or take a particular political position. But voice or inclusion in the political system could include a range of activities—such as attending rallies, volunteering for a candidate, raising money for a candidate or cause—and also actually giving money to support a candidate or a cause.[45] In asking whom should be included in the political process, it may be critical to also ask how they are included.

Return to the idea of only a citizen being allowed to have a voice. Assume we limit voting to citizens; should non-citizens be denied the right to volunteer on a campaign, attend a political rally, or engage in other activities such as giving money? Under current laws, non-citizens are barred from voting and giving money to candidates for federal office, but nothing prevents them from volunteering or engaging in other political activities. How or why is this line drawn? Maybe the idea is that only citizens should directly be able to influence elections and giving money and voting count as direct influence. Or perhaps the reason is that there is a general principle—preventing foreign influence on elections—and for good or bad the line is drawn at voting and money.

Now think about it yet another way and about the claim that only biological persons should be given a voice in politics. Does that mean, as suggested earlier, that political parties, interest groups, corporations, and unions should be barred from all types of activities? Clearly they cannot vote but should they also be prevented from airing their views on important political matters? Should they be given the right to contribute or expend money for political purposes? Moreover, should that right extend to giving directly to candidates or only to indirect giving through intermediate groups such as PACs? Or should it only extend, if at all,

---

44 558 U.S. 310 (2010).

45 Sidney Verba and Norman H. Nie, Participation in America: Political Democracy and Social Equality (1972); and Steven J. Rosenstone and John Mark Hansen, Mobilization, Participation, and Democracy in America (2002), provide an overview of the variety of ways to participate in politics in the United States.

to general issues of public concern (such as referenda) and not to a right to give to elections involving candidates for office? All of these questions raise critical questions about the First Amendment, rights of organizations, and what types of activities they should be allowed to engage in. Inclusion in the political process or the polity is thus not an easy question to define or summarize.

Robert Dahl's five values are perhaps not the sum of those essential to defining those which are critical or requisites for a democracy. One might argue that concepts such as federalism are important. By that, some would contend that political power needs to be divided up into some types of units along geographic regions. While some countries are not federal but unitary in design, federalism in large countries might make sense in terms of how it maximizes opportunities for individuals to secure the previous five values. Breaking a large polity up into smaller units or jurisdictions makes it easier for citizens to have a meaningful voice or feel like they are included or have control over the agenda. Additionally, perhaps another critical democratic value is adherence to rule of law.[46] Setting principled maxims for how controversies are to be handled—such as adhering to Aristotle's principle that equals are treated equally or likes treated alike—is important. Confining government discretion is important and it also perhaps suggests that some concept of limited government and constitutionalism may be a requisite or value of a democracy.

Finally, for many, especially the pluralists of the 1950s such as David Truman and Seymour Martin Lipset, diversity in values and allegiances are important to the protection of freedom.[47] Still others would assert that democracy needs a robust civil society to serve as a buffer on the economy and the polity.[48] Dahl, in some of his writings,[49] joins political scientists such Gabriel Almond and Sidney Verba in contending that a specific democratic political culture is needed if a democracy is to exist.[50] This is a political culture perhaps that encapsulates all of the values listed above or maybe it is a culture distinct from these values—a culture that sustains or respects the above values. The point is that there may be other values needed to make democracy work.

But of course there are two other points to think about when discussing the values of a democracy. One is that the values do not exist in isolation, but are

---

[46] David Schultz, *Democracy on Trial: Terrorism, Crime, and National Security Policy in a Post 9-11 World*, 38 GOLDEN GATE L. REV., 195 (2008); DAVID DYZENHAUS, THE CONSTITUTION OF LAW: LEGALITY IN A TIME OF EMERGENCY (2006).

[47] SEYMOUR MARTIN LIPSET, POLITICAL MAN: THE SOCIAL BASIS OF POLITICS (1960).

[48] Robert Putnam, Bowling Alone; ROBERT PUTNAM, ROBERT LEONARDI, AND RAFFAELLA NANETTI, MAKING DEMOCRACY WORK: CIVIC TRADITIONS IN MODERN ITALY (1993).

[49] Dahl, Democracy and Its Critics, 262-64; ROBERT A. DAHL, WHO GOVERNS?: DEMOCRACY AND POWER IN AN AMERICAN CITY (1961); DILEMMAS OF PLURALIST DEMOCRACY: AUTONOMY VS. CONTROL, 138-66 (1968).

[50] GABRIEL A. ALMOND AND SIDNEY VERBA, THE CIVIC CULTURE: POLITICAL ATTITUDES AND DEMOCRACY IN FIVE NATIONS (1965).

perhaps in a tension with one another.⁵¹ Second, the values are given meaning by institutions that support them. Values such as effective participation and control of the agenda, for example, may come into conflict. Giving all 310 million plus individuals in the United States, control of the agenda or a meaningful voice may be impractical. Thus the need to do tradeoffs means participation may need to be limited in some situations or perhaps simply confined to representatives. Or, another way to think about it, that tradeoffs may need to be made for different participants or activities. In *Burson v. Freeman* the Supreme Court had to confront clashing First Amendment rights.⁵² In one instance there was the right to vote and in the other the right of free expression. The question was about a law that prohibited campaigning within 100 feet of a voting place, instituted in order to prevent voter intimidation at the polls. The Court upheld the law, noting that there was a tradeoff that had to be effected here between contending rights.

Burson highlights the problem for democratic theory and then election law. Tradeoffs need to be made and values cannot be evaluated in isolation from one another. One task of a democratic theory and of election law is to effect and define the tradeoffs. It is to decide who gets to participate or have a voice in what and for what purposes. It is to decide what it means to have free and fair elections viewed in the context of the rights of others to advocate their positions. It is the tradeoff or relationship between the use of one's economic resources and how they are converted into political influence. A theory, much like a Wittgensteinian language game, defines the meaning of these values by their actual use. Critical concepts derive their meaning in part by their relationship to other values. One of the most simplistic ways to do or think about election law is simply to assert values or declare propositions—such as money is speech—in isolation from other values. Too much of the election law scholarship simply does this—offering pronouncements without getting the bigger picture. One overall needs to think about the goals of a democratic system, what one is trying to achieve, and then to ask what types of institutions can best be fashioned or implemented to secure these goals.

Thus, institutions matter. For Dahl, each of the five criteria he articulates comes with specific institutions that must be in operation.⁵³ To achieve voting equality Dahl stipulates that there needs to be elected officials and free and fair elections. Enlightened understanding requires freedom of expression, alternative information, and associational autonomy. Dahl's list of institutions run the range from a free press, voting systems, and elected officials to rights to run for office. Dahl's list is not exhaustive and, in many ways, what he considers to be institutions is strange. Saying a "right to run for office" is an institution is odd. Perhaps the right to run for office is a value—be it primary or secondary—to controlling the agenda or securing effective participation. Or perhaps something like the right to run for

---

51   Pennock, *Democratic Political Theory*, 16-17.
52   504 U.S. 191 (1992).
53   Dahl, *Democracy and Its Critics*, 222.

office is a measure or part of an index that measures inclusion or participation. But to call some of what he has on his list institutions is a stretch.

Democratic values definitely need to be operationalized or implemented. Values also need to be measured. A democracy needs specific institutions that include mechanisms to hold elections, a free press, election officials, and political parties among other things. These institutions need to be in place to give meaning to values. Perhaps they are the rules of grammar to connect the words and institutions of democracy together. But what is also needed are criteria to measure how effective these institutions operate. It is not simply enough to say parties exist or to say there are elections. Holding elections while jailing the opposition is hardly a free election. Holding an election with only one legally recognized party, or with a censored press also questions how free that election is. Declaring everyone has a voice or voting equality may be meaningless if the votes are rigged, ballot boxes stuffed, money determines the outcome of an election, or if lobbying activity effectively preempts any meaningful ballot choice. Institutions must be effective as noted, and efficacy must be evaluated according to criteria which measure how well they secure the values articulated for a democracy to exist.

All of this sounds somewhat circular. It is, in part because there is a linkage between the values, institutions, and criteria of democracy. While in general the concept of a democracy might have certain criteria, there are specific conceptions of democracy that different countries or cultures might adopt. These are conceptions that might define different tradeoffs for the values or an effort to place greater emphasis on a particular value. Specific conceptions of a democracy also simply give concrete meaning or more specification to what a value means for its culture or jurisdiction. How Canada defines inclusion may differ from the United States or France. At some point of course there needs to be an agreed-upon definition regarding what is necessary and sufficient to render a regime democratic, but beyond that it is possible to set up various schema that can legitimately be called democratic. Again, to borrow from Wittgenstein, there must be some type of family resemblance shared among all political systems referred to as democracies.

What does all this mean for democracy and election law? There is a general set of values essential for a regime to be called a democracy. These values must be embedded within a theory that describes how the people rule and express their will. A democratic theory defines the relationship among the values, with eventually institutions being necessary to implement the theory and finally, criteria adopted to measure how well the institutions perform to secure the values. Election law is the connective tissue, so to speak, linking the values and theory to the institutions. Election laws are the rules of the game that tell us how the game of democracy is played. It is the job of policy-makers and the courts to create the rules for democracy and define the tradeoffs that must be made. Ultimately, though, the people are the judge regarding how well the institutions work.

American Democratic Theory and Values

Ultimately this is not a book about democratic theory in general or in the abstract. Instead, this is a book about democratic theory and election law in the United States. The exact values that define American democracy do incorporate many of the general assumptions reflected in the discussion above, but more specificity is needed to correctly capture how the American political system operates, or at least the values that are important to it. Describing these values and assumptions about how American democracy should operate is critical to elucidating the theoretical framework that should define how our election law should work and also how the Supreme and other courts should adjudicate disputes regarding these issues.

There are two democratic theories or traditions in the United States. One which can be referred to as Madisonian democracy, named after James Madison, and the second is the pluralist tradition, finding its origins in post-World War II political science. Both theories are influential and have an impact in terms of how they affect election law. Yet both theories too owe many of the intellectual credits to American history and the experiences surrounding the disputes the American colonies had with England.

Historian Bernard Bailyn writes in his *The Ideological Origins of the American Revolution* that, as the American colonies pressed their grievances to England via the First and then Second Continental Congresses, one of the problems was that the Americans and the British were using the same language but talking past one another.[54] At root, the American Revolution was one where three political terms were in dispute—representation, constitutionalism, and sovereignty. The real revolution was over the meaning of these three terms and how they affected how Americans thought about political and governance.

Begin with the concept of representation. One of the primary objections the American colonists had with the British taxing tea and other goods was the famous claim "No taxation without representation." In making this claim, Americans asserted that the colonies did not vote for anyone serving in the British Parliament, the body that voted on taxes and other policies affecting America. Thus, the claim was that there was no one directly elected by the people in the colonies and therefore there was no representation. The British, however, did not understand this argument. Instead, they asserted that the American colonies were virtually represented in the British parliament; that the MPs who were serving there, even though not elected by anyone in the colonies, virtually could represent the interests of those back in North America. This debate over direct versus virtual representation was one of the first political disagreements between the American colonies and England. The two sides were using the same word—representation—but they meant very different things when invoking the concept. Americans demanded a direct and real voice in parliament and over their own affairs, and the British were not providing that in the way the colonists demanded.

---

54 Bernard Bailyn, The Ideological Origins of the American Revolution (1967).

A second concept over which there was debate involved the concept of sovereignty. Sovereignty refers to who holds political power. Political sovereignty refers ultimately to who is in charge in a state or nation. For the British, sovereignty resided in Parliament, it was the ultimate source of political authority and power, including in and over the colonies. British thinkers such as John Locke had argued against claims by the king that sovereignty was lodged in the monarchy. This was essentially the argument between Sir Robert Filmer and John Locke.[55] Locke's arguments invoking the social contract metaphor to explain the origin of government, as described in Chapter 2, were at the heart of this claim. The Glorious Revolution of 1688 had essentially validated John Locke's claim and therefore parliament was viewed as the sovereign body in England.

However, the colonists had a different sense of whom or what was sovereign. Instead of accepting the British view or perspective on the term they adopted an argument of Jean Bodin, a French political writer, who had argued that ultimate sovereignty resided with the people. This is the assertion that the American Founding Fathers adopted. Americans accepted Bodin's argument that the people were sovereign, and they also took as truth Locke's assertion that the people created civil society and government. Together, that meant that the people ruled or were sovereign, and that did not simply mean the people of England. Instead, the colonies, especially as a result of all of the self-rule that they had experienced, at least up until recently, were also sovereign and were entitled to a say over their own affairs. The colonies were entitled to a say over taxation, over the control of their own representatives, the selection of their governors, judges, and all the other affairs that affected their governance in North America. They resented the way Parliament and King George III treated them—like, well, a colony. Instead, as it became clear on July 4, 1776, the 13 states in North America were actually sovereign, they were their own country and entitled to rule themselves.

Finally, there is the notion of constitutionalism. Constitutionalism is an ancient term, going back to at least Aristotle in terms of its first use. Aristotle would use the term constitution to refer to forms of government depending on who ruled. Over time the concept of constitutionalism retained that basic meaning, but as it evolved it now also refers to the basic structures, "Grundnorm," or rules that constitute a government.[56] As the term evolved in Western Europe and North America, constitutionalism referred to a government of limited powers, one which often must adhere to rule of law, procedural due process or regularity, and eventually to a commitment to the protection of individual rights.[57] At the time of the American Revolution the British equated the Parliament with the Constitution. Since England lacked a written constitution, someone or something

---

55 JAMES TULLY, A DISCOURSE ON PROPERTY: JOHN LOCKE AND HIS ADVERSARIES (1983); RICHARD ASHCRAFT, REVOLUTIONARY POLITICS & LOCKE'S TWO TREATISES OF GOVERNMENT (1986).

56 HANS KELSEN, GENERAL THEORY OF THE LAW AND STATE (1961).

57 JAMES T. MCHUGH, COMPARATIVE CONSTITUTIONAL TRADITIONS, 5-10 (2002).

had to define what was constitutional. This was a task set for Parliament. It defined what was constitutional. It did not make sense to say that Parliament was acting unconstitutionally. Parliament was the final word on what was constitutional and whatever it said went in terms of what was permitted.

The American concept of constitutionalism departed from this British notion. A constitution, for Americans, was something distinct from the government. The constitution served to define the powers of the government and to place limits upon it. Parliament or the government could act unconstitutionally; that could happen when they failed to follow the limits prescribed upon them by the constitution—in this case, as the Americans came to prefer, a written constitution. Thus, when the American colonies began to argue that the King and Parliament were acting unconstitutionally, violating the rights of British citizens as Thomas Jefferson originally argued, they were again making a claim that the British just did not understand. How could the British government act unconstitutionally when the government, especially the Parliament, decided what was constitutional?

The Americanization of political discourse is significant across many fronts. Forging a unique vocabulary, the colonies developed a language of independence and grievances to support their separation from England. But also, in crafting special meanings to terms such as representation, the colonists created a set of political values that would eventually influence the drafting of the Constitution in 1787 and subsequently the Bill of Rights and then other later political debates. All this would affect American democratic theory and election law. For example, to insist on direct as opposed to virtual representation makes it hard for those opposed to female suffrage to assert that wives are virtually represented through their husbands.

But it was not only the experiences with England that defined the ideas that would eventually be incorporated into the Constitution of 1787. There are the many political cultures that influenced the American founding.[58] These included a Lockean tradition favoring equality, individual rights, and a secular limited government.[59] There was also a religious Pilgrim-Puritan one favoring religious liberty and human fallibility.[60] A third was a republican tradition emphasizing a commitment to popular government, support for a belief in a public good, and a

---

58 David Schultz, *Political Theory and Legal History: Conflicting Depictions of Property in the American Political Founding*, 37 AMERICAN JOURNAL OF LEGAL HISTORY, 464 (1993).

59 LOUIS HARTZ, THE LIBERAL TRADITION IN AMERICA: AN INTERPRETATION OF AMERICAN POLITICAL THOUGHT SINCE THE REVOLUTION (1955); GUIDO DE RUGGIERO, THE HISTORY OF EUROPEAN LIBERALISM (1959); JOHN PATRICK DIGGINS, THE LOST SOUL OF AMERICAN POLITICS: VIRTUE, SELF-INTEREST, AND THE FOUNDATIONS OF LIBERALISM (1984).

60 RICHARD HOFSTADTER, THE AMERICAN POLITICAL TRADITION AND THE MEN WHO MADE IT (1989); WILSON CAREY MCWILLIAMS, THE IDEA OF FRATERNITY IN AMERICA (1974); PERRY MILLER, THE LIFE OF THE MIND IN AMERICA: FROM THE REVOLUTION TO THE CIVIL WAR (1965).

fear of corruption rooted in a concern about how wealth affected political power.[61] Finally, there was a legal tradition indebted to William Blackstone which endorsed a commitment to rule of law.[62] These four founding traditions held sway over the Framers (and continued to do so over American history) as they developed the critical legal documents that defined the United States. This included the Articles of Confederation, America's first constitution, which was adopted in 1781. The Articles created more of a decentralized political system to govern the United States. Yet its lack of ability to raise revenue, weak control over commerce, and the ability of states to veto actions, all led a growing chorus of individuals such as Alexander Hamilton and James Madison to believe that revisions to the Articles were needed. Finally, events such as Shay's rebellion in Massachusetts, a skirmish by Revolutionary war veterans, led others to conclude that perhaps the Article government was ineffective.

It was against this backdrop that the 1787 Philadelphia constitutional convention took place. There was the fear of creating too strong a national government, less a return to the abuses experienced with England. Conversely, the Articles government had insufficient authority to act. A balance was needed. It would be impossible in this chapter to retell the story of the events that occurred at the Philadelphia convention in 1787.

Madisonian Democracy and the Problem of Politics

One way to understanding the ethics or values of the Constitution is by seeking to clarify what the Framers were trying to accomplish when they drafted the document. This is what shall be referred to here as the problem of politics. The Constitution defines a basic problem that must be solved; it is a problem based upon a psychology and sociology of human nature and power, and the Constitution itself offers a solution to both of these problems. How does one ascertain what this problem was? One way is to turn to the *Federalist Papers* for guidance.

Why the *Federalist Papers*? There are numerous reasons. The *Federalist Papers* as a whole reflect an urgent concern to limit the constraints and threats of opinion upon the American republic. There were 85 essays written by Alexander Hamilton, James Madison, and John Jay and they were presented as a defense for the replacement of the Articles of Confederation with a new constitution that

---

61 Thomas Pangle, The Spirit of Modern Republicanism: The Moral Vision of the American Founders and the Philosophy of Locke (1988); Forrest McDonald, Novus Ordo Seclorum: The Intellectual Origins of the Constitution (1985); J.G.A. Pocock, The Machiavellian Moment: Florentine Political Thought and the Atlantic Republican Tradition (2003).

62 Perry Miller, The Legal Mind in America: From Independence to the Civil War (1961); Mary Bilder, Maeva Marcus, and R. Kent Newmyer, Blackstone in America: Selected Essays of Kathryn Preyer (2009).

would be more national in character. In debating the Anti-Federalists, who claimed that the new constitution was a threat to freedom, the Federalists articulated a position that claimed that their new republic would rest upon more firm and valid principles than those of the Confederacy.[63] The Federalists argued that the new union would be more attentive to the needs of republicanism than the classic small, homogeneous, and participatory republics of the civic humanist tradition. In particular, one of the evils the new constitution could better manage would be the dangers that factions or special interests have upon growing stronger and threatening the commonweal and the virtue of the citizenry.

Moreover, the *Federalist Papers* represent to many the most definitive gloss on what the Framers were seeking to do when they drafted the Constitution. Yes, Madison did chronicle the proceedings of the constitutional convention,[64] but arguably the *Federalist Papers* provide the political theory, analysis, and philosophy behind the Constitution. Moreover, given that James Madison is considered the primary architect of the Constitution and eventually of the Bill of Rights, some also suggest that the individual *Federalist Papers* written by him provide special insights into his thoughts and ultimately on how the Constitution was supposed to operate. Thus, these essays clarify the problem of politics and the attempted solutions they devised to address the crisis or difficulties they were seeking to address in 1787. It is also important to note that the importance of the *Federalist Papers* might be oversold. After all, the essays were written to urge the New York Legislature to ratify the proposed Constitution. As such, they could be viewed as a 1787 version of the modern-day 15-second political advertisement or sound bite on television. The *Federalist Papers* might just be seen as no more than political propaganda by partisan advocates for the new constitution. Richard Hofstadter, a famous American historian, once pointed out that the constitutional Framers were political realists who had to forge compromises to secure ratification of the document. They were not omniscient angels.[65] One should always keep in mind their interests and motives when assessing their work, including the drafting of the Constitution and the *Federalist Papers*. However, it is unlikely the essays have no value in terms of informing others about the Constitution, but they also should not be viewed as the gospel; truth lies somewhere in the middle and that should be kept in mind when discussing them.

The analysis of politics in the *Federalist Papers* is not a haphazard or uninformed approach to the subject. In *Federalist* 9, Alexander Hamilton states: "The science of politics, however, like most other sciences, has received great improvement. The efficacy of various principles is now well understood, which were either not known at all, or imperfectly known to the ancients."[66] Hamilton,

---

63 Herbert J. Storing, What the Anti-Federalists Were For, 20-21 (1981).

64 James Madison, Notes of Debates: In The Federal Convention of 1787 (1985).

65 Richard Hofstadter, The American Political Tradition and the Men who Made It (1989).

66 Hamilton, Madison, and Jay, Federalist, 48.

along with Madison and Jay, believed that their analysis was based upon a solid study of politics. Their work sought to describe how best to divide political power, check political excess, and assure accountability to the people. In short, they sought to preserve the principles of popular or republican government and place it upon a firmer footing.[67] They considered themselves realists about human nature and politics. To achieve this, they sought to understand how popular governments operate and what defects threaten them. This task takes the *Federalist Papers* back to a discussion of public opinion and human nature.

What is public opinion for Madison and why is it a problem? In *Federalist* 47 and 49, Madison claims that "all government rests on opinion."[68] Public opinion is composed of the sentiments and passions of the majority of people organized together for particular purposes. Arguably the strength of republican government is that it rests upon public opinion, drawing its democratic impulse and authority from the consent of the government. This is the Lockean notion of the social contract, or later, as Abraham Lincoln would describe it, of the government "of the people, by the people, and for the people." The touchstone of a free society is the degree to which the will of the majority is generally respected. Yet, the weakness of republican government also rests upon public opinion. Alone, humans can be reasonable but not in crowds—at least this is the sentiment expressed in the *Federalist*. Crowds and the crowd sociology turn individual thoughts into restless sentiment and passion. Public opinion is both popular sentiment and popular sovereignty. The sentiment of public opinion is the ruler in a popular democracy yet this sentiment is not firm and stable but unstable, subject to frequent changes, and to fits of passion and excess. For Madison, it is unwise for a government to make frequent appeals to popular sentiment and public opinion in order to decide political issues.[69] The reason for this is grounded in human nature.

In *Federalist* 9, Hamilton states that: "men are ambitious, vindictive, and rapacious."[70] Individuals are not always virtuous, but prone to self-interest, desire, and the passions. Yet these sentiments are not good for politics. Passion should not decide public issues. Instead, some mechanism is needed to calm or repress these passions and filter them out so that more rational and calm individuals can reach public choices. Madison further describes this view of human nature and the problem of the passions in both *Federalist* 10 and *Federalist* 51. In a popular government resting on opinion, passion will usually rule because men (and presumably women) will band together in groups that Madison called factions.

What is a faction for Madison and how do factions relate to speech and public opinion? According to Madison:

---

67 *Id.* at 48-49.
68 *Id.* at 329.
69 *Id.* at 329.
70 *Id.* at 27.

> By a faction, I understand a number of citizens, whether amounting to a majority or minority of the whole, who are united and actuated by some common impulse of passion, or interest, adverse to the rights of other citizens, or to the permanent and aggregate interests of the community.[71]

Madison is saying four things about factions. First, people join factions because of some common interest or, second, because of some common passion. Third, factions can either be composed of a minority or a majority of the population. However, while Madison is concerned about both types of faction, his real concern is with majority factions because the regular votes of the majority and the weakness of the minority will prevent the latter from being a real threat to others. Finally, a faction is not defined as simply any band of people who share common impulses or interests. Their association must be destructive of the rights of others or of the interests of the entire community. The latter suggests that there is an identifiable commonweal that can be known and should be defended.[72] Individuals banding together, can do great things and pursue the public good, but they can also let their passions and interests run wild, thereby threatening the rights of others and the public good.

The tendency to form factions or pursue common interests or impulses is not some perversion of human character. Contrary to the classical republican tradition, individuals are not motivated singularly and mainly by reason or the virtues. Following the writings of British political writers such as David Hume and Bernard Mandeville, among others, humans act from passionate and self-interested motives. For Madison, who apparently accepted at least part of this moral psychology, "the latent causes of faction are sown in the nature of men."[73] In *Federalist* 51 he similarly states: "If men were angels, no government would be necessary. If angels were to govern men, neither external nor internal controls on government would be necessary."[74] Humans, whether as government officials or citizens, or both, are human, prone to misjudgments, passion, and the errors that characterize us all as imperfect beings. One cannot trust either the rulers or the ruled always to be paragons of virtue; both need to be checked in their behavior.

Individuals have a propensity to band together for common base interests and desires and this pursuit of desires can constrain or distort the rights of others including the community. This banding together in factions need not simply be equated with the hope of acquiring objects of desire. These factions can include men banding together pursuing similar opinions destructive to the republic. Factions can also be viewed as groups of individuals pursuing opinions and views that would oppress minorities. Public opinion, especially the opinions of a large

---

71 *Id.* at 54.

72 RUSSELL HANSON, THE DEMOCRATIC IMAGINATION IN AMERICA: CONVERSATIONS WITH OUR PAST, 69 (1985).

73 Hamilton, Madison, and Jay, Federalist, 55.

74 *Id.* at 337.

majority, can often be oppressive and operate to the destruction of the rational deliberation of public issues. Thus, at the core of the *Federalist Papers* is a human psychology or theory of human nature that is indebted, in part at least, to either Thomas Hobbes or the Calvinist political tradition—individuals are self-interested or sinful, and they cannot always be relied upon to do the right thing. At one point in John Locke's *Second Treatise* he argues that one of the reasons for government is individuals cannot be a good judge when it involves the enforcement of their own rights.[75] We are partial to ourselves; this sense of partiality is the core notion of what conflict of interest is all about—the conscious or unconscious bias that affects everyone. Government is necessary because we cannot be expected to be fair all the time and not favor ourselves. The human psychology of the *Federalist Papers*, and presumably of the entire Constitution, is premised upon this beginning point. It assumes humans are not angels and it seeks to build up from that truth a theory about politics that depicts factions as a threat to a republican form of government.

While the latent causes of faction are in the nature of men (Madison's choice of words), factions can be traced to the diversity in the faculties of men and in the differences in the rights to property that arise out of those different faculties. For Madison, differences in property distributions are the most "common and durable" source of factions. Inequalities, differences in occupations, and differences in talents all nourish factions.[76] Yet to remove these sources of faction would not only be impossible but injurious to liberty. The solution is not the classical republican technique of rendering the citizenry homogeneous in terms of similar tastes, interests, and beliefs. Such a task would be impossible, or at least a threat to individual liberty. The genius of American politics may be in encouraging diversity so that it controls the power of factions.

How are factions to be checked? As mentioned before, minority factions can be handled through the normal constraints of voting and by the majority. Madison seemed to believe that the power of majority rule would be enough to control the threat that minorities pose.[77] One can disagree with this claim, especially today in light of the power that well-financed and organized special interest groups or political action committees (PACs) yield. But Madison, at least in 1787, thought that the political process, through regular elections and majority rule, would take care of this problem. The real issue is how to prevent majoritarian opinions and factions from dominating.

According to Madison in *Federalist* 10, there are three competing goals that political society needs to address. First, there is the imperative to preserve a republican form of government. This is a government premised at least in part upon majority rule. The second goal is the protection of individual liberty. The

---

75 Locke, *Second Treatise*, ¶ 13.
76 Hamilton, Madison, and Jay, Federalist, 56.
77 *Id.* at 57.

third is to limit the threat of factions to both republican government and individual liberty.

Factions, if they are composed simply of a numeric minority of the population, can be handled by majority rule and elections. That is, the majority can outvote them. The real problem though is what to do with majority factions. Madison contends that one cannot eliminate the causes of faction because they are rooted in human nature. The issue is how to control their effects. Here is where Madison thus turns to a critical passage in *Federalist* 10 that summarizes the political or sociological dilemma the proposed constitution was meant to address:

> If a faction consists of less than a majority, relief is supplied by the republican principle, which enables the majority to defeat its sinister views by regular vote. It may clog the administration, it may convulse the society; but it will be unable to execute and mask its violence under the forms of the Constitution. When a majority is included in a faction, the form of popular government, on the other hand, enables it to sacrifice to its ruling passion or interest both the public good and the rights of other citizens. To secure the public good and private rights against the danger of such a faction, and at the same time to preserve the spirit and the form of popular government, is then the great object to which our inquiries are directed.[78]

The issue then is how to preserve individual liberty and republican government from the threats of majority faction. This is the core problem of politics that Madison, the *Federalist Papers*, and the constitutional Framers sought to address. Phrased otherwise, the problem, as Alexis de Tocqueville would later ask, is how the American republic can deal with the threats of the tyranny of the majority.[79] To put it another way: How to balance majority rule with minority rights? How does one allow for majority opinion to rule, as it should in a popular government, but not let it become destructive, acting impulsively or rashly when threatened? Part of Madison's solution involved abandoning three principles of classical republicanism: direct citizen control for representatives; political homogeneity for diversity; and a small democracy for a large republic.

Majority factions, then, cannot be controlled by democracies or governments where the people directly rule. Representation can check public opinions. A representative government can control the governed, and especially factions, by limiting their access to the political apparatus. A representative system allows an electoral system to substitute (at least in theory for Madison) wiser or calmer individuals for the masses so that the former could render cool, rational, and detached political decisions and not impulsive ones as the masses would make.[80] A representative system denies the passionate and irrational force of public opinion

---

78 *Id.* at 57-58.
79 Alexis de Tocqueville, *Tyranny of the Majority*, in Democracy in America, 250-53.
80 Hamilton, Madison, and Jay, Federalist, 59.

and sentiment to determine political choices. A representative government would allow for a more balanced review of public choices which would result in a greater likelihood that the public good would be promoted.

The second and third changes from classical republicanism are linked together. Because it would be impossible to render factions, inequalities, or diversities the same without obstructing liberty, there is no other option but to allow factions and opinions to exist openly. The key to controlling them though rests in doing two things. First, size and diversity must increase in the republic. While a small democracy makes it more likely that majority factions can dominate, it will be impossible for them to dominate when the number of sentiments in the polity is greater. In Madison's words:

> Extend the sphere, and you take in a greater variety of parties and interests; you make it less probable that a majority of the whole will have a common motive to invade the rights of other citizens; or if such a common motive exists, it will be more difficult for all who feel it to discover their own strength, and to act in unison with each other.[81]

A large diverse republic would make it more difficult for any one group to dominate because of all the other interests in the polity. The sheer size of the republic would also make it difficult for factious individuals to find like-minded support. In the language of contemporary economics, the search costs to finding others who agree with you would be so high that it would be nearly impossible for factions to form.

This second technique involved not just letting a thousand factions bloom, but using these factions to counteract one another. The threat of factions, including opinions, can be controlled by letting ambition counteract ambition and faction check faction.[82] In society, as in the government, the rights of others, as well as the common good, could be preserved by using factions and personal motives to countercheck and neutralize other factions and motives. The distortions of the opinions of the few, or of a tyrannical majority, could be minimized and controlled by constitutional and social mechanisms that limited the likelihood that any group could ever obtain control enough to oppress others. The solution to constraining the distortion of faction and tyranny of majoritarian opinions lies in limiting the access of these groups to all the tools they need to oppress others. It lies also in a process that impedes these groups from forming without ever restricting liberty or denying their right to form associations.

Madison and the authors of the *Federalist Papers* also describe other mechanisms to address the threat of majority factions. All of them are directed toward making it hard for them to form or, if they do form, to making it difficult for them to gather and exercise political power in a destructive fashion. There are numerous pieces to the puzzle, all directed at breaking up political power

---

81 *Id.* at 61.
82 *Id.* at 337.

and frustrating a majority from taking political control. Creating a large diverse political system that encourages groups or factions to compete against one another addresses a sociological problem, but what about the political problem. What if a faction seeks political control, how is that problem attached? Here Madison invokes checks and balances, separation of powers, federalism, and bicameralism to control the effects of factions and make it difficult for any one group to amass too much political power. Checks and balances and separation of powers work together. In *Federalist* 51, Madison connects self-interest to government, arguing that if one can link constitutional power or duties with institutional and individual self-interest, the competition among the three branches of government will serve to check one another.[83] If Congress seeks excessive power then it will be limited and checked by one of the other branches. The same is true for the executive or judicial branches. This is the concept of checks and balances. Similarly, the concept of separation of powers, derived from French political thinker Baron de Montesquieu, prevents any one branch from amassing too much political power.[84] It does that by literally preventing one branch from being judge, jury, and executioner. Congress cannot enact laws on its own without a presidential assent, except with qualified majorities. Presidents cannot take a nation to war without congressional declarations, and the judiciary is limited in the types of cases it hears and issues it addresses. No one branch can do it all.

But even beyond checks and balances and separation of powers other tools are used to check political power. Congress, or the legislative branch, was envisioned as the dominant branch of the national government. Because of the power it would hold, the Framers divided legislative power into two bodies. Yes one can view bicameralism as a product of the big and small state compromise, or even as mirroring the House of Commons and House of Lords in England. But bicameralism also served to divide up legislative power, a sort of checks and balances within Congress. Even if a faction could manage to take hold of one body, it would be much harder to dominate Congress if a group had to capture both chambers. The different election cycles for the House and Senate, two versus six years, again also ensured that if a faction was determined to take control it would take many years to secure that objective. This again frustrates the ability of majority factions.

Federalism too can be envisioned as yet another way to check political power and factions. In *Federalist* 10, Madison notes the threat that factions, such as a religious sect, may pose to the country. In describing how federalism will control them he states: "The influence of factious leaders may kindle a flame within their particular states, but will be unable to spread a general conflagration through the other states."[85] Federalism serves as a fence or border to control faction. A group

---

83   *Id.* at 337.
84   Charles de Secondat, Baron de Montesquieu, Montesquieu: The Spirit of the Laws, ed. Anne M. Cohler, Basia Carolyn Miller, and Harold Samuel Stone (1989).
85   Hamilton, Madison, and Jay, Federalist, 61.

may be successful in taking over one state such as New York, but federalism would limit its ability to affect other states or the national government. Federalism both as a system of dividing political power among states and between the states and the federal government, serves to break up political power and frustrate the ability of a faction to secure its aims.

Thus, if the *Federalist* provides any insight at all into the logic of the Constitution and the design of its Framers, one can look at it as seeking to abate the problem that majority faction renders to individual liberty, popular government, and the rights of the minorities. Because of human nature, because we are imperfect passionate and self-interested beings, potential abuses of political power occur. All of this is the central problem of politics premised upon a theory of human nature and sociology. The Constitution can be seen as a solution to the threat of the tyranny of the majority. The Constitution does not seek to suppress factions since that would be impossible. Instead it aims to use a series of mechanisms—interest competition in a heterogeneous and enlarged political society, representation, bicameralism, checks and balances, separation of powers, and federalism as tools to break up and check political power. The idea here simply is both breaking up power into many diverse hands, and in slowing down political change. If the political process is properly structured, if political ambition is channeled in the appropriate direction, then political power will check itself. Let political forces check one another. Moreover, slow down or frustrate political change. Make it difficult for any group to affect rapid political change. As Robert Dahl argued in his *A Preface to Democratic Theory*, the goal of Madisonian democracy is to avoid tyranny. It is to avoid potential situations where power is concentrated and can threaten individual liberty.

What would result if the Madisonian model worked? Quite simply, go back to the original definition of a faction as a group capable of threatening the "rights of other citizens" or "the permanent and aggregate interests of the community." The first part of the definition is obvious—factions threaten individual rights, it is the problem of majority rule versus minority rights. But the second part of the definition refers to some sort of public good that exists. This is an important and defining characteristic of Madisonian democracy—a belief that a real substantive public good does exist. The constitutional machinery that Madison proposes is meant in part to clear away those forces that threaten representatives and the political process from articulating the public good. The legislative process, so to speak, is polluted when factions or special interest groups exercise adverse political pressure. Thus, the machinery of checks and balances, separation of powers, and federalism among the other values are all aimed at solving the problem of politics and create a republic that can pursue or discover the public good.

A faction-ridden political process is a threat to individual rights and the public good. But it is important to note that this model of protecting rights relied upon the political process. By that, the Constitution had a logic to it that almost transformed the political process into a big machine.⁸⁶ Each constituent—such as Congress or the courts—had a particular role in it. The original constitutional solution was thus to use the political process to police itself against majority factions.

But the Madisonian model has potential flaws. For example, it assumes that an extended political orbit might make it difficult for factions to form. It might be difficult—the search costs high—for individuals to find like-minded supporters across the country. But in an era of telephones, cell phones, the Internet, and the social media, the search costs have practically been reduced to zero. A geographically large and diverse community may not work to prevent the forming of factions. Additionally, the rapidity of communicating information—today including the social media—might also exacerbate the movement of passionate yet tyrannical ideas, creating new space for public opinion to form and hurt minorities. New technologies create new opportunities for representation, but also new opportunities for tyranny of the majority.

Another problem with the Madisonian model is premised upon the belief that only majority factions are a threat. Minority factions were dismissed as controlled by the republican solution of regular elections. Majority rule will address and abate the problem of overzealous minority factions. But are minority factions so harmless and as easily controlled as Madison believed? Not necessarily. Political scientists and economists such as Mancur Olson have noted the power of small, cohesive, and well-organized groups. When groups get too large they are plagued by free rider and collective action problems, thereby diminishing their effectiveness. Others have also noted the influence that minority groups exert electorally.⁸⁷

Instead, smaller organizations can often exercise disproportionate influence in politics, especially if they are well organized or vote in blocks. There are numerous studies, as well as popular belief, that groups such as the National Rifle Association (NRA), the American Association of Retired Persons (AARP), and other minority groups exercise disproportionate influence in the American political process. They do that as special interest groups or PACs with lobbyists and political contributions that leverage political power and influence. The influence of Madisonian democracy upon election law might be in terms of its articulation of regulations seeking to control lobbyists or special interest groups (including PACs and other similar entities) from exercising improper influence in the political system. Moreover, as *Carolene Products* footnote number 4 attests, various forces or reasons may led to the political process closing down and preventing the moral channels of electoral or policy change from operating. Thus, Madisonian democracy provides a theory for election law and regulation of the political process.

---

86 Mihael Kammen, A Machine That Would Go of Itself: The Constitution in American Culture (1987).
87 Benjamin G. Bishin, Tyranny of the Minority: The Subconstituency Politics Theory of Representation (2009).

But the point here is that the political process does not always operate properly and it may malfunction. What to do? Enter James Madison again.

The debate over ratification of the new constitution of 1787 divided into two camps. On one side were the Federalists, such as Alexander Hamilton and James Madison who favored scrapping the Articles of Confederation and replacing it with the new document they helped draft in Philadelphia. They advocated for a new constitution, contending that the Articles government was weak and ineffective. They argued it was unable to regulate commerce, provide sufficient order to the union, and provide for a common defense. However, not everyone was in agreement that the Articles government was bad or that the new constitution was good. In particular, the Anti-Federalists opposed the new constitution for many reasons, with the most important objection for the purposes of this discussion being that they feared that the new government would be too powerful and that it would threaten individual rights. Among their major criticisms of the new constitution was that it lacked a bill of rights.

In responding to these criticisms Hamilton and Madison made several arguments that a bill of rights was unnecessary. In *Federalist* 84, Hamilton dismissed the need for a bill of rights, arguing that to include one would be to assert that the national government had some powers that it did not.[88] Hamilton's arguments were unsuccessful. Many state legislatures adopted calls for bills of rights as they ratified the new constitution. Eventually James Madison relented, promising to introduce a bill of rights in Congress if the new constitution was adopted. The states did ratify the Constitution and Madison kept his promise. In 1789, he offered 17 amendments in the House of Representatives. Ten of these amendments, once ratified in December 1791, became the Bill of Rights.

Adoption of the Bill of Rights was not only a triumph for the Anti-Federalists, but also conceptual and perhaps de facto recognition that the political process itself cannot police itself to protect rights. The adoption of the Bill of Rights represented a significant shift in how the national government was to operate. As originally envisioned in the *Federalist Papers*, the political process, through checks and balances, separation of powers, and the other constitutional mechanisms noted earlier, rights would be protected. Effectively, a well-designed political process would check abuses of power. One could rely then upon the political process and Congress perhaps to defend against the threats that public opinion and majority faction posed to the public good and the rights of minorities. Yet the Anti-Federalists were skeptical and they contended that the political process needed to be checked and that rights needed specification.

One way to think about what the Bill of Rights did is to argue that it took certain rights out of the political process and instead left it up to the courts to protect them. One cannot trust the political process to protect freedom of speech or press against the threats of majority faction. Instead, a Bill of Rights stood as a formal declaration that one cannot trust Congress and the people to respect rights.

---

88 Hamilton, Madison, and Jay, Federalist, 559.

Pure majority rule, while the basis of a representative government, might produce a tyranny of the majority that could threaten individual rights. Some check on the majority too was needed. Some substantive limits need to be imposed on the political process so that these rights cannot be abused. As Supreme Court Justice Robert Jackson stated in *West Virginia v. Barnette*:

> The very purpose of a Bill of Rights was to withdraw certain subjects from the vicissitudes of political controversy, to place them beyond the reach of majorities and officials and to establish them as legal principles to be applied by the courts. One's right to ... freedom of worship ... and other fundamental rights may not be submitted to vote; they depend on the outcome of no elections.[89]

The adoption of the Bill of Rights was a major change in how American democracy and the courts were supposed to operate. It addressed the majority faction problem very differently from the original Constitution. Neither elections nor politics should be potential threats to individual rights; the latter are not protected by the political process but are protected from it. If by some chance laws are adopted that threaten such rights, it would be the federal courts—with individuals not directly elected by the people—who would enforce and protect rights. Thus, protection of rights shifted from the regulated political process described in the *Federalist Papers* to a clear statement of individual protections defended and defined by the judiciary.

Madisonian democracy, then, is premised upon a substantive believe that a public good exists which needs to be protected from the tyranny of the majority. It develops a twofold distinction that says that in most situations majorities get their way, but in some they do not. When minority rights are threatened the courts step in to protect them. Thus when the political process seems incapable of functioning properly, this provides the rationale for judicial intervention. This perhaps is the case for court intervention into the election field.

Pluralism

Standing in contrast to Madisonian democracy, pluralism is a rival conception about American politics. It perhaps represents the dominant way that political scientists think about and describe the way American democracy operates today. The origins of pluralism can be traced to a problem of post-war American political science:

> Two political if not intellectual questions confronted political scientists and American politicians after World War II. The first was to explain how Germany had descended into a Nazi regime. The second was a question addressed the Cold

---

89 319 U.S. 624, 638 (1943).

War and why democratic countries were falling and becoming communist. Both questions were really about democratic stability. How did Fascism and Nazism develop out of ostensibly democratic states and, second, what could be done to stabilize democracies so that they would not degenerate into either authoritarian or communist states. The political science literature of the 1950s and 1960s was dominated by the question of how to maintain liberal democracies.[90]

Numerous studies sought to locate those institutions and values necessary to maintain stable democracies.[91] Factors found important included economic wealth and modernization;[92] political participation;[93] civilian control of the government;[94] and widely-supported and regularized political mechanisms to resolve conflict.[95] They stressed the importance of a democratic political culture that inculcated toleration and a reasonable balance of both social consensus and cleavage, including a respect for difference and a commitment to resolve these differences through the political process.[96] Equally important though, democracy required a social pluralism with crosscutting loyalties, expressed through multiple, competing groups.[97] The significance of overlapping loyalties among social cleavages was to prevent the emergence of social alignments polarizing a nation along race, ethnicity, religion, or other traditional lines of conflict and division.

The postwar political science paradigm argued that the trick to maintaining democratic stability rested in part on the encouragement of secular national

---

90 James W. Ceaser, *Reconstructing Political Science*, in STEPHEN L. ELKIN AND KAROL EDWARD SOLTAN, EDS., A NEW CONSTITUTIONALISM: DESIGNING POLITICAL INSTITUTIONS FOR A GOOD SOCIETY, 41, 46 (1993).

91 Arend Lijphart, *Typologies of Democratic Systems*, 1 COMPARATIVE POLITICAL STUDIES 3 (1968); Deane E. Neubauer, *Some Conditions of Democracy*, 61 AM. POL. SCI. REV. 1002 (1967).

92 Lipset, Political Man, 28, 87, 116; Robert A. Dahl, Polyarchy: Participation and Opposition, 60-62; Seymour M. Lipset, *Some Social Requisites of Democracy: Economic Development and Political Legitimacy*, 53 AM. POL. SCI. REV.,69 (1959); Samuel P. Huntington, *Will More Countries become Democratic?* 99 POL. SCI. REV. 193 (1984); W.W. ROSTOW, THE STAGES OF ECONOMIC GROWTH (1971); Dankwart A. Rustow, *Modernization and Comparative Politics: Prospects in Research and Theory*, 1 COMPARATIVE POLITICS, 37 (1968).

93 Lipset, Political Man at 116.

94 LARRY DIAMOND ET AL., EDS., DEMOCRACY IN DEVELOPING COUNTRIES: LATIN AMERICA, 344 (1989); Samuel P. Huntington, *Civilian Control and the Constitution*, 50 AM.. POL. SCI., 676 (1956).

95 ROBERT A. DAHL, DEMOCRACY IN THE UNITED STATES: PROMISE AND PERFORMANCE (1976); Almond and Verba, Civic Culture.

96 Almond and Verba, Civic Culture, 363; Lipset, Political Man, 1, 4, 78, 250; James B. Christoph, *Consensus and Cleavage in British Political Ideology*, 59 AM. POL. SCI. REV. 629 (1965).

97 Lipset, Political Man, 78.

values which all groups supported,[98] the maintenance of overlapping loyalties, and the replacement or amelioration of the divisive forces of race, ethnicity, and religion with less divisive interest politics that could be politically compromised through the electoral and political process.[99] These empirical studies stated that democracies depend on support for broad social and political toleration of diverse groups and dissident views as well as a set of regularized and peaceful mechanisms to reconcile disputes without censorship or force. Finally, these studies also emphasized that attainment of a certain level of economic conditions or affluence was required, or that a strong middle class was required, or that the gaps between the rich and the poor could not be too great such that there was unchecked class conflict or antagonisms. It was within the context of democratic stability that the role of interest groups in fostering stability made their pluralist entrance. All of these factors were structural prerequisites for democracy.

Pluralism was a political science effort to rethink what made liberal democracies stable. Drawing upon Arthur Bentley,[100] political scientists after World War II gave increasing attention to the role of interest groups in the political process. Works such as Seymour Martin Lipset's *Political Man: The Social Bases of Politics* (1963; first published in 1960), and David Truman's *Governmental Process* (first published in 1951) were among a host of many other studies that turned to de Tocqueville's *Democracy in America*. Bentley's impetus to turn to interest groups to explain how governments work, de Tocqueville's emphasis on voluntary associations as important to American democracy, and the concern to stabilize democracies and explain the rise of fascism, all contributed to the pluralists forging a theory that depicted the encouragement of interest groups as important intermediary associations critical to democratic stability.

Lipset's *Political Man* states very clearly that its goal is to locate the "social conditions making for democracy."[101] The social basis of a successful democracy resides in a tension between class conflict and social consensus and the ability of democracies to mediate this conflict and consensus. According to Lipset:

> Surprisingly, as it may sound, a stable democracy requires the manifestation of conflict or cleavage so that there will be struggle over ruling positions, challenges to parties in power, and shifts of parties in office; but without consensus—

---

98   *Id.* at 68.

99   Alvin Rabushka and Kenneth Shepsle, Politics in Plural Societies: A Theory of Democratic Instability (1972); Samuel P. Huntington, Political Order in Changing Societies (1968); David Easton, A Framework for Political Analysis (1965); William Kornhauser, The Politics of Mass Society (1959); Ian Budge, Agreement and the Stability of Democracy (1970); Arend Lijphart, Democracy in Plural Societies, 19 (1977); Pennock, Democratic Political Theory, 206-59.

100   Arthur F. Bentley, The Process of Government: A Study of Social Pressures (1949).

101   Lipset, Political Man, 1.

a political system allowing the peaceful "play" of power, the adherence by the "outs" to decisions made by the "ins," and the recognition by the "ins" of the rights of the "outs"—there can be no democracy. The study of the conditions encouraging democracy must therefore focus on the sources of both cleavage and consensus.[102]

Thus, *Political Man* is a perfect example of the pluralist concern with the stability of democratic structures that preoccupied many political scientists after World War II and in the face of the spread of communism.

Part I of the book is titled "The Conditions of the Democratic Order" and numerous passages relate to democratic stability. For example, Lipset states that the "stability of any given democracy depends not only on economic development but also on the effectiveness and legitimacy of its political system."[103] A table of social prerequisites to foster stable democracies includes an open class system, economic wealth, literacy, and a capitalist economy.[104] Sufficient economic development produces "increased income, greater economic security, and widespread higher education" that permits "the lower strata to develop longer time perspectives and more complex and gradualist views of politics."[105] In fact, Lipset cites de Tocqueville as recognizing before Marx that increased wealth and education of the lower classes make them less susceptible to extremist ideology and antidemocratic sentiments.[106]

Lipset tells the reader that it "is obvious that the conditions related to stable democracy … are most readily found in the countries of northwest Europe and their English-speaking offspring"[107] and he offers a list of stable and unstable democracies and contrasts them to stable and unstable dictatorships.[108] Overall, there is no question that democratic stability is the theme and goal of *Political Man* and the various social and economic prerequisites to democracy are important in helping states manage social conflict and consensus. Yet critical to achieving a balance between consensus and conflict are social groups and here is where Lipset notes his debt to de Tocqueville.

Lipset credits de Tocqueville as "the first major exponent of the idea that democracy involves a balance between the forces of conflict and consensus."[109] Contrasting Marx to de Tocqueville, Lipset states that, while the former saw classes as the social unit striking the balance, it was de Tocqueville who first described local communities and voluntary associations as securing this balance.

---

102 *Id.*
103 *Id.* at 64.
104 *Id.* at 61.
105 *Id.* at 45.
106 *Id.* at 51.
107 *Id.* at 57.
108 *Id.* at 32.
109 *Id.* at 4.

According to Lipset: "Private associations which are sources of restrictions on the government also serve as major channels for involving people in politics. In short, they are the mechanisms for creating and maintaining the consensus for a democratic society."[110] De Tocqueville, then, is the first pluralist, at least according to Lipset, and much of the focus of *Political Man* and the arguments in the book on using voluntary groups both as buffers between the individual and the state and as a mechanism to preserve democracy are clearly indebted to him. In fact, *Political Man* makes scores of references to de Tocqueville.

Elsewhere in *Political Man*, Lipset demonstrates how a mass society is an authoritarian one made possible by the absence of intermediary associations. Such associations act as "countervailing power" to a centralized state,[111] contributing to democratic attitudes including political tolerance and participation.[112] Voluntary associations are also credited with increased voting activity,[113] the production of crosscutting social cleavages,[114] the breakup of social conformism,[115] and the mediation of class conflict.[116]

In sum, the value of interest groups resides less in how they enhance the efficacy and participatory activity of individuals, although that does occur. Instead, democracy is less about the individual than it is about the group and how its efficacy and political activity should be encouraged. The voluntary association—not the individual—is the savior of democracy, and it was de Tocqueville's genius to first discover this.

David Truman's *The Governmental Process* is the single most important statement on pluralism, developing a theory of interest groups in a competitive political environment that serves to distribute political power. Truman defines an interest group "as a shared-attitude group that makes certain claims upon other groups in the society."[117] This definition is reminiscent of the first half of Madison's depiction in *Federalist* 10 of a faction as a number of citizens united and actuated by some common impulse, passion, or interest, yet it ignores the second half of the definition which casts factions in a negative light.

With this definition of interest group in mind, Truman begins his work by referencing *The Federalist Papers* and the importance that Madison places on factions and the need to control them.[118] Truman's claim is that *The Federalist* is "one of the most skillful and important examples of pressure group activity

---

110 *Id.* at 7.
111 *Id.* at 52.
112 *Id.* at 52-53.
113 *Id.* at 189.
114 *Id.* at 77-78.
115 *Id.* at 448.
116 *Id.* at 410.
117 DAVID TRUMAN, THE GOVERNMENTAL PROCESS: POLITICAL INTERESTS AND PUBLIC OPINION, 37 (1971).
118 *Id.* at 4.

in American history."[119] Yet Truman's sanitized reading of Madison led to the conclusion that factions carried "none of the overtones of corrupt and selfishness associated with modern groups."[120] From Madison, Truman then moves on to de Tocqueville, invoking him as further evidence of the importance of groups in the American political process. Here, he cites approvingly from *Democracy in America*: "In no country of the world ... has the principle of association been more successfully used or applied to a greater multitude of objects that in America."[121] By invoking de Tocqueville and Madison, Truman thus demonstrates the important contributions interest groups make to the political process and how democracy would not be possible without group mobilization.

Having recast interest groups in a favorable light, Truman's *Governmental Process* articulates an argument about interest groups and government power. Governmental institutions are described as centers of interest-based power where groups will seek to influence the political process by gaining access to various points of the government.[122]

Government decisions are the result of the contest and bargaining game among organized interests using many access points to advocate their members' interests in the policy process.[123] In many ways the government is almost like a blank slate, with the policies written onto it by different groups. What keeps any one group from possessing too much power is the competition from other groups similarly seeking access. Yet Truman notes that stability and equilibrium within a group is disturbed by the loss or entry of a leader,[124] and similarly, in the political arena, the entry of new groups will affect the stability and equilibrium of the interest group competitive political process. Second, overlapping group membership also serves as a stabilizing force by overcoming class stratification and the singular-minded preoccupation an individual may have with pursuing only one interest.[125]

What are the implications of Truman's arguments about interest groups? In contrast to Madison, who depicted groups often as something to be feared, the same sort of concern is not present with Truman and pluralists. At their worst groups simply exist, but at their best they are important centers of representation. Interest groups represent critical interests in society. They form around vital interests both as a way to represent their members' concerns and also to serve as critical channels of interest information to the government. Conversely, the government can reach individuals through these groups. They are, as pluralists described them, intermediate associations that serve as buffers between the government and the people. In mass societies they serve as entities to protect individual rights.

---

119   *Id.* at 5.
120   *Id.* at 6.
121   *Id.* at 7.
122   *Id.* at 506.
123   *Id.* at 507.
124   *Id.* at 26-27.
125   *Id.* at 520.

Moreover, these groups are important in terms of how they operate within a society. Under a pluralist schema, groups representing vital interests in society compete politically for power and influence. The pluralist assumption is that every important interest has its watchdog or organization that looks out for it. These various groups compete in the political arena to secure benefits or obtain whatever it is that they want. The competition among groups to secure influence is a bargaining game among them and with policy-makers. The competition with other groups prevents any one group from securing too much influence or power (prevention of tyranny to use Madisonian language). Groups little check one another and this competitive process is what facilitates the dispersion of political power.

But in addition, under a pluralist model, the competition for power and the ensuing bargain game is the essence of what public policy making is all about. By that, unlike with Madison or Madisonian democracy which assumed that a distinct public interest or good existed and therefore the purpose of the checks and balances and the other constitutional mechanisms was to make it possible for policy-makers to find it, pluralism has a procedural notion of the public interest. The public interest is byproduct of a bargaining game. Whatever is agreed upon by groups (in competition with one another) and policy-makers is the public interest. Under this model of politics, intervention and involvement by groups is not lamented but encouraged. The more involved groups perhaps the better the policy, or at least the more democratic the decision-making, because in theory more interests can be taken into consideration or accommodated.

The pluralist model emphasized group competition as an important description and perhaps even a normative statement for how a stable American democracy should work. But the competitive model did not simply end with groups. Joseph Schumpeter is often considered to be one of the proponents of what is called democratic revisionism or an elite theory of politics. Schumpeter's revision of traditional democratic theory, as noted earlier, placed emphasis on how elites competed with one another for voters in order to secure the opportunity to make policy and exercise authority. Conversely, Anthony Downs describes American democracy in economy terms, depicting voters as rational maximizers of utility preferences, and sees government and elections as perhaps no more than decision-making processes to satisfy interests.[126] If this model of elite-driven politics is combined with pluralism, then one is left with a theory that significantly displaces the individual or the voter as the ontological center of American politics. Voters do vote, but they do so to confer upon elites authority to act. Individuals also work through interest groups or organizations to communicate to the government and also to protect their interests.

In sum, the pluralist model of politics on one level offers a powerful contrast to the Madisonian model. Its endorsement of group competition and elite decision-making stands in contrast to what the original constitutional Framers espoused.

---

126 ANTHONY DOWNS, AN ECONOMIC THEORY OF DEMOCRACY, 49-50 (1957).

Pluralism is not without its criticism. Many point out that pluralism favors mobilized and better organized interests,[127] that not every interest has its watchdog, and that there are indeed many policy areas where the dominance of one or more groups fosters iron triangles that favor some interests to the exclusion of others.[128] Some of these structural limitations in the pluralist model of democracy may be unfortunate but some also might rise to a level of threatening minority or other constitutional rights. In situations where these pluralist externalities rise to the level of offending basic rights they may implicate questions about election law and democracy. Improper use of money to affect political decisions, denial of voting rights, or outright threats to minority rights or the integrity of the democratic decision-making process might be the occasion for judicial intervention.

Toward an American Democracy Theory

What is the significance of describing both the Madisonian and pluralist views for the purposes of this book and election law? Both represent complementary if not contrasting ways to think about how American democracy should operate, they also offer a set of values important to the political process. Madisonian democracy fears factions, believes in individual freedom, the public interest, the need to check political power, and the value of trying to police the law-making process to ensure that elected leaders make good choices unencumbered or unpolluted by corrupting forces of many groups. It is clearly an elite model, especially when examined in light of the absence of textually explicit language regarding the right to vote in the original Constitution. Yet for whatever fear or concern there was regarding the common person, Madisonian democracy seemed to assume that the primary political relationship in society was between the individual and the government or representative. To this day, many of us think about American politics in a Madisonian way. There is a belief in a public good, and a fear of factions (which today we describe as or call interest groups or perhaps PACs or Super Pacs). Political corruption is a constant fear, with groups, perhaps money, lobbyists, or other forces all threatening the rights of others or the public good. Conversely, pluralism provides powerful political values for the American political system. It emphasizes seeing groups as not threats but enhancements to democratic decision-making or a belief that bargaining is good. Finally, within both the Madisonian and pluralist theories, there is an expressed concern regarding balancing majority rule and minority rights—neither theory is one of direct and unmediated majority rule.

---

127 Schattschneider, The Semi-Sovereign People.
128 THEODORE J. LOWI, THE END OF LIBERALISM (1969); GRANT MCCONNELL, PRIVATE POWER AND AMERICAN DEMOCRACY (1966); HARMON ZIEGLER, INTEREST GROUPS IN AMERICAN SOCIETY (1964); FRANK R. BAUMGARTNER AND BETH L. LEECH, BASIC INTERESTS: THE IMPORTANCE OF GROUPS IN POLITICS AND IN POLITICAL SCIENCE (1998); V.O. KEY, POLITICS, PARTIES, AND PRESSURE GROUPS (1967).

These two theories of democracy often provide guidance or frameworks for how many think about American politics. Not surprisingly, many might appeal to both of these frameworks when thinking about American politics, gliding between one or another to provide a set of values to endorse a particular set of policy prescriptions. The two visions are part of perhaps a broader—but perhaps not ideologically or conceptually whole—vision about American politics.

So what is the essence of what forms or defines the contours of American democracy? The discussion of Robert Dahl provided some general framing regarding what values are important to a democracy in general, with Madisonianism and pluralism providing further specification. One could also add to this other concepts from American politics and history. For example, some would argue that the Progressive Era in American politics which ushered in the politics-administration dichotomy, neutral competence, and initiative, referendum, and recall represents a re-invention of American democracy.[129] Perhaps that is the case, or maybe the reforms represent an effort to stem political corruption caused by a political process bogged down by special interests. Moreover, implicit in the Progressive or democratic project are other values, such as transparency and open government, that have become more prominent since Watergate in the 1970s. These might be new values to the American political system, but they also could simply be specific conceptions of values implicit in Madisonian or pluralist theory.

Moreover, even if we accept Madisonian and pluralist theories, they too are not without flaws. Madison seems to underemphasize or underappreciate the powerful role that small cohesive groups (minority factions) could exert in the political process.[130] Technology has also reduced search costs, making it less likely that a big diverse republic will make it hard for like interests to find one another. In terms of pluralism, as noted above, the assumption that every interest has its watchdog, or that there is a level field upon which all groups compete equally, is not true. Many have criticized pluralism as inattentive to the impact of wealth and class upon group mobilization, or that the political system may be biased in favor of organized versus unorganized interests. Political scientists also talk of iron triangles in the policy arena, featuring policy areas where there is no effective group competition. These iron triangles form a policy triangle among interest groups, policy-makers, and administrators, making it difficult for outside groups to enter and have influence. Revolving doors—where legislators or government administrators leave to work for industries that they previously regulated—further exacerbate these concerns.

The broader point is that there are many components and concepts that form part of the American democratic system. How this applies to election law

---

129 *See:* David Schultz, *Supreme Court Articulation of the Politics/Administration Dichotomy*, in ALI FARAZMAND, ED., HANDBOOK OF BUREAUCRACY (1994), and Chapter 4 below for a discussion of the Progressive Era contributions to American democratic theory.

130 MANCUR OLSON, THE LOGIC OF COLLECTIVE ACTION (1971).

is twofold. First, the competing theories that form the boundaries of American democratic theory are the basis for the country's election laws. There may not be a fixed definition of what American democracy is, but a cluster of values that come together to define a fuzzy conception of what the practice of American democracy is supposed to look like. As noted in both this chapter and Chapter 1, election law is the mechanism by which American democracy is put into practice. How American democracy should operate forms the basis of laws and regulations regarding campaign financing, voting, ballot access, reapportionment, and a host of other issues structuring both elections and the actual policy-making process. Moreover, American democratic values are appealed to in legislative debates on these topics as well as in court decisions. Second, these values also provide or help define a theory of judicial review. If in fact there are normative values regarding American democracy that have been translated into constitutional norms or laws, part of the task of the Supreme Court and other actors is to consider them when adjudicating disputes. Yes perhaps these values influence whether the courts should be involved in the regulation of the political process, but these values also are critical in terms of indicating how it should rule when it does adjudicate.

The task of the remainder of this book is to make more explicit the values that are implicit within election law disputes in the United States. In some cases the goal will be to make an argument regarding how these values should guide specific resolution of disputes, but in other cases the aim will be simply to highlight the contrasting values and indicate how so many of the disputes really implicate clashing democratic values, to which there may not be any clear answer regarding what is the correct resolution.

Chapter 3

Voting Rights

"Demos" is the ancient Greek word for the people. The origins of the term democracy come from this word and another Greek word "kratos" meaning power. Together, democracy meant a political regime where the people rule. As simple as this concept seems to be, defining who is the demos is exceedingly difficult.

Robert Dahl's analysis of polyarchy includes the concept of inclusion.[1] Inclusion refers to defining those who get to participate in the governing and decision-making of the government. But the concept of inclusion requires more definition than simply saying that the people rule. As discussed in Chapter 2, inclusion is a complex term. Inclusion refers to asking who gets to rule and in what ways and over what. By that, one step in the process of defining who the people are who get to rule is to state that this authority is confined, as noted in Chapter 2, to biological persons, excluding legal persons or entities such as corporations. But defining democracy to include all biological persons suggests that little children and non-citizens, for example, are entitled to rule. Not all would agree with that idea, with most jurisdictions within the United States excluding non-citizens from voting and the minimum age of franchise being 18 years. Reasons for such an exclusion or minimum age requirements are based on the idea that non-citizens have less of a stake in the country than citizens, or that perhaps they are not as loyal or maybe should not be trusted compared to citizens. Or that one perk or benefit of citizenship is the right to participate. Similarly, specifying a minimum age to participate in part may be rooted in notions of maturity, knowledge, or again a sense of stake in the political process.

But non-citizens and the young may be just as knowledgeable and have as much an interest or stake as citizens as older individuals in the political system and with decisions being reached by the government. This could be the case with topics such as immigration, education, or tobacco consumption policies. Conversely, to say only biological persons may participate leads to questions about what role parties, corporations, and labor unions, among other entities, should have in the political process. To say only biological persons are part of the demos might mean that artificial entities are excluded from engagement. Given the reality that many people choose to participate in politics though groups, and also given the desirability, from a pluralist perspective, that they do so, it would be a blow to democracy to deny these entities a voice in the political process.

1　Robert A. Dahl, Democracy and Its Critics, 119 (1989).

Of course the type of voice one is talking about also matters. In the United States, civic engagement runs the range from talking about politics, voting, volunteering on a campaign, joining a group, giving money, to running for office.[2] Each of these activities carries with it certain levels of commitment and also a distinct analysis regarding who should be allowed to do what. Maybe we do not want anyone except for biological persons to vote, but does that mean that corporations, unions, or political parties should not be able to express their views on important matters of public debate? Even if we do think that corporations should not be able to speak, for example, does that mean that political parties should not? Neither are biological persons but many would contend that political parties and their role in a democracy is more important and critical than some other entities. But what is a party and how might it be different from an interest group or an organization seeking to support its candidates or interests in an election? These are questions addressed in more detail later in this book.

The point in raising all of these questions is simply to show that defining the demos is much more complicated than one might initially think. The complexity of defining the demos in election law might literally require constructing a matrix that includes a list of all possible types of participants in the political process along with a list of the entire range of political activities that are possible. The matrix would then define who gets to do what. Essentially this is the state of election law today. We have many categories of participants and for each one a set of permissible activities which they may engage in. The complexity of election law resides in the fact that many important questions have to be resolved when deciding the demos. Perhaps it would be more simple to have a "one size fits all" basic rule that defines the demos and who gets to do what. But that is probably not possible and even if it was most people would not like that. There may be good principled decisions to treat young versus old, citizen versus non-citizen, and biological versus non-biological entities differently.

This chapter does not try to tackle the entire range of demos questions. Instead, it focuses in on voting rights. More specifically it asks about who gets to vote in the United States and what the right or privilege to vote actually means. The discussion in this chapter will address how secure is franchise as a right in the United States. It examines the constitutional status of voting and it contends that, contrary to most accounts, the right to vote in the United States is hardly as protected as some think. In fact, despite constitutional language, there really is no universal right to vote in the United States.[3] There is not one demos but many

---

2 *See:* THEDA SKOCPOL AND MORRIS P. FIORINA, CIVIC ENGAGEMENT AND AMERICAN DEMOCRACY (1999), for a review of the various modes of political participation in the United States.

3 Derek T. Miller, *Invisible Federalism and the Electoral College*, 44 ARIZONA ST. L. J., 1238 (2012). Miller accurately points out that even in federal elections there are 51 different standards for determining who is allowed to vote. One can thus make the argument that there is not one single demos that casts ballots for even the president of the United

across the 50 states. Moreover, while there seems to be one trend in the United States toward enlarging the demos, there is a countertrend to shrink it, with that currently being played out with voter identification or voter ID laws being part of the second great wave of disenfranchisement in the United States. Finally, this chapter makes another simple argument—the concept of American voting and voting rights is trapped or defined by eighteenth- if not nineteenth-century legal if not political concepts. These are concepts referring to the basic right to vote, how to vote, and who is given this right. What is needed is a redefinition of voting rights for the twenty-first century that recognizes an affirmative right to vote in the United States as a condition of adult citizenship and that also is cognizant of the new technologies and political relationships in our society now challenging how we vote and what that vote should control.

The Constitution and Voting

The right of the people to rule is the essence of a democracy. In a direct democracy it would be the right to directly rule and make law or policy choices. In the case of a representative democracy it would be the right of the people to select their representatives. In either case, the idea of a democracy requires or entails the right of the people to vote. Exactly who has the franchise needs to be determined, but nonetheless the people, however defined, are supposed to have a right to it. Moreover, given that part of the dispute between the American thirteen colonies and England was over the representation and the demand of the former directly to select their own Members of Parliament, one would think that the Constitution would have language in it granting a right to vote. But that is not the case.

Look at the text of the original Constitution and the word vote does not appear anywhere in the text in reference to the right of the people to select their leaders. The word vote does appear in Article I in reference to the composition of Congress and voting rights for senators, and the right to vote also appears in Article II in reference to a discussion of the Electoral College and how electors shall choose the president and vice-president. But that is it. There is no textually explicit language in the Constitution that refers to the power of the people to vote for the president, the Senate, or the House. In fact, the Constitution is explicit in delegating to the state legislatures the authority to select the electors who will select the president, and also to decide who will be the two senators from their states. The people had no right to vote for the president and their senators, and the text of the Constitution appeared to be silent in terms of the right to vote for House of Representatives members.

States. This fact is a consequence of the Constitution primarily designating states with the responsibility of determining the time, manner, and place for federal elections along with voter qualifications.

The Constitution does not explicitly mention the right to vote. Instead, at the time of its writing, franchise rights were determined by the states.[4] In general, state laws limited franchise to white male property-owners, over the age of 21, and who were of a specific religious faith. In some cases, the religious qualification required one to be a Protestant, in others it excluded clergy. Thus, the first democratic paradox in the United States is the absence of a textually explicit right to vote in the Constitution. Stated more forcefully, a persistent paradox or problem in American democracy and election law is the lack of clarity regarding an affirmative right to vote. This lack of an affirmative right to vote raises troubling questions about the United States as a democracy.

Former Supreme Court Justice Thurmond Marshall captures this point when he declared:

> "We the People." When the Founding Fathers used this phrase in 1787, they did not have in mind the majority of America's citizens. "We the People" included, in the words of the Framers, "the whole Number of free Persons." On a matter so basic as the right to vote, for example, Negro slaves were excluded, although they were counted for representational purposes at three-fifths each. Women did not gain the right to vote for over a hundred and thirty years.[5]

But voting rights did begin to expand in the United States. Beginning in the 1820s, property qualifications were dropped and replaced with what was seen as a more democratic and fair poll tax during the Jackson an era. The end of the Civil War marked the passage of the Fourteenth and Fifteenth Amendments granting African-Americans—at least males—the right to vote. At the same time suffragette activists such as Elizabeth Cady Stanton advocated that women should have the right to vote.[6] Eventually in 1920 the adoption of the Nineteenth Amendment gave it to them. Earlier, in 1913, the Seventeenth Amendment gave citizens the right to vote for U.S. Senators. Then in 1971, during the height of the Vietnam War, adoption of the Twenty-Sixth Amendment lowered the voting age to 18 in state and federal elections. These constitutional amendments, plus the adoption of the Twenty-Fourth Amendment in 1964 banning poll taxes, the Indian Citizenship Bill of 1924 giving Native-Americans the right to vote, and the 1965 Voting Rights Act outlawing certain discriminatory voting practices directed against minorities, all further protected voting rights.

---

4 Alexander Keyssar, The Right to Vote: The Contested History of Democracy in the United States (2000); Donald Grier Stephenson, Jr., The Right to Vote: Rights and Liberties Under the Law (2004).

5 Thurgood Marshall, *Remarks of Thurgood Marshall at The Annual Seminar of the San Francisco Patent and Trademark Law Association in Maui, Hawaii* (May 6, 1987).

6 *See:* E.H. Hull, The Woman Who Dared to Vote: The Trial of Susan B. Anthony (2012), for a discussion of the history of women and voting.

But consider the language of many of the constitutional amendments regarding voting. They are phrased in the negative. The Fifteenth Amendment states that: "The right of citizens of the United States to vote shall not be denied or abridged by the United States or by any State on account of race, color, or previous condition of servitude." Former male slaves are not affirmatively granted the right to vote, the amendment merely states that their race or former status as slaves shall not be used as a disqualification to prevent them from voting. Similarly, the Nineteenth Amendment which granted women the right to vote does that in a negative way by declaring "The right of citizens of the United States to vote shall not be denied or abridged by the United States or by any State on account of sex"; and the Twenty-Sixth which extends voting rights to 18-year-olds does so equally negatively by stating: "The right of citizens of the United States, who are eighteen years of age or older, to vote shall not be denied or abridged by the United States or by any State on account of age." People of color, women, and 18-year-olds may still be denied the right to vote, just so long as it is for reasons that are not based on color, gender, and age. An affirmative right to vote would have simply declared, for example, that: "All citizens of the United States shall have a right to vote that shall not be denied or abridged by the United States or any State." There is no qualification here, simply an affirmative guarantee to franchise.

If the first paradox is the missing affirmative right to vote, the second paradox is to consider who actually votes in the United States. Despite all of the constitutional amendments and civil rights laws seeking to enable or create a right to vote in the United States—the enlargement of the demos—voting rates overall and among certain demographics remain quite low, especially when the United States is compared to its peers. Other major Western-style governments such as Germany, France, Sweden, and Malta have voting participation rates of 70 percent to 90 percent or more in their national elections.[7] The United States presidential turnout was approximately 58 percent in 2012.[8] The 2008 elections had a 57 percent turnout of those of the voting-age population, or 62 percent of those eligible to vote actually did so that year. In 1996, less than half (49 percent) of the voting-age population turned out to vote.[9] Additionally, if one were to construct a profile of the typical voter, it would tend to show how little progress has actually been made. While today females are more likely to vote than males, voter turnout generally is older, more likely white, more affluent, and more Protestant than the general adult population.[10] Phrased otherwise, the poor, less affluent and educated, those who

---

7 INSTITUTE FOR DEMOCRACY AND ELECTORAL ASSISTANCE, VOTER TURNOUT IN WESTERN EUROPE SINCE 1945: A REGIONAL REPORT (2004).

8 Michael McDonald, *2012 General Election Turnout Rates* (February 9, 2013), http://elections.gmu.edu/Turnout_2012G.html (site last visited on March 4, 2013).

9 *Id.* at http://elections.gmu.edu/voter_turnout.htm (site last visited on March 4, 2013).

10 *See, e.g.*, WARREN E. MILLER AND J. MERRILL SHANKS, THE NEW AMERICAN VOTER (1996); and MICHAEL S. LEWIS-BECK ET AL., THE AMERICAN VOTER REVISITED (2008), for a general discussion on the profile of the average American voter.

are younger, and people of color are less likely to vote. The profile of those who actually do vote today looks remarkably like the profile of those who were legally allowed the right to vote in 1787. America might still be a democracy for the few.

So how do we explain this second paradox about who does vote? Perhaps it is connected to the first paradox regarding the absence of an affirmative franchise right in the United States. Because there is no affirmative right to vote many impediments are placed in the way of people to exercise franchise. Despite the language of election law and the Supreme Court saying that there is a fundamental right to vote in the United States, the reality is that voting is a highly protected privilege. Secondarily, despite one tradition affirming and expanding a right to vote in the United States, there is also a countervailing tradition to shrink the demos and disenfranchise voters.

Creating the Right to Vote

The Framers of the Constitution appear to have left that right to vote up to the states which generally limited franchise to white male property owners, who were citizens of a certain age, occasionally of a specific religious faith.[11] For example, in *Minor v. Happersett*,[12] the United States Supreme Court rejected a claim by a Missouri woman that as a citizen the Constitution gave her a right to vote, especially as a result of the passage of the Fourteenth Amendment. Her argument was that denying her the right to vote violated the Privileges and Immunities clause. The Court dismissed her claim. The Court recognized and did rule that women including Virginia Minor could be citizens of the United States, yet the original Constitution did not include voting or franchise as one of the original rights conferred on citizens. The question was whether since then voting had become a right. According to the Court:

> It is clear, therefore, we think, that the Constitution has not added the right of suffrage to the privileges and immunities of citizenship as they existed at the time it was adopted. This makes it proper to inquire whether suffrage was coextensive with the citizenship of the States at the time of its adoption. If it was, then it may with force be argued that suffrage was one of the rights which belonged to citizenship, and in the enjoyment of which every citizen must be protected. But if it was not, the contrary may with propriety be assumed.[13]

There are two major points to be gleaned from the *Minor* opinion. The first is that, while women are or can be citizens, they do not have the right to vote. Second and perhaps equally important, the Court bifurcates citizenship and voting. By that,

---

11   Keyssar, The Right to Vote at 21-25.
12   88 U.S. 162 (1875).
13   88 U.S. at 171-72.

it declares that just because one is a citizen that does not mean one has a right to vote. Ordinarily one might think that citizenship entails that right but Court rejects that linkage. While many condemn the *Minor* decision as wrong or sexist, or point to the fact that the Nineteenth Amendment overturned the holding with regards to women voting, the truth is that the precedent of separating citizenship from voting remains valid to this day. One can be a citizen of the United States and not have a right to vote. This is true not just for minors (those under eighteen) but even for adults.

In addition to the Fourteenth Amendment, as noted above, several amendments did address voting, but not in the affirmative. It was not until the 1940s that the Supreme Court affirmatively addressed the constitutional right to vote. In *United States v. Classic*,[14] a case arising out of vote fraud in a Louisiana federal election primary, the Court was faced with the issue of whether one has a right to vote,[15] and then whether depriving a person of that right came within the meaning of a federal criminal law that made it illegal to "injure a citizen in the exercise 'of any right or privilege secured to him by the Constitution or laws of the United States.'"[16] The Court stated:

> We come then to the question whether that right is one secured by the Constitution. Section 2 of Article I commands that Congressmen shall be chosen by the people of the several states by electors, the qualifications of which it prescribes. The right of the people to choose, whatever its appropriate constitutional limitations, where in other respects it is defined, and the mode of its exercise is prescribed by state action in conformity to the Constitution, is a right established and guaranteed by the Constitution and hence is one secured by it to those citizens and inhabitants of the state entitled to exercise the right.[17]

In addition in *Reynolds v. Sims*[18] the Court embraced the principle of equal representation for equal numbers of people—one person, one vote for the purposes of reapportionment.[19] More importantly, in *Reynolds* the Supreme Court again reaffirmed that the Constitution protects the right to vote in federal elections. Furthermore, in *Reynolds* the Court drew a parallel between the right to vote and right to procreate in *Skinner v. Oklahoma*,[20] declaring the right to vote as a fundamental.[21]

---

14 313 U.S. 299 (1941).
15 *Id.* at 308.
16 *Id.* at 308, *quoting* then 18 U.S.C. 51 (1940).
17 313 U.S. at 314-15.
18 377 U.S. 533 (1964).
19 *Id.* at 558.
20 *Id.* at 561-62, *citing* 316 U.S. 535 (1942).
21 377 U.S. at 561.

Locating a constitutional text to support the right to vote in state elections is more problematic. In *Harper v. Virginia State Board of Elections*,[22] in striking down the imposition of a poll tax in state elections, the Supreme Court ruled that the right to vote in state elections was located in the First Amendment by way of the Fourteenth Amendment's Due Process and Equal Protection Clauses.[23] Although the tax met traditional constitutional standards: it was neither racially discriminatory nor indefensible as rational policy, but the Court found that it unconstitutionally singled out the poor.[24] More importantly, the Court yet again affirmed the importance of voting, stating that: "Long ago, in *Yick Wo v. Hopkins*, the Court referred to 'the political franchise of voting' as a 'fundamental political right, because preservative of all rights.' Recently, ... the Court referred to 'the political franchise of voting' as a 'fundamental political right, because preservative of all rights.'"[25] Again, as in *Reynolds*, the Court drew a parallel between voting and the right of procreation found in *Skinner v. Oklahoma*,[26] ruling that where "fundamental rights and liberties are asserted under the Equal Protection Clause, classifications which might invade or restrain them must be closely scrutinized and carefully confined."[27] Specifically, the Court cites to language in *Skinner* that dictates that efforts to interfere with the right to procreation must be subject to strict scrutiny.[28]

The legacy of *Classic*, *Reynolds*, and *Harper* is that these three cases stand for the proposition that voting is a fundamental right that must be subject to strict scrutiny. In addition to these three cases, the Court has also reached a similar conclusion elsewhere.[29] Collectively, these cases would seem to suggest that interference with, or regulation of the fundamental right to vote must be subject

---

22   383 U.S. 663 (1966).
23   383 U.S. at 664.
24   *Id.* at 666-67.
25   *Id.* at 667.
26   *Id.* at 668, 670.
27   *Id.* at 670.
28   *Id.* at 670 (*citing* 316 U.S. at 542).
29   *See, e.g.*, Illinois Bd. of Elections v. Socialist Workers Party, 440 U.S. 173 (1979); Bush v. Gore, 531 U.S. 98, 104 (2000); Oregon v. Mitchell, 400 U.S. 112, 142 (1970); Rosario v. Rockefeller, 410 U.S. 752, 767-68 (1973); Dunn v. Blumstein, 405 U.S. 330, 336 (1972); Williams v. Rhodes, 393 U.S. 23, 38 (1968) (*declaring* "When 'fundamental rights and liberties' are at issue a State has less leeway in making classifications than when it deals with economic matters") (citations omitted); Cardona v. Power, 384 U.S. 672, 676 (1966) (*ruling* that "Where classifications might 'invade or restrain' fundamental rights and liberties, they must be 'closely scrutinized and carefully confined.'"); and Storer v. Brown, 415 U.S. 724, 756 (1974) ("when legislation burdens such a fundamental constitutional right, it is not enough that the legislative means rationally promote legitimate governmental ends. Rather, 'governmental action may withstand constitutional scrutiny only upon a clear showing that the burden imposed is necessary to protect a compelling and substantial governmental interest").

to strict scrutiny, and that only if a compelling governmental interest is asserted that overrides it, may it be limited.[30] However, the Court itself has created some confusion about this point, as demonstrated in *Burdick v. Takushi*.[31]

Think about voting, even assuming there is an affirmative right to vote. What if, for example, an insomniactic individual wishes to vote in the middle of the night but the polls do not open until 7:00 a.m. Does she have a claim that her right to vote has been violated? Or what if she wishes to vote by Internet and only in-person voting is available? Has her right to vote been violated? Probably not. The reason is that government should have some ability to regulate the time, place, and manner for elections. Some reasonable administrative regulation makes sense. This is exactly what the Supreme Court has recognized—there is a difference between laws aimed at suppressing or depressing voting versus those which seek to impose reasonable administrative regulations.

In *Burdick v Takushi*, at issue was a State of Hawaii law prohibiting write-in voting.[32] In rejecting the First and Fourteenth Amendment challenges to the law,[33] the Supreme Court described its approach to regulations regarding voting rights:

> It is beyond cavil that "voting is of the most fundamental significance under our constitutional structure." *Illinois Bd. of Elections v. Socialist Workers Party*, 440 U.S. 173, 184, 99 S.Ct. 983, 990, 59 L.Ed.2d 230 (1979). It does not follow, however, that the right to vote in any manner and the right to associate for political purposes through the ballot are absolute. *Munro v. Socialist Workers Party*, 479 U.S. 189, 193, 107 S.Ct. 533, 536, 93 L.Ed.2d 499 (1986). The Constitution provides that States may prescribe "[t]he Times, Places and Manner of holding Elections for Senators and Representatives," Art. I, § 4, cl. 1, and the Court therefore has recognized that States retain the power to regulate their own elections.[34]

Because, according to the Court, states or the government need to structure elections to promote their fairness and honesty,[35] not all regulations need to be subject to strict scrutiny simply because they impose some burdens on voters:

> Election laws will invariably impose some burden upon individual voters. Each provision of a code, "whether it governs the registration and qualifications of

---

30 *See:* Steven E. Gottlieb, *Compelling Governmental Interests: An Essential but Unanalyzed Term in Constitutional Adjudication*, 68 B.U. L. Rev. 917 (1988), for a general discussion of the interplay between fundamental rights and compelling governmental interests.
31 504 U.S. 428 (1992).
32 *Id.* at 430.
33 *Id.* at 430-31.
34 *Id.* at 432-33.
35 *Id.* at 433.

voters, the selection and eligibility of candidates, or the voting process itself, inevitably affects-at least to some degree-the individual's right to vote and his right to associate with others for political ends." Consequently, to subject every voting regulation to strict scrutiny and to require that the regulation be narrowly tailored to advance a compelling state interest, as petitioner suggests, would tie the hands of States seeking to assure that elections are operated equitably and efficiently. Accordingly, the mere fact that a State's system "creates barriers ... tending to limit the field of candidates from which voters might choose ... does not of itself compel close scrutiny." [36]

Apparently replacing the strict scrutiny standard previously used to examine the right to vote, the Court proposed a different test to be used:

> A court considering a challenge to a state election law must weigh "the character and magnitude of the asserted injury to the rights protected by the First and Fourteenth Amendments that the plaintiff seeks to vindicate" against "the precise interests put forward by the State as justifications for the burden imposed by its rule," taking into consideration "the extent to which those interests make it necessary to burden the plaintiff's rights." [37]

Thus, in examining the State of Hawaii's ban on write-in voting, the Court used this new flexible standard to uphold it.[38]

However, the *Burdick* decision is confusing. While it perhaps looks as if the Court is ruling that all regulations affecting voting need to be examined from this new flexible and less rigorous standard, the language citations suggest otherwise. First, in referencing the cases where the Court says the right to vote is not absolute, it cites not to cases about voting rights per se, but to cases involving ballot access and the rights of political parties.[39] These references question the degree to which the Court is diluting its previous strict scrutiny test. Second, and more importantly, the Court casts the seeds of doubt by distinguishing between two different types of voting regulations—those which impose "severe" versus "reasonable" burdens.[40] Regulations imposing the former types of burdens would continue to be examined under the strict scrutiny standard where they must be "narrowly drawn to advance a state interest of compelling importance."[41] However, for the latter, the new standard will be used "when a state election law provision imposes only 'reasonable, nondiscriminatory restrictions' upon the First and Fourteenth Amendment rights of voters, 'the State's important regulatory interests are generally sufficient to justify'

---

36 *Id.*
37 *Id.* at 434.
38 *Id.* at 434.
39 *Id.* at 432-33.
40 *Id.* at 434.
41 *Id.*

the restrictions."⁴² Unfortunately, the Court failed to describe what constituted a severe versus reasonable burden, opening up confusion regarding when to apply which standard to what regulation.

This confusion became apparent in disputes challenging the constitutionality of voter identification laws. While voter ID will be discussed in more detail below, the question to ask is whether requiring individuals to present photo identification when they vote in person at the polls is a severe burden on their right to vote or whether it is a reasonable time, place, and manner regulation? Are voter ID laws then more like direct attempts to restrict voting or merely reasonable administrative regulations? The Supreme Court, in *Crawford v. Marion County Election Board* sought to address this.⁴³ In upholding the Indiana voter ID law in question, the Court threw into confusion whether the *Burdick* test is the one to employ when evaluating restrictions on voting rights. In *Crawford* the Court drew upon a test found in *Anderson v Celebrezze*⁴⁴ (a case involving a challenge to ballot access rules by the 1980 independent presidential candidate John Anderson). It stated: "[A] court evaluating a constitutional challenge to an election regulation [must] weigh the asserted injury to the right to vote against the 'precise interests put forward by the State as justifications for the burden imposed by its rule.'"⁴⁵

A total of six Justices affirmed the Indiana law, but only three Justices in the majority agreed to use the *Burdick* test. Justices Scalia, Thomas, and Alito affirmed the Indiana law using the *Burdick* test, while the dissenters (Souter and Ginsburg together and then a separate Breyer opinion) also opted for an *Anderson* balancing test. In theory there are thus six Justices who held that this test should be deployed when evaluating rules affecting the right to vote, although it is debatable that there is any one test that commands the majority of the Court.

The right to vote is fundamental, but it is not clear what standard to use to assess the scope and permissibility of regulations that affect it. Another question to ask is how far or deep is the right to vote. By that the Supreme Court has stated that the right extends more than to the initial allocation of franchise. Simply saying or granting someone the initial right to vote but then doing something like not counting ballots or applying different standards when counting them might pose problems that deny the right to vote. Or what about a situation where there is a gerrymander where one representative represents twice or three times as many voters as another? Here there is a dilution of voting power and in reapportionment cases such as *Reynolds v. Sims*,⁴⁶ and *Westbury v. Sanders*,⁴⁷ the Court enunciated the "one person, one vote" standard. The idea behind these cases is that democracy demands equality, at least in terms of voting, if all of us who are deemed members

---

42 Id.
43 553 U.S. 181 (2008).
44 460 U.S. 780 (1983).
45 504 U.S. at 434 (quoting Anderson, 460 U.S., at 789).
46 377, U.S. 533 (1964).
47 376 U.S. 1 (1964).

of the demos are to have the same chance to participate in the political affairs of the community.⁴⁸

But consider a few issues regarding voting. First the right to vote begs the question—for what? A simple answer is to declare that the right to vote is in elections, but all elections? No one would argue that the constitutional right to vote extends to participation in a private club or association. The rules for that club or organization, and not the Constitution, dictate what rights one has. The same is generally true in terms of corporations and the rights of shareholders, but even here there are some rules promulgated by state or federal law that do define rights. In general, however, these are all private entities and the best reading of the Constitution and the Bill of Rights limits application of the right to vote to selecting representatives in government. But as simple as this rule is, enforcing or applying it in practice is difficult, especially in a world increasingly marked by a breakdown of the traditional lines between government and the other sectors. Public-private partnerships, contracting out, and privatization increasingly make it difficult to draw clear lines between where the government begins and ends.⁴⁹

Consider two cases. The first is *Marsh v. State of Alabama*.⁵⁰ In this case a private company town owned by a corporation barred the distribution of religious materials in the business district. A member of the Jehovah's Witnesses was arrested for trespass for distributing religious materials without a permit. She was convicted in a trial and it was upheld on appeal. The Supreme Court overturned her conviction. The Court ruled that effectively the company town was acting like a government, with significant control over individuals in it. The town square in this private town effectively was like a town square in many real communities. To deny a person a constitutional right to go door to door in a real city would be unconstitutional, and the same could be argued here too. According to Justice Black in writing for the majority:

> Many people in the United States live in company-owned towns. These people, just as residents of municipalities, are free citizens of their State and country. Just as all other citizens they must make decisions which affect the welfare of community and nation. To act as good citizens they must be informed. In order to enable them to be properly informed their information must be uncensored.

---

48 *See generally*: JOHN W. CHAPMAN AND IAN SHAPIRO, DEMOCRATIC COMMUNITY, NOMOS XXXV (1993), for a discussion of various meanings of community including its relationship to equality.

49 *See:* SHEILA SEUSS KENNEDY AND DAVID SCHULTZ, AMERICAN PUBLIC SERVICE: CONSTITUTIONAL AND ETHICAL FOUNDATIONS (2010); and David Schultz, *Professional Ethics in a Postmodern Society*, 6 JOURNAL OF PUBLIC INTEGRITY 279 (2004), for a discussion of how public-private partnerships and other forms of alternative service delivery are challenging and changing the normal boundaries that distinguish the public, private, and non-profit sectors.

50 326 U.S. 501 (1946).

There is no more reason for depriving these people of the liberties guaranteed by the First and Fourteenth Amendments than there is for curtailing these freedoms with respect to any other citizen.[51]

Marsh is significant for recognizing the reality of a world where the line between private and public government has because less distinct.

Now consider the case of *Salyer Land Company v. Tulare Lake Basin Water Storage District*.[52] Here the issue was whether the principle of one person, one vote extended to a water-storage district primarily concerned with irrigation. Voting was confined to property owners, with votes allocated based on the value of land they held. Tenants and renters in the district challenged the law contending they were denied a right to vote. The Court rejected their claim, arguing that the watershed district was not a "normal governmental authority,"[53] providing a more limited array of services that do not include the range that a typical government would provide, such as schools, housing, transportation, utilities, and roads. Perhaps it was not a private organization, but the Court ruled that the State of California (which created the district and the voting rules) could have deemed it not a public governmental entity either, thereby restricting or qualifying the right to vote.

Marsh and *Salyer* offer competing perspectives on the right to vote, even if the former does not address the issue of franchise. *Marsh* recognized the trend toward a world where the lines between governmental and non-governmental were blurred. That was in 1946. The world is even more blurry now. Huge percentages of the population live in common interest communities such as private gated communities with condominiums or cooperatives. Additionally, many non-profit and private entities receive billions of dollars in contracts to perform governmental services. There are business improvement districts, special purpose districts that handle single tasks such as roads, or fire, or water and sewerage. Drawing a line that says these entities are not public or governmental and therefore the right to vote does not extend to them seems so wooden. It is to lock a model of government in the nineteenth or early twentieth century, failing to recognize the new ways or hybrid governments that have emerged. This is the difference between discussing the concept of government versus governance.

Governance is a broader term referring to the regulation of authority or process of making decisions and holding power accountable.[54] Governance is

---

51 *Id.* at 501, 508-9.
52 410 U.S. 719 (1973).
53 *Id.* at 729.
54 Jan Kooiman, Governing as Governance (2003); Donald F Kettl, Sharing Power: Public Governance and Private Markets (1993); Larry Catá. Backer, *Private Actors and Public Governance Beyond the State: The Multinational Corporation, the Financial Stability Board, and the Global Governance Order*, 18 Indiana Journal of Global Legal Studies, 751 (Summer 2011).

often talked about in reference to corporations,[55] non-profits,[56] and a host of other entities wielding power and where decisions need to be regulated and controlled.[57] Governance discusses the role that all stakeholders, however they are defined and identified, as having a say over affairs that affect their interests.[58]

The significance of discussing governance as opposed to government is that the former captures a broader spectrum of organizations that exert authority over which stakeholders should be entitled to express a voice in how decisions are made. A right to vote for the twenty-first century needs to recognize the significant authority these and other private entities have over the lives of people. To limit the concept of democracy to these old models of authority is to neglect the reality of a world where public power is increasingly wielded by private hands. This suggests that the courts need to rethink the state action doctrine when it comes to voting rights, asking more functional questions regarding what authority some erstwhile private entities possess, how the decisions they make have public ramifications, and how they affect individuals. Robert Dahl argues that the third wave of democratic theory has to include a move toward economic democracy.[59] Perhaps that is correct, but even if not, voting rights that reflect a different world of blurred edges of public and private power, as the Court saw in *Salyer*, seem necessary if franchise rights and democratic theory is to keep pace with a changing reality. To a large extent, the Supreme Court and election law have failed to capture this broader discussion of governance and the new reality of how institutions across economic sectors exercise authority. One needs to think about stakeholders as voters and think in terms of how the Constitution may need to recognize franchise rights in relationships not previously considered.

Next, consider another direction of where voting is headed. Voting was generally something that occurred on election day. Voters were expected to appear in person on the appointed day and cast their ballots that way. There was a narrow exception for some voters who because of illness, travel, or other reasons could not show up at the polls on election day. This is absentee balloting. Many states created a narrow band of excuses that would allow individuals to vote as absentees. Yet as the Minnesota Supreme Court pointed out in Minnesota Senate dispute in *Coleman v Franken*,[60] absentee voting is a privilege and not a right.

---

55   Robert A.G. Monks and Nell Minow, Corporate Governance (2008).

56   American Bar Association, Guide to Nonprofit Corporate Governance in the Wake of Sarbanes-Oxley (2005); Edward L Glaeser, The Governance of Not-for-profit Organizations (2003).

57   *See, e.g.*, Joel L Fleishman, The Future of American Political Parties: the Challenge of Governance (1982); Margaret P Karns and Karen A Mingst, International Organizations: the Politics and Processes of Global Governance (2004).

58   Ahmad Feizizadeh, *Corporate Governance: Frameworks*, 5 Indian Journal of Science & Technology, 3353 (September 2012).

59   Robert A. Dahl, A Preface to Economic Democracy (1986).

60   769 N.W.2d 453 (Minn. 2009).

One has no right to vote as absentees and therefore, as the Court stated in that case, rules prescribing absentee voting are to be strictly enforced and followed. Many states have complex rules for voting absentees, such as signature or affidavit requirements, and if they are not strictly followed then election officials may and in fact are required to reject accepting the absentee ballots.

But voting in advance of election day is becoming an ever common occurrence. In 2012 the estimates were that more than one-third of the electorate would cast ballots for the president in advance of the November 6, election date.[61] In many cases the voters would cast absentee ballots, meeting the narrow statutory requirements to do this, or under broader "no excuse" absentee ballot laws, or even under what has come to be called early voting laws.

The difference between absentee and early voting may not be apparent, but in theory allowing for early voting means perhaps that there is more constitutional or legal protection than for absentee voting, but that is not clear. Is there a constitutional right to early vote? Is there a constitutional right to absentee vote? Currently that does not seem to be the case for either. But as more and more individuals exercise early or absentee voting options, the question turns to what restrictions states can place upon this use of franchise. At a time when one-third and perhaps in the future maybe one-half or more individuals no longer cast their ballot in the old traditional way of showing up to vote, saying that the new ways of casting ballots is merely a privilege and not a right leaves open serious legal questions regarding how far the government may go in its regulations. Long ago the Supreme Court rejected the right/privilege distinction when it came to the scope of government regulation.[62] Simply asserting that something is a privilege and not a right does not give the government the ability to impose unconstitutional conditions upon a right.[63] The same should be true with voting. Over the next few years pressures to allow for internet voting will continue to grow and the technology to allow for it will no doubt be perfected. Voting may follow the road of commerce where now so much of it is taking place over the Web. A new generation of voters will emerge accustomed to doing it on-line. To freeze voting rights in an old practice and technology makes no sense. The law on voting needs perhaps to apply the *Anderson* test not simply to the initial allocation of voting that presumably takes place at the polls, but also to voting in all of its guises, including franchise activity that encompasses that activity across technologies and in times,

---

61 Elizabeth Hartfield, *Early Presidential Vote 2012: Where Things Stand in the Final Hours* (November 5, 2012), The Note, http://abcnews.go.com/blogs/politics/2012/11/early-presidential-vote-2012-where-things-stand-in-the-final-hours/ (site last visited on March 5, 2013).

62 William W. Van Alstyne, *The Demise of the Right-Privilege Distinction in Constitutional Law*, 81 Harv. L. Rev., 1439 (1968).

63 Daniel C. Kramer, The Price of Rights: The Courts, Government Largesse, and Fundamental Liberties (2004).

places, and manners that extend beyond election day and showing up and voting in person.

Additionally, the right to vote as something that extends beyond the initial allocation of franchise must also include other activities besides voting in a general election. In the famous "White Primary" cases that took place in the American South from the 1920s to the 1940s, the issue addressed the role of voting and party primaries. By that the South, as a legacy of the Civil War, was mainly Democrat. Winning the Democrat primary in a one-party region rendered the general election practically moot. The Texas Democrat Party, for example, limited to white Caucasians participation or membership in their organization. Lonnie Smith was an African-American who wanted to vote in the Texas Democratic primary. He was refused admission, with the party contending that the primary was a private affair. As a private affair the Fourteenth Equal Protection clause would not apply. The question then was is a primary event a state action? In *Smith v. Allwright*,[64] the Court said yes. The right to vote does extend to primaries, and across the United States absentee balloting is provided for absentee voting. But does the right to vote extend beyond primaries to perhaps other party events, such as caucuses? So far the Courts have not ruled that they do.

Many states use the caucus system to conduct business. Most famously, the Iowa caucuses are the beginning of the presidential selection process every four years. But beyond Iowa many other states uses caucuses to make presidential selections and conduct other business. The same is true in Minnesota, a state which consistently leads the nation in voting with presidential turnouts in recent elections above 75 percent. Imagine the Minnesota Democrat-Farmer Labor Party (DFL) adopting a rule that no people of color could participate in their caucuses, or the Republican Party adopting one barring women from attending. Could they do that? Proponents of the political parties seem to imply such a right when arguing against a law calling for primaries instead of caucuses for the selection of presidential and other candidates. While the courts have given broad deference to the First Amendment freedom of association rights of political parties, those rights are limited.

There is no question that political parties should generally be free to determine who can be a member and how they select their candidates. Over the last 20 years the Supreme Court has ruled that parties are free to associate with whomever they wish. This means, for example, that the Republican Party of Connecticut, according to the Court in *Tashjian v. Republican Party of Connecticut*,[65] could invite independents to participate in their primaries even though a state law prohibited it. Conversely, the Court *in California Democratic Party v. Jones*,[66] also voided a California law permitting voters in primaries to select candidates in any party, citing the right of political parties to limit who can participate in their

---

64 321 U.S. 649 (1944).
65 479 U.S. 208 (1986).
66 530 U.S. 567 (2000).

selection. Paraphrasing the Leslie Gore song, the reason for these decisions is that "It's my party and I'll invite whom I want to."

While these cases significantly protect party rights, the Supreme Court has never held that they are free to discriminate, as evidenced by the *Smith v. Allwright* decision. To say that individuals have a right to vote but to deny them the right to participate in party affairs effectively undermines that right. What became clear on caucus night in Minnesota and in other states with this type of gathering is how exclusionary and discriminatory the process is. While there was no official policy stating that neither women nor African-Americans could participate, many people were disenfranchised. They included those who worked second shifts or who were working second jobs, the elderly afraid to go out at night, parents with child-rearing duties, and others, such as those serving in the military in places like Iraq. None of them could participate via an absentee ballot, as would be the case in a general election. While the discrimination that occurred might not rise to the level of that found in the White Primary cases, it was nonetheless no less exclusionary and limiting in whom it effectively allowed to participate. To put it in comparison: in 2012, approximately 66,000 individuals constituting less than 2 percent of the Minnesota voting-age population attended its caucuses and cast a ballot in the presidential preference poll.[67] Conversely, in Wisconsin, a state often held in comparison to Minnesota in terms of its political culture, size, and demographics, its 2012 primary turnout was 25 percent.[68]

The point here is that in caucus states this event is an important political activity that excludes many individuals. The right to vote should include a right to vote absentee in this activity. Few would endorse the idea that illness, service to country, or work should be discounted as reasons for why individuals cannot show up in person to vote in a general or primary election. That is why there is absentee voting for these events. There is a recognition that the right to vote should be permitted for these events. Yet as noted, absentee voting is a privilege. The right to vote, if it means anything, should also entail a constitutional right to cast a ballot even if one cannot attend on election day. This is especially the case in a country where employers are not required to give paid time off to vote, let alone time off to vote at all. Voters should not have to choose between making a living or voting. The marketplace should not undermine the polity, or make voters choose between a civic duty (as some describe voting) or a constitutional right and the imperative to make a living.

A great example regarding how democracy requires making a right to vote extend to caucuses and to absentee voting can be seen in a personal example on November 6, 2012—the general election for president. I was working at a television station to cover the election and it decided to cater dinner for all of us.

---

67 Minnesota Secretary of State, *Minnesota Preference for President* (n.d.), http://caucusresults.sos.state.mn.us/ElecRsltsStateWide.asp?M=SW (site last visited on March 5, 2013).

68 Associated Press, UPDATE: *Wisconsin Primary Turnout* 25% (April 2, 2012).

They hired a company to bring the food in. The woman who brought the food in was probably making minimum wage. I asked her if she voted and she said no. I asked why not and she said that she could not afford to take time off from work. Today was a good day for her to make money, with overtime, and in the last few weeks there had not been much business. She had started work at 7 a.m. and would work way past the time the polls closed. She lived miles away from work. She had to make a choice—vote or make money to support her family. She did not know she could vote absentee. I also asked her if she ever attended the political caucuses in Minnesota. Again she said no, citing work or having to be with her children.

The point here is twofold. Democratic theory dictates that citizens have the opportunity to have a voice at all critical stages in the decision-making process. That opportunity should not be limited because of economic reasons or factors beyond an individual's control. Second, if the precedents are correct in declaring that the right to vote extends beyond the initial allocation of franchise, then the right to vote should reject the right/privilege distinction between in-person and absentee voting and recognize some form of early casting of ballots as a constitutional right. The right to vote should also extend this right to a host of political decision-making functions beyond the general and primary elections.

Overall, one reading of American history is one of seeking to expand the right to vote and franchise for all. It is a story of more and more individuals being allowed to vote, and of increased access and opportunity to cast a ballot.

A Counter-Tradition

But while there is an American tradition marked by an expansion of franchise, Alexander Keyssar notes another one characterized by efforts to deny the right to vote.[69] There are repeated periods in American history demonstrating efforts to disenfranchise voters or to scare them away from the polls.[70] For example, as noted above, after the Civil War many in the South used Jim Crow laws, poll taxes, literacy tests, grandfather laws, and not so subtle means such as lynchings, cross burnings, and other techniques to prevent newly freed slaves from voting.[71] The battle for the ballot box has definitely been long and often violent.

Today, while nearly every adult citizen age 18 or older has the right to vote, not everyone does exercise this right. In presidential races often only half of those eligible to vote do so, while outcomes in some local elections down as low as 5 percent or 10 percent. Compared to many other major European countries, the United States has quite low voter turnout, with the profile of the average voter, as previously noted, looking still much like who could legally vote in 1787.

---

69 Keyssar, The Right to Vote at xvi-xvii.
70 RICHARD K. SCHER, THE POLITICS OF DISENFRANCHISEMENT: WHY IS IT SO HARD TO VOTE IN AMERICA? (2011).
71 *See generally, e.g.*, C. VANN WOODWARD, THE STRANGE CAREER OF JIM CROW (2001).

While the Constitution and Congress have addressed voting rights, the basic determination of who possesses suffrage is still largely a matter for the states to decide, as noted above. Constitutional amendments and federal laws have somewhat limited this discretion of the states, but this is still a matter of prime state concern. This is not to say that the federal government is excluded from the field, and over a period of years the Court has attempted to determine the exact extent to which state power over the entire field of voting has been delimited by these amendments, which, as indicated, basically act as a negative on certain state suffrage activities while leaving the positive determinations of voting to the states.

But the main point to note here is one stated above—the right to vote in the United States seems highly attenuated. The constitutional amendments addressing voting are phrased in the negative. Moreover, the core holding of *Minor v. Happersett*—that citizenship does not necessarily include a right to vote—remains good law in the United States. In the United States voting rights are subject to significant regulation, and in some cases, individuals can lose the right to vote, perhaps even for life. The Supreme Court in *Richardson v. Ramirez*,[72] upheld the authority of states under the Fourteenth Amendment under Section 2 to take away voting rights for felons. Most states do that now, whether temporarily or for life as in the case of states such as Florida. Beyond the constitutional claim, the policy or democratic theory argument is that felons put themselves outside the law, thereby justifying their denial of citizenship rights. Yet this assertion argues too much. In other major democracies around the world felons do not lose their rights. Moreover, even in the United States felons do not lose all their rights once convicted of crimes. They still possess due process rights, rights to be free from cruel and unusual punishment, and rights to free exercise of religion. There seems to be no good reason to think that felons similarly should lose what should be the most basic right of a citizen—voting—even if they have been convicted of a crime. Perhaps maybe in the case of someone convicted for voter fraud; but otherwise, there seems to be no rational relationship between felony conviction and loss of voting rights.

This discussion is not meant to make the case here for arguing against felon disenfranchisement. Instead, the intention is to highlight the counter-tradition in the United States that stands for the suppression of voting rights. The suppression may be explicit—Jim Crow laws or lynchings, or more subtle, as in using claims of fraud in the late nineteenth and early twentieth centuries to change voting procedures and rules in ways that made it harder for immigrants and the working class to vote.[73] Or disenfranchisement may be even less obvious—impediments for the working class and the poor to leave work to vote. In all these cases, disenfranchisement occurs.

---

72 418 U.S. 24 (1974).

73 *See:* Ron Hayduk, Democracy for All: Restoring Immigrant Voting Rights in the United States (2006), who discusses the history of immigrant voting in the United States.

But the most recent way of disenfranchisement taking place is with the efforts institute voter identification at the polls. The claim is that there is widespread voter fraud or impersonation at the polls such that voter photo identification is needed to abate it. What is voter fraud and what evidence do we have of its existence?

Lori Minnite locates voter fraud as a subcategory of this broader concept of election fraud, defining it as the "intentional corruption of the electoral process by voters."[74] She wishes to distinguish this form of fraud from that which takes place at the hands of election officials, parties, candidates, and others who are involved in election administration and political campaigns.[75] For our present purposes, Minnite's definition of voter fraud will be employed. However, it is important to note that besides voter fraud, I will refer to other forms of election fraud as "election official fraud." The latter will include situations where election officials or parties other than voters falsely register individuals or let them vote, engage in vote buying or swapping, or engage in other forms of vote suppression or manufacturing.[76]

Even within the category of voter fraud it is important to realize that a host of activities can be included under this term. Voter fraud could include intentional efforts to falsely register to vote or actually to vote. Allegations of voter fraud include claims that illegal immigrants, ex-felons, and impersonators are stealing the identities of others, including the dead, in order that they may illegally vote. Voter fraud could also take place in several venues, such as at the polls on election day, in completing an absentee ballot, or in completing the paperwork necessary to register to vote. Given these distinctions, the evidence is clear, there is little systematic or widespread voter fraud in the United States that is changing the outcome of elections. This is at least true among the types of fraud that voter ID laws are meant to address.

The three most persistent claims of voter fraud come from the *Wall Street Journal*'s John Fund, a report from the Senate Republican Policy Committee in Congress, and the Carter-Baker Report. Fund's *Stealing Elections: How Voter Fraud Threatens Our Democracy*[77] calls for mandatory photo identification to be displayed when voting because of widespread fraud occurring in the United States. Yet what evidence exists that voter fraud is rampant? There is little systematic evidence offered here. *Stealing Elections* draws upon interviews around the country to whip up hysteria that droves of dead people, illegal immigrants, vote

---

74 *Id.* at 6.

75 *Id.*

76 *See:* Spencer Overton, Stealing Democracy: The New Politics of Voter Suppression (2007); and Dennis F. Thompson, Just Elections: Creating a Fair Electoral Process in the United States (2002), for general discussions of vote suppression and manufacturing techniques.

77 John Fund, Stealing Elections: How Voter Fraud Threatens Our Democracy (2004).

brokers, and ex-felons are cheating their ways into the voting booths, stealing elections from honest decent Republicans, and diluting the votes of red, white, and blue Americans. But when the smoke of his allegations is cleared there is little fire of voter fraud, at least of the kind he alleges.

For example, Fund alleges that the Florida 2000 presidential election demonstrated "sloppiness that makes fraud and foul-ups in election counts possible."[78] Even if one accepts all of his comments as true, the sloppiness he alleges is not voter fraud, the problems are with election officials. He also alleges that "lax standards for registration encouraged by the Motor Voter Law have left the voter rolls in a shambles in many states."[79] Again, a mere allegation that does not document which states, what shambles means, how the problems do affect voting, and whether those problems constitute voter fraud. *Stealing Elections* is rife with these types of unsubstantiated allegations of election fraud, let alone voter fraud, that he claims have actually risen to a level that affects elections. Fund seems only to offer anecdotal evidence that election officials have erred in letting some individuals register when they should not, or that a few persons have tried to vote twice in the same election, for example showing up to the polls to vote after forgetting they voted by absentee ballot. Fund, in one op-ed,[80] seems not to have learned the lessons of his ways. In that *Wall Street Journal* essay he referenced a felon named Ben Miller in Florida who voted illegally for the last 16 years and that in the Florida 2000 election, there were 5,643 voters' names that "perfectly matched the names of convicted felons."[81] However, what Fund does not say or apparently seek to investigate or prove is whether Ben Miller knew he was ineligible to vote or whether election officials incorrectly registered him. In terms of the 5,643 names, Fund fails to show that in fact these individuals were barred from voting or they were doing anything wrong. Ex-felons, after all, are not barred from voting in all states and in all circumstances as Fund's insinuations would imply. For the most part, Fund's allegations are based upon rumor, half-truths, and innuendos that fail the test of any valid social science study.

A second report by Senate Republican Policy Committee entitled *Putting an End to Voter Fraud*[82] asserts that "voter fraud continues to plague our nation's federal elections."[83] The basis of its allegations rests in assertions that the National Voter Registration Act of 1993[84] has made it difficult to maintain accurate lists to keep

---

78   *Id.* at 4.

79   *Id.* at 24.

80   John Fund, *Vote-Fraud Demagogues*, WALL STREET JOURNAL (June 13, 2007), at A19.

81   *Id.*

82   Senate Republican Policy Committee, *Putting an End to Voter Fraud* (February 15, 2005).

83   *Id.* at 1.

84   P.L. 103-31, 42 U.S.C. §1973 *et seq.* ("Motor Voter Act").

people from voting illegally,[85] that non-citizens are voting illegally,[86] and there may be risks associated with early and absentee voting.[87] What evidence is offered of voter fraud? Again, little of substance or of systematic nature that had been tested. For example, allegations of illegal voting in the 2004 Wisconsin presidential elections are cited,[88] but no firm numbers are provided to show if the allegations were true or significant. In terms of the threat of non-citizens voting, the main reference is to efforts in many jurisdictions to change the law to allow them to vote legally.[89]

A third report, *Building Confidence in U.S. Elections: Report of the Commission on Federal Election Reform*,[90] chaired by former president Jimmy Carter and former Secretary of State James Baker ("Carter-Baker Commission"), is also cited by those who argue that there is widespread voter fraud, necessitating measures, such as voter IDs, to combat it.[91] The report asserts that: "While election fraud occurs, it is difficult to measure."[92] Proof of this assertion is citation to 180 Department of Justice investigations resulting in convictions of 52 individuals from October 2002 until the release of the report.[93] Yet while the Carter-Baker Commission called for photo IDs, it also noted that: "There is no evidence of extensive voter fraud in U.S. elections, or of multiple voting, but both occur, and it could affect the outcome of a close election."[94] As with other studies, absentee voting is singled out as the place where fraud is most likely to occur, followed by registration drives by third parties.[95]

The empirical evidence supporting the Carter-Baker Commission findings of fraud are scant, at best. As noted, its own conclusion is that fraud is not extensive, but when it does cite to support its claims, it references newspaper articles and other accounts that are not corroborated or subject to critical analysis.[96] As the Brennan Center stated in its analysis and response to the Carter-Baker call for a voter photo ID: "The Report attempts to support its burdensome identification requirements on four specific examples of purported fraud or potential fraud. None of the Report's cited examples of fraud stand up under closer scrutiny."[97] Even accepting all of

---

85 *Putting an End to Voter Fraud* at 5.
86 *Id.* at 7.
87 *Id.* at 8.
88 *Id.* at 7.
89 *Id.* at 7.
90 CENTER FOR DEMOCRACY AND ELECTION MANAGEMENT, AMERICAN UNIVERSITY, BUILDING CONFIDENCE IN U.S. ELECTIONS: REPORT OF THE COMMISSION ON FEDERAL ELECTION REFORM (September 2005).
91 *Id.* at 18 (*calling* for voter IDs when voting).
92 *Id.* at 45.
93 *Id.* at 52.
94 *Id.*
95 *Id.* at 46.
96 *Id.* at fn. 19 (*citing* to section 1.1 of the report and its accompanying notes).
97 Wendy Weiser, Justin Levitt, and Catherine Weiss, *Response to the Report of the 2005 Commission on Federal Election Reform*, 9 (September 19, 2005).

the documented accounts of fraud as true, the Brennan Center points out that, in the State of Washington, for example, six cases of double voting and 19 instances of individuals voting in the name of the dead yielded 25 fraudulent votes out of 2,812,675 cast—a 0.0009 percent rate of fraud.[98] Also, assume the 52 convictions by the Department of Justice are accurate instances of fraud. This means that 52 out of 196,139,871 ballots cast in federal elections, or 0.000003 percent of the votes were fraudulent.[99] While critics might assert that these cases represent only the tip of known cases of an iceberg of fraud, it is important to underscore that the prosecutions occurred on the heels of a President Bush Justice Department taking an aggressive stance on this crime,[100] and that even a doubling, tripling, or more of successful prosecutions would find that one is in greater danger of being hit by lightning than is an election of being affected by fraud.[101]

While studies seeking to prove voter fraud offer a paucity of evidence, studies reaching the opposite conclusion are more plentiful. The United States Elections Assistance Commission (EAC), *Election Crimes: An Initial Review and Recommendations for Future Study* undertook a broad literature review and expert interviews of what was then known about voter fraud.[102] It concluded that "Many of the allegations made in the reports and books were not substantiated," even though they were often cited by many parties as evidence of fraud.[103] The same was true regarding media accounts,[104] and even stories about prosecutions lacked reliable follow-up.[105] Overall, the report noted that "impersonation of voters is the least frequent type of fraud because it is the most likely type of fraud to be discovered, there are stiff penalties associated with this type of fraud, and it is an inefficient method of influencing an election."[106] Instead of impersonation, absentee ballot voting was described as most susceptible to voter fraud,[107] but even with that the EAC called for more statistical analysis to determine its seriousness.

However, even while this version of the EAC report downplayed voter fraud while calling for more study of the subject, the original draft was more conclusive in dismissing allegations. According to the *New York Times*: "A federal panel, the Election Assistance Commission, reported last year that the pervasiveness of fraud was debatable. That conclusion played down findings of the consultants who said there was little evidence of it across the country, according to a review of the

---

98 *Id.* at 9.

99 *Id.* at 10.

100 Eric Lipton and Ian Urbina, *In 5-Year Effort, Scant Evidence of Voter Fraud*, N.Y. TIMES (April 12, 2007), at A1.

101 Weiser et al. at 10.

102 UNITED STATES ELECTIONS ASSISTANCE COMMISSION, ELECTION CRIMES: AN INITIAL REVIEW AND RECOMMENDATIONS FOR FUTURE STUDY, 2-3 (2006).

103 *Id.* at 16.

104 *Id.*

105 *Id.* at 16-18.

106 *Id.* at 9.

107 *Id.*

original report by The *New York Times* that was reported on Wednesday."[108] As reported by the *New York Times*, experts hired by the EAC to consult with them largely found that mistakes and errors on the part of election officials, as well as honest mistakes by voters have caused some problems, but overall, according to Richard G. Frohling, an assistant United States attorney in Milwaukee: "There was nothing that we uncovered that suggested some sort of concerted effort to tilt the election."[109] In effect, while the final version of the EAC report seemed tentative in dismissing fraud as a phenomenon, the experts and perhaps even the original version of the report were even more conclusive on this point.

Another study examining the extent of voter fraud in the United States was the Project Vote study *The Politics of Voter Fraud* by Lorraine C. Minnite.[110] For example, the study cites statistics provided by the Department of Justice, indicating that between 2002 and 2005 when the Attorney General made election frauds and corruption a priority,[111] only 24 individuals were convicted or pled guilty to illegal voting, including 5 who could not vote because of felony convictions, 14 non-citizens, and 5 who voted twice in the same election.[112] During that same time period, another 14 individuals were prosecuted but not convicted by the Justice Department.[113] Minnite also noted how states have heavily criminalized voter fraud,[114] and local law enforcement officials do not seem to be shying away from election fraud issues as a result of a lack of desire, ability, or resources.[115] Moreover, when Minnite examined the often told allegations of illegal voting or registration in Wisconsin during the 2004 presidential race, she found either the individuals did not know they voted illegally, that the stories were later recanted, or that prosecutions (a total of three) were dropped due to a lack of evidence.[116] Overall, the conclusion of the Minnite report is that voter fraud allegations are really partisan Republican efforts to suppress voting.[117]

Other studies have reached similar conclusions about the lack of voter fraud. While some, such as the Republican Senate Policy Committee, express concern that the Motor Voter law is a potential source of voter fraud, a major study of its

---

108 Eric Lipton and Ian Urbina, *In 5-Year Effort, Scant Evidence of Voter Fraud*, N.Y. TIMES (April 12, 2007) at A1.
109 *Id.*
110 LORRAINE C. MINNITE, THE POLITICS OF VOTER FRAUD (2007). *See also:* LORRAINE C. MINNITE, AN ANALYSIS OF VOTER FRAUD IN THE U.S. (2007), which is a later version of the original Minnite study and which reaches the same conclusions. References in this chapter are to the original study.
111 Minnite at 8.
112 *Id.*
113 *Id.* at 9.
114 *Id.* at 10.
115 *Id.* at 11.
116 *Id.* at 13.
117 *Id.* at 16.

impact did not discuss fraud.[118] *The Impact of the National Voter Registration Act* does not include this topic in its discussion of voter verification,[119] and, in fact, the report seems to suggest states have this issue under control. The biggest problem is removal from voter rolls for non-voting.[120] An Office for Democratic Institutions and Human Rights report found only isolated reports of voter fraud or impersonation.[121] Additional analysis on the impact of Motor-Voter by Davis,[122] the Carter-Baker report by Overton,[123] and a Rutgers University study of the impact of provisional voting procedures as outlined in the Help America Vote Act of 2002[124] also found little if any evidence of fraud in American elections.[125]

Finally, perhaps the most comprehensive study of voter fraud in the United States was undertaken by the Cronkite School of Journalism at Arizona State University. In August, 2012, they released perhaps the most comprehensive study to date examining the incidence of in-person voter fraud at the polls. They found that from 2000 through 2010 there were 10 proven cases of voter impersonation out of a total of 146,000,000 votes cast. The study was multistate and included interviews and analysis of 40 cities and 21 states.[126] To put the incidence of proven voter fraud in context, according to the National Weather Service, the chances of an individual being struck by lightning in a year are about one in 770,000.[127] There is a greater chance of being struck by lightning than documenting that voter fraud at the polls is a serious factor affecting the outcome of an election.

Yet, despite this paucity of evidence, the debate over voter fraud has not ended. In 2011, bills in 34 states were introduced calling for photo identification for in-person voting.[128] In 12 states both houses of the legislature passed the bill, and

---

118 UNITED STATES ELECTIONS ASSISTANCE COMMISSION, THE IMPACT OF THE NATIONAL VOTER REGISTRATION ACT (June 30, 2007).

119 *Id.* at 12.

120 *Id.* at 11.

121 OFFICE FOR DEMOCRATIC INSTITUTIONS AND HUMAN RIGHTS, UNITED STATES OF AMERICA MID-TERM CONGRESSIONAL ELECTIONS 7 NOVEMBER, 2006, 16 (March 9, 2007).

122 Jonathan E. Davis, *The National Voter Registration Act of 1993: Debunking States' Rights Resistance and the Pretense of Voter Fraud*, 6 TEMP. POL. & CIV. RTS. L. REV. 117 (1997).

123 Spencer Overton, *Voter Identification*, 105 MICH. L. REV. 631 (2007).

124 Help America Vote Act of 2002, Pub. L. No. 107-252, 116 Stat. 1666.

125 Eagleton Institute of Politics, *Appendix A: National Survey of Local Election Officials' Experiences with Provisional Voting* (July-August 2005).

126 News21, *Who Can Vote?* (August 12, 2012), located at http://votingrights.news21.com/article/about/ (site last visited on March 7, 2013).

127 Answers.Com, *What are the chances of being struck by lightning?* (n.d.), located at http://wiki.answers.com/Q/What_are_the_chances_of_being_struck_by_lightning (site last visited on March 7, 2013).

128 Wendy R. Weiser and Lawrence Norden, *Voting Law Changes in 2012* (2011), available at http://brennan.3cdn.net/9c0a034a4b3c68a2af_9hm6bj6d0.pdf (site last visited on June 2, 2012).

after vetoes, a total of 9 states now have photo identification requirements for voting. In 2012 more states will attempt to pass similar legislation. Opponents have fought voter identification bills and the decision by the Justice Department, in December 2011, to use the Voting Right Act to refuse pre-clearance to the South Carolina law guaranteed that this decision would wind up in the courts.

Clearly, the debate over voter identification laws is muddled in a methodological and evidentiary mess, conducted with little or no reliable data. But as Lorraine Minnite aptly states: there is a "dearth of literature on election fraud" with "no new empirical research published on the subject for almost two decades.[129] Most voter fraud arguments lack good empirical studies.[130] Those who contend that it is a serious and significant problem in the United States, such as John Fund, argue that the few instances of fraud are merely the tip of the iceberg; proof of far more extensive and significant fraud affecting our elections.[131] Others, such as Hans von Spakovsky, former recess appointee to the Federal Election Commission, have also alleged widespread voter fraud, but generally have not systematically produced a comprehensive study on the matter. Given the inability to detect fraud, and its lax prosecution, real evidence of its extent is difficult to grasp.[132] Conversely, Lorraine Minnite, as noted above, and David Schultz argue that the absence of more systematic evidence of fraud is proof that it is not widespread.[133] Both reach their conclusions based upon examination of current studies of voter fraud.

Perhaps the best or most authoritative statement by those who believe voter fraud exists as a problem regarding the empirical debate is by Judge Richard Posner who wrote the majority opinion in Seventh Circuit *Crawford v. Marion County Election Board*.[134] He argues:

> But the absence of prosecutions is explained by the endemic underenforcement of minor criminal laws (minor as they appear to the public and prosecutors, at all events) and by the extreme difficulty of apprehending a voter impersonator. He enters the polling place, gives a name that is not his own, votes, and leaves. If later it is discovered that the name he gave is that of a dead person, no one at the polling place will remember the face of the person who gave that name,

---

129   Lorraine C. Minnite, The Myth of Voter Fraud, 38-39 (2010).

130   *Id.* at 39.

131   Fund, Stealing Elections, 4-5.

132   John Fund and Hans von Spakovsky, Who's Counting?: How Fraudsters and Bureaucrats Put Your Vote at Risk (2012); Hans von Spakovsky, *Protecting the Integrity of the Election Process*, 11 Election L. J. 90 (2012).

133   David Schultz, *Less than Fundamental: The Myth of Voter Fraud and the Coming of the Second Great Disenfranchisement*, 34 William Mitchell L. Rev., 484 (2008); David Schultz, *Lies, Damn Lies, and Voter IDs: The Fraud of Voter Fraud*, 1 Harv. L. & Pol. Rev. On-line 1 (2008), available at http://hlpronline.com/2008/03/lies-damn-lies-and-voter-ids-the-fraud-of-voter-fraud/ (site last visited on June 2, 2012).

134   Crawford v. Marion County Election Board, 472 F.3d. 949 (7th Cir. 2007).

and if someone did remember it, what would he do with the information? The impersonator and the person impersonated (if living) might show up at the polls at the same time and a confrontation might ensue that might lead to a citizen arrest or a call to the police who would arrive before the impersonator had fled, and arrest him. A more likely sequence would be for the impersonated person to have voted already when the impersonator arrived and tried to vote in his name. But in either case an arrest would be most unlikely.[135]

For Posner, fraud detection is difficult and the costs associated with prosecution are high, thereby yielding minimal incentives to prosecute. The judge concludes: "Without requiring a photo ID, there is little if any chance of preventing this kind of fraud because busy poll workers are unlikely to scrutinize signatures carefully and argue with people who deny having forged someone else's signature."[136]

Posner parallels voter fraud to littering, contending that both are difficult to detect.[137] Others, such as Brad Smith, former chairman of the Federal Election Commission, similarly highlights the few reported or prosecuted instances of fraud as perhaps indicative of a more extensive problem (although he does admit that fraud is not extensive). His comments on the Election Law listserv draw a parallel to vehicular moving violations: "[T]he typical speeding ticket or even DWI is usually indicative of numerous other, unreported events of the same nature. But surely that is true of voter fraud as well."[138]

What do we really know about voter fraud? Yes, voter fraud does exist and there is a history of it in the United States.[139] But is voter fraud like littering and moving violations—a symptom or sign of something more significant? Or is it vastly overblown, as scholars such as Minnite and Schultz contend? How can one study voter fraud? To answer this, there is a preliminary threshold question. What can one make of Posner's assertion that because it is difficult to detect voter fraud it is hard to gather real evidence of its extent? Whatever the current status of knowledge or evidence about fraud, one thing is certain—this is an empirical question. A hallmark of modern science and social science is that it is empirical and evidence-based.[140] It requires the formulation of testable

---

135 *Id.* at 953.
136 *Id.*
137 *Id.* at 953.
138 Bradley Smith, Election Law Listserv (2010 available at http://mailman.lls.edu/pipermail/election-law/2010-October/023420.html (site last visited on June 2, 2012).
139 Tracy Campbell, Deliver the Vote: A History of Election Fraud, an American Political Tradition–1742-2004 (2005).
140 Chava Frankfort-Nachmias, and David Nachmias, Research Methods in the Social Sciences, 5-7 (2000); Alan C. Isaak, Scope and Methods of Political Science, 8 (1985).

propositions subject to rigorous methodological tools and the use of data.[141] This is the core of what the scientific method is.[142]

But even more specifically, (social) scientific research requires empirical proof to test propositions, and the form of that testing lies in falsification. As Karl Popper pointed out the hallmark of scientific and social scientific research is falsification: "But I shall certainly admit a system as empirical or scientific only if it is capable of being tested by experience. These considerations suggest that not the verifiability but the falsifiability of a system is to be taken as a criterion of demarcation."[143]

Demarcation, for Popper, is separating empirical from non-empirical theories (such as metaphysics).[144] What Popper is contending, and modern science has adopted his approach, is that empirical studies are premised not upon the confirmation of propositions but upon falsifying them. Scientific inquiry is inductive: "[It p]asses from singular statements ... such as accounts of the results of observations or experiments, to universal statements, such as hypotheses or theories."[145] It is generalizing from specific instances to broader propositions. We generalize from a survey sample to a broader population; we generalize from a few lab experiments or clinical trials to broader conclusions about drug efficacy or reaction. The same is true with social science claims: discrete data are aggregated and then generalized to produce claims about the world, whether they be about politics or some other social phenomenon.

Propositions incapable of empirical falsification are not scientific. Some types of arguments—such as deduction—may be based on logic, while others are held as belief or faith. This is true for example, with statements about God. Determining exactly what counts as evidence of God's existence is contentious, but, at least since Immanuel Kant in the late eighteenth century, the general argument has been that it is impossible to make scientific statements about God's existence.[146] Instead, it is a matter of faith.

The reference to God gets at the question of the difference between "evidence of absence" and "absence of evidence." This distinction connects back to voter fraud. Is the evidence of absence an indication that voter fraud is not a significant problem, or is the absence of evidence simply a sign, as Posner and others assert, that there is not enough information at hand due to detection problems and therefore we cannot conclude that fraud does not exist?

In some cases, evidence of absence is conclusive. A biopsy may reveal no cancer, indicating a tumor to be benign. An autopsy may demonstrate no bullet holes, therefore indicating that the victim did not die as a result of a gunshot wound. In

---

141 RICHARD J. BERNSTEIN, THE RESTRUCTURING OF SOCIAL AND POLITICAL THEORY, 15 (1976).
142 Isaak at 28.
143 KARL POPPER, THE LOGIC OF SCIENTIFIC DISCOVERY, 40 (1959).
144 Id. at 34.
145 Id. at 27.
146 IMMANUEL KANT, CRITIQUE OF PURE REASON, 29 (1965).

the nineteenth century, the famous Michaelson-Morley 1887 physics experiments with light demonstrated that aether does not exist.[147] This failed experiment was critical to providing the support Albert Einstein needed for construction of his special theory of relativity in 1905. Thus in some cases absence is evidence, but absence is still empirical and the failure to find something constitutes falsification of a claim. This is evidence of absence.

But in some instances absence of evidence is not conclusive. Failure to find evidence of God's existence has been taken not to prove that a divine being does not exist, but simply for some that we have not yet found evidence for a supreme being.[148] Those who argue that voter fraud exists take the latter view—absence of evidence is not proof that it does not exist. Instead, they offer the absence of evidence as proof of how hard it is to detect voter fraud. However, what can we really infer from an absence of evidence—that voter fraud exists in a far more significant level than thought, or that there really is very little fraud? Minnite asserts that the problem with Posner and many claims about fraud is that it is an effort to prove the negative.[149] By that, how do we prove the existence of something that we cannot detect?

What does all this mean for voter fraud studies? First, the debate has been cast the wrong way. Minnite and Schultz, as noted above, examine voter fraud studies and conclude that the absence of evidence is proof that something does not exist, at least to a large extent. Posner and Fund reach the opposite conclusion? Who is correct?

To resolve the debate it is important to restate claims about voter fraud in terms of testable (falsifiable) claims. The arguments need to be framed in ways that allow it to be tested. One needs to be able to generalize from specific instances of fraud to be able to make broader assertions. Are the few instances that are detected a good sample indicative of a broader population of fraud?

What would be a testable voter fraud claim? As one reads Fund, Smith, Posner, and others who assert its widespread existence, several claims seem to emerge. First, we do not know the extent of fraud since we do not have voter photo ID. This claim recognizes the lack of evidence and asserts the solution is to institute photo ID. Once in place, it would reveal the extent of attempted fraud. However, for those who also contend the fraud exists, once photo ID is instituted, the lack of increase in detected fraud is proof that the additional measure (photo ID) works to prevent fraud. While this may be true, proponents cannot have it both ways. The arguments are a circular logic at best; they both cannot be true at the same time. Moreover, they may not be empirical and testable propositions capable of refutation or falsification.

---

147 Simon Singh, Big Bang: The Most Important Scientific Discovery of All Time and Why You Need to Know About It, 94-97 (2004).
148 Al Seckel, Bertrand Russell on God and Religion (1986).
149 Minnite, The Myth of Voter Fraud, 156-57.

First, think about what would be valid evidence to document fraud. Paul Wyckoff describes a hierarchy of empirical evidence based on its reliability.[150] At the top of the evidence chart are controlled experiments where studies can manipulate critical variables and test them.[151] At the bottom are case studies and anecdotes where there is almost no ability to test and verify facts and control variables.[152] A critical issue in evaluating qualities or types of evidence is the ability to generalize from them to reach some larger propositions.[153] In other words, do the case studies, anecdotes, or experiments serve as good samples that represent the larger population? Generally simple stories or anecdotes are weak evidence because one cannot easily use them to make inferences about broader trends or populations unless other evidence or reasons are offered to support drawing broader conclusions. Additionally, simple stories, unless corroborated, are like hearsay and are unable to withstand truth tests to ascertain their credibility and reliability.

This is an important point because for the most part the quality of the evidence offered by Fund and others is anecdotal. As Schultz pointed out:

> Fund's *Stealing Elections: How Voter Fraud Threatens Our Democracy* calls for mandatory photo identification to be displayed when voting because of widespread fraud occurring in the United States. Yet what evidence exists that voter fraud is rampant? There is little systematic evidence offered here. *Stealing Elections* draws upon interviews around the country to whip up hysteria that droves of dead people, illegal immigrants, vote brokers, and ex-felons are cheating their ways into the voting booths, stealing elections from honest decent Republicans, and diluting the votes of red, white, and blue Americans. But when smoke of his allegations is cleared there is little fire of voter fraud, at least of the kind he alleges …
>
> *Stealing Elections* is rife with these types of unsubstantiated allegations of election fraud, let alone voter fraud, that he claims have actually risen to a level that affects elections. Fund seems only to offer anecdotal evidence that election officials have erred in letting some individuals register when they should not, or that a few persons have tried to vote twice in the same election, such as showing up to the polls to vote after forgetting they voted by absentee ballot.[154]

Thus, the first major problem with Fund and arguments regarding voter fraud is the quality of the evidence. It is unsubstantiated and of the lowest quality. Its ability to be examined and then generalizations drawn from it are questionable. Those who believe voter fraud exists and is widespread generally reference stories alleging

---

150   PAUL GARY WYCKOFF, POLICY AND EVIDENCE IN A PARTISAN AGE, 18-19 (2009).
151   *Id.* at 22-24.
152   *Id.* at 18-19.
153   *Id.*
154   Schultz, *Less than Fundamental*, 495-96.

felons, illegal aliens, or others voting or casting multiple votes. The stories quickly make the news but then upon later examination they are rejected as false or fail to secure corroboration. For example, claims of voter fraud in the 2004 Wisconsin presidential contest failed to produce evidence and prosecution.[155]

A second problem with voter fraud arguments from a social science perspective is fashioning allegations into testable empirical propositions. Again, if good social science is based upon evidence that can be tested and falsified, then a first step is formulating claims about fraud into hypotheses or assertions that can withstand empirical investigation. Given that, a first claim or hypothesis could be: "Voter fraud is a significant factor affecting the outcomes of elections." How do we test this? The best way of course would be controlled experiments or other empirical techniques where evidence of fraud is gathered and examined. However, there are no real studies that do that, but what little evidence that does fails to support this proposition. Instead, as Minnite and Schultz point out, existing studies actually falsify this claim by revealing very little detected fraud.[156] In response, Fund and Posner will argue that the current failure to have voter identification precludes that.

Given that the first proposition cannot be supported with the existing evidence, there is a fallback second claim: "Voter ID will demonstrate the extent of voter fraud." This is a claim capable of being falsified. Empirical testing of this claim would look to instances where voter ID has been instituted to see if more fraud has been detected. Perhaps also one might look to states with ID versus states with no ID to see if more fraud is detected. However, the latter is not a good test because different jurisdictions might have different levels of preexisting fraud and comparing them may be the classic problem of comparing apples to oranges.

But "before and after" (institution of photo ID) is a good way to determine levels of fraud within a jurisdiction. It speaks to how much fraud or attempted fraud there is in a jurisdiction by offering new data when it is easier to detect. However, thus far, the evidence does not support this claim—rather, the lack of increased detection of fraud falsifies this assertion. Simply put—institution of new voter photo ID requirements has yet to produce increased evidence of fraud.

Yet there is another claim offered by those who believe voter fraud is rampant to account for the lack of evidence. This would be the assertion that: "Institution of voter ID and lack of increase of fraud is proof that such identification works." However, to test this statement, one needs a baseline of fraud from before the ID was instituted and then look to see if it decreased as a result. Another way to phrase it: there must be some change in the incidence of fraud from before and after the voter ID was instituted to be able to make that claim.

Again, there is no evidence that would allow one to reach the conclusion that voter ID decreases fraud, because there was little evidence to support its existence initially. For example, in Indiana, the State conceded in the legal challenge to its

---

155 *Id.* at 497.
156 Minnite, The Myth of Voter Fraud, 57; Schultz, *Less than Fundamental*, 501.

photo ID law that it did not have a record of in-person election fraud.[157] There was no initial evidence of fraud and subsequent implementation of the ID requirements has failed to detect previously hidden fraud.

Have we resolved the problem and demonstrated that voter fraud does not exist? Not really. Those who believe fraud exists will still make the claim that it does. They will contend that the few instances we see are examples of larger populations and more extensive fraud. Is this a hasty generalization or a reasonable inductive conclusion? Is voter fraud similar to littering and moving vehicle violations in that the few instances uncovered are indicative of a larger problem? At this point those who believe voter fraud exists as a serious problem will fall to another argument, invoking analogies. Voter fraud will be paralleled or analogized to speeding or littering.

Many claim that the current rate of detection of voter fraud underreports the real or actual existence of voter fraud that exists. To assert this they argue that successful prosecution or detection of voter fraud is similar to police citation of speeding. By that, only a fraction of all speeding actually is detected and cited. The same claim is made about littering. However, this analogy is misplaced.

First, as opposed to concluding that the few instances of voter fraud are proof that the current system of detection works to root out what little fraud there is, the opposite conclusion is reached. Thus, the few instances are proof of broader and more systematic fraud. However, no evidence or proof is offered to support reaching this conclusion as opposed to the claim that there actually is very little fraud. There has to be some basis for reaching the broader claim and not the conclusion that the few reported instances are proof that current systems work to detect and root out fraud. In other words, what is the evidence supporting this generalization or inference? None is really offered to suggest that the sample is indicative of a broader population.

Second, the analogy to vehicular speeding is inapt. Speeding in a car is a continuous 24/7 activity that can occur anytime and anywhere. (The same is true about littering.) There is no single detection point or place where people can speed and therefore, with the almost infinite number of cars driving along almost infinite roads, it is virtually impossible to detect all instances of speeding. Thus, the few speed traps that are set up obviously only detect and capture a small spectrum of all speeding. Here, sampling makes sense as a way to infer a broader population. However, voting or voter fraud is a discrete activity. It can only occur at a specific point in time or place and in order to commit fraud one has to do it by going through a specific point—a voting booth. Thus, all instances of fraud must go through and exit a single detection point. To be successful, in-person fraud requires either a false registration or a false signature, and tricking an election judge. The point is that to commit voter fraud one has to get past multiple detection points or check points. One can speed without ever crossing a detection point (speed trap).

---

157 Indiana Democratic Party v. Rokita at 792.

The point here is that the analogy of voter fraud to speeding or littering, as Bradley Smith and Judge Posner assert, is inapt. One can speed or litter almost anytime or anyplace. This is what makes detection hard. The few instances detected and prosecuted are perhaps only a small sample of a larger pattern of speeding and littering that may exist. In addition, beyond detection and prosecution, other evidence, such as police using radar guns to detect speeders but not issuing a ticket, or anecdotal statements from drivers that they speed, may corroborate inferences that it is more prevalent than prosecution may suggest. With littering, proof can be found along roadsides and fields across America—the fact that there are cans, papers, and other refuse there points either to the contents of garbage cans being knocked over or intentional littering.

One can only vote in person in a finite number of places and within a finite time. To vote, especially in person, there are several steps and checkpoints in place. There is in 42 states voter registration before election day. This is one check. For all 50 states, in-person voting requires someone to show up, give a name to an election judge, and generally sign a log with which there is a signature match. There may be other requirements too.[158] What this means is that one has to go to a specific place to commit fraud and pass numerous detection or check points before one can actually submit a fraudulent ballot. One does not simply have to speed past a law enforcement officer to violate a motor vehicle law.

Because of the finite opportunities to commit in-person voter fraud, the analogy to littering and speeding is lacking in foundation. Contrary to Posner and Smith, the analogy is not correct. Moreover, given the critical differences—especially the finite opportunities to commit in-person voter fraud—one has to ask again if the few instances of detected fraud are indication that the system generally works to prevent fraud, or if they are indicative of more extensive illegality. Given the current checks in place, and given any other good evidence to the contrary, it is impossible to conclude that these few instances of fraud are empirical support of the claim that much more fraud exists.

Thus the evidence is overwhelming that voter fraud is an insignificant issue in American elections. But despite the evidence, the U.S. Supreme Court in the *Crawford* case[159] upheld a facial challenge to the Indiana voter ID law, despite admission by the state that they had no proven instances of in-person voter fraud at the polls.[160] The evidence that the Supreme Court did cite or offer to uphold the Indiana law was anecdotal and often drawn from outside of Indiana, and back to the nineteenth century.[161] The question is then why are some, and those mostly Republican, supporting or initiating voter ID laws if the evidence does not support their claims? Opponents and Democrats claim it is an effort to suppress voting, especially among people of color, the young, and the poor—coalitions or groups

---

158   Scher, The Politics of Disenfranchisement at 82-90.
159   Crawford v. Marion County Election Board, 553 U.S. 181 (2008).
160   Indiana Democratic Party v. Rokita, 458 F.Supp.2d 775, 792 (D. Ind. 2006).
161   553 U.S. at 194-97.

generally more sympathetic to and supportive of Democrats. Supporters of these laws have denied this as a motivation, yet some of them have actually admitted that this was their intention—at least this was the case in Florida.[162]

Will such laws have an impact in disenfranchising voters? Political scientists have long noted how decisions to register and vote are affected by numerous variables, including income, age, and generation,[163] as well as by social capital and trust, for example.[164] In general, the more barriers placed in front of potential voters, such as increased time periods to register to vote, the less likely they are to vote.[165] The same is true with voter ID laws, they impose a cost on citizens that may make it less likely that they will vote. At least three studies substantiate that claim.

First, Timothy Vercellotti and David Anderson examined the likely impact of voter ID laws across the United States. They found that photo ID laws would reduce the probability of voting by 3.7 percent for Whites, 6 percent for African-Americans, and nearly 10 percent for Hispanics.[166]

Second, a Brennan Center study found that 7 percent of the population lacked access to the citizenship type of papers necessary to vote, that 11 percent of the population did not have a government-issued ID, and that low income individuals were less likely to have the requisite identification to vote.[167] All told, the Brennan Center study indicated that the time, and money required to secure a valid photo ID in order to vote imposed costs on certain populations that would discourage voting.

Finally, Marjorie Hershey[168] prepared testimony as an expert witness for the plaintiffs in *Indiana Democratic Party v. Rokita*,[169] seeking to assess the likely

---

162 Dara Kam and John Lantigua, Former Florida GOP leaders say voter suppression was reason they pushed new election law, THE PALM BEACH POST (November 25, 2012), located at http://www.palmbeachpost.com/news/news/state-regional-govt-politics/early-voting-curbs-called-power-play/nTFDy/ (site last visited on March 7, 2013). *See also:* RICHARD L. HASEN, THE VOTING WARS: FROM FLORIDA 2000 TO THE NEXT ELECTION MELTDOWN (2012), for a general discussion on the partisan battle over voter fraud and IDs.

163 *See, e.g.,* Miller and Shanks, The New American Voter, 88-90, 111; M. MARGARET CONWAY, POLITICAL PARTICIPATION IN THE UNITED STATES (1991). *See also*: Marjorie R. Hershey, "Affidavit of Marjorie R. Hershey," 2005 WL 4019117 at 10-13 (*providing* a bibliography documenting this proposition).

164 ROBERT D. PUTNAM, BOWLING ALONE: THE COLLAPSE AND REVIVAL OF AMERICAN COMMUNITY (2001).

165 RAYMOND E. WOLFINGER AND STEVEN J. ROSENSTONE, WHO VOTES?, 61 (New Haven: Yale University Press, 1980).

166 Timothy Vercellotti and David Anderson, *Protecting the Franchise or Restricting It?: the Effect of Voter Identification Laws on Turnout,* 13 (2006).

167 Brennan Center for Justice, *Citizens Without Proof: A Survey of American's Possession of Documentary Proof of Citizenship and Photo Identification,* 2-3 (November 2006).

168 Hershey, "Affidavit of Marjorie R. Hershey," 2005 WL 4019117.

169 458 F.Supp.2d 775 (D. Ind. 2006).

impact of the then state's new photo ID law on voter turnout.[170] In developing her analysis, Professor Hershey indicates that perhaps the dominant mode that political scientists use to assess voting law is a rational choice or economic model that asks what costs new procedures impose upon individuals when making decisions to vote.[171] Simply put, according to Hershey: "[P]eople are likely to vote as long as the perceived costs of voting do not outweigh the perceived benefits."[172] What would be perceived as a cost to voting? The list includes time to register to vote, waiting times, financial and informational costs, registration laws, and physical barriers.[173] Hershey provides in her affidavit ample empirical evidence from political scientists to demonstrate that, as the costs of voting increase, so registration and turnout decrease.[174] Overall, her argument is that photo ID requirements for voting are a definite cost,[175] especially on some groups such as the poor,[176] those without government-issued IDs, and people of color.[177]

Taken together, these three studies, along with the political and social science literature, demonstrate that new voting requirements, such as photo IDs, impose costs upon citizens when deciding to go to the polls. These costs are likely to negatively impact voting. Couple these studies with those examining voter fraud in the United States and one conclusion becomes obvious—voter ID laws are not neutral. Not only is there negligible (at best) evidence of voter fraud to support these laws but they are also negative in that they might actually suppress real voter turnout by imposing additional burdens on voters.

Overall, there is evidence that voter ID laws could have an impact on voting. Such a concern was behind court decisions in many states over the last few years either invalidating or suspending enforcement of these laws and requirements until assured that those who needed the identification to vote would receive them.[178] In the case of Missouri, concerns that individuals would bear significant costs—not in getting the free ID but in securing the documents necessary to get do so—that would disadvantage some groups, led in part to that state's Supreme Court invalidating a voter ID law on state constitutional grounds.[179] While it was not argued that the law was a new form of a poll tax, it effectively worked as one.

---

170 Hershey at 1.
171 *Id.* at 2.
172 *Id.*
173 *Id.* at 2-3.
174 *Id.* at 3-5. For example, Hershey references studies showing how improvements in transportation in the nineteenth century had a dramatic increase in voter turnout (*id.* at 4), and how political scientists have concluded that "Registration raises the costs of voting" (*id.*).
175 Hershey at 4.
176 *Id.* at 6.
177 *Id.* at 6-7. *See also:* Texas v. Holder, 2012 WL 3743676 (D.D.C.). Here the court refused to pre-clear Texas's new voter identification law under the Voting Rights Act, noting the impact the law would have upon people of color.
178 *See:* Schultz, *Less than Fundamental*, for a review of these cases.
179 Weinschenk v. Missouri, 203 S.W.3d 201 (Mo. 2006).

Overall, voter ID laws are part of the second great wave of disenfranchisement, threatening to undermine the enlargement of the demos at a time when technology and changing social structures are forcing a rethinking of what the American democracy should be.

Conclusion

So what does the voter ID discussion tell us about voting, election law, and democratic theory? First, that despite pressures to enlarge the demos, the demand for voter ID recognizes the countertrend towards suppressing or limiting voting rights. Second, the debate and jurisprudence surrounding voter ID represents an ambivalence toward voting rights, with the Supreme Court, especially in *Crawford*, showing its willingness to permit restrictions on franchise rights for reasons that question the status of franchise as a fundamental right. Third, the debate over voter ID also seems hopelessly situated in a different era that assumes most voting takes place in person. The reality is that this is less and less of a common practice for most people and, with new technologies emerging, the idea of in-person voting could well disappear, rendering moot any concerns there may be about in-person voter fraud. New technologies may effectively outmode the practice of simply casting a ballot at a designated spot and time.

Overall, the current jurisprudence regarding voting rights is out of touch with current conceptions of democracy, social structures, and technology. The United States needs a case law that creates a positive theory of voting at all stages and which addresses changes that have been described in this chapter. Current law still seems frozen in assumptions and practices found in 1787, or in 1875 when *Minor v. Happersett* was decided.

Chapter 4
Minority Rights and the Failure of Direct Democracy

Introduction

We all grew up playing games. Be they board games, video games, sports, or whatever, games have rules and they determine how the activity should be played. We assume the rules are neutral and do not favor anyone in particular. Fair rules mean equal chances or opportunities for all to win.

Lawyers are also trained to have faith in process and rules.[1] They are trained in law school to believe in the adversarial process and that through trials and fair play according to the rules the truth will emerge and guilt, innocence, or liability will be correctly assessed.[2] Procedural justice is the hallmark of the American legal system.

Yet the rules of justice are not always neutral. The Innocence Project has demonstrated how often the criminal justice process yields false positives, convicting individuals of crimes they did not commit only to have DNA or other evidence exonerate them, often years later.[3] Increasingly, social science evidence demonstrates the unreliability of eyewitness identifications,[4] or that there is racial bias in the criminal justice system. This is demonstrated with statistics on racial profiling[5] and sentencing disparities.[6] Feminists have pointed to a persistent

---

1   *See:* Model Rule Pro. Conduct, Preamble, para. 5 (2012) (*describing* how attorneys should "demonstrate respect for the legal system"). *See also:* Frederick Schauer, Thinking Like a Lawyer (2009).

2   James J. Tomkovicz, *An Adversary System Defense of the Right to Counsel Against Informants: Truth, Fair Play, and the Massiah Doctrine*, 22 U.C. Davis L. Rev. 1, 44-47 (1988).

3   Jan Stiglitz, Justin Brooks, and Tara Shulman, *The Hurricane Meets the Paper Chase: Innocence Projects New Emerging Role in Clinical Legal Education*, 38 Cal. W. L. Rev. 413, 414-15 (2002).

4   Deborah Davis and Elizabeth F. Loftus, *The Dangers of Eyewitnesses for the Innocent: Learning from the past and Projecting into the Age of Social Media*, 46 New Eng. L. Rev. 769, 784 (2012).

5   Milt Heumann and Lance Cassak, Good Cop, Bad Cop: Profiling, Race and Competing Visions of Justice (2003).

6   Jesse J. Norris, *State Efforts to Reduce Racial Disparities in Criminal Justice: Empirical Analysis and Recommendations for Action*, 47 Gonz. L. Rev. 493 (2011-12).

patriarchal bias in the American legal system that favors a male perspective,[7] and others note how "repeat players" generally make out better in the civil law system than do those who are "one shotters."[8]

These examples point to the fact that rules are outcome determinative and processes are not neutral. The rules of justice are not neutral and the rules of the game (or of any institution) determine how the game is played and influences who wins.[9] Or that the rules can be easily manipulated or constrained by background injustices that render fair or neutral application impossible. Procedural rules actually reflect substantive values. Rules reflect values, they reflect what is deemed important. Similarly, the Constitution embodies substantive values. The original Constitution of 1787 reflected a variety of values, some good, some bad.[10] The commitments to limited government opposition to tyranny of the majority are found in the complex machinery of representation, checks, and balances, separation of powers, and federalism, all as tools to break up and limit political power. The Constitution also embodied some not so good values—such as slavery and the two-thirds compromise. John Hart Ely's *Democracy and Distrust*[11] describes the Constitution as generally process-oriented but it does embody one major substantive value—individual liberty or autonomy.

The assumption is that the rules of democracy are neutral. They embody a sense of procedural fairness or equality that does not favor any particular group. Every candidate in theory has a chance to win. All voters will have their votes counted. Tough but fair competition means that the "Ins" can be outed and replaced. Losers in one election can be winners in another. But is that true? Are the rules of democracy neutral?

The reality is that the political process is not always neutral. There is an inner morality to the law and the political process,[12] and either following the rules of the game means that certain parties will be favored,[13] or certain background

---

7   CAROLINE A. FORELL AND DONNA M. MATTHEWS, A LAW OF HER OWN: THE REASONABLE WOMAN AS A MEASURE OF MAN (2000); CATHARINE A. MACKINNON, TOWARD A FEMINIST THEORY OF THE STATE (1991).

8   Marc Galanter, *Why the "Haves" Come Out Ahead: Speculations on the Limits of Legal Change*, 9 L. & SOC. REV. 95 (1974).

9   DARON ACEMOGLU AND JAMES A, ROBINSON, WHY NATIONS FAIL: THE ORIGINS OF POWER. PROSPERITY, AND POVERTY, 79 (2012).

10 *See:* David Schultz, *Political Theory and Legal History: Conflicting Depictions of Property in the American Political Founding*, 37 AM. J. OF LEGAL HIST. 464 (1993), discussing the various values that influenced the American constitutional founding.

11 JOHN HART ELY, DEMOCRACY AND DISTRUST: A THEORY OF JUDICIAL REVIEW (1980).

12 LON L. FULLER, THE MORALITY OF LAW (1969).

13 Archibald Cox, former Solicitor General for the United States, once privately commented to me that, when it came to the issue of campaign finance reform, these rules were "the rules that determined the rules of the game which determined who won or lost elections." The same point applies here to the idea that rules are not always neutral but instead often are outcome determinative.

constraints will affect who wins or loses or how the game is played. The same is true when it comes to the rules of direct democracy. Across the country many states and local governments permit citizen initiative or referenda—allowing the people directly either to proposal their own legislation or to vote thumbs up or down on ideas submitted to them from their local legislative body. To many this is the essence of pure direct democracy—the Greek ideal of the agora or New England town democracy realized. Examples of this democracy occurred on November 6, 2012, when voters in Maine, Maryland, and Washington were asked to vote on legalizing same-sex marriage, and in Minnesota where voters were asked to amend the state constitution to prohibit the same. Surprisingly, majorities in the first three states voted same-sex marriage into law while those in Minnesota rejected the amendment. Despite the outcomes in these four states, the vote on them demonstrated a truth—the rules of initiative and referendum are not neutral, and direct democracy places minority rights at risk.

The Progressive Era reforms of initiative, referendum, and recall were adopted as a means to further democracy and break entrenched politics captured by interest groups. Ostensibly these reforms are politically neutral, yet it is not clear if these experiments in direct democracy have protected minority rights, let alone confined special interest politics. Majority rule and special interest politics can threaten individual rights, including those of people of color, the poor, and other minority groups. The constitutional Founding Fathers understood this through their articulation of Madisonian democracy.

What this chapter will argue is that the Progressive Era experiment with direct democracy has failed, at least when it comes to the protection of minority rights. Direct democracy is fundamentally askew or in conflict with the fundamental insights of constitutional Framers who better understood the problem of politics that was discussed earlier in Chapter 3. In effect, the American conception of democracy—or rather, representative democracy—was meant to balance majority rule with minority rights, and it is not clear that the Progressive Era reforms of initiative and referendum further this core set of values.

The Roots of American Democracy

Richard Hofstadter, a post-World War II American historian, quoted at the beginning of his influential book *The American Political Tradition* Horace White's assertion that the United States Constitution "is based on the philosophy of Hobbes and the religion of Calvin."[14] Hofstadter's observation identified an important point to understand about the constitutional Framers and American history—it was influenced by a set of values that helped inform the shaping of our political system. More specifically, there were four traditions or sets of values that helped frame how James Madison

---

14 RICHARD HOFSTADTER, THE AMERICAN POLITICAL TRADITION AND THE MEN WHO MADE IT, 5 (1989).

and the other founders thought about the Constitution and the political system they were creating. These traditions—indebted to religion and the Puritans and Pilgrims, Lockean-Liberalism, Republicanism, and a legal one sourced in William Blackstone—came together to define a set of ways to think about politics.[15]

In many ways these four traditions offer contrasting viewpoints on how to think about society and politics. A religious tradition de-emphasized the separation of church and state which stood in contrast to a Lockean-Liberal approach which was strictly secular. Republicanism placed greater emphasis on the public good than did liberalism, and it also worried more about maldistributions of property than did any of the other traditions. The inherent tensions across these four traditions have played out across American history in terms of how they influenced political debates and conflicts. However, at the core of the four traditions was a simple agreement on the idea of protecting individual liberty. Yes liberty for each of these traditions might mean different things, but nonetheless respect for rights is something that all of these share.

This common commitment to respect for liberty is at the core of what the Constitution and Bill of Rights are about. As described in Chapter 2, it was concern for protecting individual liberty against the tyranny of the majority that defined the theme of *Federalist* 10. And in the process of worrying about the threat of factions to liberty, Madisonian democracy created the complex constitutional machinery it did to breakup political power. A central fear of Madisonian democracy was the oppression of the people, the majority, if turned into a faction, and the damage they could do to the rights of others or the public good.

Recall from Chapter 2 that the logic of American politics and constitutionalism is well described by political scientist Robert Dahl who said that the essence of Madisonian democracy resided in efforts to check majority faction or tyranny.[16] The fundamental problem of politics is a balancing act. The issue then is how to preserve individual liberty and republican government from the threats of majority faction. This is the core problem of politics that Madison, the *Federalist Papers*, and the constitutional Framers sought to address. Phrased otherwise, the problem of politics, as Alexis de Tocqueville would later ask, is how can the American republic deal with the threats of the tyranny of the majority?[17] Another way of stating it: How to balance majority rule with minority rights?[18] How does one allow for majority opinion to rule, as it should in a popular government, but not let it become destructive, acting impulsively or rashly when threatened?

---

15   Schultz, *Political Theory and Legal History*.

16   ROBERT A. DAHL, A PREFACE TO DEMOCRATIC THEORY, 4-34 (1965).

17   ALEXIS DE TOCQUEVILLE, DEMOCRACY IN AMERICA, trans. George Lawrence, 250-53 (1969).

18   *See generally*: JAMES BRYCE, THE AMERICAN COMMONWEALTH (1891); ELISABETH NOELLE-NEUMANN. THE SPIRAL OF SILENCE (1993); and DAVID RIESMAN, INDIVIDUALISM RECONSIDERED, AND OTHER ESSAYS (1954) (*describing* the phenomena of social conformism and threat of majority preferences to minority rights in America).

The original Madisonian or constitutional solution to majority factions was a political one, residing in the creation of a complex machinery that involved an extended republic with representation, a bicameral legislature, checks and balances, separation of powers, and federalism. All of these mechanisms were set up in an effort to break up political power and slow down political change. But with the articulation of a Bill of Rights the focus shifted to a more complex system of taking some choices out of the political process, as Justice Jackson described in *West Virginia v. Barnette*, and making the courts serve as a protector of rights. There is matter for debate regarding how effective the judiciary has been as a counter-majoritarian institution, and, in fact, some such as Alexander Bickel have questioned the legitimacy of such an approach.[19] Yet one can make a strong case that Madisonian democracy, the Constitution, and the Bill of Rights collectively embodied a commitment to a set of values that sought to protect minority or individual rights.

Moreover, what all this means is that Madisonian democracy is not a commitment to direct democracy and pure majoritarianism. It is a representative model of government that seeks to mediate power and public opinion though governmental institutions. The model clearly has an elite-driven aspect too in the sense that it does not express a lot of faith in the capacity of average people to make decisions. Some of that is a reflection of the times and the biases of the Framers. But beyond these prejudices there is also a deep-seated concern about direct democracy. There are many democratic theorists ranging from Jean-Jacques Rousseau[20] though to Carol Pateman[21] who have endorsed or critically evaluated the virtues of direct democracy. John Stuart Mill sees civil engagement as containing important educational benefits,[22] and Robert Putnam finds in participation (even if not direct democracy) important values in the promotion of social capital.[23] All of these arguments about why people should be engaged are compelling. But where does direct democracy fit, if at all, into American democracy? This is the challenge of the Progressive Era.

Progressive Era Politics Direct Democracy

The Progressive Era of politics encompasses a period of American history from the end of Reconstruction to the end of World War I.[24] The era was marked by

---

19 ALEXANDER BICKEL, THE LEAST DANGEROUS BRANCH (1962). *See also:* GERALD N. ROSENBERG, HOLLOW HOPE: CAN COURTS BRING ABOUT SOCIAL CHANGE? (1991).

20 JEAN-JACQUES ROUSSEAU, THE SOCIAL CONTRACT (1977).

21 CAROLE PATEMAN, PARTICIPATION AND DEMOCRATIC THEORY (1970).

22 DENNIS F. THOMPSON, JOHN STUART MILL AND REPRESENTATIVE GOVERNMENT, 137-41 (1979).

23 ROBERT PUTNAM, BOWLING ALONE: THE COLLAPSE AND REVIVAL OF AMERICAN COMMUNITY (2001).

24 *See generally*: ROBERT H. WIEBE, THE SEARCH FOR ORDER: 1877-1920 (1967).

several characteristics, including a significant growth of corporate influence and power, and the concentration of wealth in the United States.[25] For some, this concentration of wealth led to concerns among many that the ideals and perhaps reality of American democracy were in danger of being lost.[26]

The threat to American democracy was especially manifested in how this concentration in wealth and power was a corrupting influence, affecting the purity and morality of its political institutions.[27] Thus, the capacity of legislatures across the country to act and represent the people was threatened because of the perceived plutocratic control and domination of them by big business.[28] It was out of a fear that the entrenched power of special interests had infected politics, resulting in the incapacity of legislatures to act to serve the majority, that Progressive politics was born.[29]

Progressive politics held government and big business in contempt, seeing them as teaming together to be the enemy of the people.[30] Progressives sought to restructure American political institutions[31] and to wrestle power back to serve the people.[32] The solution to doing this resided in initiative, referendum, and recall.[33] William Munro of the National Municipal League, one of the prime supporters of these three reforms, described the Progressive animus behind these reforms as lying in public loss of hope in the ability of legislators to act:

> But a large section of the public has come to the conclusion that these channels do not afford adequate facilities for the assertion of popular sovereignty. [I]t can scarcely be urged that the old machinery of democracy is fulfilling its professed ends to the satisfaction of all.
>
> Popular distrust of the present system of law-making is undeniably widespread and deep. But it is not based on the idea that the representatives of the people are incompetent to do their duty. Rather it arises from the notion that they are prevented from doing it. And these preventing influences, in the popular mind, are various organized interests—political machines and economic corporations—whose wishes do not usually run parallel to the electorate.[34]

---

25 *Id.* at 13.
26 RICHARD HOFSTADTER, THE AGE OF REFORM, 5-6 (1955).
27 *Id.*
28 *Id.* at 238.
29 *Id.* at 257.
30 *Id.* at 257; Wiebe, The Search for Order, 5.
31 Wiebe at 181.
32 Hofstadter, The Age of Reform at 259.
33 *Id.* at 261.
34 WILLIAM BENNETT MUNRO, ED., THE INITIATIVE, REFERENDUM, AND RECALL, 16-17 (1912).

According to Munro, the existing channels of legislation do not represent the "majority of the electorate";[35] initiative and referendum will be a form of direct democracy, allowing the people to bypass legislators and special interests.[36] Similarly, Teddy Roosevelt contended in the same volume that initiative and referendum are "devices for giving better and more immediate effect to the popular will."[37] Additionally, then governor and soon to be President Woodrow Wilson also wrote in that volume that Progressive politics was rooted in the need to address the concentrations of wealth damaging American political institutions,[38] and that initiative and referendum were tools to restore representative government for the people.[39] Moreover, Progressives saw in direct democracy tools to educate voters.[40]

Thus, the goal of initiative and referendum was to restore American representative democracy. It would do that by placing legislative power in the hands of the people, granting to majorities the powers to make the laws for themselves as a way of circumventing the corruption alliance of concentrated wealth and elected officials.

In juxtaposition to Madisonian democracy which sought to limit the threat of majority faction by creating a complex political machinery with representative government, Progressives placed faith in direct democracy as a way to bypass the evils of representative government and restore power to the majority. Progressive politics represented both a continuity and break from Madisonian democracy. It represented a continuity in the sense that it wanted to respect majority rule and return power to the people. It was also concerned about corruption, another theme that some scholars have noted as central to Madisonian democracy.[41] But where it broke was in its sense of placing more faith in the people to deliberate and make choices. It also seemed to embrace a greater sense of pure majoritarianism than did Madisonianism. Now perhaps that break from Madisonianism was needed. Maybe directly legislating would break up the special interest control over legislators and make them more responsible to the people. Given fears that Americans have that the government does not always serve their interests then perhaps Progressive reforms were needed. But the question is to evaluate how these reforms have played themselves out. What has been the legacy of initiative and referendum? The simple answer is that the Progressives did not get what they hoped for, and they also got something that they perhaps did not bargain on—a pair of election mechanisms that threaten minority rights.

---

35 *Id.* at 20.
36 *Id.*
37 Theodore Roosevelt, *Nationalism and Popular Will*, in Munro at 52, 64.
38 Woodrow Wilson, *The Issue of Reform*, in Munro at 69, 85.
39 Wilson at 87.
40 Munro at 21, 24.
41 J.G.A. Pocock, The Machiavellian Moment: Florentine Political Thought and the Atlantic Republican Tradition (2003).

Failure of the Progressive Solution: The Threat to Minority Rights

In some cases initiative and referendum might be legitimate expressions of majority rule, in many cases it is not. Depending on one's political views, direct democracy has produced many important recent reforms including medical marijuana and the decriminalization of that drug,[42] physician-assisted suicide,[43] and important or political reform initiatives.[44]

Progressive Era politics may be noble in its goals to break the entrenched corruption of state politics at the close of the nineteenth and rise of the twentieth centuries by seeking a direct majority appeal to the people. Yet Progressives forgot or ignored the essential insights of the constitutional Framers who saw in majoritarianism a threat to minority and individual rights.

Minority Rights Generally Lose

Generally minority rights lose in ballot initiatives. This is true despite the fact that in the 2012 elections same-sex marriage was voted into law in Maine, Maryland, and Washington, and an effort to in Minnesota to constitutionally ban it was also rejected by the voters. These four victories for supporters of gay rights come after 31 states had already limited via ballot initiatives the rights of same-sex couples to marry.[45]

Derrick Bell argues that, while ballot initiatives for Whites may be an expression of democracy at its finest, for the poor and people of color ballot propositions are a threat to their rights.[46] Use of initiative and referenda, while often seemingly neutral on their face, discriminate against specific groups.[47] Bell contends that, while the Court will police direct democracy when the balance between majority rule and minority rights has been tipped too much against the latter he also asserts that the judiciary has generally not taken an aggressive enough action to look beyond apparent neutral processes to guard against abuses.[48] Bell's conclusion is

---

42 California Proposition 215 in 1996 added Section 11362.5 to the California Health and Safety Code legalizing the use of marijuana for medical purposes.

43 Measure 16 of 1994 established the state of Oregon's Death with Dignity Act (ORS 127.800-995).

44 For example in 1974 California voters enacted Proposition 9, enacting the Political Reform Act and creating the Fair Political Practices Commission.

45 Nicole Neroulias, Gay marriage foes to fight expected Washington state law, http://www.reuters.com/article/2012/02/03/us-gay-marriage-washington-idUSTRE81204 O20120203 (site last viewed on December 10, 2012).

46 Derrick A. Bell, Jr., *The Referendum: Democracy's Barrier to Racial Equality*, 54 WASH. L. REV. 1 (1978-79).

47 *Id.* at 7.

48 Bell at 7-9 (*criticizing* the approach the Court took in City of Eastlake v. Forest City Enterprises, Inc., 426 U.S. 668 (1976) and James v. Valtierra, 402 U.S. 137 (1971) where it respectively upheld laws requiring public approval for zoning changes to build a

that the initiative and referendum process is structurally biased against minority rights and therefore should be eliminated in light of the warnings of majoritarian tyranny that James Madison cautioned.[49]

Thomas Cronin notes in *Direct Democracy*[50] that minority rights are often targets of initiatives and referenda. While it is no doubt the case that some ballot measures have supported minority rights, the truth is that more often than not ballot measures have become another means for special interest groups to push their agenda, often at the expense of individual rights. For Cronin, it is unlikely that debates on the rights of unpopular or minority groups or other politically salient issues can be adequately undertaken in a media campaign where dollars buy sound bites.[51] Deliberation of public policy requires more than that.

Numerous studies examining ballot initiatives have documented their hostility to minority rights.[52] David B. Magleby reviewed ballot measures between 1898 and 1978 and found that only 33 percent of them were supported by the voters. But Magleby does not indicate what percentage of those targeting minority rights were successful. Instead, one of the most comprehensive studies regarding the hostility of direct democracy to minority rights was undertaken by Barbara Gamble.[53] Gamble examined local and state ballot measures related to AIDS testing, gay rights, language, school desegregation, and housing/public accommodations desegregation from 1960 to 1993. She found that 78 percent of the 74 civil rights measures in her study opposed minority interests.

Additionally, Sylvia Vargas updated and corroborated the Gamble study, examining ballot initiatives from 1960 to 1998. According to Largos: "In the eighty-two initiatives and referendums surveyed in this Article, majorities voted to repeal, limit, or prevent any minority gains in their civil rights over eighty percent of the time." Conversely, in efforts to extend civil rights protections, they success rate was barely one in six.[54]

---

high rise apartment building and before a state public body could create a federally financed public housing project).

49 Bell at 28-29.

50 Thomas Cronin, Direct Democracy: The Politics of Initiative, Referendum, and Recall, 90-99 (1999).

51 *Id.* at 116-23.

52 David B. Magleby, *Let the Voters Decide? An Assessment of the Initiative and Referendum Process*, 66 U. Colo. L. Rev. 13, 26-27 (1995). *See also:* Daniel C. Lewis, Direct Democracy and Minority Rights: A Critical Assessment of the Tyranny of the Majority in the American States (2012); Elizabeth Garrett, *Direct Democracy*, in Daniel A. Farber and Anne Joseph O'Connell, eds., Research Handbook on Public Choice and Public Law, 137 (2010).

53 Barbara S. Gamble, *Putting Civil Rights to a Popular Vote*, 41 Am. J. Pol. Sci. 245, 246 (1997).

54 Sylvia R. Lazos Vargas, *Judicial Review of Initiatives and Referenda in which Majorities Vote on Minorities' Democratic Citizenship*, 60 Ohio St. L. J. 399, 42-43 (1999).

Gays, lesbians, and other minority groups generally lose in ballot initiatives.[55] For example, in 1977 St Paul, Minnesota adopted anti-gay discrimination legislation, only to see voters repeal it in a 1978 ballot initiative.[56] In addition to the 31 state initiatives since 2004 that successfully targeted gay rights, Donald P. Haider-Markel and Kenneth J. Meier looked at the passage rates of ballot initiatives seeking to limit or extend rights to gays and lesbians.[57] They found that that 77 percent of the time efforts to repeal the rights of gays and lesbians were successful whereas only 16 percent of the efforts to extend rights were adopted. This anti-gay hostility did not stop after 1996 when the Supreme Court ruled in *Romer v. Evans* that a Colorado ballot initiative rescinding local gay rights laws was unconstitutional because the law singled out a specific group and imposed upon them a "broad and undifferentiated disability on a single named group."[58]

Overall, minority rights are held hostage to ballot initiatives and they should not be. In *Reitman v. Mulkey*,[59] the Supreme Court invalidated a California ballot initiative that sought to repeal recently adopted legislation aimed at addressing racial discrimination in the real estate market. The Court ruled that the ballot measure had an "ultimate effect" in furthering state discrimination, thereby violating the Equal Protection clause. Ballot initiatives may be letting the people decide, but the people have no right to commandeer the government to discriminate.

Money Spent for Initiatives and Referenda Cannot Be Limited

In its 1978 decision *First National Bank v. Bellotti*,[60] the United States Supreme Court declared that money on ballot initiatives was core political speech. *Bellotti* along with other decisions such as *FEC v. Massachusetts Citizens Concerned for Life*,[61] *Federal Election Commission v. National Right to Work Committee*,[62] *California Medical Association v. Federal Election Commission*,[63] and *Federal*

---

55 *See generally*: AMY L. STONE, GAY RIGHTS AT THE BALLOT BOX (2012) (*arguing* that in general anti-gay interests have been successful in using initiative and referendum to the detriment of gay rights); and Cronin, Direct Democracy, 94-95.

56 Cronin at 95.

57 Donald P. Haider-Markel and Kenneth J. Meier, *Legislative Victory, Electoral Uncertainty: Explaining Outcomes in the Battles Over Lesbian and Gay Rights* (unpublished manuscript presented at the 1995 annual meeting of the Midwest Political Science Association, Chicago, April 1995).

58 517 U.S. 620, 632 (1996). *See also:* William E. Adams, Jr., *Can We Relax Now? An Essay About Ballot Measures & Lesbian, Gay, and Bisexual Rights After Romer v. Evans*, 2 NAT'L J. SEXUAL ORIENTATION L., 188, 190 (1996).

59 387 U.S. 369 (1967).

60 435 U.S. 765 (1978).

61 479 U.S. 238 (1986).

62 459 U.S. 197 (1982).

63 453 U.S. 182 (1981).

Election Commission v. National Conservative Political Action Committee,[64] collectively stand for the proposition that limits on the amount of money spent or contributed to support ballot initiatives are unconstitutional More importantly, the Court stated in *Bellotti* that limits on corporate spending for issue advocacy violated the First Amendment.[65]

The importance of *Bellotti* for ballot initiatives is that when the people get to vote, the state cannot limit the amount of money spent by any party, including corporations. Hence, use of initiative and referendum opens an enormous hole in the existing campaign finance laws, permitting corporations and any other party to spend unlimited amounts of money to influence the outcome. The result is less a ballot proposition being a statement about populism and direct democracy and more one potentially about the ability of corporate interests to use their resources and interests to push their favored agendas.

Money Spent on Initiative and Referenda Circumvent Populism

Thomas Cronin indicates in his book *Direct Democracy* that money has a decisive influence on the outcome of ballot measures. For example, he notes that corporate-backed sponsors win 80 percent of the ballot initiatives and that when big money opposes a poorly funded ballot measure "the evidence suggests that the wealthier side has about a 75% or better chance of defeating it."[66] In addition, evidence demonstrates strong correlations between the amount of money spent and the number of votes cast and that, while money cannot guarantee victory, the amount of money spent is decisive in defeating a ballot proposition.[67]

Overall, the evidence suggests that a popular ballot measure is more often than not defeated by corporate and special interest money. Elisabeth Gerber reaches a similar conclusion that the role of money is that of defeating but not passing ballot measures.[68] Thus, she sees ballot initiatives both as targeting minority rights[69] and also at the same time undermining majoritarian preferences because of the ability of wealthy individuals to use money to thwart popular preferences.[70]

Big Money Distorts Public Deliberation

What big money buys in debates on ballot measures is media exposure. According to several studies, media exposure is the single most important factor influencing

---

64   470 U.S. 480 (1985).
65   435 U.S. at 784.
66   Cronin, Direct Democracy, 109.
67   *Id.* at 110-13.
68   ELISABETH R. GERBER THE POPULIST PARADOX, 137-38 (1999).
69   *Id.* at 142-43.
70   *Id.* at 144.

and swaying voter decisions.[71] Given the cost of the media, for the most part, the public will be asked to make critical public policy decisions based upon 15-second sound bites financed by interests that have the most money to spend on the media. Clearly our constitutional Framers and the original supporters of initiative and referendum did not envision policy-making premised upon sound bites and the cash nexus yet the evidence, as Cronin and Gerber indicate, suggests in California and other states that this is exactly what has happened.

Moreover, consider the structural differences between legislative deliberations and ballot initiatives. Legislators are able to compromise, bargain, negotiate, and can find ways to take potentially incompatible propositions in legislation and make them work together. Voters are given ballot initiatives as all-or-nothing propositions, and cannot vote for part of one.[72] Ballot propositions generally must adhere to a single subject,[73] yielding problems of compromise or reconciliation of occasionally incompatible legislation. Additionally voters may be asked to vote on contradictory propositions,[74] again without the legislators' ability to forge compromises or affect tradeoffs to render them compatible. Thus, the deliberative nature of representation that Madison and the Constitutional Framers desired may often be missing in ballot initiatives. The result is the creation of faulty legislation that too may fail to adequately capture public sentiment on any of the propositions they are asked to render decisions upon.

Initiative and Referendum Has Little Impact on Breaking Up Special Interests

Advocates of initiative and referendum claimed that letting the voters decide would help break the grip that special interests had upon legislatures. It would do that in part by mobilizing citizens to outvote citizens. Only part of this Progressive hope has been realized. While some contend that ballot initiatives do not increase voter turnout,[75] more recent evidence contradicts that and finds that they do in fact mobilize more individuals to participate.[76] However, research also indicates that

---

71 Cronin, Direct Democracy, 116-23.

72 Chris Chambers Goodman (*M)ad Men: Using Persuasion Factors in Media Advertisements to Prevent a "Tyranny of the Majority" on Ballot Propositions*, 32 HASTINGS COMM. & ENT L. J. 247, 249 (2010).

73 *See generally*: Daniel H. Lowenstein, *California Initiatives and the Single-Subject Rule*, 30 U.C.L.A. L. REV., 936 (1983); Daniel H. Lowenstein, *Initiatives and the New Single Subject Rule*, 1 ELECT. L. J. 35 (2002); and John G. Matsusaka and Richard L. Hasen, *Aggressive Enforcement of the Single Subject Rule*, 9 ELECT L. J. 399 (2010) (*discussing* the single-subject rule).

74 Michael D. Gilbert and Joshua M. Levine, *Less Can Be More: Conflicting Ballot Proposals and the Highest Vote Rule*, 38 J. LEGAL STUDIES, 383 (2009).

75 Cronin, Direct Democracy, 226-27.

76 Daniel A. Smith and Caroline Tolbert, *The Instrumental and Educative Effects of Ballot Measures: Research on Direct Democracy in the American States*, 7 STATE POL. & POL'Y Q. 416, 430-31 (2007).

interest groups have become effective in using direct democracy to further their causes, thus questioning a central tenet of initiative and referendum advocates that their use would break entrenched interests.[77]

Courts Do Not Always Defer to Ballot Measures

Another way in which the spirit of populism is frustrated by initiative and referendum is in the lack of deference the courts often have towards ballot measures.[78]

In general, courts will defer to the will of legislatures so long as there is a rational basis to the policy adopted and there is some legislative finding of fact to support the policy. However, in the case of ballot measures, there is often very little if any finding of fact or legislative hearings to support the initiative or referendum.[79] Therefore, the courts are unwilling to afford the same deference to initiative and referendum as they would to acts of a state legislature.[80] Thus, any expression of populism that appears to occur as a result of ballot measures disappears once they face judicial review and challenges.

Ballot Measures Undermine Accountability

The Latin root for republic is two words—res and publica. Together they translate as the "public thing." A republic is a public form of government with the idea that decisions made in the polis are done publicly and in an open and accountable fashion. As discussed in Chapter 2, the concepts of transparency, openness, and accountability, are central to any concept of a popular government, including the United States. The authors of the Declaration of Independence viewed with disdain the British Star Chamber and the idea that judicial hearings could take place in secret. Judges and juries need to be accountable for their decisions, hence open courts and judicial proceedings.[81] The same principle also applies to all other legislative proceedings. As a rule, the making of policy is something that is done

---

77 *Id.* at 432.

78 *See:* Cody Hoesly, *Reforming Direct Democracy: Lessons from Oregon*, 93 CAL. L. REV. 1191 (2005) (*noting* the decreased deference state courts were giving in Oregon to ballot measures) *See also:* Michael D. Gilbert, *Does Law Matter? Theory and Evidence from Single Subject Adjudication*, 40 J. LEGAL STUDIES 333 (2011).

79 Mihui Pak, *The Counter-majoritarian Difficulty in Focus: Judicial Review of Initiatives*, 32 COLUM. J. L. & SOC. PROBS. 237 (1999) (*discussing* the problems regarding standards of review the courts should take toward ballot initiatives).

80 Cronin, Direct Democracy, 219-20. *See also:* MATT MANWELLER, THE PEOPLE VS. THE COURTS: JUDICIAL REVIEW AND DIRECT DEMOCRACY IN THE AMERICAN LEGAL SYSTEM (2004) (*finding* that the courts treat ballot initiatives differently from ordinary legislation and that they are less likely to defer to and uphold the former compared to the latter); KENNETH MILLER, DIRECT DEMOCRACY AND THE COURTS (2009).

81 Richmond Newspapers, Inc. v. Virginia, 448 U.S. 555 (1980).

within public purview, with legislators accountable for the votes they tender. The basis of representative government rests upon the idea that, if the public does not like or endorse a position that their representatives have on a particular issue, voters have a right to vote against them at the next election. Accountability resides in the ability to have open deliberations, votes, and then elections.

But government by ballot measure can undermine accountability in several ways. First and most obvious is in the sense of holding someone responsible. There is no one. Yes there is accountability in the sense that voters can reject a ballot initiative, but one of the defects of at least referenda is that it lets elected officials off the hook. Instead of them making the decisions or choices they were put into office to make they can instead put proposition on the ballot and let the people decide. Public officials can then either avoid having to make a decision or more cynically place something on the ballot and then say that, whatever the result, it was the people and not them that made the choice. Alternatively, with initiatives, elected officials may also use them to avoid making decisions, rationalizing that if the people want something they can put it on the ballot themselves. In either case, legislators are able to duck responsibility for what the people ultimately do.

But there is another way in which accountability is undermined and that is with holding the people, especially with initiatives, responsible for their actions. First, unlike legislators, supporters of ballot initiatives cannot be unelected. This applies both in the case of those who have started the ballot initiative (the sponsors or initiators) and among those who also are signatories of the petitions to get items on the ballot. Often little is known about the former in terms of their identity, motives, or other factors that one might know when it comes to legislators voting on or initiating legislation. Additionally, as noted, except for voting down a ballot initiative there is little a voter can do to hold these individuals accountable and to prevent them from seeking to place additional items on the agenda in the future. This is in contrast to legislators whom voters hold accountable at elections for actions the voters do not endorse.

But there is another sense of accountability that is at stake here for both ballot sponsors and initiators and even for those who sign petitions to get proposals on the ballot. This is the issue of privacy and the battle being fought against disclosure. There is a principle of democracy that favors disclosure. In the famous campaign finance case of *Buckley v. Valeo*,[82] the Supreme Court upheld disclosure requirements for political contributions and expenditures. It ruled that three compelling governmental interests— providing information to voters, preventing corruption, and ensuring compliance with the law—supported disclosure.[83] Yet in ruling in this case the Court did note that in some circumstances disclosure might not be appropriate or compelling. That situation harked back to *NAACP v. Alabama* where the State of Alabama during the nascent rise of the civil rights

---

82   424 U.S. 1 (1976).
83   *Id.* at 66-67.

movement sought disclosure of the membership lists of the NAACP.[84] The purpose of such disclosure was obvious—to intimidate supporters of NAACP and break the back of it and the civil rights movement. The Court voided the state disclosure law as an unconstitutional violation of the First Amendment rights of the NAACP. According to the Court:

> [C]ompelled disclosure of affiliation with groups engaged in advocacy may constitute as effective a restraint on freedom of association as the forms of governmental action in the cases above were thought likely to produce upon the particular constitutional rights there involved. This Court has recognized the vital relationship between freedom to associate and privacy in one's associations.[85]

In some cases First Amendment considerations weigh against disclosure. The Court in *Buckley* argued that while disclosure is constitutionally permissible, the compelling interests to disclose must be weighed against the rights of the group and then it must show a relevant correlation or substantial relation between the interest and the information sought. Disclosure when it affects First Amendment expressive interests must be narrowly tailored.

NAACP v. Alabama is not the only case supporting the proposition that certain types of disclosure might chill speech. Efforts to require religious solicitors to get permits or wear identifications have also been invalidated. The point here is that, when it comes to ballot propositions, disclosure and anonymity are two sides of a First Amendment coin that need to be respected and the Supreme Court has wrestled with this tension. First, in *Buckley v American Constitutional Law Foundation*,[86] the Court invalidated a Colorado law requiring petition circulators to wear name badges. The Court found that this disclosure was unconstitutional in that there were less restrictive alternative ways to gather information about who the petition circulators were. The Court did not directly state that the public did not have a right to know who was circulating petitions, but it came close to saying so because it acknowledged that some circulators felt afraid or harassed because their names were on the badge.

Now consider the case of *Doe v. Reed*.[87] Here individuals who signed a petition to place a referendum on the ballot to repeal a state law granting unmarried couples domestic benefits objected that their names would be made public. The ostensible concern was one of privacy or, more correctly, a chilling of speech. The complaint was that if they signed the petition and their name was made public then they would face harassment. In effect, they would be chilled in their speech and perhaps unlikely to sign a petition had they known that their names would be disclosed.

---

84 357 U.S. 449 (1958).
85 *Id.* at 462.
86 525 U.S. 182 (1999).
87 130 S.Ct. 2811 (2010).

The Supreme Court rejected their argument. The Court failed to find any significant evidence of harassment here and that the disclosure requirements here were sufficiently tailored to ensure the integrity of the electoral process.

While the opinion was 8-1, it was a fractured one with many concurrences. But one of the most interesting was that of Justice Scalia in commenting on disclosure and political courage. First, in terms of disclosure he noted a historical tradition in the United States of disclosing petition signatories and thus the long-standing practice lent constitutional validity to the transparency requirement:

> The public nature of federal lawmaking is constitutionally required. Article I, § 5, cl. 3 requires Congress to legislate in public: "Each House shall keep a Journal of its Proceedings, and from time to time publish the same, excepting such Parts as may in their Judgment require Secrecy; and the Yeas and Nays of the Members of either House on any question shall, at the Desire of one fifth of those Present, be entered on the Journal." State constitutions enacted around the time of the founding had similar provisions. See, e.g., Ky. Const., Art. I, § 20 (1792); Ga. Const., Art. I, § 15 (1798). The desirability of public accountability was obvious. "[A]s to the votes of representatives and senators in Congress, no man has yet been bold enough to vindicate a secret or ballot vote, as either more safe or more wise, more promotive of independence in the members, or more beneficial to their constituents.[88]

The constitutional validation for disclosure is located in an American tradition that had always required signatories to stand publicly behind the petitions they sign. But this public nature, Scalia stated, was also rooted in a sense of a courage for one's convictions:

> Requiring people to stand up in public for their political acts fosters civic courage, without which democracy is doomed. For my part, I do not look forward to a society which, thanks to the Supreme Court, campaigns anonymously (McIntyre) and even exercises the direct democracy of initiative and referendum hidden from public scrutiny and protected from the accountability of criticism. This does not resemble the Home of the Brave.[89]

According to Scalia, being required to stand up publicly for one's beliefs fosters a democratic spirit. It encourages individuals to be accountable for their views and to demonstrate a sense of courage or real conviction for their beliefs. A democratic spirit requires that people actively believe in their values and be willing perhaps to be criticized for them and then defend the stands that they take. The ancient Greek democracies did not allow for anonymous debate in the agora, and New England

---

88 *Id.* at 2833-34.
89 *Id.* at 2837.

town democracies do not permit it either. Both recognized the publicness of debate and, in fact, even went so far as to require public voting.

The point of Scalia's dissent is really first to recognize that political advocacy in a free society is public and transparent. It is about political openness and the willingness to engage publicly for positions and not in a clandestine way. Moreover, Scalia recognizes that democracy or democratic debate is not always peaceful. It might include shouting, criticism, and name calling. It would be nice if this did not occur but, as the Supreme Court once noted in *Cohn v. California* case:

> Additionally, we cannot overlook the fact, because it is well illustrated by the episode involved here, that much linguistic expression serves a dual communicative function: it conveys not only ideas capable of relatively precise, detached explication, but otherwise inexpressible emotions as well. In fact, words are often chosen as much for their emotive as their cognitive force. We cannot sanction the view that the Constitution, while solicitous of the cognitive content of individual speech has little or no regard for that emotive function which practically speaking, may often be the more important element of the overall message sought to be communicated. Indeed, as Mr. Justice Frankfurter has said, "(o)ne of the prerogatives of American citizenship is the right to criticize public men and measures—and that means not only informed and responsible criticism but the freedom to speak foolishly and without moderation."[90]

The point here is that democratic debate does not always follow the niceties of the rules of etiquette. It gets rough, heated, and emotional, and words and actions are often used to get the attention of others. Yes lines need to be drawn to prevent real harassment and threats of intimidation, but at some point the concept of robust and open debate means debate will be heated. There may be a fine line between harassment and robust debate, but democratic theory is about taking positions that others may not always agree with and being willing to defend them. This is the reason why legislators cannot take secret votes—they are expected to be accountable to their colleagues and voters for their positions and the same should be expected among those who are petition signatories.

Why is this debate about the disclosure of signatories of ballot measures important and germane here? First, signing a petition is not like voting. The courts have come to recognize a right to a secret ballot, but that has only come about in the last century or so in American history.[91] Signing ballot initiative petitions is less like voting and more like legislating or proposing legislation (sponsoring a bill?), with the latter recognized as a public act. Legislating is a public act and the

---

90 Cohen v. California, 403 U.S.15, 26-27 (1971).
91 Rogers v. Lodge, 458 U.S. 613, 647, fn. 30 (1082), where the Court stated: "[T]he very purpose of the secret ballot is to protect the individual's right to cast a vote without explaining to anyone for whom, or for what reason, the vote is cast."

process of placing a proposition on the ballot too is a public act and individuals too should be held accountable for their acts.

Yet there is a demand in some circles, as seen by Clarence Thomas' dissent in *Doe v. Reed*, to insulate signatories from having to publicly disclose their names. Beyond the concerns or reasons expressed in majority opinions about disclosure needed to ensure protection for the integrity of the electoral process and prevent corruption, there is also the notion that anonymity here can be used to shield or insulate prejudice or bigotry, or to prevent democratic debate from being open and transparent. If individuals wish to engage in actions that do not affect others, to paraphrase John Stuart Mill, their actions are private and no one else's concern. But if they wish to legislate in ways that affect others, especially minorities, then it is the public's business in requiring these individuals to be accountable for their views.

The point here is then is twofold. First, if ballot initiatives are meant to be the people legislating, then they should be held to the same standard of disclosure as legislators when proposing bills. If on the other hand there are genuine concerns that in self-legislating supporters or opponents of propositions will be chilled in their speech then maybe direct democracy is not the appropriate way to legislate on a matter. If it is impossible to police the chilling of First Amendment individual speech when engaging in direct democracy, then the collective First Amendment interests in public debate, transparency, and accountability might suggest that the process of initiative and referendum might be in conflict with, or ill-suited as, a decision-making process in some circumstances.

Conclusion

Direct democracy and majoritarian politics inconsistent with the broader substantive values of the Constitution and Bill of Rights which seeks to preserve minority rights. American constitutionalism is not about pure majoritarianism and it never was. The United States is a country of checks and balances, limited power, and respect for individual and minority rights. The majoritarian politics reflected in constitutional amendments addressing minority rights reveals the darker and uglier side of America, one that seeks to enable prejudice, often times under the cloak of a anonymity. We need to understand that the rules of direct democracy are sometimes unfair. In some ways they do not further democratic values as they have evolved in the United States which require respect for minority rights and debates which take place in a way that further transparency and accountability. Majoritarian politics produced slavery, Jim Crow, and Stonewall. The time has come to recognize that the Progressive Era embrace of direct democracy has generally failed when it comes to minority politics, and in many ways it also has failed to further majority rule. As Justice Jackson so eloquently stated, certain rights should not be decided at the ballot box and going forward, initiative and referendum should exclude votes on any propositions that deal with minority rights.

Chapter 5
Representation and Reapportionment

By definition, representation is at the center of contemporary conceptions of democratic theory and popular government in that they are generally described as representative government. If at one point for the Ancient Greeks democracy signified direct voting or engagement of the citizens in the agora, the practicality if not the desirability of such a political system today is in dispute. While there is something powerfully attractive in the traditional notion of a New England town meeting, or perhaps in a futuristic electronic Internet-based commonwealth,[1] both of these ideals challenge other important values associated with democratic theory.

The strength of direct democracy resides in the ability of all citizens to directly participate in the making of rules that will govern their behavior. This is Jean-Jacques Rousseau's dream in his *Social Contract*. There is also a powerful Kantian notion of autonomy associated with such a governance model, enabling individuals to act according to laws that they will themselves. Second, the lure of direct democracy is defensive and self-interested—individuals can best protect their interests by representing themselves. As the old adage goes, if you want to know if the shoe pinches, ask the wearer. Individuals, as the Utilitarian philosophers would say, are the best judge of their own self-interest and preferences and, if for no other reason, direct political participation ensures that each person represents and defends his or her own interests.

But direct participation supposedly has an educative aspect. For John Stuart Mill and others the act of participation fosters growth and self-development.[2] Alexis de Tocqueville saw several institutions in America, including participation in voluntary associations and participation on juries, as fostering what he called self-interest rightly understood.[3] As citizens engage, they learn and therefore are better able to transcend self-interest and work with others. John Dewey, for example, saw powerful linkages between education and democratic engagement.[4]

---

[1] JEFFREY B. ABRAMSON, F. CHRISTOPHER ARTERTON, GARY R. ORREN, THE ELECTRONIC COMMONWEALTH: THE IMPACT OF NEW MEDIA TECHNOLOGIES ON DEMOCRATIC POLITICS (1990).

[2] DENNIS F. THOMPSON, JOHN STUART MILL AND REPRESENTATIVE GOVERNMENT, 137-41 (1979); CAROLE PATEMAN, PARTICIPATION AND DEMOCRATIC THEORY, 28-35 (1970).

[3] ALEXIS DE TOCQUEVILLE, DEMOCRACY IN AMERICA, ed. J.P. Mayer, trans. George Lawrence, 525-28 (1969).

[4] JOHN DEWEY, DEMOCRACY AND EDUCATION (1944); JOHN DEWEY, RECONSTRUCTION IN PHILOSOPHY (1957); ROBERT B. WESTBROOK, JOHN DEWY AND AMERICAN DEMOCRACY (1991); R.W. Hildreth, *Word and Deed: A Deweyean Integration of Deliberative and Participatory Democracy*, 34 NEW POL. SCI., 297 (2012).

Jürgen Habermas,[5] John Dryzek,[6] and Benjamin Barber[7] similarly believed that political participation and deliberation would have educative or socially transformative effects. Moreover, direct participation connects to the development of social capital and trust, two traits that are essential and necessary to making democracy work.[8] Overall one can cite to these and perhaps other factors to why direct democracy and engagement for all citizens is valuable.

Yet there is a practical problem with direct democracy. In larger republics or countries such as the United States, it would be impossible to convene town forums to deliberate on matters that affect the entire country, let alone a state or perhaps most cities. The sheer number of people would challenge the ability to hold debates, allow for votes, or otherwise give most people a meaningful opportunity to engage. The economy or efficiency of direct democracy challenges it as a viable primary way to make decisions, leading John Stuart Mill in *Considerations on Representative Government* to argue that representative government was necessary.[9] Robert Dahl too contended that representation was one of the first great transformations in democratic theory, making such a theory of governance practical for communities beyond the size of the Greek polis.[10]

But as the chapter on initiative and referendum discussed (above Chapter 4), direct democracy may be biased against minority rights. Additionally, if the rationale for direct democracy and straight majority rule resides in a utilitarian calculus that it produces the greatest good for the greatest number, John Rawls' critique in *A Theory of Justice* is profound—any theory of justice that could justify the enslavement of some to serve the interest of the majority is deficient.[11] Political majority rule in some cases does threaten rights. Direct democracy, as James Madison worried about in *Federalist* 10, runs the risk of majority faction or the tyranny of the majority. Individuals are often torn by passion and act hastily, with James Madison concluding that representatives could filter the passions of the people and do a better job promoting the public good. While we might question such faith in representatives, needless to say the American political system has opted for a form of democracy that relies upon representation.

The concept of representation is complex for democratic theory. What does it actually mean to represent? As discussed in Chapter 2, Bernard Bailyn first points

---

5   Jürgen Habermas, The Structural Transformation of the Public Sphere (1989).

6   John Dryzek, Deliberative Democracy and Beyond: Liberals, Critics, Contestations (2002).

7   Benjamin R. Barber, Strong Democracy: Participatory Politics for a New Age (1984).

8   Robert Putnam, Bowling Alone: The Collapse and Revival of American Community (2001); Robert Putnam, Robert Leonardi, and Raffaella Nanetti, Making Democracy Work: Civic Traditions in Modern Italy (1993).

9   John Stuart Mill, *Representative Government* in Utilitarianism, Liberty, and Representative Government, 291-2 (1951).

10 Robert A. Dahl, Democracy and Its Critics, 213-25 (1989).

11 John Rawls, A Theory of Justice (1971).

to the Americanization of the term.[12] Part of the dispute between the American colonies and the British when the former demanded "no taxation without representation" was that both sides were using the same words but with different meanings. The British already thought that the colonies had representation in Parliament—they were virtually represented their by members elected in England. The Americanization of representation was in the insistence that virtual representation was not enough—the colonies wanted their own representatives that they selected themselves. Choice and geography were important. The colonists wanted representatives that they chose, but also those from geographically closer to home. Thus, contrary to what the Supreme Court would later say in *Reynolds v. Sims* that representatives do not represent trees or acres,[13] they actually do in the sense (or at least Americans think so) in that we do prefer them to be geographically closer as opposed to more distant. Few in Montana would accept the idea that a member of Congress from New York is their representative. The fact that each state is guaranteed one House of Representative member and two senators speaks to something about the power of geography in defining what representation means.

But representation is also nuanced in other ways. What does it mean to represent? Edmund Burke won an election when he proclaimed in his famous 1774 Speech to the Bristol Electors that his duty as an MP was to exercise his best judgments and not necessarily be a simple delegate for what the people want.[14] It is surprising that he won with a speech like that. But the reality is that Burke might have been partially correct. To represent may at times means doing exactly what the people want, to listen to them,[15] whereas in other cases it is exercising best judgments (delegate v trustee role).[16] As Kenneth Arrow pointed out, there may not be a majority preference among voters thereby compromising the ability of any representative to do what they want.[17] Politics is about the aggregation of minorities rule;[18] few districts and electorates are of one voice and opinion on a single topic or issue that makes it possible for someone to simply divine what the majority preference is and therefore execute it. Some judgment about what to do is inevitable. Especially when representatives may have greater access to knowledge and therefore may be better informed than many voters.

---

12 BERNARD BAILYN, THE IDEOLOGICAL ORIGINS OF THE AMERICAN REVOLUTION (1967).

13 Reynolds v. Sims, 377 U.S. 533, 562 (1964).

14 Edmund Burke, Speech to Bristol Electors (1774), http://almostchosenpeople.wordpress.com/2011/08/15/edmund-burke-speech-to-bristol-electors-1774/ (site last visited March 14, 2013).

15 Rebakah Herrick, *Listening and Representation*, 13 ST. POL. & POL'Y Q., 88 (2012).

16 J. ROLAND PENNOCK, DEMOCRATIC POLITICAL THEORY, 323 (1979).

17 KENNETH J. ARROW, SOCIAL CHOICE AND INDIVIDUAL VALUES (1963).

18 ROBERT A. DAHL, WHO GOVERNS?: DEMOCRACY AND POWER IN AN AMERICAN CITY (1961).

Further, representation may also mean something in a descriptive sense. By that, does Congress demographically represent the United States in terms of race, gender, class, and other similar traits? The answer is no. Does that demographic divide render it impossible for Congress or any specific member of legislature to represent the values of those who do not share similar physical or demographic traits? The jury is out on this one, with some contending that White Caucasians are incapable of understanding and therefore representing people of color. Others disagree on this issue, pointing to how many white politicians—such as former Senator Ted Kennedy—were able to represent individuals who looked nothing like them and perhaps came from very different social economic situations.

Finally, even if one can sort out what representation means, defining whether it is effective or "working" is another question too.[19] If a member of Congress does not always vote the way I would want them to, does that mean the representation is ineffective? Do representatives only represent the individuals who voted for them, or do they have a duty to represent all of their constituents or perhaps even the country? At a time when many in the United States Congress are criticized for their failure to compromise and do what is in the best interest of the country, this is an especially meaningful question. Instead of acting for the public good, electoral incentives and messages from their supporters (if not personal ideology or party affiliation) may be driving how one votes. Or for Madisonian democracy, if the presence of persistent special interests and lobbyists corrupts the legislative deliberative process, does that render representation ineffective? Conversely, for pluralist views on democracy, ignoring the important role of groups may point to the ineffectiveness and breakdown of a representation system. Representation may or may not be effective here, depending on one's perspective.

What this discussion points to is the complexity of what the term representation means, and the multiplicity of values implicated by that term. But despite the complexity and debate, it does not negate the central role of representation to the American conception of democracy. The American political system is built upon a foundation of a sound representative government, one that provides for voters to select individuals who will make choices for them, and by which the former hold the latter accountable through free and fair elections.

---

19 *See, e.g.*, HANNA F. PITKIN, THE CONCEPT OF REPRESENTATION (1971), for a discussion of various notions of representation and what it means for it to be effective. *See also:* DAVID K. RYDEN, REPRESENTATION IN CRISIS: THE CONSTITUTION, INTEREST GROUPS, AND POLITICAL PARTIES (1996); JULIET ROPER, CHRISTINA HOLTZ-BACKA, AND GIANPIETRO MAZZOLENI, THE POLITICS OF REPRESENTATION: ELECTION CAMPAIGNING AND PROPORTIONAL REPRESENTATION (2004); DAVID SCHULTZ, EVICTED! PROPERTY RIGHTS AND EMINENT DOMAIN IN AMERICA (2009); DAVID SCHULTZ, PROPERTY, POWER, AND AMERICAN DEMOCRACY (1992); Paul Boudreaux, *Eminent Domain, Property Rights, and the Solution of Representation Reinforcement*, 83 DENVER U. L. REV., 1 (2005); Jane Mansbridge, *Clarifying the Concept of Representation*, 105 AM. POL. SCI. REV., 621 (2011).

In crafting a congressional representation system to help secure this objective, the House of Representatives allocates seats in Congress based on population. The apportionment of the lower house of Congress based on the population of a state was the original Virginia plan proposed at the 1787 Constitutional Convention. Population mattered. As a result, the Constitution mandates a decennial census. The purpose of the census is, in part, to determine the population of states and therefore the allocation of seats for Congress. But how should new congressional district lines and, for that matter, state legislative lines be drawn? This is one of the most vexing and important questions in politics. Legislatures, entrusted with the duty to draw both, have often resorted to a variety of tricks when engaging in reapportionment. They do so because the drawing of district lines can have an impact on who is elected and on who has power. From the earliest days of the American republic efforts have been undertaken to manipulate district lines. In the early nineteenth century Elbridge Gerry, a signer of the Declaration of Independence and later governor in Massachusetts, sought to draw lines in a way that was to his own benefit. One district, which looked like a salamander, led a newspaper to coin the term gerrymander to describe the process of drawing district lines to favor a specific group, such as incumbents.[20]

The drawing of district lines is a controversial topic that by default has fallen to the courts to undertake due to the failure of the political process to perform it adequately and fairly. While gerrymandering has deep roots in American history, is it unconstitutional or simply an accepted fact of politics? This chapter examines the topics of racial and partisan gerrymandering, redistricting commissions, and the criteria and processes that should be employed when district lines are drawn. Its goal will be to try to address some of the democratic theory roots or issues within these controversies surrounding representation and reapportionment. While clearly it would be impossible for this book to resolve and adjudicate all the issues regarding what is the proper meaning of representation within American democratic theory, the aim is to review some of the controversies regarding redistricting and apportionment as they affect representation. The argument will be that, while the Court has generally done a good job in examining many of the values or variables affecting representation and reapportionment, it has failed to examine the role of neutrality and conflict of interest in terms of how both affect the fairness and effectiveness of the former. The argument of this chapter suggests that a different approach or solution to representation needs to be considered. It is one that recognizes that it is a conflict of interest for legislators to draw their own district lines, and suggests that alternative districting schema, such as multimember districts and proportional representation, are needed to address problems such as partisan and racial gerrymandering.

---

20 GARY W. COX AND JONATHAN N. KATZ, ELBRIDGE GERRY'S SALAMANDER: THE ELECTORAL CONSEQUENCES OF THE REAPPORTIONMENT REVOLUTION (2002).

Redistricting and the Federal Courts

State politics dating back to the earliest days of the republic reveal twin characteristics: first, continued efforts to gerrymander; second, responses to control those gerrymanders.[21] As is often forgotten, the term "gerrymander" is an amalgam of Elbridge Gerry and salamander.[22] Gerry was a second-term governor of Massachusetts in 1810 when his political party attempted (much like Tom DeLay in Texas nearly 200 years later) to redraw district lines to their advantage in order to retake control of the state legislature.[23] The resulting shape of one of the districts looked like a salamander to some, leading Gilbert Stuart to label it and other similarly-shaped districts a "gerrymander."[24] Besides giving birth to a new word, this incident confirmed that efforts to control the districting process for partisan or other reasons has a long history in the states.

Alan Tarr[25] and Jim Gardner document many of the ways that state constitutions historically have tried to address gerrymandering. Provisions such as requiring that districts be contiguous or compact are often constitutionally mandated,[26] or that the districts have equal or near equal populations.[27] Other states also stipulate that local governments cannot be divided in some situations,[28] while others such as Iowa express criticism regarding the capacity of legislators to draw district lines, entrusting the duty instead to a non- or bi-partisan redistricting commission.[29] Overall factors referred to as "traditional districting principles" used for apportionment in *Shaw v. Reno*[30] along with structural requirements such as commissions were legislated as responses to gerrymandering.

But beyond more naked efforts to gerrymander districts by cutting them into irregular geographic shapes or sizes, another type of malapportionment became more common in the late nineteenth and early twentieth centuries. This was the failure of states to redraw boundaries or allocate representatives based upon the shift in population from rural to urban areas and efforts to carve up districts to disempower freed slaves and African-Americans after the Civil War. Thus, drawing lines in ways that either did not reflect population changes or which used race in discriminatory ways were two frequent tools employed to gerrymander

---

21 Jim Gardner, *State Constitutional Lecture*, 5 (March 9, 2006 draft) (copy on file with the author).

22 DONALD GRIER STEPHENSON, JR., THE RIGHT TO VOTE: RIGHTS AND LIBERTIES UNDER THE LAW, 243-44 (2004).

23 *Id.* at 244.

24 *Id.* at 244.

25 ALAN TARR, UNDERSTANDING STATE CONSTITUTIONS, 118-21 (1998).

26 Gardner, Lecture (2006) at 14.

27 *Id.* at 15.

28 *Id.* at 15.

29 James A. Gardner, *Voting and Elections* in G. ALAN TARR AND ROBERT F. WILLIAMS, EDS., STATE CONSTITUTIONS FOR THE TWENTY-FIRST CENTURY, v. 3, 145, 163 (2006).

30 509 U.S. 630, 642 (1993).

and compromise the effectiveness of representation. One measure involved the dilution of voting power, the other ranged from diminished to perhaps even no voice in the selection of representatives.

As immigration and an exodus of people from farms swelled the number of city dwellers, once populous rural districts saw a corresponding decline. Had normal redistricting followed the decennial census, political power and representation would have flowed to the urban centers with more members of Congress (House of Representatives) and state legislators being apportioned to represent these areas. However, this was not the case. Rural legislators in control of reapportionment, refused to redraw district lines to reflect the demographic shifts in population. Often this failure to redistrict lasted decades.

In the second case, while the Fifteenth Amendment granted freed slaves (male ones, at least) the right to vote, many states, mostly in the South, undertook a variety of measures to ensure that they did not exercise this franchise.[31] Notorious among measures to discourage African-Americans from voting were poll taxes, literacy tests, grandfather clauses, felon disenfranchisement laws, and outright intimidation and lynching by the Ku Klux Klan.[32] Lesser known but still a widely-used practice is racial gerrymandering. Specifically, racial gerrymandering is using race in redistricting to limit the ability of African-Americans to form a voting bloc large enough to elect a representative of their own.[33] The failure to carry out reapportionment after a census, and the use of racial gerrymandering as issues began to come to a head after World War II, pressuring the Supreme Court to address these problems.

The Supreme Court Responds

Colgrove v. Green[34] is the first case to reach the Supreme Court regarding the first type of redistricting problem, *i.e.*, a failure to reapportion after the decennial census to reflect population shifts. In this case, petitioners brought suit challenging the drawing of the congressional district lines under the federal Reapportionment Act of 1929.[35] Specifically, the failure of the Illinois legislature to redraw congressional district lines since 1901 to reflect subsequent changes in population had resulted in districts of varying sizes such that they were in violation of the 1929 Act.[36]

---

31 *See, e.g.*, C. VANN WOODWARD, THE STRANGE CAREER OF JIM CROW (2001).
32 DAVID T. CANON, RACE, REDISTRICTING, AND REPRESENTATION: THE UNINTENDED CONSEQUENCES OF BLACK MAJORITY DISTRICTS, 61-62 (1999); DAVID LUBLIN, THE PARADOX OF REPRESENTATION: RACIAL GERRYMANDERING AND MINORITY INTERESTS IN CONGRESS (1997).
33 *Id.*
34 328 U.S. 549 (1946).
35 *Id.* at 549.
36 *Id.* at 549.

Justice Frankfurter, writing for the Court, rejected a plea to intervene in this matter because it was not a justiciable controversy. In rebuffing a request to issue an injunction preventing the use of these 1901 district lines in the coming election, Frankfurter stated:

> An aspect of government from which the judiciary, in view of what is involved, has been excluded by the clear intention of the Constitution cannot be entered by the federal courts because Congress may have been in default in exacting from States obedience to its mandate. The one stark fact that emerges from a study of the history of Congressional apportionment is its embroilment in politics, in the sense of party contests and party interests. The Constitution enjoins upon Congress the duty of apportioning Representatives' among the several States according to their respective Numbers, Article I, s 2. Yet, Congress has at times been heedless of this command and not apportioned according to the requirements of the Census. It never occurred to anyone that this Court could issue mandamus to compel Congress to perform its mandatory duty to apportion. "What might not be done directly by mandamus, could not be attained indirectly by injunction."[37]

Congressional districting, for the Court, was a matter constitutionally delegated to Congress and the states, and not to the Courts.[38] For the Courts to intervene would be to take them into the political thicket which they should not enter. Frankfurter reached this opinion despite acknowledging in his appendix that there were significant disparities in population across congressional districts.[39]

Gomillion v. Lightfoot represented the second type of malapportionment, *i.e.*, racial gerrymandering.[40] But unlike in *Colgrove* where the Court refused to assent to the justiciability of the case, in *Gomillion* they let the case proceed. Here, at issue was a challenge to an Alabama act of 1957 which had defined the boundaries of the City of Tuskegee.[41] Specifically, African-American voters challenged under the Fifteenth Amendment a redrawing of the municipal boundaries of the City. Prior to the Act Tuskegee's boundaries were square but as a result of the 1957 Act, they constituted a 28-sided figure.[42] The complaint alleged that the intent of the new line-drawing was to prevent most if not all of the 400 African-American voters from participating in the City's elections.[43]

---

37 328 U.S. at 555.
38 *Id.*
39 328 U.S. at 557.
40 364 U.S. 339 (1960).
41 *Id.* at 340.
42 *Id.* at 341.
43 *Id.*

Again writing for the Court, Justice Frankfurter did permit the case to be heard in federal Court. The Court, in distinguishing the controversy in *Gomillion* from *Colegrove* stated that:

> That case involved a complaint of discriminatory apportionment of congressional districts. The appellants in *Colegrove* complained only of a dilution of the strength of their votes as a result of legislative inaction over a course of many years. The petitioners here complain that affirmative legislative action deprives them of their votes and the consequent advantages that the ballot affords. When a legislature thus singles out a readily isolated segment of a racial minority for special discriminatory treatment, it violates the Fifteenth Amendment. In no case involving unequal weight in voting distribution that has come before the Court did the decision sanction a differentiation on racial lines whereby approval was given to unequivocal withdrawal of the vote solely from colored citizens. Apart from all else, these considerations lift this controversy out of the so-called 'political' arena and into the conventional sphere of constitutional litigation.[44]

Here, there was more than an allegation of inaction. Instead, Alabama had affirmatively acted, and it did so in a way that directly affected a minority population. These two features, for the Court, were enough to suggest that perhaps there was a violation of the Fifteenth Amendment, making it no longer a political dispute but one involving the Constitution, and therefore within the sphere of authority for the Court to address.

Gomillion's holding would permit the courts to address one type of malapportionment it would not allow for the other type involving disparities in district sizes that *Colgrove* left in place. Perhaps the argument could be that the remedy for malapportionment was to be found in the political process, yet how was that to occur? Clearly the beneficiaries of the malapportionment—such as rural legislators and areas—had no incentive to change because they were enriched with the political power they reaped or retained. Conversely, the losers could not affect changes in reapportionment easily since they lacked the political power or votes to force a change. Effectively, the political process had shut them out. Their options for bringing about political change were limited since they were denied effective (equal) representation.

Thus in *Baker v. Carr* the Court was asked to revisit its *Colgrove* decision.[45] Here, the State of Tennessee had last apportioned its state legislative seats in 1901 but had not reallocated seats to reflect changes in population since that date.[46] As a result, between 1901 and 1961 the state's population had increased from a little over to two million to over three-and-one-half million citizens.[47] In addition to

---

44   *Id.* at 346-47.
45   369 U.S. 186 (1962).
46   369 U.S. 186, 187-88.
47   *Id.* at 192.

the population growth, the population had shifted geographically and the number of eligible voters has grown by approximately fourfold.[48] Hence, districts were of various populations, leading plaintiffs to assert a violation of the Fourteenth Amendment equal protection clause.[49]

While the federal district court rejected hearing the dispute because it presented a nonjusticiable dispute under *Colgrove*,[50] Justice Brennan, writing for the majority, reached a contrary conclusion. Instead, he undertook an analysis of the Article III power of the Supreme Court under the Constitution,[51] seeking to understand exactly what a "political question" was and what types of issues it was forbidden from taking.[52] Brennan rejected claims that the mere assertion of a political right constituted a non-justiciable political question.[53] Yet the Court did argue that claims arising under the Guaranty Clause were non-justiciable.[54] What is a non-justiciable political question?

> We have said that "In determining whether a question falls within (the political question) category, the appropriateness under our system of government of attributing finality to the action of the political departments and also the lack of satisfactory criteria for a judicial determination are dominant considerations. *Coleman v. Miller*, 307 U.S. 433, 454-455, 59 S.Ct. 972, 982, 83 L.Ed. 1385.' The nonjusticiability of a political question is primarily a function of the separation of powers. Much confusion results from the capacity of the 'political question' label to obscure the need for case-by-case inquiry. Deciding whether a matter has in any measure been committed by the Constitution to another branch of government, or whether the action of that branch exceeds whatever authority has been committed, is itself a delicate exercise in constitutional interpretation, and is a responsibility of this Court as ultimate interpreter of the Constitution.[55]

The political question doctrine was a matter of separation of powers, asking whether the constitutional text had committed the resolution of a specific issue to any particular branch of the national government. More exactly, the Court outlined several characteristics regarding what constituted a political question:

> It is apparent that several formulations which vary slightly according to the settings in which the questions arise may describe a political question, although each has one or more elements which identify it as essentially a function of the

---

48 *Id.*
49 *Id.* at 194-95.
50 *Id.* at 198-99, 202.
51 *Id.* at 200-202.
52 *Id.* at 209-10.
53 *Id.* at 209.
54 *Id.* at 209.
55 *Id.* at 210-11.

separation of powers. Prominent on the surface of any case held to involve a political question is found a textually demonstrable constitutional commitment of the issue to a coordinate political department; or a lack of judicially discoverable and manageable standards for resolving it; or the impossibility of deciding without an initial policy determination of a kind clearly for nonjudicial discretion; or the impossibility of a court's undertaking independent resolution without expressing lack of the respect due coordinate branches of government; or an unusual need for unquestioning adherence to a political decision already made; or the potentiality of embarrassment from multifarious pronouncements by various departments on one question.[56]

Overall, unless the Constitution clearly committed the issue to another branch for resolution, or it required the Court to make a prior policy judgment, or there were no clear standards for resolving the matter, then the federal courts were not precluded from hearing the case.[57] In the dispute at hand, the Court did not find any of these conditions to obtain, thereby freeing the lower courts to hear the redistricting claim.[58] Thus, as with *Gomillion* for racial gerrymandering, malapportionment could now be addressed by the judiciary.

Left unresolved in *Baker* though was the establishment of a standard by which to judge if malapportionment had occurred. If no manageable standard for resolving the claim could be found, then by the logic of *Baker* the reapportionment controversy would still be deemed non-justiciable.[59] The construction of that would occur in *Reynolds v. Sims*. But the manageable standard and *Reynolds* did not immediately follow from *Baker*.[60] Following *Baker* the Court first in *Gray v. Sanders*[61] struck down a voting procedure which, while counting each vote the same, weighed rural votes more heavily than those that came from other areas. In this "county unit system" for voting, each county was given a unit vote equal to that of the size of its representation in the state house. This yielded a situation where the largest counties received three unit votes and others fewer votes. Then in *Wesbury v. Sanders*[62] the Court mandated that congressional districts must be of equal population. But in neither of these cases did the Court declare a clear standard for judging the constitutionality of apportionment systems.[63]

In *Reynolds v. Sims* the Court did finally describe its manageable standard: "The conception of political equality from the Declaration of Independence, to

---

56 *Id.* at 217.
57 369 U.S. at 217.
58 *Id.*
59 RICHARD HASEN, THE SUPREME COURT AND ELECTION LAW: JUDGING EQUALITY FROM BAKER V. CARR TO BUSH V. GORE, 50-53 (2006).
60 *Id.*
61 372 U.S. 368 (1963).
62 376 U.S. 1 (1964).
63 Hasen, The Supreme Court and Election Law at 51-53.

Lincoln's Gettysburg Address, to the Fifteenth, Seventeenth, and Nineteenth Amendments can mean only one thing—one person, one vote."[64] In reaching that conclusion the Court noted how "[l]egislators represent people, not trees or acres. Legislators are elected by voters, not farms or cities or economic interests"[65] and that the right to vote was diluted:

> if a State should provide that the votes of citizens in one part of the State should be given two times, or five times, or 10 times the weight of votes of citizens in another part of the State, it could hardly be contended that the right to vote of those residing in the disfavored areas had not been effectively diluted. It would appear extraordinary to suggest that a State could be constitutionally permitted to enact a law providing that certain of the State's voters could vote two, five, or 10 times for their legislative representatives, while voters living elsewhere could vote only once. And it is inconceivable that a state law to the effect that, in counting votes for legislators, the votes of citizens in one part of the State would be multiplied by two, five, or 10, while the votes of persons in another area would be counted only at face value, could be constitutionally sustainable. Of course, the effect of state legislative districting schemes which give the same number of representatives to unequal numbers of constituents is identical.[66]

Thus, *Reynolds* established the basic standard for reapportionment that would dominate subsequent redistricting decisions—promotion of the one person, one vote standard.[67]

While one person, one vote was the general standard for all of its apportionment decisions, the Court subjected it to subsequent refinement and articulation. First, in *Lucas v. Forty-Fourth General Assembly of Colorado*[68] the Court confronted a districting schema similar to that found at the congressional level. By that, while the lower house of the Colorado legislature would be apportioned by population, the upper house, or senate, would be apportioned like the United States Senate in that geography would be a factor in the allocation of seats.[69] As they did in *Reynolds*,[70] the Court in *Lucas* rejected the federal analogy,[71] finding no logical

---

64 377 U.S. 533, 558.
65 *Id.* at 562.
66 *Id.* at 563-64.
67 The standard of one person, one vote seems clear, but surprisingly not all find it so and the Supreme Court has not unambiguously declared that the apportionment is made on the basis of actual population, the number of adults, or voters in a jurisdiction even though the issue has been addressed at the appellate state. *See:* Chen v. City of Houston, 206 F.3d 502 (5th Cir.2000) and Lepak v. City of Irving, Texas, 453 Fed.Appx. 522 (5th Cir. 2011).
68 377 U.S. 713 (1964).
69 *Id.* at 719.
70 *Id.* at 571-76.
71 Stephenson, The Right to Vote at 234.

basis for apportioning one house by population and another by a different method.[72] Finally, in *Avery v. Midland County*[73] the Court mandated that the one person, one vote, standard also be extended to local government units.

But notice something important in these decisions—the apparent rejection of geography when it came to apportionment. On one level geography was important for the purposes of a district being compact and contiguous. But geography was rejected in terms of the federal analogy and in terms of what the Court said in *Reynolds* rejecting the idea that legislators represent trees and acres. Yet geography or place is important to many. As noted earlier, no person from Montana would consider herself adequately represented by someone from New York. The concept of place is critical to many senses of self-identification. Geographic proximity seems to be important at some level in American democratic theory for a theory of representation and it is not completely clear that the Supreme Court in its *Reynolds* line of cases determined the best way to balance one person, one vote with this concern.

While one person, one vote was the official mathematical standard, the Court initially applied it differently to congressional versus state and local government seats. In *Kirkpatrick v. Preisler*,[74] *White v. Weiser*,[75] and most notably *Karcher v. Daggett*[76] the Court rejected even minor deviations from the one person, one vote standard for congressional seats, appearing to mandate near mathematical equality.[77] However, when it came to apportionment of state and local government seats, the Court seemed more willing to tolerate some variance—10 percent from the least to the most populous districts was permitted if needed to prevent the dividing up of subunits of government.[78] Yet recently, in *Tennant v. Jefferson County*,[79] the Court seemed to back off on the mathematical identity or equality standard at the federal level, seeming to follow the rule it had for state and local districting that permitted consideration of local government boundaries when drawing lines. While it is too soon to tell, the current Supreme Court may be moving to adopt identical rules for congressional and non-congressional districting.

A final question when it comes to the one person, one vote standard relates to timing. Specifically, how often must redistricting occur in order to be compliant with the *Reynolds* standard? On the one side, while the Supreme Court has not ruled on this issue, several federal courts have held that, while adherence to the one person, one vote standard is mandatory, the interests of stability and letting

---

72   377 U.S. 713 at 738-39.
73   390 U.S. 474 (1968).
74   394 U.S. 526 (1969).
75   412 U.S. 783 (1973).
76   462 U.S. 725 (1983).
77   Stephenson, The Right to Vote at 236-37.
78   *See, e.g.*, Abate v. Mundt, 403 U.S. 182 (1971); Mahan v. Howell, 410 U.S. 315 (1973); and Gaffney v. Cummings, 412 U.S. 735 (1973).
79   —— U.S. ——, 133 S.Ct. 3 (2012).

incumbents complete their current terms do not require immediate elections based upon new population figures obtained in the most recent decennial census.[80] Yet conversely, the Supreme Court, in the recently decided *League of United Latin American Citizens v. Perry*,[81] held that the Constitution does not bar mid-decade redistricting, even when done solely for partisan motives.[82] Thus, states are free to redistrict more frequently than once per decade to meet the one person, one vote standard, but they also have some freedom beyond the decennial period to depart from it if promoting the stability of existing districts and letting incumbents finish terms are offered as competing interests.

So what do we learn from these cases when it comes to representation and reapportionment? The most important and perhaps the most quantifiable is the one person, one vote standard. Numeric or mathematical equality is the gold standard to ensure that voting power and representation is not diluted. But that standard needs to be balanced against other considerations that include compactness, contiguity, and increasingly respect for local governmental subdivisions. These are all traditional and acceptable redistricting criteria. These are all formal redistricting criteria. They do not speak to a more difficult question regarding the adequacy of representation. Perhaps this is a more substantive issue that is a matter of political debate. Determining or assessing whether representation is truly adequate may be up to the voters to decide. They may do that in terms of whether they feel their views or preferences are being considered. Yet there is also a sense here that the adequacy or effectiveness of representation is more than a political preference issue. For individuals perpetually in the minority in a district and where their representatives consistently vote contrary to their preferences, they may feel they are not adequately represented and opt to vote with their feet.[83] There is evidence across the United States of a geographic sorting that is creating areas that are solidly of one party preference versus another.[84] This might solve one problem regarding the adequacy problem by simply getting people to move to where they feel a sense of political identity or political belonging. But it creates a different problem—a lack of competitiveness of elections.

Competitive elections are critical to democratic theory, as noted in Chapter 2. They help ensure that officeholders and elected officials remain accountable to the voters. If there are competitive elections, voters have a choice, they can literally "Throw the bums out" if they do not like the current elected official.

---

80 *See, e.g.*, Political Action Conference of Illinois v. Daley, 976 F.2d 335 (7th Cir.1992) and French v. Boner, 963 F.2d 890 (6th Cir.1992).

81 548 U.S. 399 (2006).

82 *Id.* at 416-20.

83 BILL BISHOP, THE BIG SORT: WHY THE CLUSTERING OF LIKE-MINDED AMERICA IS TEARING US APART (2009).

84 *Id. But see:* Samuel J. Abrams and Morris P. Fiorina, *"The Big Sort" that Wasn't: A Skeptical Reexamination*, PS, 203 (April, 2012), arguing that the evidence for the geographic sorting of political or partisan polarization is lacking.

The threat of being ousted from office is the disciplinary tool to ensure that representatives remain accountable. Yet the geographic sorting that America is experiencing means that the number of truly swing congressional districts—those where there is a serious chance of an incumbent being ousted by an opposing party—is diminishing. Nate Silver, for example, argues that in 1992 there were 103 swing seats in Congress, by 2012 that number had decreased to 35.[85] If his analysis is correct, barely 8 percent of the seats in the House of Representatives are really swing where the threat of a serious challenge from the opposite party is real. Perhaps part of the issue is malapportionment but an equally challenging problem is the geographic sorting of neighborhoods along partisan preferences and identities. Micro-targeting in political messaging is premised upon the realization that there are significant overlaps in party preferences, identity, and consumerism. Geography matters to politics.[86]

If this political geography is correct, even absent gerrymandering it might be difficult to draw legislative or other offices in ways that promote competitive elections. It might require drawing lines in ways that compromise other important values such as compactness and continuity. Conversely, if the goal were to maximize competitiveness then there would be a problem with stability, another crucial value associated with democratic theory and representation. By that, if every race were competitive then the possible turnover of officeholders in every election would perhaps produce unstable governance. Madisonian democracy sought to slow down political change like this to prevent threats to liberty. But putting the brakes on change also means more continuity in office. Large turnovers of elected officials, as occurs with term limits, can lead to scenarios where there is a brain drain, loss of expertise, and perhaps overall damage to the ability of elected officials to have the collective skills necessary to do their job.

The broader point here is that the Supreme Court in its reapportionment jurisprudence has undervalued both geography and accountability as important redistricting criteria. In ignoring or undervaluing both it has failed to develop a jurisprudence that reflects two important values that should be addressed when representation and reapportionment are considered.

Partisan Gerrymandering

The concern with promoting competitive elections is not simply about accountability and the effectiveness of representation, it is also about seeking to discourage entrenchment by incumbents. All things being equal, incumbents

---

85   Nate Silver, *As Swing Districts Dwindle, Can a Divided House Stand?* N.Y. TIMES (December 27, 2012), located at http://fivethirtyeight.blogs.nytimes.com/2012/12/27/as-swing-districts-dwindle-can-a-divided-house-stand/ (site last viewed on March 14, 2013).

86   Renee Boucher Ferguson, *Candidates "microtarget" voters*, 25 EWEEK 18 (March 17, 2008).

would like to stay in office and they use the redistricting process to entrench themselves or their party.[87] This has been done ever since the early years of the American republic making it, perversely, a traditional criterion or practice used in redistricting. Yet such a value is not one that generally promotes democratic values. The question then first is whether it is acceptable for elected officials to use partisan affiliation or consider their re-election when redistricting? This gets to a difficult question the Court has sought to address in the last 20-30 years—partisan gerrymandering.

If venturing into reapportionment was not already a political thicket, confronting its most brazen form—partisan gerrymandering—definitely thrust the federal courts into the middle of controversy. If violation of the one person, one vote mandate and racial gerrymandering could be actionable under either the Fourteenth or Fifteenth Amendment, why could gerrymandering solely for the sake of partisan advantage not also be a constitutional violation? After all, was not the redrawing of lines to help incumbents or one particular party a practice that went all the way back to Ellbridge Gerry's day? To address partisan gerrymandering has been the object of three Supreme Court decisions that have done no more than muddle the issues.

First, in *Davis v. Bandemer*[88] at issue was a suit brought by Indiana Democrats contesting the constitutionality of a 1981 state redistricting plan. The specific allegation was that the plan drew legislative lines and seats in such a way to disadvantage Democrats. It did so by dividing up cities such as South Bend in arguably unusual ways.[89] The Democrats filed suit, contending that these districts violated their rights as Democrats, under the Fourteenth Equal Protection Clause.[90] The district court had ruled in favor of the Democrats, in part, because of evidence and testimony suggesting that the Republican Party had in fact drawn the lines to favor themselves.[91] When the case reached the Supreme Court a central issue was whether this was a justiciable controversy.[92] The Court held that it was.

To support its conclusion it returned to discussion of the political question doctrine that it had in *Baker v. Carr*.[93] It quoted from *Baker* its famous formulation of its view on what a political question was,[94] noting that, unless a matter was textually committed to another branch, required a specific type of policy determination not appropriate for the Court, or there were missing manageable standards for resolving the controversy, the issue should be addressed by the federal

---

87   DAVID MAYHEW, CONGRESS: THE ELECTORAL CONNECTION (2004).
88   478 U.S. 109 (1986).
89   478 U.S. 109 at 115.
90   *Id.*
91   *Id.* at 117.
92   *Id.* at 117-18.
93   *Id.* at 121.
94   *Id.* at 121-22 (*quoting* Baker at 396 U.S. at 217).

judiciary. Finding that none of the characteristics outlined in *Baker* existed in the political gerrymandering case before it, it held that the matter was justiciable.[95]

Yet while the case was deemed justiciable, it did not uphold *in toto* the lower court's determination that there was a constitutional violation in *Bandemer*. Instead, the Court articulated several stipulations that had to be met to sustain a political gerrymandering claim. First, there had to be proof of intentional discrimination against the one party, here, the Democrats.[96] Second, "a group's electoral power is not unconstitutionally diminished by the simple fact of an apportionment scheme that makes winning elections more difficult, and a failure of proportional representation alone does not constitute impermissible discrimination under the Equal Protection Clause."[97] Instead, the Court stated that the political process must frustrate political activity in a systematic fashion:

> As in individual district cases, an equal protection violation may be found only where the electoral system substantially disadvantages certain voters in their opportunity to influence the political process effectively. In this context, such a finding of unconstitutionality must be supported by evidence of continued frustration of the will of a majority of the voters or effective denial to a minority of voters of a fair chance to influence the political process.[98]

Finally, the Court contended that showing frustration or dilution of political influence in one election was also insufficient.[99] Instead, it would need to be shown that it took place over several elections.[100] In sum, to support a constitutional claim for partisan gerrymandering the *Bandemer* Court stated that one would have to demonstrate intentional discrimination against a party that systematically frustrated and diluted their ability to influence the political process across several elections.[101] What emerged from *Bandemer* was perhaps the manageable standards called for in *Baker* that would allow the federal judiciary to resolve a controversy. Yet the three conditions of the case proved to be anything but manageable, and the federal courts had never invalidated a redistricting plan as a partisan gerrymander.[102] This led to demands for the Court to rethink the question of the justiciability of partisan gerrymandering. It did that first in *Vieth v. Jubelirer*[103] and then again in *League of United Latin American Citizens v. Perry*.[104]

---

95 *Id.* at 126-27.
96 *Id.* at 127-28.
97 *Id.* at 131.
98 *Id.* at 132.
99 *Id.* at 135.
100 *Id.*
101 Stephenson at 246.
102 *Id.* at 246-47.
103 541 U.S. 267 (2004).
104 548 U.S. 399 (2006).

In *Vieth* at issue was the constitutionality of a Pennsylvania districting plan that drew the seats for its congressional delegation after the 2000 census. Prior to the census the state had 21 representatives but after 2000 it was only entitled to 19 seats.[105] Republicans controlled both houses of the Pennsylvania legislature as well as the governor's office.[106] State Democrats contended that the district lines drawn constituted both a violation of the one person, one vote standard and, more importantly here, a partisan gerrymander.[107] The district court dismissed the partisan or political gerrymandering claim[108] (with some of the other issues addressed or resolved in other litigation in the case) and it was appealed to the Supreme Court. It what was clearly a split decision if ever one existed, the Supreme Court ruled several things. First, a four-person plurality opinion written by Justice Scalia reviewed the history of partisan gerrymandering in the United States, concluding that such a practice went back to the early days of the republic.[109] Given this history, there had also been numerous efforts to address it, with the Court first in *Baker v. Carr* seeking to demonstrate why redistricting issues were justiciable.[110] The Court keyed in on the *Baker* discussion that judicially manageable standards or a clear rule was needed for the judiciary to resolve a controversy.[111] Scalia argued that the standards for addressing partisan gerrymandering in *Bandemer* had proved unworkable[112] and therefore that case should be overturned. In effect, a four Justice plurality ruled that partisan gerrymanders were not justiciable and therefore in the case before them the claims of the Democrats should be rejected.

However, only four Justices agreed that the Democrats had not proved that a partisan gerrymander existed in the case before and that this type of issue was not justiciable. Justice Kennedy concurred that there was no partisan gerrymander here, but he refused to go along with overruling *Bandemer*.[113] He agreed that neutral rules for resolving and adjudicating partisan gerrymanders were needed but he did not agree with the majority that it would never be possible to find them.[114] This thus created a five Justice majority to reject the plaintiff's claims. However, four Justices in several dissents, joined by Kennedy, refused to overrule *Bandemer*, making at least in theory partisan gerrymanders justiciable issues. What the dissenters could not agree on were what constituted acceptable or manageable standards for adjudicating a partisan gerrymander dispute. The hope

---

105 541 U.S. at 272.
106 *Id.*
107 *Id.* 272.
108 *Id.* at 273.
109 *Id.* at 274.
110 *Id.* at 278.
111 *Id.* at 278.
112 *Id.* at 278.
113 *Id.* at 306-7.
114 *Id.*

was that *League of United Latin American Citizens v. Perry* (*LULAC*) would do that, but it did not.

LULAC arose out of a high-profile partisan struggle in the Texas legislature that involved U.S. Representative Tom DeLay and a battle for the state legislature and its congressional delegation. The 2000 census indicated that the State of Texas should receive two additional seats in the House of Representatives beyond the current 30 that it had.[115] At the time of redistricting, the Texas Republican Party controlled the State Senate and governor's office but the Democrats controlled the State House of Representatives.[116] As the parties were unable to agree to adopt a redistricting scheme, litigation eventually led to the creation of a court-ordered one.[117] This plan produced a 17-15 Democratic majority in the Texas congressional delegation.[118] But in 2003 state elections gave Republicans control of both houses of the state legislature as well as control of the governor's office.[119] With the encouragement of Tom DeLay, and after a long struggle—including Democrats in the legislature hiding out in Oklahoma to avoid a special session—the state passed a new redistricting plan in 2003.[120] In 2004, elections using this new plan gave Republicans 58 percent of the statewide vote compared to 41 percent for Democrats. Republicans also captured 21 of the congressional seats to the 11 won by the Democrats.[121] LULAC challenged the 2003 plan in court, claiming, *inter alia* that it was a partisan gerrymander and that the state and federal constitutions barred a second redistricting scheme following a decennial census.[122] Judgment was for the appellees but, in light of the *Vieth v. Jubelirer* decision, the Supreme Court vacated that decision and remanded to reconsider.[123] The district court solely considered the political gerrymandering claim and again ruled in favor of the appellees.[124] Before the Supreme Court were arguments that the 2003 redistricting schema was a partisan or political gerrymander, that it violated the Voting Rights Act (VRA), and that the mid-decade redistricting violated the one-person, one-vote requirement under the Fourteenth Amendment.[125] While the Court did find that one of the districts did violate the VRA,[126] it rejected claims that a mid-decade redistricting violated the Constitution and it also ruled that the appellants had failed to state a claim upon which relief could be granted for the political gerrymander.

115 548 U.S. 399, 410-12.
116 *Id.*
117 *Id.*
118 *Id.* at 412-13.
119 *Id.*
120 *Id.*
121 *Id.*
122 *Id.*
123 *Id.*
124 *Id.*
125 *Id.*
126 548 U.S. 399, 441-42 (*finding* that district 23 did violate the VRA). For the purposes of this analysis, the VRA claim shall not be discussed.

Justice Kennedy, writing for yet another divided Court when it came to the partisan gerrymander claim, specifically noted that the theory of the plaintiffs was that a mid-decade redistricting when solely motivated by partisan objectives violated the Fourteenth Amendment.[127] A majority of the Court rejected this claim,[128] stating that not every line drawn was done based on partisan objectives.[129] Yet even if mixed motives were not present in this case, Kennedy asserted that one challenging a gerrymander as partisan would have to show how it burdened, according to a reliable standard, their representational rights.[130] The simple fact that a mid-decade redistricting schema took place is rejected as a *per se* standard to show burden.[131] Similarly, the claim that a mid-decade redistricting violates the one-person, one-vote requirement if done for partisan purposes is also rejected.[132] Overall, while Kennedy clearly stated that this decision did not revisit the justiciability of partisan gerrymandering, he rejected the tests offered in this case to define a standard for resolving disputes averring this as a claim.[133]

The decision in *LULAC* offered little clarification on what a partisan gerrymander is when compared to the *Jubelirer*. Partisan gerrymandering is still justiciable but no manageable standard exists upon which the Court can provide relief. This is no different than where the Court was after *Jubelirer*. The Court also appears as fractured as before regarding the justiciability, and there is still no majority willing to overturn *Bandemer*. Perhaps the only clarity to result from the decision is that it does not appear that mid-decade redistricting is barred by the Constitution, whether done from mixed motives or only for partisan purposes.

Partisan Gerrymandering and the First Amendment

The Supreme Court remains divided after *LULAC* regarding what to do with partisan gerrymandering. The litigation following the 2010 census and redistricting failed to address this issue too. While in theory partisan gerrymanders are justiciable, there is no manageable standard that has been accepted by the Court to define when a violation has occurred. The Court does not seem even to be able to agree what a partisan gerrymander is or even if such a phenomenon constitutionally exists, let alone whether it is illegal. Does this mean that the Court should stay out of the partisan gerrymandering thicket? Not necessarily. There is a different approach that can be taken, drawing upon the Liberal concept of political neutrality. This argument would follow the direction

---

127 548 U.S. 399, 416-17.
128 *Id.*
129 *Id.*
130 *Id.*
131 *Id.*
132 *Id.* at 421.
133 *Id.* at 414.

suggested by Kennedy and Stevens in *Vieth* and Stevens in *LULAC* and use the First Amendment as the constitutional hook to address these claims?

In *Vieth* Justice Kennedy responds to criticism from Scalia's plurality opinion that he sought to resolve the dispute in this case by an appeal to fairness and not a standard.[134] Yet in searching for a standard to address the case he notes that perhaps another "subsidiary standard" besides the equal protection clause might be more appropriate:

> Though in the briefs and at argument the appellants relied on the Equal Protection Clause as the source of their substantive right and as the basis for relief, I note that the complaint in this case also alleged a violation of First Amendment rights. The First Amendment may be the more relevant constitutional provision in future cases that allege unconstitutional partisan gerrymandering. After all, these allegations involve the First Amendment interest of not burdening or penalizing citizens because of their participation in the electoral process, their voting history, their association with a political party, or their expression of political views.[135]

Justice Kennedy suggested that within the First Amendment jurisprudence, especially in the patronage decisions such as *Elrod v. Burns*,[136] or some of the political party associational rights decisions such as *Democratic Party v. Jones*,[137] might offer a basis for making this claim in that he sees these cases as supporting the propositions that the state cannot enact a law burdening individuals' representational rights or considering their political views absent a compelling governmental interest.[138] Kennedy also offers a brief but undeveloped analysis of how a First Amendment jurisprudence would work in comparison to an equal protection approach, noting how the former looks to the burden on representational rights while the latter looks to the permissibility of the classification.[139]

In addition to these brief words by Kennedy in *Vieth*, Justice Stevens in both this case and *LULAC* drops similar hints about a First Amendment analysis as applies to political gerrymandering. In *Vieth* he argues that the Constitution requires neutrality regarding individuals' political beliefs, and he also cites the patronage cases for the proposition that it is not legitimate for the government to discriminate on the basis of politics, political affiliation, or speech.[140] In *LULAC* Stevens again makes the same point both when he cites to Kennedy's *Vieth* discussion and when

---

134 *Id.* at 313-14.
135 *Id.* at 314.
136 427 U.S. 347 (1976).
137 *Id.* (*citing* 427 U.S. 327 (1976) and 530 U.S. 567 (2000)).
138 541 U.S. at 314.
139 *Id.*
140 *Id.* at 317, 324.

he seeks to blend a First Amendment and Equal Protection analysis to partisan gerrymanders:

> The requirements of the Federal Constitution that limit the State's power to rely exclusively on partisan preferences in drawing district lines are the Fourteenth Amendment's prohibition against invidious discrimination, and the First Amendment's protection of citizens from official retaliation based on their political affiliation. The equal protection component of the Fourteenth Amendment requires actions taken by the sovereign to be supported by some legitimate interest, and further establishes that a bare desire to harm a politically disfavored group is not a legitimate interest. See, *e.g., Cleburne v. Cleburne Living Center, Inc.,* 473 U.S. 432, 447, 105 S.Ct. 3249, 87 L.Ed.2d 313 (1985). Similarly, the freedom of political belief and association guaranteed by the First Amendment prevents the State, absent a compelling interest, from "penalizing citizens because of their participation in the electoral process, ... their association with a political party, or their expression of political views."[141]

Unfortunately, beyond this brief fragment, Stevens does little to develop his blended First Amendment/Equal Protection analysis in a way that offers a clear manageable standard accepted by a majority of the Court for adjudicating political gerrymanders.

After *Vieth* there was a flurry of authors who examined the First Amendment challenges of Kennedy and Stevens. These authors—many of them the leading authors in the field of constitutional and election law—were almost unanimous in their dismissal of the shift from the equal protection clause to the First Amendment in addressing partisan gerrymanders.

One line of criticism is that regulation of partisan gerrymanders is not a judicial function. Peter Shuck,[142] for example, writing after *Bandemer*, best captured this sentiment and appeared to anticipate Justice Scalia's arguments in *Vieth* when he argued that partisan gerrymanders are nonjusticiable and that the Court should not try to adjudicate them. For Shuck: "Judicial regulation of partisan gerrymandering would be a cure worse than the disease."[143] According to Shuck, the Constitution does not require political perfection and instead the gerrymandering that exists in our society is the price we pay for a robust political environment that is open and free. Gerrymandering, as a long-standing practice, is something that is politically legitimate and congruent with our political norms.[144] In short, his advice: Learn to live with partisan gerrymanders.

---

141 126 S.Ct. at 2634.
142 Peter H. Shuck, The Thickest Thicket: Partisan Gerrymandering and Judicial Regulation of Politics, 87 COLUM. L. REV. 1325 (1987).
143 *Id.* at 1330.
144 *Id.*

Shuck would withdraw the Court from the political thicket of partisan gerrymanders. Others, including Nathaniel Persily, agreed.[145] Yet others writing after *Vieth*, did not go quite that far, instead confining their criticism of the opinion and the First Amendment turn to other matters. Rick Hasen[146] carps that *Democratic Party v. Jones* does not support Kennedy's associational harm argument or that it is about people who are subject to disfavored treatment based on their views.[147] This case, he contends, is about forced association. In terms of referencing the patronage cases, Hasen states that there the burden or harm is tangible—individuals lose their jobs—but the harm is not so clear in cracking or packing party members in the partisan gerrymandering cases.[148] Thus, citing to or referencing the patronage cases as precedent the way Kennedy does is illegitimate or incorrect for Hasen.

Issacharoff and Karlan make a similar claim about the patronage cases,[149] but they ground their argument in a broader philosophical context. The inapplicability of the patronage cases to partisan gerrymanders lies in the fact that the injury in the former resided outside of the political process. By that, their harm "did not require the reviewing court to articulate a political philosophy or to decide in the abstract what constituted a fair employment or contracting policy."[150] In contrast, they contend, as a second criticism of the First Amendment approach, that "in a political gerrymandering case, the question whether 'an apportionment has the purpose and effect of burdening a group of voters' representational rights' requires deciding what voters' 'representational rights' are."[151] Missing from the First Amendment analysis is a broader democratic theory that explains what representational rights are,[152] or a political philosophy that informs constitutional theory regarding the scope of majoritarian politics and what is permissible in popular politics.[153] Lacking this broader theory, their criticism of Kennedy is simply put:

> [T]he distinction between relying on the Equal Protection Clause and relying on the First Amendment lies in the fact that "equal protection analysis puts its emphasis on the permissibility of an enactment's classifications" while First Amendment analysis "concentrates on whether the legislation burdens the

---

145   Nathaniel Persily, *In Defense of Foxes Guarding Henhouses: The Case for Judicial Acquiescence to Incumbent-Protecting Gerrymanders*, 116 HARV. L. REV. 649, 652-53 (2002).

146   Richard L. Hasen, *Looking for Standards (In All the Wrong Places): Partisan Gerrymandering Claims after Vieth*, 3 ELECTION L. J. 626 (Winter 2004).

147   *Id.* at 636.

148   *Id.*

149   Samuel Issacharoff and Pamela S. Karlan, *Where to Draw the Line?: Judicial Review of Political Gerrymanders*, 153 U. PENN. L. REV. 541, 563 (2004).

150   Issacharoff and Karlan at 563.

151   *Id.*

152   *Id.* at 564.

153   *Id.* at 543, 560.

representational rights of the complaining party's voters," as Justice Kennedy would have it, simply ignores the question that "representational rights" are as yet undefined.[154]

In addition to Issacharoff and Karlan, others such as Driver,[155] Berman,[156] Charles,[157] and Lewis[158] made similar appeals to broader political theories or approaches as a prerequisite to the articulation of clear standards.

Absent a clear political theory that explains what or why partisan gerrymandering is wrong leads to a third criticism of the judicial attempts to correct partisan gerrymanders—a lack of clear and manageable standards. This lack of clear standards is why Shuck contends that this issue should be left to the political process to address.[159] Hasen would pull a Bork[160] and wait for clear standards to emerge through an evolving social consensus,[161] while, as noted, Issacharoff and Karlan would have us wait for a democratic theory to provide guidance in ascertaining clear and manageable standards.[162]

A fourth criticism, most vigorously made by Rick Pildes, is that the First Amendment protects individual rights but that partisan gerrymandering is a structural problem.[163] Specifically, Pildes argues that individual rights adjudication either is not appropriate for addressing structural issues such as gerrymandering, or such an individualistic rights-based strategy is categorically different than the broader principles demanded to bring about structural reform.[164] Issacharoff and Karlan's appeal to a broader theory similarly seems to make the same assumption.[165] All three of them roughly draw a dichotomy between individual rights and governmental structure, as if the two are distinct and as apparently unrelated as a

---

154 *Id.* at 564.

155 Justin Driver, *Rules, the New Standards: Partisan Gerrymandering and Judicial Manageability after Vieth V. Jubelirer*, 73 GEO. WASH. L. REV. 1166, 1179 (2005).

156 Mitchell N. Berman, *Managing Gerrymandering*, 83 TEX. L. REV. 781, 783(2005).

157 Guy-Uriel Charles, *Judging the Law of Politics*, 103 MICH. L. REV. 1099, 1131-39 (2005).

158 Erika Lewis, *Trailblaze or Retreat? Political Gerrymandering after Vieth v. Jubelirer*, 27 U. HAW. L. REV. 269, 271 (2004).

159 Shuck at 1330.

160 *See:* Robert Bork, *Neutral Principles and Some First Amendment Problems*, 47 IND. L. J. 1 (1971) (*arguing* that if the Court cannot resolve a case by neutral principles given to it by another body it should not hear the case).

161 Hasen at 628.

162 Issacharoff and Karlan at 543, 560, 563.

163 Richard H. Pildes, *The Constitutionalization of Democratic Politics* 11 HARV. L. REV. 28, 58 (2004). *See also:* Charles, *Judging the Law of Politics* 103 MICH. L. REV. 1099, 1132 (2005), for a similar understanding of Pildes' arguments.

164 Pildes at 58-59.

165 Issacharoff and Karlan at 543, 560, 563.

Kantian antinomy.[166] In making these arguments, they seem to be aping Scalia's points in *Vieth* that there is a problem moving from individual claims at the district level about representational rights to statewide assertions regarding impermissible First Amendment motives.[167]

On top of the above four points, others criticized the First Amendment approach to addressing partisan gerrymandering for a variety of reasons. Richard Briffault appears to agree with Scalia that a First Amendment approach to addressing partisan gerrymanders would imprudently eliminate all political criteria from the districting process.[168] Conversely if such an approach did not do that then it would leave less clear criteria in place regarding when partisan considerations were permissible,[169] short of falling into the trap of proportional representation as the adjudicated remedy.[170] For some, the First Amendment either provides standards no more exact than the Equal Protection clause[171] or that any standards that might result would not be clear no matter what.[172]

Overall, scholars and election law specialists have been critically unsympathetic to using the First Amendment to adjudicating partisan gerrymanders. Joann Kamuf, in one of the few articles defending the First Amendment turn,[173] nicely summarizes criticisms of this approach to addressing partisan districting. For Kamuf, claims that redistricting is a task for the political branches to address, or that no manageable standards can be found, or that reapportionment require the courts to make policy decisions, are all potential objections.[174] In addition to what Kamuf lists, lack of a theory to guide the Court, the gap between individual rights and government structure, and the inapposite use of the patronage and party cases by Kennedy to support his propositions, round out the criticisms of the First Amendment turn.

---

166   IMMANUEL KANT, CRITIQUE OF PURE REASON, trans. Norman Kemp Smith, 328, 396 (1965) (*describing* how certain paired assertions or propositions such as reason and empiricism stand in apparent contradiction or separation from one another).

167   541 U.S. at 284.

168   Richard Briffault, *Defining the Constitutional Question in Partisan Gerrymandering*, 14 CORNELL J. L. & PUB. POL'Y 397, 408 (2005); *Compare* to Scalia at 541 U.S. at 294.

169   Briffault at 409.

170   *Id.*

171   Driver at 1179; *The Supreme Court, 2003 Term, Leading Cases Constitutional Law*, 118 HARV. L. REV. 343, 351 (2004).

172   Hasen 2004 at 628; Adam Raviv, *Unsafe Harbors: One-person, one-vote and Partisan Redistricting*, 7 U. PA. J. CONST. L. 1001, 1050 (2005).

173   Joann D. Kamuf, *Should I Stay or Should I Go?: The Current State of Partisan Gerrymandering Adjudication and a Proposal for the Future*, 74 FORDHAM L. REV. 163, 204-11 (2005) (*arguing* that the First Amendment may in fact provide a viable alternative to the equal protection analysis).

174   Kamuf at 198-201.

Is the First Amendment fundamentally flawed as a tool for adjudicating partisan gerrymanders as critics contend? Despite some nitpicking and more serious criticisms, a turn towards a First Amendment approach is still worth a try. At the worst it would produce results no worse than presently yielded with the Equal Protection clause and at best, it would resolve a vexing problem that the Court has sought to resolve since *Bandemer*. In offering a First Amendment approach to the partisan gerrymandering problem, one can argue with many of the criticisms of Issacharoff and Karlan that a broader political philosophy or democratic theory is needed to justify or support the constitutional argument. The theory that provides this foundation is classical Liberalism. However, in offering that theory, the argument here makes two other points. First, Scalia and others who argue that politics or partisanship are relevant criteria in redistricting are wrong. Instead, Liberal thought, as it will be shown, demands political neutrality, especially in terms of the construction of the basic institutions of government. Second, Pildes and other who argue that a First Amendment rights strategy is inappropriate or an unsatisfactory means to bringing about structural changes are incorrect because rights and structure are connected ontologically, legally, and conceptually.

Democracy, Liberal Theory. and Partisan Neutrality

American political and democratic theory is heavily influenced and defined by Liberalism and a liberal tradition.[175] According to John Rawls, neutrality is a central concept of liberal thought.[176] In making this claim Rawls appeals to one of the precepts of classical Liberal thought which contends that the state or the government should remain neutral regarding the life choices and preferences of its citizens.[177] This notion of neutrality, grounded in epistemological objectivity,[178] religious toleration,[179] and the political premises of equality and liberty for all,[180] represents a belief that the government should generally not substitute its concept of the good or the good life for that determined by each individual citizen.

---

175 LOUIS HARTZ, THE LIBERAL TRADITION IN AMERICA: AN INTERPRETATION OF AMERICAN POLITICAL THOUGHT SINCE THE REVOLUTION (1955); JOHN PATRICK DIGGINS, THE LOST SOUL OF AMERICAN POLITICS: VIRTUE, SELF-INTEREST, AND THE FOUNDATIONS OF LIBERALISM (1984); David Schultz, *Political Theory and Legal History: Conflicting Depictions of Property in the American Political Founding*, 37 AMERICAN JOURNAL OF LEGAL HISTORY, 464 (1993).

176 JOHN RAWLS, POLITICAL LIBERALISM, 190 (1993).

177 GUIDO DE RUGGIERO, THE HISTORY OF EUROPEAN LIBERALISM, 363 (1959); Rawls, A Theory of Justice, 254.

178 RICHARD RORTY, PHILOSOPHY AND THE MIRROR OF NATURE, 131-65 (1979).

179 RICHARD ASHCRAFT, REVOLUTIONARY POLITICS & LOCKE'S TWO TREATISES OF GOVERNMENT, 37-41 (1986).

180 FRANKLIN L. BAUMER, MODERN EUROPEAN THOUGHT: CONTINUITY AND CHANGE IN IDEAS, 1600-1650, 218-36 (1977).

John Locke locates the concept of neutrality both within his writings on government neutrality towards religion,[181] the idea of toleration,[182] and a natural law framework that respects the inherent rights of all individuals to make claims against the government and political society from interfering with their life, liberty, and estate.[183] With Kant, the concept of neutrality is grounded in the individual capacity of citizens to use their own public reason to render political judgments.[184] Similarly, John Rawls situates this neutrality within a Kantian respect for the inherent dignity of rational beings to make choices regarding the ends or goals of their life,[185] and for his eventual prioritization of the right over the good,[186] and respect for the equality of conscience of all.[187] Finally, Jürgen Habermas would see neutrality as grounded in non-hierarchal bargaining and communication that takes place in the public sphere, making possible democratic decision-making.[188] While many sources could be cited for this proposition, it is sufficient to state that John Rawls is correct in his basic point that neutrality is important to Liberal thought, eventually manifesting itself in the law in several ways, including the concepts of free speech, religious toleration, equal protection, and equality before the law.[189]

Neutrality demands thus a sense of disinterestedness by the state in its attitude towards the political and often moral preferences of its citizens. As Rawls recognized in *Political Liberalism*, citizens approach the public sphere from a diversity of moral, religious, and political perspectives; the task of reaching political agreement is respect for this diversity, building upon it an overlapping consensus that must start with an understanding that the state may not favor the views of some at the expense of others.[190] How does this concept of neutrality translate over into politics, or more specifically, into the use of partisanship or

---

181   John Locke, *The Spirit of Toleration*, In STERLING P. LAMPRECHT, ED., LOCKE SELECTIONS, 43 (1956): "Absolute Liberty, just and true liberty, equal and impartial liberty, is the thing that we stand in need of."

182   JOHN LOCKE, A LETTER CONCERNING TOLERATION, 29-30, 49 (1979).

183   John Locke, *An Essay Concerning the True Origin, Extent, and End of Civil Government*, in JOHN LOCKE, TWO TREATISES OF GOVERNMENT, para. 54, 87 (1963).

184   Immanuel Kant, *An Answer to the Question: What is Enlightenment?*, 54, 55-59, in HANS REISS, ED., KANT'S POLITICAL WRITINGS (1979) (*arguing* that the hallmark of the Enlightenment is a monarch deferring to citizens to make public use of their own reason).

185   Rawls, A Theory of Justice at 254.

186   *Id.* at 446-52.

187   *Id.* at 211-16.

188   JÜRGEN HABERMAS, THE STRUCTURAL TRANSFORMATION OF THE PUBLIC SPHERE, 198-205 (1989).

189   *See, e.g.*, RODNEY A. SMOLLA, FREE SPEECH IN AN OPEN SOCIETY, 46, 183-85 (1992); and OWEN M. FISS, LIBERALISM DIVIDED: FREEDOM OF SPEECH AND THE MANY USES OF STATE POWER, 109-20 (1996) (*describing* in both books how the concept of neutrality in embedded in the law, especially the First Amendment).

190   Rawls, Political Liberalism at 145-46, 190.

political preferences in the drawing of district lines? Here is where one can appeal to Liberalism, Rawls, and his construction of the basic rules of justice.

A Theory of Justice seeks to construct the rule of justice that will govern the basic institutions of a society.[191] Drawing upon classical social contract theory which situates individuals in a prepolitical state of nature who are asked to devise a government for themselves, Rawls asks what type of basic institutions of justice would rational but mutually disinterested individuals construct for themselves when they are placed under a veil of ignorance.[192] Behind this veil of ignorance individuals have general knowledge of their society but they do not know certain facts such as "his place in society, his class position or social status; nor does he know his fortune in the distribution of natural assets and abilities, his intelligence, and strength, and the like."[193]

In effect, stripped of knowledge of personal attributes such as our gender, race, and religion, and therefore rendering them as impartial decision-makers stripped of personal bias—therefore neutral—individuals are called upon to construct the rules of justice that will govern their society. Moreover, Rawls depicts individuals as self-interested and rational maximizers, wanting more as opposed to less social goods,[194] which therefore means that they might be unlikely to base social distributions based upon immutable characteristics which they cannot control and which they have no personal knowledge of under the veil of ignorance.[195] Under these constraints, Rawls contends that individuals would opt for his two principles of justice over a utilitarian theory of distribution.[196] The two principles of justice thus embody a sense of right over good as well as political neutrality. They state that "each person is to have an equal right to the most extensive basic liberty compatible with a similar liberty for others" and "social and economic inequalities are to be arranged so that they are both (a) reasonably expected to be to everyone's advantage, and (b) attached to positions and offices open to all."[197]

What are we to make of the veil of ignorance, the Rawlsian bargaining game, and the two principles of justice that he claims individuals would construct to order their society? Imagine individuals behind Rawls' veil of ignorance asked to devise rules of justice that will order their society, including their political and governmental institutions. Would such individuals, unaware of their partisan preferences, be willing to let such partisan values or preferences factor into the organization of the government? The answer is probably not, at least when it comes

---

191   Rawls, A Theory of Justice at 54-60.
192   *Id.* at 137.
193   *Id.*
194   *Id.* at 142-49.
195   *Id.* at 17-22, 142-49.
196   *Id.* 17-22.
197   *Id.* at 60. Rawls will subsequently offer various formulations of these two rules, with (b), the difference principle, eventually modified to require inequalities to work to the advantage of the least advantaged n society. *See, e.g.*, Rawls, A Theory of Justice at 96-98.

to the rules determining the awarding of political representatives. A Rawlsian individual behind the veil of ignorance would probably be unlikely to let partisan considerations drive districting, for fear that, once the veil of ignorance is lifted, seats and boundaries would potentially be drawn to their political disadvantage.

The point with this Rawlsian construct and appeal to Liberalism is simple: It is unlikely that partisan preferences would be an acceptable criterion for the drawing of district lines either under the principle of neutrality inherent in Liberal thought or in a situation where individuals were in a bargaining game, asked to design the basic institutional rules of justice, and they did not know what their partisan identity is. Partisanship, contra to Scalia, Shuck, Briffault, and others who contend that it is not an illegitimate factor in redistricting, simply have it wrong. Nonpartisan districting is dictated by a political philosophy that lies at the heart of American constitutional theory and the First Amendment[198] and there is nothing inconsistent in arguing that such an imperative should apply in an all-or-nothing fashion.

A second objection leveled at a First Amendment turn towards addressing partisan districting is that a rights-based strategy is inappropriate for bringing about structural changes such as in representation. Critics who make this argument, or some permutation of it, both misunderstand the nature of litigation and the relationship between rights and governmental or political structures.

Consider first the nature of litigation. Charles has pointed out that a rights-based strategy has changed the structure of reapportionment already when it comes to the one person, one vote standard and in terms of the racial gerrymandering.[199] The judiciary has been exceedingly successful since *Baker v. Carr* in forcing states to undertake decennial redistricting that conforms to the one-person, one-vote mandate, and since *Gomillion v. Lightfoot* and the adoption of the Voting Rights Act the courts have also been very successful promoting minority voting and representation.[200]

Second, one can also read the rights-structure argument as a claim about judicial efficacy, specifically, that the courts are not effective in undertaking efforts to redraw district lines and therefore would not be effective in seeking to effect nonpartisan districting. This objection, if empirical, can be rejected by looking at

---

198 *See:* Stephen E. Gottlieb, *Fashioning A Test for Gerrymandering*, 15 J. LEGIS. 1, 11 (1988-89); and Stephen E. Gottlieb, *The Speech Clause and the Limits of Neutrality*, 51 ALB. L. REV. 19 (1986) (*describing* the role neutrality plays in the First Amendment).

199 Guy-Uriel Charles, *Judging the Law of Politics*, 103 MICH. L. REV. 1099, 1131-39; and Guy-Uriel Charles, *Racial Identity, Electoral Structures, and the First Amendment*, 91 CAL. L. REV.1209 (2003) (*contending* that a First Amendment analysis might be appropriate when it addresses the political activity of racial minorities).

200 *See, e.g.*, CHANDLER DAVIDSON AND BERNARD GROFMAN, EDS., QUIET REVOLUTION IN THE SOUTH: THE IMPACT OF THE VOTING RIGHTS ACT, 1965-1990 (1994) (*discussing* the impact of the Voting Rights Act on representation and voting among African-Americans in the South).

the 40 years of history the courts have had in redistricting since *Baker*. By that, there is no evidence that the courts have done a worse job than legislatures in districting and, in fact, given that the political branches have foot-dragged and fought the one person, one vote standard and the efforts to root out racism in this process, the courts come out looking quite good. Yet if the objection is normative (the courts ought not to address partisan districting), then one is arguing nothing more than a question about the proper role for judges in our society. Ultimately, judicial role hangs both on the type of debate Justice Brennan engaged in over the justiciability of reapportionment in *Baker v. Carr*, or in a discussion about the courts and their relationship to the political process in a democratic society.[201] Normative disagreements are differences in kind from empirical ones.

A third sense about what the rights-structure argument means looks at the nature of litigation. All litigation is really rights-based in the sense that some type of injury must be demonstrated for a party to have standing. One cannot simply sue claiming a deficient process or structure unless ultimately one shows an injury. In terms of the First Amendment, several authors have developed elaborate arguments discussing how free speech or association claims are linked to structural conceptions of how society operates.[202] Thus, litigation can have numerous goals, sometimes among which is an effort to bring about social change or institutional reform.[203]

Yet a fourth sense in which rights and structure are connected can be understood from the perspective of looking at the underlying or internal connections that exist in the law. These connections can be understood in several ways. Perhaps the most simple is Wesley Hohfeld's claim that there are basic connections among and between legal concepts such as rights and duties or powers and liabilities.[204] Hohfeld's famous article sought to demonstrate the "intrinsic meaning and scope"

---

201 *See, e.g.*, JOHN HART ELY, DEMOCRACY AND DISTRUST: A THEORY OF JUDICIAL REVIEW (1980) (*examining* the impact of the *Carolene Products* footnote number 4 upon the Warren Court's jurisprudence).

202 *See, e.g.*, STEVEN H. SHIFFRIN, THE FIRST AMENDMENT, DEMOCRACY, AND ROMANCE, 58-63 (1990) (*connecting* First Amendment litigation to limits on majority power); David Schultz and Stephen E. Gottlieb, *Legal Functionalism and Social Change: A Reassessment of Rosenberg's The Hollow Hope*, 169, 186, in DAVID SCHULTZ, ED., LEVERAGING THE LAW: USING THE COURTS TO ACHIEVE SOCIAL CHANGE (1998)) (*noting* how not all rights litigation is the same, embodying the same functionalist or structural goals ,and how the purpose of rights claims is often to induce structural responses from the courts or other government actors); and Stephen E. Gottlieb and David Schultz, *Empirical Analysis and Fundamental First Amendment Principles*, 19 J. L & POL. 145 (2003) (*examining* the impact of First Amendment litigation upon social toleration).

203 *See, e.g.*, David Schultz, *Courts and Law in American Society*, in DAVID SCHULTZ, ED., LEVERAGING THE LAW: USING THE COURTS TO ACHIEVE SOCIAL CHANGE, 1 (1998) (*reviewing* the literature and research on the use of litigation to effect social and institutional change).

204 Wesley Newcomb Hohfeld, *Some Fundamental Legal Conceptions as Applied in Judicial Reasoning*, 23 YALE L. J. 16, 30-31 (1913).

of several critical legal concepts, as well as "their relations to one another and the methods to which they are applied."²⁰⁵ Hohfeld demonstrated interconnections in legal terms and, although "rights" were not connected to "structure" in his essay, it is impossible to understand the former without seeing it as a limit upon the latter. By that, if the Constitution confers a power upon the federal government, such as an ability to tax and spend money for the general welfare, a First Amendment right might serve as a limit upon it if expenditure is to serve a religious purpose.²⁰⁶ Thus, rights imply a relational standing to government structure; change one and the meaning of the other also changes.

Another way to comprehend this relationship is to view the law as a Wittgensteinian language game.²⁰⁷ Here we can draw an analogy, stating that law resembles language in several ways.²⁰⁸ First, both law and language are a collection of concepts.²⁰⁹ These concepts acquire their meaning both in terms of how they are used²¹⁰ and in their relationship to one another within a specific language game.²¹¹ Social conventions also determine the meaning of words, with an agreement on the use of a word critical to deciding how it shall be used within a language.²¹² Finally (for the purposes of this article) language is ultimately grounded in social practices and conventions which Wittgenstein refers to as a "form of life."²¹³ Applying this simplified language model to law, legal concepts such as rights, constitution, and representation acquire a meaning based on use and within a context of how other words are defined. Agreements on the meaning of terms is critical to the process of legal interpretation or legal hermeneutics, offering rules on how to read legal texts and render the meaning of terms based, in part, on the structure of sentences and the terms they contain. Finally, if language ultimately sources its meanings in practices that are part of a form of life, one could argue that law itself arrives at its meanings in a set of social practices, customs, and perhaps even a political philosophy, such as Liberalism.

The point in pushing a Wittgensteinian parallel of law and language is that legal terms such as rights, redistricting, and government structure are part of a similar or the same language game. Instead of seeing rights litigation and governmental or political structures as distinct entities, in many cases they are part of one language game such that the meaning of one term has an impact upon

---

205   Hohfeld at 58.
206   *See:* Flast v. Cohen, 392 U.S. 83 (1968).
207   JOHN W. DANFORD, WITTGENSTEIN AND POLITICAL PHILOSOPHY, 113-14 (1976) (*drawing* parallels between law, language, and political philosophy).
208   LUDWIG WITTGENSTEIN, PHILOSOPHICAL INVESTIGATIONS, para. 67 (1968) (*discussing* the idea of family resemblances among different discourses).
209   *Id.* at para. 1-15.
210   *Id.* at para. 43, 82, 122, 340, 381, 384, 432.
211   *Id.* at para. 130.
212   *Id.* at para. 146, 198-205, 224-27.
213   *Id.* at 23, 241.

another. Change what a right is, or the scope of what "neutrality" means, or what representation is, and other words, as suggested by Hohfeld, will also change. We can also potentially view linguistic social conventions, rules, agreements, or forms of life as a political philosophy or theory that helps to inform meanings in the law. Thus, in response to Issacharoff and Karlan who say that a theory is needed to explain what constitutes harm to representational rights,[214] the language game of Liberalism, with its commitment to neutrality, as well as individual liberty and equality, fit that bill, providing the definition that links individual rights claims to political and governmental structures.[215]

Besides the parallel of law to a language game, there are two other ways that one can see rights and structure related. First Kant and then eventually Hegel saw connections in apparent opposites. Kant's antinomies between reason and empiricism, for example find a unity in opposition or connection via transcendental reason.[216] More famously, Hegel drew connections between apparent antithetical concepts such as Being and Nothing and Subject and Object in his dialectical method of analysis.[217] For both Kant and Hegel, internal connections or relations may actually exist between or among concepts (or Notions for Hegel) that are initially seen. Finally, to make the connection to law most exact, Ronald Dworkin's concept of rights as trumps places limits on the political process,[218] shifting from the majoritarian branches to the judiciary the responsibility for the protection of individual claims.[219] Simply put, rights claims have a structural impact upon how the government operates in terms of who acts and who responds and how.

Democracies and political systems define the background for individual rights. For Dworkin, they operate "in an abstract way against decisions taken by the community or society as a whole," with "more specific institutional rights that hold against a decision made by a specific institution."[220] These background rights serve

---

214 Issacharoff and Karlan at 56.

215 It should also be pointed out that Issacharoff and Karlan at 563, are both wrong and right in their assertion that defining injury in the patronage cases did not require the courts to construct a theory of fair employment or injury. Yes, the courts did not have to construct they theory *ab initio*, but they did have to rely on prior determinations of what did constitute unfair employment or an injury and then they had to apply that theory to the facts at hand, deciding if the concept of fair employment fell under the language game of the First Amendment. In ruling that it did, the Court essentially constructed a new theory to decide what constituted fair employment when the government was the employer.

216 Kant at 328, 396.

217 G.W.F. HEGEL, HEGEL'S LOGIC, trans. William Wallace, 285 (1982); HEGEL'S PHENOMENOLOGY OF SPIRIT, trans. A.V. Miller, 28-31 (1977).

218 RONALD DWORKIN, TAKING RIGHTS SERIOUSLY, xi (Harvard University Press 1977) (*stating* that "Individual rights are political trumps held by individuals"). *See also:* LAURENCE A. TRIBE, AMERICAN CONSTITUTIONAL LAW, 1677-82 (1988) (*describing* how rights claims can have structural impacts).

219 RONALD DWORKIN, LAW'S EMPIRE, 356 (1986).

220 Dworkin, Taking Rights Seriously at xi.

as general principles that define rights within a community, with the embodiment of these rights in the law representing specific claims against political institutions to perform certain functions or tasks. To simplify Dworkin's point: Theories (such as about democracy) represent abstract rights regarding how a legal regime should operate, with constitutional law serving as a concrete embodiment of rights in definite institutions and structures.[221] As Iredell Jenkins states: "Legally, the recognition that certain persons have a certain right has two immediate and important consequences: it imposes corresponding duties on other persons, and it enlists the state in the protection of these rights."[222] Individual rights claims then, thus contrary to assertions by Pildes, are not only related to political and governmental structures, but pursuing them is the most logical and appropriate way to bring about institutional changes, including with how reapportionment and redistricting occur. These claims are also organized by a political or democratic theory, with Liberal political neutrality serving as the map upon which we give content and meaning to the Constitution, individual rights, an even the concept of representation.

Political Neutrality and the Politics/Administration Dichotomy

Critics of the First Amendment turn to adjudicating partisan gerrymandering assailed Justice Kennedy's appeal to the patronage and party cases as support for the proposition that partisanship or political preferences are illegitimate preferences to be considered when the state acts. While conceding that the *Jones* case cited by Kennedy may not support his argument, Hasen and others are both right and wrong when it comes to the patronage cases. They are maybe right that the cases do not provide a clear statement of the harm implicated in partisan gerrymandering, but they are wrong in their assertions that they do not stand for the proposition that the state should not be allowed to consider partisanship in its decision-making. Moreover, where Kennedy and perhaps Stevens erred in their referencing of the patronage cases was that they focused too narrowly on them and not on a broader role the Court has had in articulating Liberal neutrality in its decisions. In particular, Liberal neutrality in public administration manifests itself in a Progressive Era concept called neutral competence or the politics/administration dichotomy.[223] This dichotomy called for a removal of politics in the administration of government, leaving politics to the realm of elected officials who make policy.

---

221 *Compare:* G.W.F. HEGEL, HEGEL'S PHILOSOPHY OF RIGHT, trans. T.M. Knox, 160-74 (1967). *See also:* David Schultz, *Hegel's Constitutionalism*, 4 COMMONWEALTH 26 (1990) (*examining* Hegel's concept of constitutionalism and constitutional law).

222 IREDELL JENKINS, SOCIAL ORDER AND THE LIMITS OF LAW, 241 (1980).

223 *See: Neutral Competence* and *Politics-Administration Dichotomy*, in DAVID SCHULTZ, ED., ENCYCLOPEDIA OF PUBLIC ADMINISTRATION AND PUBLIC POLICY, 287, 331 (2004).

Efforts to depoliticize the administrative apparatus of the government can be traced to the late nineteenth-century civil service reform movements that were directed at rooting out the corruption and spoils that had emerged in Andrew Jackson's time and which fully blossomed during Lincoln's and Grant's administrations.[224] Political patronage and spoils, which during the Jacksonian era was heralded as a reform movement to improve political accountability, strengthen political parties, and improve the representative quality of the federal bureaucracy, had by the 1850s become viewed as a corrupt practice that undermined the moral integrity of the government. Thus, starting as early as the 1840s, some in Congress sought to establish competitive examinations for some positions and by 1856 there were demands for a professionalized civil service.[225] After the Civil War, Congress, and especially representative Thomas Jenckes from Rhode Island, began pushing for civil service exams and other reforms. While claims that spoils were inefficient were articulated, the primary focus of these early reformers was moralistic and aimed at the purification of the federal employment that was tainted by politics.[226]

The first serious movement towards reform of spoils came in 1871 when Congress issued a joint resolution authorizing President Grant to create a Civil Service Commission (CSC).[227] This Commission classified some positions, issued guidelines for competitive examinations, and also recommended a ban on political assessments (the practice of employees paying yearly fees in return for continued federal employment). The Commission died in 1873 for lack of funding. However, the Grant Commission had created many regulations and terminology that would eventually become the basis for the 1883 Pendleton Act which was the first major federal civil service reform act.

Further action towards the reform of the civil service took place throughout the 1870s. In 1873, for example, Grant issued an executive order forbidding civil servants from holding state or local offices.[228] Although the order did not preclude campaigning, it did place some limits upon the individual's own political career. In 1877, President Hayes issued an order limiting the political activities of federal employees by banning their involvement in the management of political organizations, caucuses, conventions, and elections, although their right to vote or speak out on issues was not affected.[229]

The 1883 Pendleton Act represented a first and small triumph over spoils and the articulation of the position that political control of administration did not further democratic ideals but instead threatened the neutral administration of justice, the moral integrity of government, and the efficiency of administration.

---

224 David Schultz and Robert Maranto, The Politics of Civil Service Reform, 50-53 (1998).
225 Ari Hoogenboom, Outlawing the Spoils (1961).
226 Schultz and Maranto at 54-58.
227 Id.
228 David Rosenbloom, Federal Service and the Constitution (1971).
229 Id.

Three years subsequent to its adoption, President Cleveland strengthened earlier efforts towards political neutrality by issuing an order that reiterated the ban on political activity by federal employees.[230]

After the Pendleton Act's passage the civil service reform movement underwent several important changes. First, passage of the Act was not a complete remedy for all the social and political ills facing the federal government. There were still other problems, and the Pendleton Act could not address them because the Act covered only a very small percentage of the positions in the federal government (entry level and clerical positions in urban centers and where custom houses were located). Also, the reform spirit somewhat lapsed on the federal level after 1883 and some hostility against the Act developed in Congress leading to unsuccessful efforts to repeal it.

However, neither did the desire for reform die nor did the demand to take politics out of administration subside. Reformers at this time believed that the only way to eliminate spoils was to depoliticize the civil service. Hence, the reform movement changed in a couple of important ways. First, starting in the late 1890s and into the early twentieth century, there was a new focus to reform. Partly as a result of the Populist movement, reformers became preoccupied with efforts to reconcile the operation of the federal bureaucracy with the basic political values of Madisonian democracy and popular government.[231] Reformers asked how a politically neutral merit system and a tenured civil service could operate within a political system that respected representative democracy and the public accountability of public officeholders through competitive elections. One solution to this problem would be to try to distinguish politics from administration and push the goal of neutral competence.

The experiences of foreign regimes offered later nineteenth- and early twentieth-century Americans a model for civil service reform and efforts to purge politics from the administration of government. Woodrow Wilson, writing in his 1885 "Notes on Administration," contended that "the task of developing a science of administration for America should be approached with a larger observance of the *utilities* [Wilson's emphasis] than is to be found in the German or French treatment of the subject."[232] In this essay Wilson stated for the first time that "*administration* should be subservient to the *politics* [Wilson's emphasis]," a distinction that he would make more forcefully in his now famous 1887 essay "The Study of Administration."[233] Administrative questions, for Wilson, are distinct from political questions because while political questions are policy questions, public administration is simply the "detailed and systematic execution

---

230 Schultz and Maranto at 88.
231 *Id.* at 8, 11-13.
232 Woodrow Wilson, *Notes on Administration*, in ARTHUR LINK. ED., THE PAPERS OF WOODROW WILSON, v 5, 49 (1968).
233 *Id.* at 359.

of public law."[234] In borrowing from German writers, Woodrow Wilson argued that administration was the detailed execution of general government policies and "lies outside the proper sphere of politics."[235] Policies should be set by elected leaders and their appointees. Administration is the province of politically neutral, permanent officials selected for their expertise.

Though Wilson's essay had little influence until decades after his death, Frank J. Goodnow's 1900 *Politics and Administration* was perhaps the most influential book upon early twentieth-century administrative thinking.[236] It sought to clarify the various functions of the state which he described as politics and administration. Politics is defined as the "expressions of the state will" while administration is the "execution of these policies."[237] However, while these are distinct functions, there is a need for a harmony between the expression and execution of the law because a popular government must be able to control the execution of the law if its will is to be expressed. Yet, while politics should control administration, there is a limit to how much politics should penetrate into administration lest the latter becomes inefficient.

The spoils system had produced a coordination of politics and administration, yet the spoils had two glaring deficiencies: (1) it led to the impairing of administrative efficiency; and (2), and far more important for Goodnow, it was a threat to popular government and competitive elections because it supported the ruling party and kept it in power. The spoils system, a consequence of strong political parties and a decentralized administrative system, was a threat to democracy because "the party in control of the government offices had made use of them not merely to influence the expression of the popular will, but to thwart it when once expressed."[238]

While Goodnow did recognize the importance of political parties in a popular government and sought to strengthen them in America, he rejected party (political) control over administration as the best way to harmonize the expression and execution of the popular will. Goodnow rejected perhaps the hallmark Jacksonian defense of spoils that it sustained strong parties and democratic control of the bureaucracy. Moreover, Goodnow also repudiated earlier claims that open competitive exams would end this corruption because these exams were a small part of the reform movement. The solution to preventing administration (party control of offices) from thwarting the political will was to remove it from political and party control.

> That it (popular government) shall not be lost in our case, depends very largely on our ability to prevent politics from exercising too great an influence over administration, and the parties in control of administration from using it to influence improperly the expression of the public will.[239]

---

234 *Id.* at 372.
235 *Id.*
236 FRANK GOODNOW, POLITICS AND ADMINISTRATION (1967).
237 *Id.* at 18.
238 *Id.* at 131.
239 *Id.* at 131-32.

The best way to assert a new harmony between the expression and the execution of the laws would be by creating a hierarchal and centralized administration with the President at the head to direct the operations of the government. Such a centralized system with superiors overseeing subordinates would limit the discretion of the latter and, thus, prevent them from acting politically.

While this model of organization sought to subordinate administration to politics, this subordination did not mean that politics should control administration. Instead, Goodnow makes it clear that this type of control is inefficient. There are certain areas of administration, moreover, that should be insulated from politics. As well as purely administrative management issues, these areas include the administration of justice, and technical, scientific information gathering.[240] These functions should be performed by politically neutral, tenured and competent individuals who are to act in a semi-scientific, quasi-judicial, and quasi-businesslike fashion.[241] Such efficient behavior would only be upset by politics.

Central to the arguments of Wilson and Goodnow was that politics and patronage threatened the administrative efficiency of government and that, in general, administrative and political questions were and should be distinct. The former should be addressed by technically competent civil servants insulated from politics. Thus, in these writings we see the emergence of a neutral competence ideology that stressed a politics/administration dichotomy in order to promote efficiency and limit the threats parties posed to popular government. Yet an important part of the crusade, particularly on the local level where most of the public sector existed, was a direct attack on political parties and the evil of partisanship, and that the spoils system represented an acceptable relationship among the party, administration, and popular government. Instead, the reformers believed that spoils damaged administrative efficiency and popular government and did little for the health of parties. Neutral competence ideology sought to depoliticize the civil service, and it was grounded in a Liberal commitment of neutrality and attempts to reconcile bureaucratic power with the values of American representative democracy.

The Supreme Court jumped on the bandwagon of civil service reform and enforcement of neutral competence ideology in several decisions. In *Ex Parte Curtis*[242] at issue was the constitutionality of an 1876 Act that prohibited all members of the Executive branch who had received Senate confirmation from "requesting, giving to, or receiving from, any other officer or employee of the government, any money or property or other thing of value for political purposes." Curtis was a federal employee who was convicted of violation of this Act in district court for receiving money from employees. He appealed contesting its constitutionality. Additionally, in *United States v. Wurzbach*[243] the Court upheld a

---

240 *Id.* at 78-82.
241 *Id.* at 85, 87.
242 106 U.S. 371 (1882).
243 280 U.S. 397 (1929).

1925 Corrupt Practices Act that made it illegal for officers and employees of the United States to promote their candidacy or reelection in a party primary. Justice Holmes, writing for the Court, ruled that Congress could provide measures that would limit the political pressure that employees might face to contribute money if they were to retain employment.

The Hatch Act cases represent another line of decisions where the Court sought to depoliticize the machinery of government. Starting in 1939, Congress passed a variety of acts that sought to place limits upon the ability of the Roosevelt administration to use the federal bureaucracy for political/partisan purposes. The Act, specifically Section 9, forbid employees and officers of the executive branch from taking any active part in political management or in political campaigns. First in *United Public Workers v. Mitchell*,[244] and then again in *United States Civil Service Commission v. National Association of Letter Carriers*,[245] the Court upheld against First Amendment challenges the political activity bans in the Hatch Act.

In *Mitchell* the Court stated that "the interference with free expression is seen in better proportion as compared with the requirements of orderly management of administrative personnel."[246] For the Court, several factors contribute to the need to limit the political activity of workers in order to promote good administrative management. First, it notes how, if political activity of federal workers hurts the civil service, its damage is no less than if the activity occurs after work hours.[247] Second, the Court indicated how free speech rights had to be balanced against the needs to protect a democratic society against the evils of political partisanship in the federal service.[248] Specifically, the Court, in citing public administration scholarship as authority,[249] argued that there was a need to limit political activity in order to promote "political neutrality for public servants as a sound element for efficiency."[250] Elsewhere, the Court also noted how an "actively partisan governmental personnel threatens good administration,"[251] hurts political neutrality and that, overall, partisan political activity is a threat to efficiency, political neutrality, and discipline.

United States Civil Service Commission v. National Association of Letter Carriers ("*Letter Carriers*") was also a challenge to Section 9 of the Hatch Act and again the Court upheld the Act. Here the majority stated that "federal service should depend upon meritorious performance rather than political service, and that the political influence of federal employees on others and the electoral process should be limited."[252] The basis of this claim rested in the majority's recounting

---

244   330 U.S. 75 (1947).
245   413 U.S. 548 (1973).
246   330 U.S. at 94.
247   *Id.* at 95-96.
248   *Id.*
249   330 U.S. at 97, fn 32.
250   330 U.S. at 97.
251   *Id.* at 98.
252   413 U.S. at 548.

the nineteenth-century reforms directed against spoils and in their agreement that "partisan political activities by federal employees must be limited if the Government is to operate effectively and fairly."[253] Political neutralization is thus required by the First Amendment. For the majority:

> The argument that political neutrality is not indispensable to a merit system for federal employees may be accepted. But because it is not indispensable does not mean that it is not desirable or permissible. Modern American politics involves organized political parties. Many classifications of Government employees have been accustomed to work in politics—national, state and local—as a matter of principle or to assure their tenure. Congress may reasonably desire to limit party activity of federal employees so as to avoid a tendency toward a one-party system. It may have considered that parties would be more truly devoted to the public welfare if public servants were not over active politically.[254]

The Hatch Act's decisions stated that the political neutrality of federal employees was dictated by the First Amendment. The patronage decisions[255] pushed the point even further by placing limits upon the government using political affiliation as a factor in hiring, firing, and promotion decisions. In these decisions the Court engaged in extensive debate concerning the merits of patronage with arguments over the supposed contributions that spoils had to the maintenance of democracy, political parties, public accountability, and administrative control. These debates made significant reference to political science and public administration scholarship on these topics. These debates regarding the merits of patronage occurred within the rhetoric of the neutral competence. In all five of these decisions the Court finds that the consideration of partisan affiliation or party activity in the hiring, firing, promotion, or letting of contracts was a violation of the First Amendment. It does so by declaring the use of partisanship or party preference is not a compelling governmental interest in employment decisions.[256] In all of these decisions, the Court also appeals to the ideology of neutrality and neutral competence.

For example, in *Elrod v. Burns* Justice Brennan begins his opinion by offering a history of the spoils system in America, noting how the impetus for the Pendleton Act and civil service reform could be traced to the "corruption and inefficiency" of patronage employment.[257] He contends that patronage is a threat to democracy and

---

253 *Id.* at 547.
254 330 U.S. at 100.
255 *See, e.g.*, Elrod v. Burns, 427 U.S. 347 (1976); Branti v. Finkel 445 U.S. 507 (1979); Rutan v. Republican Party of Illinois, 497 U.S. 62 (1990); Board of County Commissioners v. Umbehr, 518 U.S. 668 (1996); and O"Hare Truck Service Inc. v. City of Northgate, 518 U.S. 712 (1996).
256 427 U.S. at 362; 445 U.S. at 514-15; 497 U.S. at 69, 74, 78; 518 U.S. at 674-77; 518 U.S. at 716-17.
257 427 U.S. at 354.

popular government because of the advantage it gives to one party in the electoral process:

> It is not only belief and association which are restricted where political patronage is the practice. The free functioning of the electoral process also suffers. Conditioning public employment on partisan support prevents support of competing political interests ... As government employment, state or federal, becomes more pervasive, the greater the dependence on it becomes, and therefore the greater becomes the power to starve political opposition by commanding partisan support, financial or otherwise. Patronage thus tips the electoral process in favor of the incumbent party, and where the practice's scope is substantial relative to the size of the electorate, the impact on the process can be significant.[258]

The *Branti* Court reaffirmed their holding in *Elrod*. In the latter Justice Stevens' majority opinion stated that the real question in the case was "whether the hiring authority can demonstrate that party affiliation is an appropriate requirement for the effective performance of the public office involved."[259] It found that, except in a few narrow circumstances, partisanship was not an appropriate requirement. In *Rutan* Justice Brennan stated: "Today we are asked to decide the constitutionality of several related political patronage practices—whether promotion, transfer, recall, and hiring decisions involving low-level public employees may be constitutionally based on party affiliation and support. We hold that they may not."[260]

Overall, if one reads the patronage, Hatch Act, *Wurzbach*, and *Curtis* cases together they demonstrate that the Court had been a consistently strong defender of the First Amendment's commitment to political neutrality.[261] For the last 100 years the Court has deferred to Congress in its attempts to limit forced monetary contributions within the bureaucracy and to place limits upon the political activity of federal employees. The patronage decisions, on the other hand, represent a direct attempt by the Court to limit use of spoils in hiring, firing, and transfers. Together, these decisions represented a rejection of the use of partisanship or party membership in the performance of governmental duties and adoption of the principles of neutrality inherent in the Liberal tradition within American democratic theory.[262] More importantly, they offer support to the claims of

---

258   *Id.* at 356.
259   445 U.S. at 518.
260   497 U.S. at 65.
261   *See:* Stephen E. Gottlieb, *Fashioning A Test for Gerrymandering*, 15 J. LEGIS. 1, 11 (1988-89); Stephen E. Gottlieb, *The Speech Clause and the Limits of Neutrality*, 51 ALB. L. REV. 19 (1986); Kenneth Karst, *Equality as a Central Principle in the First Amendment*, 43 U. CHI. L. REV. 20 (1975); Geoffrey R. Stone, *Content Regulation and the First Amendment*, 25 WILLIAM & MARY L. REV. 189 (1983).
262   *See also:* Keyishian v. Board of Regents, 385 U.S. 589 (1967); Perry v. Sindermann, 408 U.S. 593 (1972); Speiser v. Randall, 357 U.S. 513 (1958); and Sherbert

Kennedy and Stevens that consideration of partisanship can constitute a valid and real harm to citizens because it may lead to the suppression of First Amendment free speech or associational rights.

Defining the First Amendment Harm

Given the arguments so far made, there are five remaining questions:

1. What is the theory defining the harm in partisan gerrymandering?
2. What is the harm in partisan gerrymandering?
3. How do we know when the harm has occurred?
4. Why should partisan gerrymandering be compared to the patronage decisions?
5. Are there ever any circumstances when partisanship should be considered in the drawing of district lines?

To answer the first question, the theory defining the harm is Liberalism. Liberalism demands of the state that it act neutral with regards to its citizens. If we accept neutrality as the yardstick of measurement for eventually determining harm, one need not address the messy problem of defining or assessing what constitutes a burden to representational rights, as Issacharoff and Karlan contend.[263]

Second, the harm in partisan gerrymandering is a state violation of neutrality—more specifically, using partisan factors when drawing of district lines or in the allocation of representative seats. There are two ways to conceptualize this harm. First, the malapportionment of district lines based on partisanship is analogous to being a Democrat in Texas, a Republican in New York, or someone anywhere voting for a third-party candidate for president of the United States. In these three cases many allege that these votes are wasted.[264] These are clear disincentives in all three cases to voting as one would prefer, creating harms that range from deciding not to vote to the belief that their vote will not make a difference. Similarly, a Democrat who votes party line in a solidly Republican district will also feel little point in voting, and feel her voice is not heard, much in the same

---

v. Verner, 374 U.S. 398 (1963) as examples where the Court has ruled as illegitimate the conditioning of hiring decisions based on the suppression of First Amendment rights. In none of these cases was the relinquishment of First Amendment rights accepted as a compelling governmental interest.

263   Issacharoff and Karlan at 563.

264   GEORGE C. EDWARDS, III, WHY THE ELECTORAL COLLEGE IS BAD FOR AMERICA (2004) (*arguing* that the Electoral College serves to disenfranchise many voters not living in competitive states); Thomas M. Durban, *The Anachronistic Electoral College: The Time For Reform*, 39 FED. B. N. J. 510 (1992).

way the remaining minorities in Tuskegee, Alabama felt in *Gomillion v. Lightfoot* after they were redistricted out of the city.

A traditional analysis would assert that they face a one person, one vote Equal Protection violation, yet a First Amendment analysis would assert instead that (at least with the Democrat in a Republican district and a racial minority in Tuskegee) the state violated the principle of both equality and neutrality, producing a form of viewpoint discrimination.[265] In transforming the harm into a First Amendment claim, the Court can draw upon its well-developed line of jurisprudence holding as presumptively invalid content-based, viewpoint discrimination.[266] In using a First Amendment content-based viewpoint analysis to examine partisan gerrymandering, the Court could employ this jurisprudence[267] to define the range of harms to voters from directly malapportioning to cracking and packing voters based on partisanship (if one can be sure of partisan identity), to automatic presumptions of the invalidity and harm of partisan-based lines much in the same way O'Connor made the argument about race in *Shaw v. Reno*.[268] The point is one can simply postulate that partisan-based gerrymandering is *per se* unconstitutional unless it survives strict scrutiny.

A third question to address is how do we know when the harm has occurred? More specifically, the issue that has plagued the Court since *Bandemer* has been how to construct judicially-manageable standards that the courts can apply neutrally that will allow for them to adjudicate claims of partisan gerrymandering.[269] It is over the failure of the Court to find these standards that Justice Scalia in *Vieth* wanted to overturn *Bandemer* and declare partisan gerrymanders nonjusticiable.[270] Two possible responses are possible here.

First, as just noted, the Court could use its traditional First Amendment jurisprudence that focuses on intent as an effort to uncover partisan gerrymandering. Under this form of analysis, the use of party membership or partisanship as a criterion in the drawing of redistricting lines would be ruled unconstitutional. The reason for this is that, as contended above, its use would never be considered a

---

265 Stone, 1983 at 201-2.

266 *See, e.g.*, Simon & Schuster, Inc. v. Members of N.Y. State Crime Victims Bd., 502 U.S. 105, 115 (1991); Consolidated Edison Co. of N.Y. v. Public Serv. Comm'n of N.Y., 447 U.S. 530, 536 (1980); Police Dept. of Chicago v. Mosley, 408 U.S. 92, 95 (1972); Ward v. Rock Against Racism, 491 U.S. 781(1989); R.A.V. v. St. Paul, 505 U.S. 377, 391 (1992); Perry Ed. Assn. v. Perry Local Educators' Assn., 460 U.S. 37, 46 (1983); Texas v. Johnson, 491 U.S. 397, 406 (1989); Rosenberger v. Rector and Visitors of University of Virginia, 515 U.S. 819 (1995). *See also:* Richard L. Hasen: *Bad Legislative Intent*, 2006 WISC. L. REV. 843 (2006) (*describing* how "bad" legislative intent may be used to adjudicate a range of First Amendment issues, including potentially partisan gerrymandering).

267 *See:* Smolla at 48-50 (*reviewing* the various notions of harm defined under the First Amendment).

268 509 U.S. 630 (1993).

269 541 U.S. at 307-9.

270 *Id.* at 281.

compelling governmental interest. Under this type of analysis, while compactness and shape of districts would be acceptable criteria to use in redistricting, partisanship would not be. Drawing upon O'Connor's arguments regarding the use of race in *Shaw v. Reno*, if a districting schema could not be explained otherwise except by the inclusion of partisanship as a criterion for boundaries, then the reapportionment would be presumed to be done on the basis of party membership unless defendants could rebut that presumption.

Yet while First Amendment scholarship has developed a sophisticated analysis of intent, these tests may not be adequate or objective enough to detect more subtle uses of partisanship in redistricting. If the intent analysis found in First Amendment jurisprudence is unsatisfactory, a second and more objective test to detect harm is grounded in the "symmetry standard" that was proposed by one of the amicus briefs in the *LULAC* case.[271] Based on political science research dating back over three decades,[272] King states:

> The symmetry standard measures fairness in election systems, and is not specific to evaluating gerrymanders. The symmetry standard requires that the electoral system treat similarly-situated political parties equally, so that each receives the same fraction of legislative seats for a particular vote percentage as the other party would receive if it had received the same percentage. In other words, it compares how both parties would fare hypothetically if they each (in turn) had received a given percentage of the vote. The difference in how parties would fare is the "partisan bias" of the electoral system.[273]

For Gottlieb, "symmetry provides an equivalent opportunity for both parties to win elections."[274] In using the symmetry standard, one examines the swing ratio, or the rate at which legislative seats change when votes change.[275] If, for example, for every one percent change in vote a party picks up X number of seats, one wants to look to see if that ratio is the same for all political parties.[276] If there

---

271 *Brief of Amici Curiae Professors Gary King, Bernard Grofman, Andrew Gelman, and Jonathan N. Katz, in Support of Neither Party*, 2006 WL 53994 ("Gary King Brief"). Justice Stevens at 126 S.Ct. 2637 cites to the symmetry standard.

272 *See, e.g.*, Richard G. Niemi, *The Relationship Between Votes and Seats: The Ultimate Question in Political Gerrymandering*, 33 U.C.L.A. L. Rev., 185 (1985); Edward R. Tufte, *The Relationship Between Seats and Votes in Two-Party Systems*. 67 Am. Pol. Sci. Rev. 540 (1973); Bernard Grofman, *Measures of Bias and Proportionality in Seats-Votes Relationships*, 9 Am. Pol. Sci. Rev. 295, 327 (1983); Andrew Gelman and Gary King, *A Unified Method of Evaluating Electoral Systems and Redistricting Plans*, 38 Am. J. Pol. Sci. 514 (1994).

273 Gary King Brief at 4-5.

274 Gottlieb, J. Legis. at 12.

275 Niemi at 195.

276 *Id.*

is a statistical difference in the swing ratios, that is a sign of partisan bias.[277] Simplified, the symmetry standard requires that if Democrats win 70 percent of the seats when they receive 55 percent of the vote, Republicans should receive the same number of seats when they receive the same percentage of the vote.[278] Thus, partisan gerrymandering occurs when each party does not have the same chance of electing its members when compared to others.[279] Overall, the strength of the symmetry standard is its objectiveness. It avoids the messy search for intent, defining a neutral barometer for partisan bias.

However, the *LULAC* Court rejected the symmetry standard alone,[280] both because it failed to provide for a sense of fairness[281] and because it was based on a hypothetical state of affairs.[282] Perhaps, then, another alternative would be to combine an intent and symmetry test together. One could define a partisan gerrymander as one where district lines could not be explained except for the impermissible consideration of partisanship in the drawing of lines (intent), supplemented by evidence that there was a lack of symmetry (effect). Together, the test would try to show that the intent was to engage in a partisan gerrymander and that there was some evidence of representational harm in terms of how votes followed seats. Together, the two factors demonstrate a First Amendment harm.

Fourth, once we know what the harm is, is the drawing of district lines more politics and policy or more like administration? By that, the politics/administration dichotomy and neutral competence drew the lines of partisanship to exclude decisions by elected officials. If elected officials are doing the redistricting, does it not make it policy and therefore permissible to use partisanship in drawing lines? Several responses can be offered here. First, if the arguments about the First Amendment that have been presented above are accepted, then it does not matter if the redistricting decisions by legislatures are politics or policy; in both cases the consideration of partisan affiliation or party membership is never a valid governmental interest that should employed when drawing district lines. The concept of viewpoint discrimination as enunciated by the Court does not simply apply to administrative decisions. In the case of *R.A.V. v. St. Paul*, it also extended to laws passed by elected officials to ban cross burning.[283] Second, the appeal to the Hatch Act and patronage cases were meant to serve as examples where the Court has issued decisions to take politics out of the basic institutions involved in the administration of government. District boundaries, it is submitted, are more like the basic administrative institutions of government than they are like policy pronouncements of elected officials because the fairness and impartiality in

---

277 *Id.* at 199.
278 Gary King Brief at 5.
279 *Id.*
280 548 U.S. 399, 418-20.
281 *Id.*
282 *Id.*
283 505 U.S. 377 (1992).

constructing districts assure the proper operations of elections and representation (fair outcomes), much in the same way that impartiality in administration assures a fair and just outcome in decisions reached by public administrators. Overall, partisan gerrymandering is no more legitimate than permitting a legislature to directly reserve specific seats on the basis of party membership. While it is the prerogative of voters to decide to make their decisions on a partisan basis, the principles of political neutrality and the First Amendment preclude the government from doing that, especially when setting the ground rules for an election. The First Amendment, like the Equal Protection clause, demands that the government act neutrality and that it respect an equality among viewpoints. According to Geoffrey Stone:

> It has been suggested that the concept of equality "lies at the heart of the first amendment's protections against government regulation of the content of speech." Indeed, it has been argued that, "just as the prohibition of government-imposed discrimination on the basis of race is central to equal protection analysis, protection against governmental discrimination on the basis of speech content is central among first amendment values."[284]

Finally, are there any situations when partisanship should be permitted in the drawing of district lines? There are two possible responses. First, one could argue a hard version of the thesis being advocated here that party affiliation is never a compelling government interest in any decision made by the government. In this case, no exceptions are permitted and therefore party membership may never be considered in districting. However, a softer version of the argument would be that the government may only use party membership or partisan affiliation if it could demonstrate a compelling government interest that survived strict scrutiny. One circumstance of the latter can be identified and it occurs when a state might consider partisanship to comply with the requirements of the Voting Rights Act. Specifically, in *Easley v. Cromartie*[285] the Court upheld North Carolina's new districting plan, finding that race was not considered to the exclusion of other factors when drawing congressional boundaries. Here, the Court noted that the burden is on the plaintiffs who challenge a redistricting plan as a racial gerrymander to show that race was the predominant factor in explaining the plan.[286] But the Court was not persuaded by the evidence that race and not politics was the issue that determined the line-drawing.[287] Specifically, Justice Breyer, writing for the majority, argued that past voting behavior and not necessarily race was used to determine the lines and even though race and voting may correlate, the use of the former is permissible and a

---

284 Stone 1983 at 201-2.
285 532 U.S. 234 (2001).
286 *Id.* at 241-42.
287 *Id.* at 243.

possible explanation for the shape of the districts.[288] Hence, if voting behavior was the factor to explain the districts, then race was not a factor and therefore no racial gerrymander occurred. As a result of *Easley v. Cromartie* one can effectively create minority-majority districts so long as one can show that voting or other political behavior determined the districting, even if those criteria correlate with race. For the purposes of this argument, the decision in *Cromartie* would permit the consideration partisan factors in order to meet the demands of the Voting Rights Act. Beyond this, a First Amendment turn towards adjudicating partisan gerrymanders would prevent party from being a factor affecting the drawing of district lines.

So what does all this mean in terms of partisan gerrymandering? At a minimum, Liberal-democratic theory argues in favor of neutrality as a overall political principle when it comes to the government. This neutrality at the very least must mean something when it comes to the formal drawing of lines in the apportioning of legislative and other seats. The rules of the game cannot systematically favor one party or side. Nor should they favor incumbents. Does this mean that the courts should police for partisan gerrymanders? Perhaps yes, but there is also a different answer. Maybe legislators should not be allowed to draw district lines for themselves or for other elected officials. Asking them to act like angels and not consider self-interest when doing something so fundamental as drawing district lines may not make any sense. Instead, again drawing upon the concept of Liberal neutrality, one can argue that letting elected officials draw district lines for themselves or other elected officials is a conflict of interest. It is allowing them to effectively be judges in their own instance, giving them the authority to draw lines in a way that favors their own personal interests. At the heart of what a conflict of interest is about, it is using public authority for personal benefit or in cases where one's own judgments are clouded by self-interest, favoritism, or bias.

The argument here then is toward taking the responsibility of reapportionment out of the prerogative of state or other relevant legislators and turning it over to a different body—such as a non-partisan redistricting to do that job. Effectively, with the federal and state courts having done much of the redistricting since the 1960s, that is what has occurred. But instead of making the judiciary the ad hoc court of last resort (literally) to perform this task, the duty should fall to a more permanent body that is assigned within each state to undertake this function. It would be a body that would draw upon the redistricting values discussed in this chapter so far (and below), seeking to ensure that at the least the formal requisites of representation have been met.

Race, Redistricting, and the Constitution

But there is still one more important issue when it comes to thinking about redistricting and representation. This is the issue of race. Starting with *Gomillion*

---

288   532 U.S. 234 at 243-44.

v. Lightfoot the federal courts began to address racial gerrymandering. While initially limited to claims under the Constitution, the 1965 adoption of the VRA allowed plaintiffs to raise race issues under both.[289] In terms of understanding how the Court has sought to address racial gerrymandering under the Constitution, several decisions offer a good overview.

If *Gomillion* stands for the proposition that the use of race for discriminatory purposes is impermissible in redistricting, then in *United Jewish Organizations of Williamsburg, Inc. v. Carey*[290] the Court had to address whether race could be used for the purposes of promoting representation. Specifically, following the adoption of its 1972 reapportionment plan the State of New York concluded that parts of Manhattan and Brooklyn became subject to Sections 4 and 5 of the VRA.[291] To secure compliance with the VRA in time for the 1974 elections the state amended its 1972 redistricting plan to allow for the creation of more nonwhite state legislative seats.[292] In the process of securing that objective parts of the white population, including part of the Hasidic community, were reassigned to an adjoining district, resulting in this community being divided across a couple of senate and assembly districts.[293] According to the Court, members of the Hasidic Jewish community of Williamsburgh alleged "that the 1974 plan 'would dilute the value of each plaintiff's franchise by halving its effectiveness,' solely for the purpose of achieving a racial quota and therefore in violation of the Fourteenth Amendment. Petitioners also alleged that they were assigned to electoral districts solely on the basis of race, and that this racial assignment diluted their voting power in violation of the Fifteenth Amendment."[294] This redistricting plan was upheld in court and the Supreme Court affirmed.

Writing for the Court, Justice White stated that among the issues at stake was whether the use of race was ever permissible in redistricting if it was being used for remedial purposes to remedy the residual effects of past unconstitutional reapportionments.[295] In upholding the reapportionment plan under the VRA, White quickly dismissed plaintiffs' constitutional claims, stating that "neither the Fourteenth nor the Fifteenth Amendment mandates any per se rule against using racial factors in districting and apportionment. Nor is petitioners' second argument valid. The permissible use of racial criteria is not confined to eliminating the effects of past discriminatory districting or apportionment."[296] Contrary to

---

289 *See:* ALEXANDER KEYSSAR, THE *RIGHT TO VOTE*: THE CONTESTED HISTORY OF DEMOCRACY IN THE UNITED STATES, 287-98 (2000) (*discussing* the VRA, constitutional claims, and racial gerrymandering).
290 430 U.S. 144 (1977).
291 *Id.* at 148-49.
292 *Id.* at 151.
293 *Id.*
294 *Id.* at 152-53.
295 *Id.* 144 at 155-56.
296 *Id.* at 161.

what *Gomillion* seemed to suggest, race may be used in some redistricting plans, and with the passage of the VRA Congress was signaling that after inaction for nearly a century in foot-dragging it was prepared to "shift the advantage of time and inertia from the perpetrators of the evil to its victims."[297] Left unclear in the decision, though, was how much race could be considered in redistricting for remedial purposes.

In *City of Mobile, Alabama v. Bolden*,[298] the Court was asked to consider whether an at-large municipal election system in place since 1911 violated the Fourteenth and Fifteenth Amendments.[299] In ruling that it did not Justice Stewart wrote for the Court. He declared that while the Court had declared it was impermissible for states to discriminate on the basis of race when it came to voting, a "racially discriminatory motivation is a necessary ingredient of a Fifteenth Amendment violation."[300] Moreover, he contended that the Fifteenth Amendment does not guarantee the "the right to have Negro candidates elected," it merely bans discriminatory purposes.[301] He then argues that in the past the Court has upheld at-large election systems, again insisting that the Fourteenth Amendment only precludes intentional discrimination.[302] But because there was evidence that at least two Blacks had been elected in the at-large elections, and because the Court did not see sufficient evidence that the election schema was dissuading voter registration among African-Americans, it did not find either a Fourteenth or Fifteenth Amendment violation here.[303]

Finally, the majority rejected a claim raised by Justice Marshall in dissent who argued that "every 'political group,' or at least every such group that is in the minority, has a federal constitutional right to elect candidates in proportion to its numbers."[304] The Court rejected the argument for proportional representation, stating that neither the Fifteenth Amendment nor the one person, one vote standard of *Reynolds* grants an affirmative right to vote, let alone a guarantee to a proportionate right to elect representatives of one's own race.[305] Thus, under *Bolden*, race would only be banned in redistricting under the Constitution if used for discriminatory purposes, but race also did not guarantee one would in fact elect representatives proportionate to the racial demographics of a community.

---

297   *Id.* at fn. 19.
298   446 U.S. 55 (1980).
299   *Id.* at 58.
300   446 U.S. 55 at 62 (*citing* Gomillion v. Lightfoot among other cases for this proposition).
301   *Id.* at 64.
302   *Id.* at 66-67.
303   *Id.* at 73-74.
304   *Id.* at 75.
305   *Id.* at 79-80. In addition, the VRA expressly prohibits proportionality as a remedy.

However, beginning with *Shaw v. Reno*,[306] the Court undertook a difficult process of revisiting some of the claims made in *Gomillion, Carey*, and *Bolden* in the context of the creation of minority-majority districts primarily in North Carolina. Many states, often at the urging of the United States Attorney General per his authority under the VRA, created minority-majority districts in order to maximize Black representation.[307] After the 1990 census the State of North Carolina was entitled to an additional (twelfth) congressional seat.[308] The original redistricting plan based on this census created one minority-majority seat but after the United States Attorney General objected to the plan on VRA grounds it was amended to create a second minority-majority seat.[309] At the time the voting-age demographics of the state was 78 percent White and 20 percent Black, with the latter dispersed throughout the state.[310] As the Supreme Court described these two districts:

> The first of the two majority-black districts contained in the revised plan, District 1, is somewhat hook shaped. Centered in the northeast portion of the State, it moves southward until it tapers to a narrow band; then, with finger-like extensions, it reaches far into the southern-most part of the State near the South Carolina border. District 1 has been compared to a "Rorschach ink-blot test," and a "bug splattered on a windshield ..." The second majority-black district, District 12, is even more unusually shaped. It is approximately 160 miles long and, for much of its length, no wider than the I-85 corridor. It winds in snakelike fashion through tobacco country, financial centers, and manufacturing areas "until it gobbles in enough enclaves of black neighborhoods."[311]

As a result of the changes made to create the second minority-majority district, several individuals and the State Republican Party brought suit claiming the new plan was a political gerrymander under *Bandemer*.[312] When that suit was dismissed by a lower court[313] a new suit was brought claiming the plan was an unconstitutional racial gerrymander under the Fourteenth Amendment because it considered race in the drawing of district lines at the exclusion of other factors

---

306   509 U.S. 630 (1993).
307   *See, e.g.*, DAVID LUBLIN, THE PARADOX OF REPRESENTATION: RACIAL GERRYMANDERING AND MINORITY INTERESTS IN CONGRESS, 99, 112 (1997 (*contending* that the creation of minority-majority seats, while enabling African-American descriptive representation, hurt the substantive interest representation of Blacks). *See also:* DAVID T. CANON, RACE, REDISTRICTING, AND REPRESENTATION: THE UNINTENDED CONSEQUENCES OF BLACK MAJORITY DISTRICTS (1999), for another view on the impact of minority-majority districts.
308   509 U.S. 630 at 633.
309   *Id.*
310   *Id.* at 633-34.
311   *Id.* at 635-36 (internal Court citations omitted).
312   *Id.* at 636.
313   Pope v. Blue, 809 F. Supp. 392 (1992), *affirmed* 506 U.S. 801 (1992).

such as compactness, contiguity, and respect for subdivisions.[314] The lower courts dismissed their claims, and the Supreme Court reversed and remanded.[315]

Writing for the Court Justice O'Connor noted that, despite the plea for a color-blind Constitution from the days of *Plessy v. Ferguson*,[316] the use of race in some government decision-making is permissible. However, the issue in this case was whether the use of race here constituted an "effort to segregate the races for purposes of voting, without regard for traditional districting principles and without sufficiently compelling justification."[317] Contending that the shape of the two districts in North Carolina were so irregular that they could only be explained on account of race,[318] O'Connor proceeded to use strict scrutiny to examine their constitutionality.[319] In looking for an explanation for the appearance of the districts she argued:

> Put differently, we believe that reapportionment is one area in which appearances do matter. A reapportionment plan that includes in one district individuals who belong to the same race, but who are otherwise widely separated by geographical and political boundaries, and who may have little in common with one another but the color of their skin, bears an uncomfortable resemblance to political apartheid. It reinforces the perception that members of the same racial group—regardless of their age, education, economic status, or the community in which they live—think alike, share the same political interests, and will prefer the same candidates at the polls. We have rejected such perceptions elsewhere as impermissible racial stereotypes.[320]

Given the appearance of the two districts, the Court concluded that it need not decide on whether the districts could be explained in nonracial terms; instead it first stated that plaintiffs had stated a claim upon which a case could proceed.[321] Second, in its remand for reconsideration the Court indicated that the lower courts would need to use strict scrutiny in considering the plan and, if race were used to the exclusion of other traditional districting criteria,[322] then the plan should be held unconstitutional even if the state sought to justify its plan based upon seeking compliance with the VRA.[323]

---

314   *Id.* at 636.
315   *Id.* at 640.
316   163 U.S. 537 (1896).
317   509 U.S. 630 at 642.
318   *Id.* at 640-41 (*citing Gomillion*).
319   *Id.* at 642-43.
320   *Id.* at 647.
321   *Id.* at 649.
322   *Id.* at 642.
323   *Id.* at 655-56.

The repercussions of the *Shaw v. Reno* decision played themselves out in subsequent cases. In *Miller v. Johnson*,[324] the Court faced a challenge to the creation of the minority-majority in Georgia and the same in Texas.[325] In the latter case the Court confronted oddly-shaped districts in the construction of a districting plan drawn after the 1990 census. Again employing strict scrutiny because race appeared to be a predominant factor (at the exclusion of traditional districting criteria) when they were developed,[326] three districts were invalidated under the Fourteenth Amendment. Rejected were claims that they had to so consider race to secure compliance with the VRA.[327] In *Miller* Justice Kennedy again confronted a "bizarre-shaped"[328] minority-majority district that was challenged as a racial gerrymander under the Equal Protection clause. However, the Court did not find that bizarre shape to be a threshold requirement for challenging a plan as a form of racial gerrymandering.[329] Other evidence may also be used to show that race for its own sake, at the exclusion of other criteria, affected the drawing of the lines.[330] Given this statement, the Court appeared poised to expand the implications of its *Shaw* opinion and potentially invalidate any district, regardless of shape, if race was the predominant factor in districting. In addition, the Court also appeared on the brink of not only rejecting compliance with the VRA as a compelling governmental interest supporting the use of race in redistricting, but also of declaring the Act to be unconstitutional.[331] In doing that, the Court anticipated arguments that would be made years later in *Shelby County v. Holder*[332] where the former contended that the Section 5 pre-clearance provision of the VRA was unconstitutional in that it exceeded Congressional authority under the Fifteenth Amendment single out some states to secure permission before changing their voting procedures.

Shaw v. Reno, *Bush v. Vera*, and *Miller v. Johnson* may well have represented the high-water mark of the Court's efforts to root out racial gerrymandering. In *Shaw v. Hunt*[333] the Court again invalidated a North Carolina redistricting scheme because it found that race was used at the exclusion of other districting criteria. But in *Easley v. Cromartie*[334] the Court upheld the State's new plan, finding that race

324 515 U.S. 900 (1995).
325 Bush v. Vera, 517 U.S.952 (1996).
326 *Id.* at 975-76.
327 517 U.S. 952 at 976.
328 515 U.S. 900 at 912.
329 *Id.* at 912-13.
330 515 U.S. 900 at 913.
331 *Id.* at 927. *Compare,* Keith Reeves, *Prospects for Black Representation after Miller v Johnson,* in DAVID A. BOSITIS, ED., REDISTRICTING AND MINORITY REPRESENTATION, 161, 162 (1998) (*discussing* the implications of the *Miller* case in terms of electing African-American Representatives).
332 679 F.3d 848 (Ct. App. D.C., 2012), *cert.* granted, 133 S.Ct. 594 (2012).
333 517 U.S. 899 (1996).
334 532 U.S. 234 (2001).

was not considered to the exclusion of other factors when drawing congressional boundaries. Here, the Court noted that the burden is on the plaintiffs who challenge a redistricting plan as a racial gerrymander to show that race was the predominant factor in explaining the plan.[335] Further, the Court was not persuaded by the evidence that race and not politics was the issue that determined the line-drawing.[336] Specifically, Justice Breyer, writing for the majority, argued that past voting behavior and not necessarily race was used to determine the lines and, even though race and voting may correlate, the use of the former is permissible and a possible explanation for the shape of the districts.[337] Hence, if voting behavior was the factor to explain the districts, then race was not a factor and therefore no racial gerrymander occurred. Thus, as a result of *Easley v. Cromartie* one can effectively create minority-majority districts so long as one can show that voting or other political behavior determined the districting, even if those criteria correlate with race. The shifting of the burden to plaintiffs noted in the case, additionally, seemed to represent a backing away of strict scrutiny of the type used in *Shaw v. Reno* and *Bush v. Vera* type cases.

Rethinking Representation

Yet even with the retreat from *Shaw*, the Court has yet to ascertain where to locate race within the paradigm of redistricting and overall reapportionment. Commencing with *Gomillion v. Lightfoot* in 1960, the Supreme Court and the federal judiciary launched a reapportionment revolution in the states. Using the Fourteenth and Fifteenth Amendments, often along side with the VRA, federal courts applied the concept of one person, one vote to a constitutional examination of state legislative and congressional districting schemas in order to root out racial gerrymandering and malapportionment. In the process, it applied the one person, one vote to congressional, state, and local districting plans, requiring near-mathematical identity for the congressional plans but permitting more deviation to the others in order to protect subunits of government. This federal model did not altogether ban the use of race in redistricting, but in the 1990s the Court became more suspect about its application when its use came into conflict with other traditional apportionment criteria. While redistricting became mandatory after a decennial census, more frequent apportionment was not forbidden, even if done with partisan motives, and the courts did not mandate immediate elections following redistricting, permitting officeholders to complete as opposed to truncate terms. Finally, while in theory the Supreme Court has found partisan or political gerrymanders to be justiciable, it remains confused over how to define them and construct manageable standards to enforce. Thus, by the end of the day the Court

---

335   *Id.* 234 at 241-42.
336   *Id.* at 243.
337   *Id.* at 243-44.

has failed to adequately address where race and partisanship fit, if at all, into an overall theory of redistricting that promotes democratic representation. Part of the problem, as highlighted in *Shelby County v. Holder*, are the imposed limits built into the debate surrounding redistricting.

Whatever the Supreme Court's decision in that case, race, redistricting, and minority representation is at a crisis stage. The case involves the constitutionality of Section 5 of the VRA—the pre-clearance provision—one of the most powerful and successful civil rights tools in American history. The battle over its constitutionality is part of the second great disenfranchisement in American history, one that began after Florida 2000.

America's history tells two stories. There is the United States represented by "We the people," the first three words of the Constitution. A country that promises an inclusive democracy, liberty, and equality for everyone. But, as discussed in Chapter 3, former Supreme Court Justice Thurgood Marshall pointed out in a 1987 speech commemorating the bicentennial of the Constitution, "We the people" excluded many. African-Americans were slaves, Native-Americans were three-fifths persons, and by the laws across the thirteen states, women, the poor, and many others were denied the right to vote and share equally in the promise of American democracy. For Marshall, it took a civil war and numerous constitutional amendments to bring the ideal of "We the people" within the grasp of those excluded.

But the Reconstruction Congress after the Civil War represented the first major civil rights era. It included, as the 2012 movie *Lincoln* depicted, the 1865 adoption of the Thirteenth Amendment that banned slavery. But this same Congress adopted the Fourteenth Amendment in 1868 which aimed to guarantee, among other things, equal protection for all, and it also ratified in 1870 the Fifteenth Amendment, granting voting rights to former male slaves. This Reconstruction Congress passed a flurry of civil rights acts in 1866, 1870, 1871, and 1875, with the later three passed pursuant to the authority that the Fourteenth and Fifteenth Amendments gave to them to adopt appropriate legislation to enforce these amendments.

Reconstruction was successful. Across the South, African-Americans were elected to state houses and Congress. Yet slowly the civil rights era ended. The presidential election between Republican Rutherford B. Hayes and Democrat Samuel Tilden in 1876 resulted in disputed electoral votes going to the former in return for federal troops being withdrawn from the South. Enforcement of Reconstruction laws ended and the Jim Crow Era began as the states of the former Confederacy devised a host of ways to undermine civil and voting rights for African-Americans. The Supreme Court in the *Slaughterhouse Cases*[338] and the *Civil Rights Cases*[339] further dismantled the force of the three constitutional amendments and four civil rights laws, with the infamous 1896 *Plessy v. Ferguson*[340]

---

338   Slaughterhouse Cases, 83 U.S. 36 (1873).
339   Civil Rights Cases, 109 U.S. 3 (1883).
340   163 U.S. 537 (1896).

upholding "separate but equal" as a constitutional doctrine until overturned by the Court in 1954 in *Brown v. Board of Education*.[341]

When it came to undermining the Fifteenth Amendment right to vote, the South was crafty. It used literacy tests, poll taxes, grandfather clauses, and felon disenfranchisement laws as tools to deny franchise. If all else failed, the KKK simply burned crosses or murdered those who dared exercise their rights.

But maybe it was the 1954 *Brown* decision or perhaps it was in 1955 when Rosa Parks refused to go to the back of the bus that the second civil rights era began. As with the first civil rights era it was marked by constitutional amendments and legislation from Washington, including the 1965 Voting Rights Act. The VRA sought to restore and protect the voting rights that the Fifteenth Amendment promised, and one of the central features of the act was Section 5. Section 5 required either the Justice Department or a Washington, D.C. federal district court to pre-clear any changes in voting procedures sought to be made by the 22 jurisdictions covered by Section 4 of the Act. Essentially Section 5 covered most of what was part of the Confederacy. Exactly what practices were covered by Section 5 was not specified, but, as Chief Justice Earl Warren declared in the 1969 *Allen v. State Board of Elections* decision which upheld Section 5, the VRA "aimed at the subtle, as well as the obvious, state regulations which have the effect of denying citizens their right to vote because of race."[342]

The power of pre-clearance resides in the concepts of presumption and burden of proof. The law is full of both. When accused of a crime, there is a presumption of innocence and the government carries the burden to show guilt beyond a reasonable doubt. Civil trials hinge on the plaintiff demonstrating by a preponderance of evidence that the defendant was liable. Laws affecting constitutional rights are presumptively suspect unless the government can demonstrate a compelling interest for their validity. Section 5 works the same way. Changes to voting procedures are presumed invalid unless a covered jurisdiction can show why they should be allowed. Such a presumption, in nearly 50 years, has invalidated hundreds if not thousands of laws that would have hurt voting rights.

The result, as told by Chandler Davidson and Bernard Grofman in *Quiet Revolution in the South*, is that the VRA has been monumentally successful in enhancing voting rights.[343] The original 1965 Act and its reauthorizations in 1970, 1975, 1982, and 2007 have dramatically expanded minority voter registration, turnout, and election of candidates across the South. But that success is part of its problem. There are now many who claim that Section 5 pre-clearance is no longer needed. We have a Black president, and minority registration and voting equals or in some cases exceeds that of Whites. The South has been punished enough and it can now be trusted with minority voting rights.

---

341 347 U.S. 483 (1954).
342 393 U.S. 544, 565 (1969).
343 Davidson and Grofman, Quiet Revolution in the South (1994).

Constitutionally, the Shelby County argument is that Congress's Fifteenth Amendment enforcement is outweighed by a state's rights under the Tenth Amendment. Congress, in reauthorizing the VRA in 2007, used outdated data to support Section 5 and therefore the pre-clearance requirements are disproportionate to the authority the federal government has to enforce this act.

Oral arguments in February, 2013 suggested that the Supreme Court was prepared to strike the law down by a 5-4 vote, with the five Republican-appointed Justices forming the majority, leaving the four Democrat-appointed ones in dissent. This is exactly what happened in June 2013 when the Supreme Court by a 5-4 majority declared that the coverage formula of Section 4 is unconstitutional, thereby effectively voiding Section 5 pre-clearance. The Court ruled that Section 5 limits on state sovereignty could not be justified by voting data and evidence that was outdated. Pre-clearance could only be justified based upon current or present voting statistics, and the Court contended that voter registration and voting patterns no longer demonstrated that there was a "blight of racial discrimination in voting" across the South that needed to be prevented or addressed by pre-clearance. The majority decision overlooked, as the dissent pointed out, the hundreds of voting changes that the Justice Department refused to pre-clear, and it also ignored how the threat of pre-clearance had deterred other forms of racial discrimination when it came to voting. Proof that pre-clearance was needed could be seen in the aftermath of *Shelby Country*—states such as Texas, Florida, and North Carolina moved quickly to implement voter ID or make other changes that make it harder to vote. Thus, *Shelby County* looks like yet another partisan 5-4 decision in recent years that will further erode the legitimacy of the Supreme Court, making it appear that it is ideology and not the law driving its decisions.

Shelby County may be part of the second great disenfranchisement in American history. It needs to be viewed in context of the 2013 *Fisher v. University of Texas, Austin* decision which appeared to make it harder for schools to consider race when making admission decisions. *Fisher* and *Shelby County* together make it harder to address problems or racial discrimination, and no doubt will lead to new partisan battles over voting rights and fraud. Since Florida 2000 there has been a barrage of legislation across the country (discussed in Chapter 3) to require voter photo identification at the polls in order to abate voter fraud. There have also been allegations of increased voter lines and intimidation of voters aimed at discouraging them from voting. It is not necessary to rehash the debate here.

What is critical to note is how *Shelby County* speaks to a host of issues surrounding race and representation.[344] Some would argue that Section 5 is no longer needed in that minority voter registration in the South is effectively equal to that for white Caucasians. Others argue that reauthorization of the VRA in 2007 exceeded Congress's constitutional authority because it relied on old

---

344 *See generally:* Daniel McCool, The Most Fundamental Right: Contrasting Perspectives on the Voting Rights Act (2012), a collection of articles offering support and criticism of the pre-clearance provision.

data and therefore pre-clearance was no longer congruent and proportional to its enforcement authority.[345] If Section 5 is struck down then a powerful tool to remedy discrimination is lost, but even if upheld, the VRA may have reached the end of what it can accomplish. By that, a generation ago Lani Guinier was one of several critics of the VRA, contending that its overall creation of majority-minority districts under Section 2 has not only led to the creation of token districts for people of color, but also safe ones for Whites.[346] Moreover, once elected, minority legislators are often marginalized in office.[347] Overall, minority candidates and legislators may not be able to appeal to white voters or secure support from other white representatives, thereby limiting the influence they have. Thus, even if the VRA were to survive in its present form, it may have already accomplished about as much as it can in its present form. The problem may be that the VRA is wedded to notions of representation that are inadequate for a demographically evolving or multi-cultural country. There need to be alternative schemas that consider the use of proportional representation and multimember districts.

Section 2 of the VRA prevents the use of proportional representation as a remedy for violations. Additionally, federal law bars the use of multimember districts for Congress,[348] even though, through the 1990s, 13 states used it for state legislative races.[349] The significance of these two facts is that perhaps if multimember districting and proportional representation were permitted or more frequently employed it might address some of the racial and partisan problems associated with redistricting, while at the same time furthering other critical representation values. Keep in mind that some of the problems surrounding redistricting stem from a geographic political sorting of the population. People live with political likes or with those whom they share political interests. Because of that it is difficult to draw competitive legislative seats that are accountable to the voters while at the same time protecting and empowering minority interests.

Moreover, one valid concern of the Court in the *Shaw v. Reno* line of cases has been to address the proper role of race in redistricting. There is a fine line between

---

345 It is not entirely clear what test should be used to determine the scope or Congress' authority to enforce the VRA. Under South Carolina v. Katzenbach, 383 U.S. 301, 324 (1966), the Court ruled that the standard was that the legislation must represent a "rational means to effectuate the constitutional prohibition," whereas in City of Boerne v Flores, 521 U.S. 507, 520 (1997) the standard is that there must be a "congruence and proportionality between the injury to be prevented or remedied and the means adopted to that end." In Northwest Austin Municipal Utility District Number One v. Holder, 557 U.S. 193 (2009), the Supreme Court, in avoiding ruling on Section 5, failed to clarify this issue.

346 LANI GUINIER, THE TYRANNY OF THE MAJORITY (1994).

347 Lani Guinier, *The Triumph of Tokenism: The Voting Rights Act and the Theory of Black Electoral Success*, 89 MICH. L. REV. 1077 (1991); *Groups, Representation, and Race-conscious Districting: a Case of the Emperor's Clothes*, 71 TEX. L. REV. 1589 (1993); *No Two Seats: The Elusive Quest for Political Equality*, 77 VA. L. REV. 1413 (1991).

348 2 USC § 2c (2011).

349 NATIONAL CONFERENCE OF STATE LEGISLATURES, REDISTRICTING LAW 2000 (1999).

using race as a discriminatory tool and taking it into consideration as a form of a community of interest. Moreover, Section 2 of the VRA addresses concerns about voter dilution. The problem here is how to maximize minority voting power and representation. As some writers such as Lani Guinier pointed out years ago,[350] the VRA may have been successful in getting some people of color elected but it did little in many cases to give them significant influence in legislatures, especially if they represented token seats. Getting elected in mostly minority districts they never learned how to appeal to white voters or build coalitions. Their influence and strength might only extend as far as the people of color they represent. Effectively, even though the VRA prohibited it, the law might have endorsed proportional representation as some of its critics contended.[351] Guinier's recommendation, among others, was the creation of multimember districts. Her approach was not adopted and instead the Supreme Court in *Georgia v. Ashcroft*[352] seemed to try to address these concerns with the distinction between majority-minority and influence districts as together counting toward compliance with Section 5. Ultimately that approach was rejected in the 2007 reauthorization of the VRA.[353]

Simple proportional representation alone may not address concerns of minority representation or partisan gerrymandering. Proportional representation alone freezes voting preferences along one dimension. By that, it assumes that people of color or partisans vote only on the basis of race or party preference. That is not always the case. Additionally, simple proportional representation still may not address the problem of tokenism and it may also be ineffective in combating the geography issue. In a single-member district that is drawn in a compact and contiguous fashion, it may be difficult, no matter what, for minority party members to elect a candidate of their choice. It may also be that it would be impossible to draw districts so as to protect minority interests in ways that ensure that candidates are accountable to their interests.

Certainly it is not a panacea, but serious consideration should be again given at least to the creation of multimember districts in Congress and in state legislatures. Such an approach would better address partisan gerrymandering problems by giving members of the minority party a chance to vote for someone who represents them. The same is true for people of color in areas with small minority populations. Multimember districts create incentives for some candidates to appeal to diverse voters, perhaps mitigating racially polarized and partisan voting. Perhaps combining multimember districts with some form of proportional

---

350 Lani Guinier, *The Representation of Minority Interests: The Question of Single-Member Districts*, 14 CARDOZO L. REV. 1135 (1993).
351 ABIGAIL THERNSTROM, WHOSE VOTES COUNT? AFFIRMATIVE ACTION AND MINORITY VOTING RIGHTS (1987).
352 539 U.S. 461 (2003).
353 Daniel McCool, *Meaningful Votes*, in DANIEL MCCOOL, ED., THE MOST FUNDAMENTAL RIGHT: CONTRASTING PERSPECTIVES ON THE VOTING RIGHTS ACT, 1 (2012).

representation might address some of the problems noted with current forms of representation in this chapter.

Of course, employment of multimember districts will not work everywhere. In states which have only one member of Congress this idea makes no sense. But the point here is that the current method or schema of representation often fails to protect minority interests and it encourages legislators to gerrymander districts to partisan or personal advantage. The geographic sorting out of partisan preferences also seems to discourage competitive elections that are necessary for democratic accountability. In an era when partisan voting in Congress and across the country seems to be on the rise, the current representation and redistricting systems appear unable to provide for ways that allow for effective governance and decision-making.

A serious debate needs to take place about how to enhance representation beyond the current preoccupation of one person, one vote and the other formal trappings of traditional districting criteria. The failure of the election law jurisprudence is that it is stuck in the past. It remains committed to a formal model of representation that looks only to one person, one vote and other similar criteria to measure the adequacy of representation. That is not adequate if a richer meaning of the term is to be appreciated. Additionally, it is stuck in the past by remaining committed to single-member and first-past-the-post theories of representation. Third, election law jurisprudence has failed to appreciate how the Constitution and the law constitute and mediate representation. By that, the interests that are served and how they are represented—be it from a Madisonian or pluralist perspective— are defined and determined by the law. Non-proportional interests and election systems, for example, represent different types of interests in contrasting ways.[354] Fourth, election law has failed to appreciate how the concept of liberal neutrality may dictate how redistricting is done, mandating perhaps that it is a conflict of interest for legislators to draw their own lines.

Finally, perhaps the biggest flaw may lie in an American concept of representation that remains committed to the current structure of Congress. A 50-state bicameral system that was created in 1787 as a result of a compromise between the big and small states may have been an expedient political mechanism to save the union, but it is now not so clear that it provides adequate representation in a multi-cultural age of the Internet. Many interests may not be able to be represented because they are sacrificed in part to federalism concerns. While the Madisonian democratic vision placed federalism among the solutions to limiting majority faction, it may be a component of American democratic theory that now does more to impede development of representational schema that may better facilitate other important

---

354 DAVID K. RYDEN, REPRESENTATION IN CRISIS: THE CONSTITUTION, INTEREST GROUPS, AND POLITICAL PARTIES (1996); JULIET ROPER, CHRISTINA HOLTZ-BACKA, AND GIANPIETRO MAZZOLENI, THE POLITICS OF REPRESENTATION: ELECTION CAMPAIGNING AND PROPORTIONAL REPRESENTATION (2004); G. BINGHAM POWELL, JR., ELECTIONS AS INSTRUMENTS OF DEMOCRACY: MAJORITARIAN AND PROPORTIONAL VISIONS (2000).

political values. Similarly, from a pluralist perspective, it is not clear that Cong current structure facilitates adequate interest representation. In either case, this chapter ends by arguing that the current election law representation jurisprudence is flawed or incomplete, necessitating a significant rethinking.

Chapter 6
Political Parties

Americans are of two minds regarding political parties and partisanship—love or hate. At the time of the nation's birth and selection of the first president and Congress in 1787-88, political parties did not formally exist in the United States. Perhaps one could describe the Federalist and Anti-Federalist split over the ratification of the Constitution as a form of party or partisan rivalry, but if one thinks in terms of candidates running under party labels and banners as one major characteristic of what it means to be a political party,[1] then these two groupings failed the test. President George Washington thus was unburdened by partisan politics during most of his two terms in office.

Yet with the election of 1796 and the split between John Adams and Thomas Jefferson there emerged the beginnings of the first two major parties in the country—the Federalists and the Democratic-Republicans. Washington, himself, was not pleased with these developments, declaring in his farewell address:

> I have already intimated to you the danger of parties in the State, with particular reference to the founding of them on geographical discriminations. Let me now take a more comprehensive view, and warn you in the most solemn manner against the baneful effects of the spirit of party generally.
>
> This spirit, unfortunately, is inseparable from our nature, having its root in the strongest passions of the human mind. It exists under different shapes in all governments, more or less stifled, controlled, or repressed; but, in those of the popular form, it is seen in its greatest rankness, and is truly their worst enemy.
>
> The alternate domination of one faction over another, sharpened by the spirit of revenge, natural to party dissension, which in different ages and countries has perpetrated the most horrid enormities, is itself a frightful despotism. But this leads at length to a more formal and permanent despotism. The disorders and miseries which result gradually incline the minds of men to seek security and repose in the absolute power of an individual; and sooner or later the chief of some prevailing faction, more able or more fortunate than his competitors, turns this disposition to the purposes of his own elevation, on the ruins of public liberty.[2]

---

1 Martin Wattenberg, The Decline of American Political Parties: 1952-1996, 1 (1998).

2 George Washington, "Farewell Address," located at http://avalon.law.yale.edu/18th_century/washing.asp (site last visited on March 18, 2013).

George Washington saw in political parties a spirit no more noble than and perhaps as destructive as the factions that James Madison warned of in *Federalist* 10. They were a source of revenge, disunion, and dissension. They would put their interests ahead of that of the country and serve as a destructive force. For those observing the state of party politics and gridlock in Washington, D.C. and across many state legislatures across the United States, Washington's comments were prescient of the future. Yet even during Washington's time, the evils that he foretold came soon. With John Adams as president, the Federalists passed the Alien and Sedition Act, prompting Thomas Jefferson and James Madison anonymously to pen the Virginia and Kentucky Resolutions to urge states to nullify this federal law.[3] Party politics became so intense under the Adams administration that opposition members were denounced as traitors, with some jailed for their speech. The election of 1800, which resulted in Thomas Jefferson and the Democratic-Republicans winning, was an intense and hard fought campaign, the like of which has seldom been seen since.

But there is a second view on political parties in the United States. Political scientist E.E. Schattschneider declared: "The parties created democracy, or perhaps more accurately, modern democracy is a by-product of party competition."[4] Parties make it possible to control the government. They perform many useful functions in terms of mobilizing support for candidates and specific public policies. Effectively, they make governing possible by aggregating interests into a majority. For Schattschneider, they form the second Constitution for the United States.[5] In addition to Schattschneider, political theorists such as Robert Dahl,[6] Paul Beck and Frank Sorauf,[7] Anika Gauja,[8] and Gerald Pomper[9] too described the central importance of parties to democracy.

As noted earlier, parties not only mobilize constituencies to form majorities, but they also serve as the proverbial loyal opposition, acting as an important check to the ruling coalition. Credible party competition is critical to democratic practice—it ensures that the party in power remains accountable to the people and the voters have an alternative to support if they do not like the policies or performance of those currently in charge. One-party government or scenarios where there is no credible opposition or realistic opportunity to oust the incumbents, is the recipe

---

3 JAMES MACGREGOR BURNS, THE VINEYARD OF LIBERTY, 125-33 (1982); ALFRED H, KELLY, WINFRED A. HARBISON, AND HERMAN BELZ, THE AMERICAN CONSTITUTION: ITS ORIGINS AND DEVELOPMENT, vol. 1, 129-33 (1991).

4 E.E. SCHATTSCHNEIDER, PARTY GOVERNMENT, 4 (1942).

5 *Id.* at 2.

6 ROBERT A. DAHL, DEMOCRACY AND ITS CRITICS, 157-58 (1989).

7 PAUL A. BECK AND FRANK J. SORAUF, PARTY POLITICS IN AMERICA (1991).

8 ANIKA GAUJA, POLITICAL PARTIES AND ELECTIONS: LEGISLATING FOR REPRESENTATIVE DEMOCRACY (2010).

9 GERALD M. POMPER, PASSIONS AND INTERESTS: POLITICAL PARTY CONCEPTS OF AMERICAN DEMOCRACY (1992); VOTERS, ELECTIONS AND PARTIES: THE PRACTICE OF DEMOCRATIC THEORY (1988).

for an oppressive or authoritarian government. Genuine party competition is a necessary component for democracy to exist. Thus, the partisan disagreements seen in Washington, D.C. and across the United States are less signs of gridlock and more a healthy indication of party politics at work, serving to provide checks and balances upon the opposition or ruling party.

But, as noted in previous chapters, there are many places across the United States where serious party competition has almost disappeared. The geographic sorting of partisan preferences, gerrymandering, and perhaps other factors have contributed to scenarios where there are fewer and fewer competitive Congressional and perhaps state legislative and local government races in the United States. In many ways, the description of America as Red and Blue (Republican and Democrat) seems accurate. Competition, if it exists at all, is intra- and not inter-party. Democrats and Republicans have more to fear from challenges within their parties and less from outside it. Primaries or endorsing conventions may be more determinative of who wins than the general elections.

If parties are either the savior or scourge of democracy, then either the lack of robust competition or their partisan excess is something of concern. Political parties need to be regulated. But what does the Constitution explicitly state about them? Simply put, nothing. Political parties, as noted, did not exist at the time of the writing of the Constitution or even with the Bill of Rights. Thus looking for express language on them is futile. Additionally, to divine the intent of the Framers would also be difficult. George Washington's comments suggest a dislike of them that necessitate they be regulated. Additionally, depending on whether one treats political parties as *sui generis* or no differently than factions, James Madison too would have viewed them negatively and perhaps also endorsed significant regulation of them to control their effects.

The absence of clear language and intent regarding the constitutional status of political parties means that the law—and more significantly, the Supreme Court—has had to frame the role for them in American democratic theory and practice. Many questions exist when it comes to thinking about what constitutional protection and rights should be given to them. Among these questions include constitutionally clarifying what is a political party and distinguishing it from other groups in society. Second, as Dan Lowenstein has asked, there is the question of who the party is. By that, when it comes to asserting constitutional rights, who gets to assert or claim harm or rights? Third, are parties public or private entities? Fourth, if parties can be regulated, are there limits to government control? For example, is there a difference between the internal operations of a party versus its external impact? All of these are important questions, and, as will become clear, the Supreme Court and the judiciary in general has failed to develop a coherent jurisprudence when it comes to the constitutional status of political parties. This failure may be rooted in terms of a larger overall failure of democratic theory to provide a coherent theory about parties. The goal of this chapter is to examine some of the questions surrounding the role that political parties should have within an American democratic theory of election law.

What Parties Do

As noted earlier, Robert Dahl and E.E. Schattschneider, along with other theorists, describe political parties as essential to the maintenance of democratic societies. For Schattschneider, they provide a mobilization function and help forge majorities to govern. For Dahl, parties perform a similar function but also operate to maintain voter choice and facilitate political accountability. Political parties thus are entities or a means to express political views and ideas. The Supreme Court noted this importance for political parties in *California Democratic Party v. Jones* when it declared: "Representative democracy in any populous unit of governance is unimaginable without the ability of citizens to band together in promoting among the electorate candidates who espouse their political views.[10]

But parties perform a host of functions that transcend what Dahl and Schattschneider describe. Martin Wattenberg[11] lists more than a dozen functions that include providing political symbols, organizing interests, mobilizing majorities, educating and socializing voters, organizing dissent, recruiting candidates, channeling conflict, overriding sectionalism, implementing policies, legitimizing decisions, and fostering stability. Add to this list also that parties increasingly provide financial and other forms of assistance to their candidates, that they organize voter registration drives, and facilitate get out the vote campaigns, among other tasks.

Parties undertake a host of functions that are critical to democracy. On one level they are the intermediate or voluntary associations that pluralists and de Tocqueville praised. They are entities that aggregate preferences and organize interests. In a mass society where it is difficult for individuals acting on their own to achieve a sense of efficacy, parties fill that void. They bring similarly-minded individuals together to support causes and candidates. They provide bottom-up information to candidates and the government regarding political preferences and top-down communication from leaders to rank-and-file. In many ways, parties are the missing link that connects the people to the government. Viewed in this regard, political parties serve roles consistent with the aims of pluralist democratic theory. They may operate, along with interest groups, as yet another institution that serves to facilitate interest aggregation and mobilization.

But not to be ignored are two other critical features of parties that Wattenberg and others note. The first is that parties implement policies, the second is that they provide stability. In terms of implementation, parties can be seen as both a formal and informal source of political power. Formal in the sense that majority parties passing legislation thereupon will be called on to implement governmental policy. In the days before the Pendleton Act and civil service reform, party governance and implementation was more direct. Majority

---

10   530 U.S. 567 (2000).
11   Wattenberg, The Decline of American Political Parties at 1-3.

parties were able to staff government bureaucracies with their members.[12] To a larger extent governmental bureaucracies have been politically neutralized and patronage-based hiring has been limited as a result of First Amendment concerns.[13] However, formally majority parties are still in the expected position to execute policies in a formal fashion, especially if they control the executive branch. Parties, as Schattschneider points out, are held accountable in elections for their ability or failure to govern.[14]

But parties also implement policies informally. In a world of intergovernmental federalism, the party in control at the national government may rely upon state parties in control to support their policies. Party control across units of government may provide important signals and support for programs. For example, a president may expect governors of the same party to support and implement their initiatives. Moreover, partisan support for policies simply lessens opposition and encourages party mobilization of ideas as part of a platform unifying them.

Promoting stability is another important function of a party.[15] It does that by channeling opposition.[16] How? Think of the alternative to organizing opposition if parties did not exist? It could include riots, armed resistance, violent confrontation, and, at the most extreme, rebellion. In countries where there is no space or forum for formal opposition, political change is not peaceful but often violent. What political parties, especially opposition ones, make possible is the channeling of dissent into more peaceful and stable forms of disagreement. Instead of scenarios where the choice is between supporting the ruling party and the government versus regime change, voters and those who do not share the same political views can compete for power in elections. If and when the ruling majority or party is ousted the regime itself does not change. Instead, the change is limited to the personnel and to those making policy. Political stability is produced by the regularization of elections, party change, and an orderly process for articulating disagreement and transitioning power from one group to another. If stability is one goal of democracy, then maintenance of competitive party structures is important.

Of course, even though parties may have ideological disagreements over policy, there still needs to be some consensus regarding the legitimacy of the regime. In many countries the opposition party questions not simply the ruling party but

---

12 *See generally:* DAVID SCHULTZ AND ROBERT MARANTO, THE POLITICS OF CIVIL SERVICE REFORM (1998), for a general discussion of spoils and patronage staffing of the government.

13 SHEILA KENNEDY AND DAVID SCHULTZ, AMERICAN PUBLIC SERVICE: CONSTITUTIONAL AND ETHICAL FOUNDATIONS, 120-27 (2010).

14 Schattschneider, Party Government at 193, 199.

15 ALAN GITELSON, AMERICAN POLITICAL PARTIES: STABILITY AND CHANGE (1984); RUSSELL J. DALTON, DAVID M. FARRELL, AND IAN MCALLISTER, POLITICAL PARTIES AND DEMOCRATIC LINKAGE: HOW PARTIES ORGANIZE DEMOCRACY (2011).

16 Wattenberg, The Decline of American Political Parties at 2.

the very legitimacy of the government. Short of that, it is also possible for two parties to have widely divergent views on the role of government in society. One of the classic traits of American political parties has been that they generally were more coalitional and less ideological.[17] At one time, perhaps even as recently as a generation ago, it was more likely to find a range of ideological perspectives in the two dominant parties in the United States. But one of the more recent trends in American politics now seems to be that the Republican and Democratic parties have adopted more of an ideological basis, as evidenced by party-line votes in Congress and by public opinion polls and surveys revealing clear differences in the policy preferences and demographics between the two.[18] Again, for those who view the current political disagreements in Washington and across the country as a sign of gridlock, this partisan polarization is a problem. It is perhaps also a sign that James Madison was correct in his fears of factions. Perhaps political parties are no different than factions, mobilizing against the rights of others or the public good. This is the sentiment regarding political parties that seems to be expressed by George Washington in his farewell address.

But for those who see the partisan disagreement as producing genuine choice and checks on governmental and political power, this is good. The point of this discussion is not to settle this issue. Instead, it is simply is to note that the two major parties offer contrasting views on the role of government and the policies it should pursue, and it does not appear that either of them engage in questioning the legitimacy of the American political system. Despite their differences, they share some consensus on many American values, as is necessary to maintain overall democratic stability.[19]

In sum, without making this chapter a significant discourse on political parties, it is clear that from a general theory of democracy, they serve an important role performing a host of functions as described by Dahl, Schattschneider, Wattenberg, and others. But there is another important question to ask—how are parties different from other groups or entities?

Consider several other groups that exist in the United States. Exclude the private clubs and other voluntary organizations that de Tocqueville wrote about and restrict the list to groups that are interested in politics. These might include political action committees, interest groups that lobby the government, and perhaps other ad hoc or more permanent entities concerned with political issues.

---

17 EVERETT CARLL LADD AND CHARLES D. HADLEY, TRANSFORMATIONS OF THE AMERICAN PARTY SYSTEM: POLITICAL COALITIONS FROM THE NEW DEAL TO THE 1970s (1976).

18 PEW RESEARCH CENTER, THE GENERATION GAP AND THE 2012 ELECTION (2011).

19 *See generally:* LOUIS HARTZ, THE LIBERAL TRADITION IN AMERICA: AN INTERPRETATION OF AMERICAN POLITICAL THOUGHT SINCE THE REVOLUTION (1955), for a discussion of the Lockean consensus on political values. *See also:* DANIEL J. BOORSTIN, THE LOST WORLD OF THOMAS JEFFERSON (1993), DANIEL J. BOORSTIN, THE AMERICANS: THE COLONIAL EXPERIENCE (1964); and CLINTON ROSSITER, SEEDTIME OF THE REPUBLIC: THE ORIGINS OF THE AMERICAN TRADITION OF POLITICAL LIBERTY (1953).

How are these organizations different from political parties? Many of these groups are interested in furthering public policy, maybe they provide financial support directly or indirectly to political candidates or causes. These groups might also engage in voter registration and education, they might seek to organize individuals, they may oppose or support policies. In many ways, these organizations may perform many of the tasks that political parties perform. How do we distinguish them from political parties? Perhaps one could argue that these entities do not nominate and run candidates under their label, but what is the difference between a candidate running for office as a Republican who has received the endorsement of the National Rifle Association opposed to actually running as an NRA Party candidate?[20] It is not clear in some circumstances what the real difference is. On one level, there may be no real ontological difference between parties and other groups—it is simply a matter of legal construction.[21]

Additionally, Schattschneider sees distinguishing features of political parties in the fact that they govern and are held accountable in elections.[22] There is significant merit to this argument. While interest groups may support candidates for office, and while it may be argued that someone is a candidate favoring or favored by the NRA or the AARP, these organizations do not have their members caucus, run for office, or serve in government under these interest group or organizational labels. They also do not appear on the ballot as NRA or AARP candidates. They do all of that as Republicans, Democrats, or under some other label. Thus, there is some difference between being an organized interest versus being a party, even if nothing would or could in theory prevent the NRA or the AARP from organizing itself as a party if they so wished.

But why should we care? It matters because of the special status or position that parties are assigned in American society and in democratic theory in general. They are given the ability to nominate candidates, secure ballot access for their members, engage in certain unique types of fundraising, and otherwise be allowed to immunize themselves from some types of regulations or be allowed to do things that these other entities may not do. They are held out as different, but maybe they should not be. For many individuals who do not like political parties, or who do not subscribe to the current menu of policy positions that the current major parties endorse, political engagement through another entity or interest

---

20 *See:* Republican Party of Minnesota v. White, 416 F.3d 738, 759-60 (8th Cir. 2005). Here the court, in ruling on whether a candidate for judicial office may affiliate with a political party or accept their nomination, questioned whether there was much difference in doing that versus affiliating or accepting the endorsement of specific groups such as the NRA or the NAACP.

21 DAVID K. RYDEN, REPRESENTATION IN CRISIS: THE CONSTITUTION, INTEREST GROUPS, AND POLITICAL PARTIES (1996).

22 Schattschneider, Party Government at 199.

group may be a more attractive feature.[23] Many people may be more interested in supporting a single-issue group than a political party. Thus, to give special status to political parties as opposed to other entities may be a form of First Amendment discrimination. By that, it forces individuals to politically associate in a particular format or organization as opposed to another if they want to express themselves in a specific way, such as supporting or nominating a candidate for office and then achieving ballot access for that person.

Now also compare political parties to other entities such as corporations, labor unions, and non-profits. For example, since the 1907 Tillman Act corporations have been barred from making direct political contributions to candidates for federal office. The Taft-Hartley Act of 1947 imposed the same restriction upon labor unions. Taft-Hartley also barred both unions and corporations from making express advocacy independent expenditures to advocate for the election or defeat of a federal candidate for office. This latter restriction remained in place until the 2010 *Citizens United v. Federal Election Commission* decision voided it.[24] Now unions and corporations at the federal level can make express advocacy independent expenditures. But even prior to that decision several Court decisions had granted corporations a variety of rights to expend money for political purposes, depending on whether it was a for-profit or non-profit or depending on whether it was a ballot proposition or a candidate campaign. These cases included *FEC v. Massachusetts Citizens Concerned for Life*,[25] *Federal Election Commission v. National Right to Work Committee*,[26] *California Medical Association v. Federal Election Commission*,[27] and *Federal Election Commission v. National Conservative Political Action Committee*.[28] Additionally non-profit corporations, depending on whether they are classified under IRS tax law as a 501 c 3 or 501 c 4, face differing restrictions on partisan political activity and the amount of lobbying they can do.

The point here is that the law classifies entities or organizations in many different ways, giving them varying rights to speak in the political process. Classification matters, unless of course one argues that all entities should be treated the same, including political parties. This may be a worthy or valid argument, but it is not one that seems generally well supported by democratic and legal theorists. Conceptually, ordinary language or usage of the term political party seems to

---

23   Gallup Politics, Americans Renew Call for Third Party (September 17, 2010), http://www.gallup.com/poll/143051/Americans-Renew-Call-Third-Party.aspx (site last visited on March 19, 2013), describing how 58 percent of those surveyed believed that the two major parties did a poor job representing the American people. In 2011 a similar Gallup Poll survey revealed that 52 percent of the public still held this view (May 9, 2011), http://www.gallup.com/poll/147461/Support-Third-Party-Dips-Majority-View.aspx (site last viewed on March 19, 2013).

24   558 U.S. 310 (2010).
25   479 U.S. 238 (1986).
26   459 U.S. 197 (1982).
27   453 U.S. 182 (1981).
28   470 U.S. 480 (1985).

assume that in fact they are somehow different from these other entities in terms of their purposes. For-profit corporations are there to make money, unions to advocate for the rights of workers, and political parties to advocate for candidates and political causes of their choosing.

Even some on the Supreme Court seem to have assumed, rightly or wrongly, that political parties are unique. Consider the cases of *Colorado Republican Federal Campaign Committee v. Federal Election Commission* (Colorado Republican I)[29] and *Federal Election Commission v. Colorado Republican Federal Campaign Committee* (Colorado Republican II).[30] In Colorado Republican I, in 1986, the Colorado Republican Party (CRP) sought to expend money to oppose the re-election of the incumbent U.S. Senator Tim Wirth well in advance of the time when the party had selected a candidate of its own to oppose the incumbent. The FEC charged the CRP with violation of a section of the 1971 Federal Election Campaign Act which imposed spending caps on party expenditures.[31] Since the CRP had already exceeded its spending limits pursuant to §441a(d)(3), the Democratic Party complained to the FEC that the expenditures made in connection with Tim Wirth's race were in violation of the FECA spending caps. The CRP argued that the party expenditures made against Tim Wirth were uncoordinated expenditures and should be treated like any other political expenditures as dictated by *Buckley* such that the §441a(d)(3) limits on party spending were a facial and as applied violation of the First Amendment.[32]

Justice Breyer's majority opinion did not address the CRP facial challenge to §441a(d)(3) but it did strike down the application of this section of FECA to CRP.[33] In reaching that holding Breyer drew heavily upon the *Buckley* distinction between money spent to advertise one's views independently and money given to a candidate for his campaign purposes.[34] In accepting the basic expenditure/contribution distinction drawn by the *Buckley* Court, Breyer again noted that independent expenditures do not create the same problems of *quid pro quo* corruption or preventing its appearance as do contributions,[35] and, as a result,

---

29   518 U.S. 604, 135 L. Ed.2d 795 (1996).

30   533 U.S. 431 (2001).

31   2 U.S.C. §441a(d)(3) limited party expenditures in U.S. Senate races to the greater of $20,000 or "2 cents multiplied by the voting population of the state," as adjusted for inflation from 1974.

32   135 L.Ed.2d at 803-4.

33   *Id.* at 804, 810. Specifically, the CRP sought to challenge the entire party expenditure limit as unconstitutional, and it also sought, in the case of political parties, to challenge the restrictions placed on coordinated expenditures. While the Court declined to address this question, *id.* at 810, the force of CRP's assertion was that at least in the context of party activity, there is no constitutional difference between expenditures for coordinated and uncoordinated activity (a.k.a. contributions and expenditures). Justice Thomas's dissent did, however, seek to address the broader claims of the CRP.

34   *Id.*

35   *Id.* at 805.

regulation and limitation on expenditures are a more direct and greater burden on free speech than are regulations upon contributions given to and coordinated with candidates and their campaigns.[36] Hence, since the CRP expenditures were not coordinated with any candidate (since they had no candidate at the time), the Court held that these party expenditures were protected political expression under the First Amendment.[37] Further, the Court noted that, lacking any evidence that party expenditures poses a special form of corruption not previously noted or associated with independent expenditures,[38] the absence of any candidate coordination between a party and a candidate removed the danger that any of the expenditures by the party are a form of *quid pro quo* arrangement.[39]

In a partial concurrence and dissent, Justice Thomas, joined by the Chief Justice Rehnquist and Justice Scalia, reached the broader claims of the CRP, striking down the party expenditure limits as unconstitutional.[40] In rendering that opinion, Thomas made two claims. First, he saw no overall threat of corruption associated with party expenditures.[41] In fact, given the structure of parties as dealing with numerous candidates and the absence of any evidence that party expenditures would implicate a *quid pro quo* problem, Thomas would invalidate §441a(d)(3) as facially unconstitutional.[42] In effect, the majority, and Justice Thomas in particular, did not see how independent expenditures and the interrelationship between the parties and candidates could be corrupting. In fact, Breyer declared in his majority opinion: "We are not aware of any special dangers of corruption associated with political parties."[43] Parties were not to be treated differently from any other entity when it came to the making of independent expenditures.

Finally, in dissent, Justices Stevens and Ginsburg would have upheld the FECA limits.[44] Of special note, however, is both Justices would treat all money spent by parties as a contribution and therefore subject to the regulative standards and analysis found under *Buckley*.[45] Without directly reaching the broader contribution/expenditure distinction raised in *Buckley*, both of the Justices nonetheless found that the spending caps imposed on parties are necessary both to address the problems associated with corruption and its appearance, and, more importantly, to prevent individuals from circumventing the $1,000 contribution limit to candidates by instead giving to parties.[46] For the very fact that parties and

---

36 *Id.*
37 *Id.*
38 *Id.* at 806.
39 *Id.* at 805.
40 *Id.* at 815, 825.
41 *Id.* at 823-24.
42 *Id.* at 822.
43 518 U.S. 604, 616 (1996).
44 *Id.* at 825.
45 *Id.* at 825-26.
46 *Id.* at 826.

candidates are closely linked is a reason to worry about the corruption that can take place.

Colorado Republican II addresses an issue carrying over from the previous case: Does the First Amendment permit the coordination of expenditures between the parties and candidates? The Court said no, refusing to distinguish parties yet again from any other entity. In reaching this answer Souter wrote for the majority contending the this regulation really asks a basic question about the relationship of candidates to parties:

> There are two basic arguments here. The first turns on the relationship of a party to a candidate: a coordinated relationship between them so defines a party that it cannot function as such without coordinated spending, the object of which is a candidate's election. We think political history and political reality belie this argument. The second argument turns on the nature of a party as uniquely able to spend in ways that promote candidate success.[47]

Effectively, the majority was asking how we view parties, especially in comparison to other entities, perhaps such as corporations and maybe other large donors. Are parties and candidates effectively linked and therefore the latter is unable to corrupt the latter, or is there a different type of relationship? Again the Souter opinion seems to answer that question:

> When we look directly at a party's function in getting and spending money, it would ignore reality to think that the party role is adequately described by speaking generally of electing particular candidates. The money parties spend comes from contributors with their own personal interests. PACs, for example, are frequent party contributors who (according to one of the Party's own experts) "do not pursue the same objectives in electoral politics" that parties do … In fact, many PACs naturally express their narrow interests by contributing to both parties during the same electoral cycle, and sometimes even directly to two competing candidates in the same election, Parties are thus necessarily the instruments of some contributors whose object is not to support the party's message or to elect party candidates across the board, but rather to support a specific candidate for the sake of a position on one narrow issue, or even to support any candidate who will be obliged to the contributors.
>
> Parties thus perform functions more complex than simply electing candidates; whether they like it or not, they act as agents for spending on behalf of those who seek to produce obligated officeholders. It is this party role, which functionally unites parties with other self-interested political actors, that the Party Expenditure Provision targets. This party role, accordingly, provides good reason to view limits on coordinated spending by parties through the same lens

---

47 533 U.S. at 449.

applied to such spending by donors, like PACs, that can use parties as conduits for contributions meant to place candidates under obligation.[48]

Political parties are not simply arms of candidates or vice versa, and they are additionally viewed by the Court as more than simply alter egos of candidates. Parties are like other special interests prepared to use money and resources to purpose their objective and exact influence, even on their own candidates. Thus, parties can be corrupted (by other interests) and are capable of corrupting. Accepting such a view is perhaps somewhat consistent both with a Madisonian and pluralist view of parties. In the former, parties may be no more than another potential faction that poses a threat to the political process, whereas for pluralists they are no more than another way to express interests on individuals and other groups.

But in dissent Justice Thomas sees a different relationship between parties and its candidates:

> The dearth of evidence is unsurprising in light of the unique relationship between a political party and its candidates: "The very aim of a political party is to influence its candidate's stance on issues and, if the candidate takes office or is reelected, his votes." [Citation omitted] If coordinated expenditures help achieve this aim, the achievement "does not ... constitute 'a subversion of the political process.'" It is simply the essence of our Nation's party system of government.[49]

For Thomas, neither is there evidence of party corruptibility nor of a party being able to corrupt its candidates, the two are expected to work together. Instead, there seems to be a belief that parties are different from other groups. Parties in some ways can control or filter the influences of interest groups. This picture of political parties reflects a widely held view (though not proven) that, in areas where political parties are strong, interest groups are weak, and vice versa.[50]

The two *Colorado Republican* decisions offer contrasting views on the relationship among political parties, candidates, other special interests, and money. The majority opinion in both cases refuses to treat parties as really different from any other special interest group when it comes to the corrupting influence that its money may (with coordinated) or may not (independent) have with expenditures it makes on behalf of candidates. Parties are more than tools of candidates and needed to be treated as distinct ontological entities. The importance of this debate in these

---

48 *Id.* at 450-51.
49 *Id.* at 476-77.
50 *See, e.g.*, KAY LEHMAN SCHLOZMAN JOHN T. TIERNEY, ORGANIZED INTERESTS AND AMERICAN DEMOCRACY (1986); Ronald Hrebenar and Clive Thomas, "*Who's Got Clout? Interest Group Power in the States*," 25 STATE LEGISLATURES 30 (April 1999); Schattschneider, Party Government at 192, 198-201, "A strongly led party able to discipline its members and able to hold its line on controversial questions will be able to defy the guerilla tactics of the pressure groups."

two cases is that it suggests that some on the Court see parties as different from other entities and therefore should be permitted to do things others may not. These two cases fail to resolve the debate over how parties are different, and other opinions across many issues affecting political parties continue to reveal judicial confusion.

Are Political Parties Private Affairs?

There is a 1960s Leslie Gore song titled "It's My Party and I'll Cry if I Want To." In some ways the song speaks to the jurisprudence of political parties. Political parties generally have broad leeway under the First Amendment freedom of association clause to govern their own internal affairs by determining who may participate in their business. But is this authority unlimited? Could they create a party for Whites or males only? Could Democrats invite independents in or prevent Republicans from participating in their conventions, primaries, or caucuses? Could states, in an effort to increase voter turnout or eliminate discrimination, mandate who may participate? These are some of the questions raised when party associational rights are considered. The starting point for understanding the scope of regulation over parties begins by asking this question. If parties are private entities then the Constitution does not cover them in terms of whether they can violate Equal Protection mandates. If parties are deemed to be public (or public accommodations) then the Constitution and anti-discrimination laws may be applicable, unless overridden by First Amendment factors. Consider the case of *Smith v. Allwright*.[51]

At issue in *Smith* was a challenge by an African-American citizen in Texas who wished to participate in its state democratic primary. However, the Texas Democratic Party confined membership to "all white citizens of the State of Texas who are qualified to vote under the Constitution and laws of the State."[52] On one level the issue was quite simple: Can the Democratic Party exclude Lonnie Smith from participation in their primary because of his race? At a time before the 1964 Civil Rights Act existed and questions regarding whether the Party was a public accommodation could be asked, the issue came down to whether the Party was a government actor or not. If it were a government actor in some way then perhaps the Fourteenth and Fifteenth Amendments would have applied, thereby affirming the rights of Smith to participate.

But *Smith* took place during the 1940s, in the middle of a series of cases known as the White Primary cases in the South. The South was solidly Democratic—a one-party region—and victory in the primary was tantamount to winning office. The primary was perhaps more important than the general election. *Smith* also took place in the context of a separate but equal segregated South during a time when the NAACP was challenging discrimination. Given all this, the exclusion from

---

51 321 U.S. 649 (1944).
52 *Id.* at 656.

participating in a primary is significant. Had the State of Texas formally denied Smith or any African-American the right to vote in the general election it arguably would have violated the Fourteenth and Fifteenth Amendments. In *United States v. Classic*,[53] an earlier White Primary case from Louisiana, the Court had stated that there was a right to vote in federal elections. Yet states did figure out ways to deny individuals the right to vote though a series of Jim Crow laws and techniques that were discussed earlier in Chapter 3. But another way to disenfranchise was to preclude participation in the primary, declaring such activities to be private events and to consider the political party to be no different than a private club.

In fact, the Texas Democratic Party was a private association according to how the State Supreme Court classified it.[54] But in examining the primary process in Texas, the U.S. Supreme Court noted that primaries were conducted under state authority:

> The county executive committee selects precinct election officials and the county, district or state executive committees, respectively, canvass the returns. These party committees or the state convention certify the party's candidates to the appropriate officers for inclusion on the official ballot for the general election. No name which has not been so certified may appear upon the ballot for the general election as a candidate of a political party. No other name may be printed on the ballot which has not been placed in nomination by qualified voters who must take oath that they did not participate in a primary for the selection of a candidate for the office for which the nomination is made.[55]

This extensive intertwining of the Democratic Party and the State, along with other statutes and provisions set by the latter assessing candidates for office the cost of running the primary,[56] places the party in "agency of the state in so far as it determines the participants in a primary election."[57]

Notice that the Supreme Court does not actually say that the Texas Democratic Party is a state actor per se. Instead, because of the extensive state involvement with the party, and due to the fact that the primary places candidates on the ballot for the general election,[58] the party is cloaked with enough state action to render it an agent of the state when it comes to the operation of its primaries.[59] In some

---

53 313 U.S. 299 (1941).
54 321 U.S. at 654.
55 *Id.* at 764-65.
56 *Id.* at 765.
57 *Id.*
58 *Id.* at 664-65.
59 The parallel here seems to be to business deemed to be heavily regulated industries such as public utilities where the courts have upheld laws requiring them to serve the public interest or serve all comers. Munn v. Illinois, 94 U.S. 113 (1877) is a classic example of this point.

ways this is a narrow opinion declaring that in at least this case of running a primary, a party has enough state involvement—somewhat like a heavily regulated industry—that it qualifies as a state actor and therefore may not discriminate. This narrow reading that does not outright declare parties to be government actors left open the possibility that if parties were not intertwined with state action, if it were not a primary, but instead a club that selected individuals to participate in the primary, then this one-step removal might make a difference and allow for exclusion on account of race. This was the issue effectively in *Terry v. Adams*, but the Court rejected this argument.[60]

So why is *Smith* an important case? It represents a situation where, Leslie Gore's song title notwithstanding, a party could not do what it wants. But *Smith* raises other great questions. Presumably a party would also be barred from excluding women from its primary for the same reasons.[61] And one could perhaps also make good arguments that religious affiliation[62] and nationality[63] would be impermissible grounds for exclusion. But think about other grounds for exclusion and other activities and it becomes a more difficult question.

First, what if a party wished to exclude someone from participating in a primary because of sexual orientation? What if the party had a strong anti-gay platform? Or what about a hypothetical Male Misogynist Party wanting to exclude women? Or what if a party in the United States wanted to follow the direction of some European ones and form a Christian Party. Assume that occurs and the party requires Christian orientation as a condition of membership and participation in a primary. Would all of these stipulations be unconstitutional under *Smith*? A quick answer would be to say no, that they are forms of discrimination impermissible

---

60   345 U.S. 461 (1952).

61   *See:* Roberts v. U.S. Jaycees, 468 U.S. 609 (1984). While the case does not address party exclusion based on gender it does reject a First Amendment argument by a group to prevent women from joining their organization. In Bachur v. Democratic Nat. Party, 836 F.2d 837 (4th Cir. 1987) the court rejected an Equal Protection challenge by a delegate that claimed that a ballot requiring him to allocate his votes for candidates to attend the national convention based on gender was unconstitutional. Here the court noted that parties have broad authority to select their delegates free from state control, but the case does not directly address if a party could simply just decide to refuse to admit women at all to their functions.

62   If party functions were deemed to be a state activity then presumably Article VI of the Constitution, baring religious tests as a qualification for any public office in the United States, might apply along with the Equal Protection clause and perhaps laws on public accommodation.

63   Excluding someone because of their national heritage may be a violation of Equal Protection clause and laws on public accommodation ("No Irish-Americans are allowed to attend a convention or vote in a primary") but excluding someone because they are not a citizen is arguably constitutional (especially if the party function is a primary) since these individuals may not be allowed to vote or serve in office.

under *Smith*, the Constitution, or applicable civil rights laws. Yet think again about how to reclassify these cases.

Could the Texas Democratic Party limit primary participation to members of its own party and exclude Republicans? The answer surely seems yes even though, on the face of it, it looks like either viewpoint- or content-based discrimination against some individuals on grounds of their political orientation. The right freedom of association under the First Amendment would suggest that. In cases such as *Tashjian v. Republican Party of Connecticut*,[64] *California Democratic Party v. Jones*,[65] and *Eu v. San Francisco County Democratic Central Committee*,[66] the Supreme Court seemed to assert broad First Amendment rights of political parties to decide what individuals or groups they get associate with. *Tashjian* declares that parties have broad rights to decide whom they can invite to their events, although *Clingman v. Beaver* seemed to retract somewhat on that right to invite members of other party members from participation in events.[67] But read these cases a different way—the First Amendment grants individuals and associations the right to disassociate themselves from individuals whose messages they do not support. This is what the Court declared in *Hurley v. Irish-American Gay, Lesbian and Bisexual Group of Boston*.[68]

Could a party exclude someone from its activities unless they agreed with its ideological platform? Could Republicans exclude the Log Cabin Republicans or TEA Party members because of ideological reasons? One thinks yes.[69] A party should be able to define its own political orthodoxy and exclude those whom it does not agree with, or those who do not agree with it. But what if political views overlap with racial, religious, or gender issues. What if the Male Misogynist Party which opposes political rights for women decides on political principle to exclude women from its primary, may it do so? *Smith* suggests no, but the First Amendment analysis might suggest otherwise.

It is probably easy to make the argument that the party can hold any views it wants but that it cannot discriminate in practice. This type of distinction would be

---

64 479 U.S.208 (1986).
65 530 U.S. 567 (2000).
66 489 U.S. 214 (1989).
67 544 U.S. 581 (2005). *Tashjian* involved the Connecticut Republican Party wishing to invite independent voters to their events while *Clingman* involved the Libertarian Party wanting to invite members of other political parties to their events. In the latter case the Court ruled that prevent of party raiding and promoting stability and providing clear information to voters were compelling state interests that overrode party interests in inviting these individuals to their events.
68 515 U.S. 557 (1995).
69 However, in Ammond v. McGahn, 390 F. Supp. 655 (D. N.J. 1975) a federal district court seemed to suggest some limits on a party legislative caucus being able to exclude one of its members because the former objected to political views of the latter. This case seems an outlier in terms of the broad authority of parties to maintain orthodoxy and define their political messages.

similar to the one made in *Reynolds v. United States*[70] where the Court ruled that notwithstanding religious duty or belief in polygamy, the government could ban such a practice. The reasoning here is that the Court drew a distinction between faith and action. *Reynolds* is not generally respected as precedent because it drew a narrow notion to what religious faith was. In cases such as *Boy Scouts v. Dale*[71] the Court recognized the importance of values and mission in terms of freedom of association and the choice of the Scouts to exclude individuals based on their sexual orientation. Given a decision such as this, perhaps the Male Misogynist Party could exclude women.

Additionally, racial or gender-based discrimination when it comes to who is invited to a primary seems different from ideological or viewpoint-based discrimination. We do not expect parties to be neutral when it comes to political views. In some cases, the Constitution forbids parties from discriminating for certain reasons because it is a state actor, conversely the Constitution permits parties to discriminate in ways the government may not because they are more akin to private associations.

A second question left open by *Smith* is in regards to what party functions beyond primaries are considered cloaked with state action. In part, this question has already been raised in Chapter 3. Many state parties have conventions and caucuses, often with meeting dates and times proscribed by state law. These events in many cases may lead to the selection of candidates who appear on the general election ballot. Because of that, are they events that should be subject to the same rules regarding anti-discrimination as those which apply to primaries? In Chapter 3 the discussion was upon the issue of absentee voting for these events. The issue was over who can be required to be admitted to a party for the purposes of establishing a right to vote. But now here the argument is about which events are private that would allow parties to exclude individuals or otherwise restrict or condition membership or entrance.

Is there a black letter rule that can be constructed to define under what circumstances parties are state versus private actors and which also draw lines regarding when the government can regulate to protect a right to vote? The case law is not clear. But the question is important because it affects the degree to which the government may regulate parties and how independent the latter may be in the governance of their affairs.

Internal and External Affairs

Another way to think about the status of political parties and the scope of government regulation is to distinguish between internal and external affairs. Conceptually it may make sense to say that how a political party conducts its internal affairs is of

---

70 98 U.S. 145 (1878).
71 530 U.S. 640 (2000).

no business to anyone outside of it and therefore the government has no business in regulating its activities. This type of argument is a variation of the public/private distinction perhaps initially made famous by John Stuart Mill in *On Liberty* where he seeks to distinguish the scope of governmental authority over the individual. For Mill, behavior that affects no one else is private and therefore the government has no right to intervene to prevent or promote specific acts. Perhaps the same distinction can be applied to political parties.

There is some evidence that this type of distinction has affected Supreme Court political party jurisprudence. First in *Tashjian v. Republican Party of Connecticut*,[72] the Court ruled that a state closed primary law which required individuals to be a member of a party to participate in its primaries was unconstitutional. Here, the Connecticut Republican Party wished to invite independents to participate in their primaries and the state sought to prevent that from occurring, asserting as compelling interests to ensure "the administrability of the primary system, preventing raiding, avoiding voter confusion, and protecting the responsibility of party government."[73] Connecticut also asserted its constitutional authority under Article I, Section 4, Clause 1 to regulate the time, manner, and place of elections.[74]

The Supreme Court rejected the Connecticut argument, ruling in favor of the First Amendment association rights of the party. While Justice Thurgood Marshall's majority opinion recognized all of these interests as compelling, they did not override the interests of the Republican Party in how it managed its internal affairs. According to the Court:

> Under these circumstances, the views of the State, which to some extent represent the views of the one political party transiently enjoying majority power, as to the optimum methods for preserving party integrity lose much of their force. The State argues that its statute is well designed to save the Republican Party from undertaking a course of conduct destructive of its own interests. But on this point "even if the State were correct, a State, or a court, may not constitutionally substitute its own judgment for that of the Party." The Party's determination of the boundaries of its own association, and of the structure which best allows it to pursue its political goals, is protected by the Constitution. "And as is true of all expressions of First Amendment freedoms, the courts may not interfere on the ground that they view a particular expression as unwise or irrational."[75]

The Court rejects party paternalism here. Whether or not the decision by the Republicans to invite independents to their primary was wise, it is their party and the Republicans could invite whom they want. There seems to be, regarding the internal operations of the party, a line beyond which the government may not

---

72 479 U.S. 208 (1986).
73 *Id.* at 217.
74 *Id.*
75 *Id.* at 224.

venture, leaving it up to the former to decide how best to associate with others or govern itself.

A second case highlighting the internal/external distinction is *Eu v. San Francisco County Democratic Central Committee*.[76] In this case, a California law that prevented elected officials from endorsing candidates for office was declared a violation of the First Amendment. The same law also imposed term limits and rotation for some party officers. Here again the Court struck the law as unconstitutional. First, the Court noted that the law did not prevent other political entities such as labor organizations and political action committees from doing pre-primary endorsements and it did not require them to rotate officers. Thus, there was an issue in singling out political parties with these requirements.[77] The Court again rejects promoting party stability and preventing voter-confusing as compelling interests to support the ban on endorsements, finding the interests insufficient here to override the First Amendment rights of the parties.[78] More important for the purposes here, the Court returns to the external-internal distinction. After declaring that a state has a right to promote the integrity of the political process, the Court cites a litany of situations and cases where that justification has allowed for some regulation of internal party affairs:

> A State indisputably has a compelling interest in preserving the integrity of its election process. Rosario v. Rockefeller, 410 U.S. 752, 761, 93 S.Ct. 1245, 1251-1252, 36 L.Ed.2d 1 (1973). Toward that end, a State may enact laws that interfere with a party's internal affairs when necessary to ensure that elections are fair and honest. Storer v. Brown, 415 U.S., at 730, 94 S.Ct., at 1279. For example, a State may impose certain eligibility requirements for voters in the general election even though they limit parties' ability to garner support and members. See, e.g., Dunn v. Blumstein, 405 U.S., at 343-344, 92 S.Ct., at 1003-1004 (residence requirement); Oregon v. Mitchell, 400 U.S. 112, 118, 91 S.Ct. 260, 261-262, 27 L.Ed.2d 272 (1970) (age minimum); Kramer v. Union Free School Dist. No. 15, 395 U.S. 621, 625, 89 S.Ct. 1886, 1888-1889, 23 L.Ed.2d 583 (1969) (citizenship requirement). We have also recognized that a State may impose restrictions that promote the integrity of primary elections. See, e.g., American Party of Texas v. White, 415 U.S., at 779-780, 94 S.Ct., at 1305-1306 (requirement that major political parties nominate candidates through a primary and that minor parties nominate candidates through conventions); id., at 785-786, 94 S.Ct., at 1308-1309 (limitation on voters' participation to one primary and bar on voters both voting in a party primary and signing a petition supporting an independent candidate); Rosario v. Rockefeller, supra (waiting periods before voters may change party registration and participate in another

---

76 489 U.S. 214 (1989).
77 *Id.* at 217.
78 *Id.* at 226-28.

party's primary); Bullock v. Carter, 405 U.S., at 145, 92 S.Ct., at 856-857 (reasonable filing fees as a condition of placement on the ballot).[79]

But this list of exceptions is meant to underscore that regulation of a party's affairs is different and that: "In sum, a State cannot justify regulating a party's internal affairs without showing that such regulation is necessary to ensure an election that is orderly and fair."[80]

Finally, consider *California Democratic Party v. Jones*.[81] Here the Court struck down a state ballot measure creating a blanket primary system where voters, regardless of their party affiliation, could vote in primaries for candidates of any party affiliation. The Court ruled that such a measure violated the associational rights of the party. Scalia, in writing for the Court, addressed previous cases, including *Smith*, where some regulation of internal party affairs was permitted. According to Scalia:

> What we have not held, however, is that the processes by which political parties select their nominees are, as respondents would have it, wholly public affairs that States may regulate freely. To the contrary, we have continually stressed that when States regulate parties' internal processes they must act within limits imposed by the Constitution.[82]

What Scalia seeks to distinguish here is a situation where in *Smith* the Court appeared to endorse regulation of internal party affairs, especially who a party can be forced to associate with. The Texas Democratic Party did not wish to associate with African-Americans but compelling interests to enforce the right to vote overrode that associational choice. Conversely, in *Tashjian* the State of Connecticut was telling Republicans whom they may not associate with. *Jones* is a case about forced association—requiring parties to associate with voters of potentially different parties with whom they do not want to associate. A political party should be able to select "a standard bearer who best represents the party's ideologies and preferences,"[83] and California blanket primary law endangers the ability of the party to secure that objective. The law permits individuals to participate in internal party decision-making who may turn out to be hostile to the principles of the party.[84] In sum, defining party orthodoxy and who is the best person to represent its values is a matter of internal party decision-making.

Tashjian, *Eu*, and *Jones* all establish an important point about party autonomy. If political parties are to be able to organize and develop platforms and ideas and select

---

79   *Id.* at 231.
80   *Id.* at 233.
81   530 U.S. 567 (2000).
82   *Id.* at 572-73.
83   *Id.* at 575 (quoting the *Eu* opinion).
84   *Id.* at 577.

candidates for office, their internal party affairs generally need to be left free from government regulation. This claim seems consistent with democratic theory that indicates that parties generally need to be free to operate. But at the same time the Court in these three opinions consistently noted compelling governmental interests as to when party internal affairs may be regulated. The list provided in *Eu* seemed so long that the exceptions appeared to consume the rule against regulation of internal affairs. Additionally, one could argue that in all of these cases the Court failed to offer convincing reasons why promotion of stability or preventing voter confusion were not compelling enough interests to prevail. They did not seem to offer a clear principle or rule to indicate why regulation of internal affairs was not allowed here.

That failure to offer a principled distinction shows up first in *Clingman v. Beaver*.[85] *Clingman* involved the constitutionality of an Oklahoma law that prevented the Libertarian Party in that state from inviting members from any other party to participate in its primary. On first impression this case simply looks like *Tashjian* all over again. Yet in *Clingman* the Court upheld the law. It distinguished the facts at hand from those in *Tashjian*, noting that in Connecticut the Republican Party only wanted to invite independents but that here in Oklahoma the Libertarians wanted also to open up its primary to members of other parties. Consistent with *Tashjian* the Court should have declared that the choice to do this is a matter of internal party governance, regardless of whether it was a wise choice. But here the Court was instead willing to recognize preservation of party stability and prevention of voter confusion and party as compelling interests[86] that here placed only a marginal burden on associational rights of the parties.[87]

Second, the *Clingman* Court was also concerned about voter confusion issues along with party stability. According to the Court:

> If the LPO is permitted to open its primary to all registered voters regardless of party affiliation, the candidate who emerges from the LPO primary may be "unconcerned with, if not ... hostile to," the political preferences of the majority of the LPO's members. It does not matter that the LPO is willing to risk the surrender of its identity in exchange for electoral success. Oklahoma's interest is independent and concerns the integrity of its primary system. The State wants to "avoid primary election outcomes which would tend to confuse or mislead the general voting population to the extent [it] relies on party labels as representative of certain ideologies."[88]

There are a couple of remarkable arguments here. First, despite the fact that the Libertarian Party of Oklahoma is willing to let others in and perhaps risk a change in political philosophy or orthodoxy, the State and the Supreme Court will not let

---

85   544 U.S. 581 (2005).
86   *Id.* at 594-97.
87   *Id.* at 590-92.
88   *Id.* at 594.

it do that. There is an incredible amount of party paternalism here, looking out for the best interests of the party. Moreover, the State's interest in party stability seems misplaced. Stability means preventing threats to the status of political parties in general within its jurisdiction, not stability in terms of how the current or specific parties align or define themselves. Parties change in part by making appeals to non-members to join them and the Court seems just not to understand that.

The defense of preventing voter confusion also seems inapt. If individuals accept the LPO invitation to participate in their affairs and then nominate candidates, that is the choice of the party in terms of how it wishes to represent itself at the ballot. The Court again seems wedded to the notion that it is up to them and not the party to decide what is appropriate information or what it means to be a libertarian party. However one examines the decision, the Court effectively seems to be implicitly articulating a new compelling interest for the government to regulate internal party affairs—to promote the stability and policy orientation of specific parties.

Finally, consider *New York State Board of Elections v. Lopez Torres*,[89] where the Supreme Court overturned a lower court decision which had declared unconstitutional the state's use of judicial conventions to select candidates for the position of New York Supreme Court Justice. In a 9-0 opinion the Court (again with Scalia writing the majority opinion) ruled that the First Amendment gives broad protection to political parties regarding how they select and endorse judicial candidates. Juxtapose *Lopez Torres* to *Washington State Grange v. Washington State Republican Party*.[90] By a 7-2 vote, the Supreme Court upheld a State of Washington law that identifies candidates by party affiliation on the primary ballot, lets voters select any candidate, and the two candidates who receive the most votes, regardless of affiliation, will proceed to have their names advanced to the general election. Political parties had objected to the law, claiming that their First Amendment rights under *Jones* had been violated. The Court rejected this, claiming that party associational rights were not burdened. More importantly, what the Court seems to do in this case is say that we do not care how your members selected the nominees to appear on the primary ballot, but once there they have no right to appear on the general election ballot.

In reviewing all of these cases the Court ostensibly declares a line to be drawn between regulation of internal and external party affairs. Yet no clear line is provided that defines external versus internal and, even for the latter, the Court seems willing to create numerous exceptions to the hands-off policy it has divined. Looked at from this perspective, the Court seems confused in its treatment of parties.

---

89 552 U.S. 196 (2008).
90 552 U.S. 442 (2008).

Who is the Party?[91]

To add to the confusion, briefly look at all of the cases just discussed and now ask the question, who is the party? Defining who the party is is an important question in many respects. From one point of view it is important in terms of questions regarding who has standing to sue on behalf of the party, or be served, standing, or waiving attorney-client privilege. It is about who is the client from a representation point of view. But there is another way to think about the party in terms of the specific persons recognized by the judiciary as the party and whose specific interests are being defended.

In *Smith v. Allwright* the Democratic Party of Texas was its leadership or its existing members. This leadership was composed of white Caucasians. The same is true of its existing members. Yet they lost out because of the Court defending the rights of a voter who wanted to become a member of the party. He was neither a current member nor was he white. In *Tashjian* the party was the leadership seeking to define who would be permitted to participate in their functions. In *Jones* the party was again the leadership, and in *Eu* the same was again true. Yet in *Clingman* the Court ignored the wishes of the party leadership to protect the interests of the rank and file or the general voter. In *Lopez Torres* the party was those who show up to pick judicial candidates. But in *Washington State Grange* the party is almost ignored and instead the entire voting electorate gets to decide who appears on general election ballot.

Think about a political party as composed of many constituencies. The party will have its executive director and paid staff. There are then those who attend conventions, those who attend caucuses (if they exist in that jurisdiction), primary voters and general election voters who cast ballot for their candidates, just to name some of the different constituencies. Which of these is the party? The easy answer is to say that all of them are, but this is not a good response. In some cases the legal interests of any of these groups will conflict, forcing the law and the judiciary to have to make a choice over who will win. The Court here again seems unclear and unguided by a rule that defines who the party is. This might reflect contrasting visions of the party even from the point of view of democratic theory—do we define party from an elite or a mass perspective?[92]

---

91 *See:* Dan Lowenstein, *Associational Rights of Major Political Parties: A Skeptical Inquiry*, 71 TEX. L. REV. 1741 (1993), who first and correctly raised this question about the Supreme Court's jurisprudence when it came to questions regarding whose associational rights in political parties are recognized or not.

92 *See:* Joseph Schlesinger, *On the Theory of Party Organizations* 46 JOURNAL OF POLITICS, 369 (1984); ROBERT MICHELS, POLITICAL PARTIES: A SOCIOLOGICAL STUDY OF THE OLIGARCHICAL TENDENCIES OF MODERN DEMOCRACY (1958); and JOSEPH A. SCHUMPETER, CAPITALISM, SOCIALISM, AND DEMOCRACY, 269-73 (1975) who take an elitist view of parties and argue that voters are not part or in control of them but instead cast ballots to decide which party shall exercise power.

Is there a simple way to resolve the questions regarding who is the party? Perhaps not. But it, along with determining if a party is a public or private entity and then determining the scope of government regulation, are all tough election law if not democratic theory questions. However, parties do appear to be more public than private entities, especially if we accept Schattschneider's argument that they are publicly accountable via elections. Even parties that are not in office are accountable electorally since they are competing for votes and hoping, we presume, that their objective is to participate in governing. Perhaps the way to think about parties is to borrow a distinction from municipal law where cities are classified in terms of when they act in their governmental or proprietary capacities, or in terms of when governments act in their regulatory or market participant roles (such as being an employer or purchaser of goods and services).[93] The law recognizes different rules and authority depending on the roles. Such distinctions recognize that governments have contrasting roles and tests are set up to try to distinguish when they are fulfilling one capacity versus another.

The same may be parallel to political parties. Governments are always public but still may be acting in different capacities. Parties are always public entities because of their real or potential capacity to govern. Yet just because they are public does not mean they there is no autonomy for them to act or make some distinctions—such as imposing residency requirements. Parties should generally be presumed to be public entities, open without discrimination to all who wish to participate. Yet parties should be given relatively free rein to decide ideological orthodoxy, with the general presumption being that the leaders of party, subject to the rules of the organization, decide how the entity is to be governed.

Does this depiction of parties provide clear answers to the problems posed in this chapter about the party? Probably not, but it does at least indicate that there are other areas of law where governmental entities are viewed in dual capacities and therefore it should not be foreign to think of parties that way too. Moreover, in light of the earlier discussion of voting in Chapter 3 that pointed out that the lines between governmental and non-governmental entities is becoming more blurred, the same may be true with political parties. The line between what is or is not a party is getting more difficult to determine as more and more individuals choose alternative entities to affiliate with and engage through. Changes in participatory vehicles may already be forcing the law to rethink election law, as non-profits and voluntary organizations are perhaps replacing parties for many people. Traditional party functions now may be performed by many entities not often seen as party organs. That change alone is forcing a rethinking of election law and how to regulate a range of entities.

---

93 *See:* Hughes v. Alexandria Scrap Corp., 426 U.S. 794 (1976) for a discussion of the differences between being a market regulatory and a market participant. *See also:* Janice C. Griffith, *Local Government Contracts: Escaping from the Governmental/proprietary Maze*, 75 Iowa L. Rev. 277 (1990) for a review of the distinction between governments acting in these different capacities.

What it also means is that, as the lines among the public, private, and non-profit sectors change, defining a party simply as public or private may not make sense. It also may not make sense simply to say a party is ontologically defined as one specific person or group all the time. Democratic theory—and with that, election law—has not kept pace with changes in how people use organizations for political engagement purposes. This is perhaps the biggest reason for the confusion in the law.

Ballot Access and Third Parties

The Supreme Court has recognized promoting stability and preventing factionalization as compelling interests justifying party regulation. But, as noted above, the Court seems confused about both of the interests, conflating a general interest in strong parties with a specific interest in maintaining current party stability. Additionally, the Court's interest in defending the party elite and in facilitating them in preventing factionalization seems to be creating a different problem—preventing parties from evolving and changing. A healthy democracy must allow for parties to evolve and change otherwise they ossify and become irrelevant to the electorate.

Survey research and voting patterns demonstrate that membership in the two major parties in the United States is on decline as more and more individuals list themselves as independents.[94] Among the reasons for party decomposition are claims by voters that the two parties do not align along the mix or choice of policy preferences they favor, or that the parties have become captured by interest groups and extremist politics.[95] There may be other reasons for this too. Surveys also suggest that many voters express preferences for third parties or third-party candidates, although when push comes to shove few voters exercise this option, perhaps out of fear that supporting their preferred candidate will lead to the election of their least desired one. One can call this the Nader effect. The reference is to many Democrats claiming that, were it not for the votes for Ralph Nader in Florida in 2000, Al Gore and not George Bush would have been president. The logic of the Electoral College in 48 states as a winner-take-all contest creates disincentives to vote for third-party candidates.

---

94 *The Party's (Largely) Over*, THE ECONOMIST (March, 20, 2013), http://www.econo mist.com/node/17306082 (site last viewed on March 20, 2013).

95 Kathleen Bawn, et al., *A Theory of Political Parties: Groups, Policy Demands and Nominations in American Politics*, 10 PERSPECTIVES ON POLITICS, 571 (2012), discusses the relationship between interest groups and political parties in presidential nominations and party platforms and finds that the former have helped drive changes or debates in both. The implications are to suggest that parties are far less independent from interest groups that one might be assumed and therefore the line between parties and organized interests in less conceptually clear than may be thought.

Yet over time membership, labels, and even the identities of the major parties have changed over time. Political scientists such as Walter Dean Burnham once described critical realignments, or realigning elections, as, until recently, have occurred about every 30-40 years in American politics.[96] Realignments were triggered by changing economic conditions or a crisis that slowly built up to a very intense election that redefines the major political agenda and parties in American politics for the next couple of generations. Among the characteristics of such elections were short-lived but very intense disruptions of traditional patterns of voting behavior. Major parties become minorities; politics which was once competitive becomes non-competitive, or vice versa. Former one-party areas become arenas of intense partisan competition; large blocks of voters shift their partisan allegiance.

Second, critical elections are characterized by abnormally high intensity. This intensity includes ideological polarization within and among parties and an abnormal rise in voter participation. This intensity spills over into party nominations and platforms where "rules of the game" are changed and/or the party becomes polarized. Party coalitions shift or existing parties decompose and new or third parties emerge to reflect changes in coalitions and voting.

Finally, critical elections produce new majority parties and policy programs and agendas that dominate the institutional structure of American government. These parties will continue to dominate for a couple of generations until the next realignment occurs.

Burnham has identified several critical elections over time, with the first in 1800. Here the Jeffersonian Democratic-Republican and the Adams Federalist parties emerge. The Democratic Republicans win the presidency and take over the two houses of Congress. This party is composed of mainly farmers, former Anti-Federalists, and those from the Southern and Middle Southern states.

The second critical election is in 1828. The Jacksonian Democrats emerge as the major party. The Democrats now are composed of Southerners and Westerners representing rising middle-class merchants and investors. The third is in 1860 when the Republican Party of Lincoln emerges. The Republicans represent the Northern anti-slavery states and those committed to the supremacy of national power over states' rights. The fourth critical election is in 1896 when Democrats no longer simply represent the Southern slave states but they include the prairie states and farmers. The Republicans take on the Progressive banner of reform. Finally, there is the critical election of 1936. The FDR landslide creates a pro-government and emerging civil rights-orientated Democratic Party consisting of unions, workers, Blacks, Catholics, and Jews. The Republicans are pro-business and anti-government.

The point in reciting this discussion on realignments is that since 1936 political scientists have been waiting for their realigning Godot. Some claim this occurred

---

96 WALTER DEAN BURNHAM, CRITICAL ELECTIONS: AND THE MAINSPRINGS OF AMERICAN POLITICS (1971).

in the 1960s when Barry Goldwater drove the Republicans to the right and Lyndon Johnson signed civil rights legislation that lost the South for the Democrats. Or maybe it occurred with the election of Reagan and the emergence of Reagan blue-collar Democrats. One could even make the case that Obama's 2008 election was a critical realignment that moved the Democrats in one direction and forced the Republicans further to the right as the party of Sarah Palin. But, whether a realignment did or did not occur, the fact remains that the Republican and Democrat parties presently are the two major ones, and an argument can be asserted that they have ossified. We have not seen either of these two parties go by way of the Whig or Federalist parties.

Part of the reason for this may be due to the treatment of third parties and ballot access in addition to the way the law and the courts seem to be entrenching the current two parties in place. Ballot access is all about simply allowing candidates and parties to get on the general election ballot.

In most states, once a party has achieved major party status it either automatically or easily can get its candidate on the ballot for the general election. The problem though is with third parties. How do they secure ballot access? In general there are two ways to achieve ballot access. The first is for the candidate or party to pay a fee, the other is to demonstrate some sign of support such as by obtaining a certain number of signatures. In *Bullock v. Carter* the Court struck down a Texas law requiring the payment of a filing fee to appear on a ballot.[97] Such fees, the court ruled, burdened the rights of poor candidates. As a result of this decision, states generally give candidates the options of filing fees or of gathering signatures on a petition as a way of securing ballot access.

The *Bullock* case implicates an important question: Is there a constitutional right to appear on the ballot? Should any individual be allowed to appear on any ballot for any election or should there be some minimum threshold that needs to be met? Perhaps there needs to be some minimum number of voters who support the candidate before one should be allowed on the ballot? The simple answer is that while a candidate has a First Amendment right to run for office, the right to appear on a general election ballot is limited by state interests to prevent voter confusion. In theory, everyone who wanted to run could appear on the ballot, and maybe that is good. Yet some minimum threshold of support is needed to rule out individuals who are not serious candidates, or those who support is so *de minimis* that they really have no chance of prevailing. In response one might argue that in a democracy the people, rather than some ballot access rules, should decide who is a serious or viable candidate, unless one assumes the rules themselves are an appropriate means to answer these concerns. Thus, the issue is how to balance access against viability and seriousness, or access against preventing voter confusion. Such balances need to be struck to make sure that the major parties are not entrenched and that minor parties have a chance to grow and elect their candidates to office.

---

97 405 U.S. 134 (1972).

This question about ballot access is important because it looks to how laws may inhibit or discourage perhaps third parties or alternative candidates in the electoral process. For example, in 1980 Republican Illinois Congressman John Anderson ran for president but lost the nomination to Ronald Reagan. He then decided to run as an independent for president. However, like Alabama Governor George Wallace before him when he decided to run for president as a third-party candidate in 1968, Anderson faced numerous state laws that appeared to block his efforts, forcing him to go to court in many states to secure ballot access.

Look first at *Williams v. Rhodes*.[98] The case involved a challenge to an Ohio law requiring a new party wishing to appear on the ballot to obtain signatures equivalent to 15 percent of the voters in the previous gubernatorial election. Among the parties challenging this law was the Ohio American Independent Party, the party of George Wallace. In striking down this requirement as unconstitutional the Court first notes how the law is biased in favor of the two major parties:

> No extended discussion is required to establish that the Ohio laws before us give the two old, established parties a decided advantage over any new parties struggling for existence and thus place substantially unequal burdens on both the right to vote and the right to associate. The right to form a party for the advancement of political goals means little if a party can be kept off the election ballot and thus denied an equal opportunity to win votes. So also, the right to vote is heavily burdened if that vote may be cast only for one of two parties at a time when other parties are clamoring for a place on the ballot.[99]

The law does more than favor two parties, it favors two specific parties at the expense of a marketplace of ideas among many parties competing for votes. It does little to force them to compete against outsiders for voters and support:

> [T]he Ohio system does not merely favor a 'two-party system'; it favors two particular parties—the Republicans and the Democrats—and in effect tends to give them a complete monopoly. There is, of course, no reason why two parties should retain a permanent monopoly on the right to have people vote for or against them. Competition in ideas and governmental policies is at the core of our electoral process and of the First Amendment freedoms. New parties struggling for their place must have the time and opportunity to organize in order to meet reasonable requirements for ballot position, just as the old parties have had in the past.[100]

The law does favor the two major parties, but Ohio asserts that it has a compelling interest either in promoting a two-party system and political compromise, or in

---

98 393 U.S. 23 (1968).
99 *Id.* at 31.
100 *Id.* at 32.

preventing a winning candidate from achieving 50 percent of the vote, or simply in preventing voter confusion.[101] While the Court does acknowledge that Ohio does have these legitimate interests it also notes that they must be weighed against the First Amendment rights of parties:

> In determining whether or not a state law violates the Equal Protection Clause, we must consider the facts and circumstances behind the law, the interests which the State claims to be protecting, and the interests of those who are disadvantaged by the classification. In the present situation the state laws place burdens on two different, although overlapping, kinds of rights—the right of individuals to associate for the advancement of political beliefs, and the right of qualified voters, regardless of their political persuasion, to cast their votes effectively.[102]

The Court does not provide clarification in this case regarding what an acceptable minimum signature threshold would be. But in *Munro v. Socialist Workers Party* the Court did answer that question.[103] Here the question was whether a state law requiring a minor or third party to secure 1 percent of the vote in the primary in order to appear on the general election ballot violated its constitutional rights. The Court said no. Here the Court indicated that the 1 percent was sufficient to secure the state interests of protecting the major parties and preventing confusion. Does the state have an interest in regulating the number of names on the ballot? Is such favoritism permissible? In *Storer v. Brown*[104] the Court did acknowledge that such an interest was okay.[105]

At issue in *Storer* was a California law preventing an independent candidate for public office if he was a member of another party within one year of the preceding primary election. The Court upheld the requirement, contending that it was a valid measure on the part of the state to promote the integrity of the election process.[106] Yet, as the dissent pointed out in that case, a candidate wishing to run for office and appear on the general election ballot would have to have disaffiliated from another party fully 17 months in advance of the election.[107] Yet in reality candidates running for office, including independents, make their decisions to run premised upon who else is running and the issues they are articulating. Yet the California law in question, a variation of a "sore loser rule," makes it difficult to bolt from a major party to run for office.

---

101   *Id.* at 31-32.
102   *Id.* at 30.
103   479 U.S. 189 (1986).
104   415 U.S. 724 (1974).
105   *Id.* at 732.
106   *Id.* at 733.
107   *Id.* at 758.

But then in *Anderson v. Celebrezze*[108] the Court appeared to agree that many of these laws were burdensome obstacles. The Court here articulated one of the tests now used to judge whether ballot access laws are unfair or burdensome to the candidate:

> Constitutional challenges to specific provisions of a State's election laws therefore cannot be resolved by any "litmus-paper test" that will separate valid from invalid restrictions. Instead, a court must resolve such a challenge by an analytical process that parallels its work in ordinary litigation. It must first consider the character and magnitude of the asserted injury to the rights protected by the First and Fourteenth Amendments that the plaintiff seeks to vindicate. It then must identify and evaluate the precise interests put forward by the State as justifications for the burden imposed by its rule. In passing judgment, the Court must not only determine the legitimacy and strength of each of those interests; it also must consider the extent to which those interests make it necessary to burden the plaintiff's rights. Only after weighing all these factors is the reviewing court in a position to decide whether the challenged provision is unconstitutional.[109]

This case involved challenges by John Anderson's unsuccessful presidential run for president, again in the state of Ohio. While Anderson did not prevail, his legal challenges facilitated later campaigns by Ross Perot in 1992 and Ralph Nader in 2000. Yet they too had to fight in court to secure ballot access.

Overall the point being made here is that the laws for ballot access across the United States continue to discourage third parties and party change. Cases such as *Burdick v. Takushi* make it difficult for write-in candidates.[110] *Timmons v. Twin Cities Area New Party* complicates the ability of third parties to cross endorse candidates and grow themselves in some cases by legitimately stealing votes from other parties.[111] And then there are cases such as *Arkansas Educational Television Commission v. Forbes*[112] that place third parties in a box: They need a certain threshold of support to be invited to a televised presidential debate but lacking coverage they will burdened in reaching that threshold. At the same time *Buckley v. Valeo*[113] upheld withholding public funding from minor party presidential candidates until they proved viability—a similar paradox as found in *Forbes*.

The broader point to be made here is that the Court and the law remain biased against third parties in many ways. This bias in favor of the two dominant parties

---

108 460 U.S. 780 (1983).
109 *Id.* at 789.
110 504 U.S. 428 (1992).
111 520 U.S. 351 (1997).
112 523 U.S. 666 (1998).
113 424 U.S. 1 (1976).

has actually produced perhaps the counter of what the aim was supposed to be—democratic stability. It has confused support for the status quo parties with that of overall democratic stability and an orderly change in party composition and structure over time. Instead of allowing third parties and candidates greater opportunity to form, appear on the ballot, and secure funding and publicity, the law and courts have hampered these efforts, perhaps overall resulting in the weakening of parties. This weakening is demonstrated in the increased potency of interest groups and non-party political entities. Perhaps even the intra-party fighting that occurs in the Republican and Democrat Parties is a sign that the law makes it more difficult to break away and form a new party than it does to preserve the existing parties and fight from inside them. *Tashjian* speaks to the Court allowing a major party to grow and maintain itself while *Clingman* points to how third parties are restricted. The suffocation of healthy party change and evolution may be one of the reasons why so many voters are disaffiliating from the two major parties now.

Conclusion

Political parties are critical institutions to the maintenance of a stable democratic regime. Yet the Supreme Court's jurisprudence more often than not is riddled with decisions that fail to define an appropriate role for parties, all of them and not just the major ones, within the American electoral system. The decisions seem unable to decide if parties are public or private entities, how much they can be regulated in their internal affairs, who the party is, and how major versus minor parties should be treated. At even the most basic threshold level, the Court seems unable to distinguish and clarify how parties are different from other political entities and whether they are entitled to special treatment. The argument here is that the problem is due to a lack of theory guiding its jurisprudence.

The problem may not entirely be the fault of the judiciary. Democratic theory and party scholars seem challenged in answering these questions too. It may be that Schattschneider was correct when he described parties as linkages that make governance possible. His description suggested parties are public and private, autonomous and subject to regulation, and composed of many subparts to form a whole. Political parties are important to democracy but a theory of parties is missing both from the law and theory.

Chapter 7
Money, Politics, and Campaign Financing

"Come on, come on, listen to the money talk." So goes the lyrics to the AC/DC song "Money Talks." But while money may talk, the real question is whether it speaks. More specifically, the issue is whether money contributed or expended for political purposes is protected as free speech under the First Amendment? The way this constitutional question has been framed, at least since 1976, has been simply to ask "Is money speech?" For those who believe money is speech, the claim generally is that there should be no restrictions on who and how much money can be deployed for political purposes, with at most disclosure being the only acceptable regulation. Conversely, for those who do not believe money is speech, both political contributions and expenditures can be regulated if not limited. Yet framing the debate as an on-off light switch is hardly edifying and does little to answer some more-fundamental and broader questions about the role of money in politics.

The real issue is reconciling democracy and capitalism. More specifically, the question is one of the connection between economic power and resources and political influence. Should resources amassed in the economic marketplace be fungible and transferable into political influence? The debate surrounding whether money is speech is really about the connection between the economic and political spheres, querying the legitimacy of letting the logic of the marketplace determine how a democratic political system should operate. For the most part this is the broader question that has not been asked by the Supreme Court, at least not since Justice Holmes famously mused in *Lochner v. New York* that the Constitution does not enact a specific economic theory.[1] Yet, as this chapter will argue, that is precisely what the debate about money and politics has become—a referendum on whether the Constitution endorses not only a free market theory of democracy but in the process accepts the legitimacy of the economic marketplace defining how the political process should operate. The argument of this chapter will be that American democratic theory and, with that, election law, should not be one that accepts as legitimate the right of an individual or any entity to convert economic resources over into political power or advantages. Instead, there needs to be a sharp wall of separation between the economic and political marketplaces.

---

1 198 U.S. 45 (1905).

Money in American Politics: A Short History

Money, as former California politician Jesse Unruh reputedly once said, is the "Mother's milk of politics." So much of politics, or at least campaigns and elections, involves money. It costs money to run for office or communicate a message, necessitating in most if not all parts of the United States that candidates, political parties, and other groups both raise and spend money to achieve their political objectives. However, while money is critical to political success and it can be a valuable tool for many purposes, it also potentially corrupts the political system as it raises the fear of bribery and extortion. Dating back to the days when George Washington was a candidate for the Virginia Assembly there were allegations that he spent too much money on rum that he gave to voters. Thus, there has always been a fear that money posed dangers to the political process.

The fear about money and politics on one level is about corruption in a couple of ways. First there is simply the idea of vote buying. This is the fear of someone offering voters something of value to induce them to vote in a particular way. This is either bribing voters to cast their votes in a specific manner or doing the same with elected officials. The latter leads to another sense of corruption—*quid pro quo*. It is the fear that money deployed for political purposes—such as donated to an elected official—will be used for the purposes of seeking influence. I give to an elected official with the expectation that I will receive something in return, such as a favorable contract from the government or an appointment to an official post.

In fact, exchange of money for government employment was effectively politics as usual in nineteenth-century America. The Jacksonian Era ushered in with the election of President Andrew Jackson the spoils system.[2] The spoils system entailed a politics where donors gave money and their time in the hope of receiving favors and jobs if candidates were elected. Federal and state government jobs were freely traded for contributions and support, and often times these offices served as a basis of funding campaigns, as salaries were often "assessed" to help pay for political expenses. But several laws were adopted to restrict this practice. First, beginning with the 1883 Pendleton Act, civil service reforms gradually replaced the spoils with a merit system for the staffing of federal positions. Many states followed suit with their own civil service reclassifications.

In addition, the Progressive Era of the early twentieth century, as noted in Chapter 4, feared the role of special interests, especially corporations, as efforts began to reform the spoils system and limit the role of money in politics. For example, in 1907 Congress, at the urging of President Theodore Roosevelt, passed the Tillman Act which banned corporations from giving money to federal candidates for office. Then in 1947 the Taft-Hartley Act did the same with labor unions. Taft-Hartley also barred unions and corporations from making independent expenditures to affect federal elections. Fear of excessive power by corporations and unions prompted

---

2 *See generally:* DAVID SCHULTZ AND ROBERT MARANTO, THE POLITICS OF CIVIL SERVICE REFORM (1998).

these laws. Moreover, in 1925 Congress passed the Federal Corrupt Practices Act which banned political assessments. This Act was upheld in *U S v. Wurzbach*.[3]

Throughout the 1950s, and more in the 1960s and early 1970s, Congress sought to reform the way campaigns are funded and conducted. Efforts were undertaken to impose contribution or expenditure limits, to provide public financing, or to increase disclosure requirements on donors and campaigns. These efforts mostly failed. However, when revelations of President Nixon's 1972 fundraising scandals surfaced, it gave new life to the cause of campaign finance reform, resulting in the adoption of the 1974 amendments to the Federal Election Campaign Act (FECA). These amendments provided for a major overhaul of federal elections, and included spending and contribution limits, disclosure rules, public financing, and the creation of a new federal agency to regulate campaign activity.

Yet these amendments raised significant constitutional questions. For example, given the importance of money to campaigns, was money speech for the purposes of the First Amendment? Or could the government impose expenditure or contribution limits in order to equalize the political playing field and make elections more competitive? These questions were all implicated in *Buckley v. Valeo*.[4]

In *Buckley*, at issue were several challenges to the 1997 FECA Amendments. Specifically, for our purposes, at issue were challenges to the expenditure and contribution limits that the Amendments imposed.[5] In examining limits on contributions and expenditures, a *per curiam* opinion of the Court applied very different lines of constitutional analysis. First, the Court noted that Congress had broad power to regulate federal elections,[6] yet the question in this case was whether the contribution and expenditure limitations violated the First Amendment free speech clause.[7] The Court of Appeals, in upholding the FECA contribution and expenditure limitations,[8] ruled that the restrictions were directed towards conduct and not speech and that, accordingly, the frame of analysis as dictated by *United States v. O'Brien*[9] should apply.[10] The Court rejected the assertion that contribution and expenditure limits were conduct and not speech,[11] stating:

> We cannot share the view that the present Act's contribution and expenditure limitations are comparable to the restrictions on conduct upheld in *O'Brien*. The expenditure of money simply cannot be equated with such conduct as destruction

---

3 280 U.S. 396 (1930).
4 424 U.S. 1 (1976).
5 *See:* 18 U.S.C. 608 (a)-(e).
6 424 U.S. at 13.
7 *Id.* at 13-14.
8 Buckley v. Valeo, 519 F.2d 821, 840 (1975).
9 391 U.S. 367 (1968).
10 424 U.S. at 15-16. *See:* 391 U.S. at 377 (*describing* the basic substantial interest test the Court employs to examine regulation of conduct draped with speech).
11 424 U.S. at 16.

of a draft card. Some forms of communication made possible by the giving and spending of money involve speech alone, some involve conduct primarily, and some involve a combination of the two. Yet this Court has never suggested that the dependence of a communication on the expenditure of money operates itself to introduce a nonspeech element or to reduce the exacting scrutiny required by the First Amendment.[12]

Hence, the Court seemed to regard the giving of money for political purposes as a form of protected speech. Yet one needs to be clear, the Court never says that money is constitutionally protected speech in *Buckley*. The broadest statement that the Court issues is to declare: "In sum, although the Act's contribution and expenditure limitations both implicate fundamental First Amendment interests, its expenditure ceilings impose significantly more severe restrictions on protected freedoms of political expression and association than do its limitations on financial contributions."[13] What the Court seems to be saying here are two things. First, that there is some connection between money contributed or expended for political purposes: and second, the Court sees the connection differently for each. The Court has never in *Buckley* nor in any of its case law since provided real details regarding exactly how expenditures and contributes exactly implicate First Amendment concerns. Its decisions have offered a more ad hoc approach to this issue, but never anything that rises to the level of a real theory about the role of money in a democracy.

Turn first to contribution limits. The Court described contributions as a means of expressing support for a candidate or otherwise indicating one's preference for political candidates such that restricting political contributions also imposed First Amendment associational limitations upon political dialogue.[14] Yet the Court indicated that restrictions upon them were allegedly justified by three claims:

> [T]he primary interest served by the limitations and, indeed, by the Act as a whole, is the prevention of corruption and the appearance of corruption spawned by the real or imagined coercive influence of large financial contributions on candidates' positions and on their actions if elected to office. Two "ancillary" interests underlying the Act are also allegedly furthered by the $1,000 limits on contributions. First, the limits serve to mute the voices of affluent persons and groups in the election process and thereby to equalize the relative ability of all citizens to affect the outcome of elections. Second, it is argued, the ceilings may to some extent act as a brake on the skyrocketing cost of political campaigns and thereby serve to open the political system more widely to candidates without access to sources of large amounts of money.[15]

---

12   *Id.* at 16.
13   *Id.* at 23.
14   *Id.* at 21, 24.
15   *Id.* at 25-26.

The Court rejected the muting of wealthy voices and the controlling of the skyrocketing costs of elections as compelling enough to justify restrictions on contributions, yet preventing corruption was sufficiently compelling enough to justify restrictions upon contributions.

> It is unnecessary to look beyond the Act's primary purpose to limit the actuality and appearance of corruption resulting from large individual financial contributions in order to find a constitutionally sufficient justification for the $1,000 contribution limitation. Under a system of private financing of elections, a candidate lacking immense personal or family wealth must depend on financial contributions from others to provide the resources necessary to conduct a successful campaign. The increasing importance of the communications media and sophisticated mass-mailing and polling operations to effective campaigning make the raising of large sums of money an ever more essential ingredient of an effective candidacy. To the extent that large contributions are given to secure a political quid pro quo from current and potential office holders, the integrity of our system of representative democracy is undermined. Although the scope of such pernicious practices can never be reliably ascertained, the deeply disturbing examples surfacing after the 1972 election demonstrate that the problem is not an illusory one.[16]

Similarly, in addition to recognizing the prevention of corruption as a compelling governmental interest to limit contributions, preventing the appearance of corruption was also accepted by the Court as a legitimate reason to limit contributions:

> Of almost equal concern as the danger of actual quid pro quo arrangements is the impact of the appearance of corruption stemming from public awareness of the opportunities for abuse inherent in a regime of large individual financial contributions. In *CSC v. Letter Carriers, supra,* the Court found that the danger to "fair and effective government" posed by partisan political conduct on the part of federal employees charged with administering the law was a sufficiently important concern to justify broad restrictions on the employees' right of partisan political association. Here, as there, Congress could legitimately conclude that the avoidance of the appearance of improper influence "is also critical ... if confidence in the system of representative Government is not to be eroded to a disastrous extent." (Citations omitted)[17]

Thus, the interest of preventing corruption or its appearance was enough to uphold the $1,000 limit on individual contributions and, by the same logic, the

---

16 *Id.* at 27-28.
17 *Id.* at 28-29.

Court upheld the $5,000 contribution limit on political committees[18] and the overall $25,000 contribution limit during any calendar year.[19]

With expenditures, the Court saw the restrictions as a "substantial rather than merely theoretical restraints on the quantity and diversity of political speech."[20] First, the Court indicates that the expenditure restrictions, while neutral, still restrict the "quantity" of the speech individuals, groups, and candidates may express.[21] However, while preventing corruption or its appearance was compelling enough to restrict contributions to candidates, these two justifications did not obtain in terms of independent and other expenditures that were not made in coordination with a candidate:

> We find that the governmental interest in preventing corruption and the appearance of corruption is inadequate to justify § 608(e)(1)'s ceiling on independent expenditures. First, assuming, arguendo, that large independent expenditures pose the same dangers of actual or apparent quid pro quo arrangements as do large contributions, § 608(e)(1) does not provide an answer that sufficiently relates to the elimination of those dangers. Unlike the contribution limitations' total ban on the giving of large amounts of money to candidates, § 608(e)(1) prevents only some large expenditures. So long as persons and groups eschew expenditures that in express terms advocate the election or defeat of a clearly identified candidate, they are free to spend as much as they want to promote the candidate and his views. The exacting interpretation of the statutory language necessary to avoid unconstitutional vagueness thus undermines the limitation's effectiveness as a loophole-closing provision by facilitating circumvention by those seeking to exert improper influence upon a candidate or office-holder. It would naively underestimate the ingenuity and resourcefulness of persons and groups desiring to buy influence to believe that they would have much difficulty devising expenditures that skirted the restriction on express advocacy of election or defeat but nevertheless benefited the candidate's campaign. Yet no substantial societal interest would be served by a loophole-closing provision designed to check corruption that permitted unscrupulous persons and organizations to expend unlimited sums of money in order to obtain improper influence over candidates for elective office.[22]

---

18 *Id.* at 35-36.
19 *Id.* at 38.
20 424 U.S. at 19. *See also:* 424 U.S. 19 n. 18 where the Court made the analogy that "[b]eing free to engage in unlimited political expression subject to a ceiling on expenditures is like being free to drive an automobile as far and as often as one desires on a single tank of gasoline."
21 424 U.S. at 39.
22 *Id.* at 45-46.

Because independent expenditures are not tied into candidates or otherwise not coordinated with candidates, the Court felt the there was no danger of *quid pro quo* corruption or its appearance. The independent expenditure ceiling thus failed to serve any substantial governmental interest and was therefore unconstitutional in terms of its application to individual expenditures,[23] expenditures by candidates from personal or family resources,[24] and total campaign expenditures.[25]

Finally, the Court rejected as a valid compelling interest the restriction on expenditures to equalize the influence of individuals and groups upon the political process. Such restrictions, for the Court, were invalid because "the concept that government may restrict the speech of some elements of our society in order to enhance the relative voice of others is wholly foreign to the First Amendment" since the basic goal of the First Amendment was to enhance political dialogue and the widest amount of dialogue, including views from antagonistic groups.[26] Hence, while preventing corruption and its appearance were considered compelling enough to justify restrictions on contributions, it appeared that no such compelling justifications could be found to justify restrictions on expenditures. In essence, the Court categorically stated that restrictions on contributions were permissible in some cases, while categorically stating that no restrictions on expenditures could be justified in 1976.

However, the Court articulated two caveats to its discussion of independent expenditures. First, the Court noted that independent expenditures do "not *presently* appear to pose dangers of real or apparent corruption comparable to those identified with large campaign contributions."[27] Second, the *per curiam* opinion also asserted that "independent expenditures may well provide little assistance to the candidate's campaign and indeed may prove to be counterproductive."[28] In making these two claims the Court held out the possibility that at some point independent expenditures may be restricted if evidence could be provided that they posed dangers of corruption or its appearance and, two, if it could be shown that such expenditures had some impact or assistance to a candidate campaign then some restrictions might be permissible. However, circa 1976, no evidence had been presented to the *Buckley* Court to demonstrate either. As subsequently interpreted by commentators, *Buckley* effectively equated speech with money, ruling that the expenditure of money for political purposes is a protected First Amendment activity that cannot be limited or restricted.[29]

---

23 *Id.* at 50-51.
24 *Id.* at 52.
25 *Id.* at 57.
26 *Id.* at 48.
27 *Id.* at 46 (italics added here for emphasis).
28 *Id.* at 47.
29 J. Skelly Wright, *Politics and the Constitution: Is Money Speech?*, 85 YALE L. J. 1001, 1004-5 (1976).

Buckley raised more questions than it answered. Most importantly, it did not say that money is speech but it did say that money contributed or expended for political purposes raises important free speech concerns. The Court then distinguishes contributions from expenditures, finding that limits on the former were permissible in order to prevent corruption or its appearance. This corruption stemmed from the concern about how money could be exchanged for political favors—a *quid pro quo* model for corruption.[30] However, while abating corruption or its appearance was found to be a compelling governmental interest that could justify limits on contributions, the absence of such a possibility for corruption precluded expenditure limits. The Court thus seemed to give more constitutional protection to the latter than to contributions; or at least it saw less evidence that justified restrictions on expenditures. But bottom line, neither in *Buckley* nor in any other case has a majority of the Court held that money is speech for First Amendment purposes. It is something short of that, but what exactly in not clear.

But as noted, several other issues remain unclear after this decision. *Buckley* seemed to create several ambiguities or loopholes in the law. Many if not all of the most important comments in *Buckley* appear in footnotes. See footnotes 52 and 65, for example. The Court holds out in note 65 that voluntary public financing of campaigns is possible and would permit expenditure limits as a condition of accepting public money.

Second, the Court articulates a distinction between express advocacy and issue advocacy in footnote 52—this footnote referring to what came to be called the "magic words." So long as political advertisements lacked the magic words such as "vote for" or "vote against," they were considered issue advocacy and therefore protected under the First Amendment. This express versus issue advocacy distinction provided a way for corporations and unions to communicate their political views in federal elections without being limited by the Tillman and Taft-Hartley Acts.

A 1975 opinion by the FEC also opened up a new hole in the FECA regulations. It ruled that a corporation could expend money to solicit contributions from employees and stockholders. More importantly, the decision opened the way for unions and corporations eventually to give money to political parties for the purposes of voter registration, get out the vote, and party building. These exceptions allowed for a dramatic increase in money these groups could spend. Thus, *Buckley*, the 1975 FEC opinion, and other Court cases created a new distinction in the law between hard and soft money. Hard money constituted regulated and disclosed contributions to candidates, soft money was unregulated (in terms of dollar amounts) to parties. The problem of soft money would grow until the passage of BCRA.

Another question was regarding whether the contribution-expenditure distinction was categorical or not. By that, when the Court declared that independent expenditures do not "presently" pose dangers of corruption or its appearance, was

---

30 Thomas F. Burke, *The Concept of Corruption in Campaign Finance Law*, 14 CONSTITUTIONAL COMMENTARY 127 (1997).

the Court signally that it might be willing to uphold some expenditure limits at some point? Did the decision also suggest that the Court might not always uphold contribution limits? The Court sent signals that both might be the case.

Consider first *Austin v. Michigan of Commerce*.[31] At issue in this case was a Michigan law prohibiting independent corporate campaign expenditures. The majority opinion upheld the Michigan law which prohibited any direct corporate treasury funds being spent to support or oppose any candidate for office. The Michigan law stated that corporations could make expenditures only from separate, segregated funds used solely for political purposes (PACs). Thus this case appeared to support the idea that the Court might be willing to consider some restrictions on expenditures. It did so in part by expanding the notion of corruption beyond that of *quid pro quo*. Specifically, in upholding the Michigan law the Court recognized the state interest in seeking to address the unique or special threat that of corporate domination of the political process.[32] This type of corruption may be more structural—a mobilization of bias to use Schattschneider's term—than it is a concern about a direct *quid pro quo*.

Conversely, consider *Nixon v. Shrink Missouri Government PAC*.[33] Here the Court had been called upon to adjudicate the constitutionality of a Missouri law setting contributions limits as low as $250 for some state offices.[34] David Souter wrote for the Court upholding these limits. Again, in doing this, he cited to *Buckley* for the proposition that a state may impose contribution limits.[35] However, he rejected arguments that the precedent from *Buckley* was that the floor on these limits was $1,000, the same as was upheld back in 1976.[36] To clarify what the floor was, Souter argued that left unclear in *Buckley* was the exact level of analysis or standard of review that should be afforded to contribution limits. He noted how *Buckley* had rejected both intermediate scrutiny and time, manner, and place forms of analysis.[37] Souter then again recounted the distinction the *Buckley* Court had made between expenditures and contributions, and in how addressing corruption or its appearance counted as compelling reasons to limit the former but not the latter.[38] Thus, so far, *Shrink Missouri* broke no new ground. However, when it came to the evidentiary standard to support limits, this is where some changes might have occurred.[39] First, Souter rejects claims by the respondents

---

31 494 U.S. 652 (1990).
32 *Id.* at 658.
33 528 U.S. 377 (2000).
34 Mo. Rev. Stat. § 130.032 (1994).
35 528 U.S. at 381.
36 *Id.* at 385.
37 *Id.* at 386.
38 *Id.* at 387-9.
39 Some commentators saw *Shrink Missouri* as lowering the evidentiary burden to sustain contributions. *See:* David Schultz, *Proving Political Corruption: Documenting the Evidence Required to Sustain Campaign Finance Reform Laws*, 18 Tex. Rev. Litigation 86 (1998).

that since *Buckley* the Court had modified the standards to require demonstration "that the recited harms are real, not merely conjectural."[40] However, Souter also dismissed claims that mere conjecture was enough to count as evidence to sustain a contribution limitation.[41] Instead, the degree of evidence necessary to sustain a limitation is left unspecified here, although the opinion implies that it might vary depending on the counterevidence offered.[42] But in contrast to previous lower court decisions that seemed to demand jurisdiction-specific evidence of corruption,[43] the *Shrink Missouri* Court seemed more flexible, permitting newspaper accounts of corruption and survey results, as evidence.[44]

A second potential change or clarification from *Buckley* addressed how low contribution limits may be set. While the $1,000 *Buckley* floor was rejected[45] and the $250 limit was accepted in this case, the Court refused to set a specific dollar amount as a threshold, instead stating that the Court would look to the "outer limits of contribution regulation by asking whether there was any showing that the limits were so low as to impede the ability of candidates to 'amas[s] the resources necessary for effective advocacy.'"[46] However, Souter did not see either the evidentiary or dollar threshold issues as rejections of *Buckley*, and instead rejected pleas from the dissenters to overturn that precedent.[47] Given this decision, it would appear the Court would be willing to uphold all contributions limits, but that was not the case.

Now look at *Randall v. Sorrell*.[48] At issue was a Vermont Law referred to as Act 64[49] which imposed contribution limits as low as $200 for state offices such as representative, and $400 for statewide positions such as governor.[50] It also enacted expenditure limits for campaigns, with, for example, the governor capped at $300,000 for a two-year election cycle.[51] In overturning the law and rejecting both the contribution and expenditure limits, the Court split along some surprising and not so surprising lines. Moreover, in contrast to its earlier decisions which seemed to adopt a categorical distinction between expenditures and contributions, the *Randall* Court demonstrated a more flexible use of the *Buckley* precedent as it applied it to Act 64.

---

40 528 U.S. at 392.
41 *Id.*
42 *Id.* at 392.
43 *See:* Kruse v. City of Cincinnati, 142 F.3d. 907 (6th Cir. 1998) (*rejecting* survey data and newspaper accounts of corruption as evidence justifying departing from the *Buckley* framework).
44 528 U.S. at 393.
45 528 U.S. at 397.
46 *Id.* at 397.
47 *Id.* at 397.
48 548 U.S. 230 (2006).
49 Vt. Stat. Ann. Tit. 17, § 2801 *et seq.* (2002).
50 *Id.* at §2805a.
51 *Id.* at §2805a (a).

Justice Breyer, joined by Chief Justice Roberts and Justice Samuel Alito, used the *Buckley* framework to strike down both the contribution and expenditure limits. In first examining the expenditure limits Breyer first notes how under *Buckley* the Court decided to treat them differently from contributions, seeing restrictions on the former as imposing "significantly more severe restrictions on protected freedoms of political expression and association than "do contribution limitations."[52] He then noted no governmental interest had been found to be compelling enough to justify expenditure limits, with subsequent Court decisions consistently reaffirming that proposition.[53] In seeking to address the *Buckley* ruling, the Court states that respondents asked either to overturn the precedent as unworkable or to distinguish it from the facts at issue here.[54] However, this plea is rejected in defense of *stare decisis*:

> *Stare decisis* thereby avoids the instability and unfairness that accompany disruption of settled legal expectations. For this reason, the rule of law demands that adhering to our prior case law be the norm. Departure from precedent is exceptional, and requires "special justification." Arizona v. *Rumsey,* 467 U.S. 203, 212, 104 S.Ct. 2305, 81 L.Ed.2d 164 (1984). This is especially true where, as here, the principle has become settled through iteration and reiteration over a long period of time ... We can find here no such special justification that would require us to overrule *Buckley*. Subsequent case law has not made *Buckley* a legal anomaly or otherwise undermined its basic legal principles. Cf. *Dickerson v. United States,* 530 U.S. 428, 443, 120 S.Ct. 2326, 147 L.Ed.2d 405 (2000). We cannot find in the respondents' claims any demonstration that circumstances have changed so radically as to undermine *Buckley's* critical factual assumptions. The respondents have not shown, for example, any dramatic increase in corruption or its appearance in Vermont; nor have they shown that expenditure limits are the only way to attack that problem. Cf. *McConnell v. FEC,* 540 U.S. 93, 124 S.Ct. 619, 157 L.Ed.2d 491. At the same time, *Buckley* has promoted considerable reliance. Congress and state legislatures have used *Buckley* when drafting campaign finance laws. And, as we have said, this Court has followed *Buckley*, upholding and applying its reasoning in later cases. Overruling *Buckley* now would dramatically undermine this reliance on our settled precedent.[55]

The constitutionality of expenditure limits is simple for the Court to address; *Buckley* seems to have come to mean that they are per se unconstitutional. Moreover, the Court quickly disposes of the argument to distinguish the limits here from those in *Buckley* by asserting a new compelling governmental interest—

---

52 548 U.S. at 241 (*quoting Buckley*).
53 *Id.*
54 *Id.* at 242-43.
55 *Id.* at 243-44.

reducing the time needed to fundraise.[56] The Court rejects the invitation to accept a new limit, finding that even if it had been asserted in *Buckley* the decision would have still been the same as it was.[57]

Turning to contribution limits, the Court again draws on *Buckley* and *Shrink*, asking if the caps are so low that they make it difficult to amass the resources necessary for effective advocacy.[58] The Court concluded that the spending limits are beyond this minimum threshold, in fact, lower than ever approved by the Court so far, or in comparison to those permitted in *Buckley*, and therefore unconstitutional.[59] Writing separately, Alito makes two points in his concurrence. First, he does not see how either of the limits are consistent with *Buckley*, and, more importantly, the respondents have not persuasively made the case to re-examine this precedent.[60]

Moving beyond the three Justice plurality opinion, there was little movement among the rest of the Court from their earlier opinions on *Buckley*. Kennedy again expressed his disagreement with *Buckley*, but declined the invitation to overrule it yet again.[61] Scalia and Thomas again voted to overturn *Buckley* and use strict scrutiny for both contributions and expenditures.[62] In dissent, Stevens, Ginsburg, and Souter applied *Buckley* to uphold the contribution limits,[63] but they would have remanded back to the Second Circuit to ascertain if there is enough evidence to sustain the expenditure limits under *Buckley*.[64] The basis for this reasoning? They clearly did not read *Buckley* as a per se ban on expenditure limits, but instead as one that failed in 1976 due to lack of evidence but which may be found in this case.[65]

The only Justice changing his mind in *Randall* was Stevens in a separate dissent—he voted to overturn *Buckley* and uphold expenditure limits.[66] Stevens' reason for this is his claim that the *Buckley* Court never considered the impact of endless fundraising upon candidates.[67] Nor did the Court consider a long history of expenditure limits in America.[68] Nor did that Court foreclose all expenditure limits.[69] Moreover, while the Court had on numerous occasions considered *Buckley*

---

56 *Id.* at 245.
57 *Id.*
58 *Id.* at 248.
59 *Id.* at 252-53.
60 *Id.* at 263.
61 *Id.* at 265.
62 *Id.* at 266.
63 *Id.* at 279-80.
64 *Id.* at 283.
65 *Id.*
66 *Id.* at 274 (*stating* "I am convinced that *Buckley's* holding on expenditure limits is wrong, and that the time has come to overrule it").
67 *Id.*
68 Id. at 277.
69 *Id.* at 279-80.

as *stare decisis* for contribution limits, it had not done so for expenditures.[70] Finally, in what could be read as a poke at originalists such as Scalia and Thomas, Stevens invokes the intent of the Framers to support expenditure limits:

> Nevertheless, I am firmly persuaded that the Framers would have been appalled by the impact of modern fundraising practices on the ability of elected officials to perform their public responsibilities. I think they would have viewed federal statutes limiting the amount of money that congressional candidates might spend in future elections as well within Congress' authority. And they surely would not have expected judges to interfere with the enforcement of expenditure limits that merely require candidates to budget their activities without imposing any restrictions whatsoever on what they may say in their speeches, debates, and interviews.[71]

Sorrell stood for two propositions. First, the Court suggested that in some cases contribution limits would not be upheld. Second, the Court rejected yet again expenditure limits of any kind, seemingly suggesting that what might have been a flexible distinction in *Buckley* between contributions and expenditures had become more categorical. By that, the Court seemed to declare that it would never uphold expenditure limits. Reading *Randall* alongside *Citizens United v. Federal Election Commission* where the Court overturned *Austin*,[72] there appears to be now a near categorical distinction. No expenditure limits will be upheld whereas most contribution limits appear constitutional.

In addition, *Buckley* and its progenies did not specifically clarify how money is related to speech. Another question left either unanswered or muddled was who can speak. As noted in Chapter 4 on direct democracy, the Court has opened up the category of entities allowed to speak. While at one point corporations and labor unions were barred by law from expending money to affect federal races, that limit has been all but eliminated by the time *Citizens United* was decided. Over time for-profit corporations were allowed to expend money in ballot initiatives along with ideological non-profit ones. Then for-profit corporations along with labor unions were allowed to make independent expenditure express advocacy expenditures. The only real bar on them now is direct contributions to candidates for office. The point is that the Court has come to expand the range of actors allowed to speak in American politics by using money. Thus, money increasingly is viewed as a valid commerce of communication, even if it is not directly viewed as speech itself.

Finally, if we look at the Supreme Court's treatment of the regulation of money in politics since *Buckley*, we see what appears to be a growing hostility toward most efforts to regulate. For example, to stem the dramatic increase of money being spent for political purposes in the 1980s and 1990s, and to address many of

---

70   *Id.* at 281.
71   *Id.* at 280-81.
72   558 U.S. 310 (2010).

the loopholes and problems in the law caused by *Buckley* and subsequent Supreme Court decisions, Senators Russ Feingold and John McCain worked for nearly a decade to achieve passage of the Bipartisan Campaign Reform Act of 2002 (BCRA or "McCain-Feingold Act"). BCRA sought to close the soft money loophole that had been opened up by post-*Buckley* FEC and courts decisions and which allowed corporations and unions to make political contributions to political parties for the purposes of party building, get out the vote, and voter education and registration drives. This soft money loophole along with the express-issue advocacy seemed to allow for an enormous amount of money to be expended or contributed by corporations and unions, Tillman and Taft-Hartley notwithstanding. NCRA also redefined the line between express and issue advocacy, improved disclosure, and placed some limits on the ability of wealthy candidates to use their money to affect elections.

BCRA was a controversial piece of legislation that was challenged by numerous groups who argued that it violated their First Amendment rights. To the surprise of many, when the Supreme Court ruled in *McConnell v FEC*,[73] it upheld almost all of the major provisions. The net result of the decision was to uphold the soft money ban and to endorse the closing of the express v. issue advocacy distinction that *Buckley* had created in footnote 52.

After the *McConnell* decision many critics of *Buckley* thought that the Court might be prepared to overturn that decision and uphold expenditure limits and even lower contribution limits than were permitted in the *Shrink* case. Vermont, in an effort to limit the impact of money in politics, passed Public Act 64 which imposed both expenditure and contribution limits. Yet as discussed, *Randall v. Sorrell* dashed that hope. Then in *Federal Election Commission v. Wisconsin Right to Life Committee*,[74] the Court ruled that as applied, the BCRA definition on electioneering communication that effected declared certain advertisements express advocacy when they take place within 30 days prior to an election violated the First Amendment. This decision effectively reinstated the express and issue advocacy distinction found in *Buckley*. Then, in *Davis v. Federal Election Commission*,[75] the Court struck down the provision of BCRA known as the "millionaire's amendment" which sought to offset expenditures made by wealthy candidates. Finally, *Citizens United* permanently voided the electioneering communications provision of BCRA.

Where does all this leave the Court and the First Amendment when it comes to money, speech, and campaign finance? First, more or less the *Buckley* framework remains the law of the land when it comes to how expenditures and contributions are treated under the First Amendment. It appears most contribution limits are permitted and all expenditures limits (except voluntary) are unconstitutional. Second, the Court has made a mess out of laws and efforts to regulate money in politics, regardless of

---

73   540 U.S. 93 (2003).
74   551 U.S. 449 (2007).
75   554 U.S. 724 (2008).

whether one supports such regulation or not. Distinctions between express and issue advocacy, generally allowing corporations and unions to expend but not contribute money, and even the distinction between what an expenditure versus a contribution are, all seem confusing.[76] Moreover, by the time *Citizens United* was decided, the Court had generated other problems leading to new or expanding entities being allowed to use money for political purposes. With *Citizens United* as a precedent, a court permitted in *Speechnow.org. v. FEC*[77] unlimited contributions to independent expenditure only political action committees, thereby creating what has now has come to be known as Super PACS. Thus, even in some cases, corporations and unions can now make contributions to other entities.

Think about where the law is now regarding money and politics. Assume that you are an individual or an entity wishing to disburse money to leverage political influence for yourself. How to allocate that money is effectively a portfolio investment strategy that gives you a range of ways to invest to maximize influence. There are direct contributions to candidates which is what is known as hard money. This is money, except if given in small amounts, which is highly transparent and subject (at the federal level) to contribution limits. But one can also give to PACs and Super PACs, subject to certain limits, and depending on whether your contributions are as an individual or through an entity. The same is true for donations to political parties. Then there are options to contribute to Super Pacs, non-profits, be that be 501 c 4s (which may endorse candidates) or 501 c 3s (which may not endorse candidates but can do issue advocacy up to a limit), and even 501 c 6 (business groups). One can also make independent expenditures that are for issue or express advocacy, and one can also spend money directly on lobbying. There may be other ways to contribute or expend money to leverage influence. There are a range of options to contribute or expend money, with the choice of how to distribute the money up to a particular agent's needs and desires. Each of these means of using money has its own set of rules determined both by legislation and the courts, and the rules also vary between federal and state and across state jurisdictions.

The point here is that the rules for how to use money for political purposes are confusing. Moreover, it is also questionable whether they are effective in doing

---

76 The range of confusion post *Citizens United* is extensive. *See, e.g.*, Erwin Chemerinsky, Richard Hasen, and James Sample, *Citizens United Impact on Judicial Elections*, 60 DRAKE L. REV. 685 (2012) (judicial elections); Benjamin I. Sachs, *Unions, Corporations, and Political Opt-out Rights after Citizens United*, 112 COLUM. L. REV. 800 (2012) (individual and entity rights); Jonathan Romiti, *Playing Politics with Shareholder Value: the Case for Applying Fiduciary Law to Corporate Political Donations Post-citizens United*, 53 B. C. L. REV. 737 (2012) (shareholder rights); Roger Colinvaux, *The Political Speech of Charities in the Face of Citizens United: a Defense of Prohibition*, 62 CASE W. RES. L. REV. 685 (2012) (non-profit law); Jason S. Campbell, *Down the Rabbit Hole with Citizens United: Are Bans on Corporate Direct Campaign Contributions Still Constitutional,?* 45 LOY. L.A. L. REV. 171 (2011) (constitutionality of bans on direct corporate contributions to candidates).

77 599 F.3d 686 (D.C. Cir. 2010 (en banc)).

anything simply because there are so many ways for money to get into the political system such that you would have to be an idiot not to figure out a way to get around limits. In addition, if the goal is to prevent corruption or the appearance of *quid pro quo* corruption, it is not clear they have solved that problem. While the number of actual political bribery cases in the United States may be quite small, public opinion remains high in the belief that money does corrupt the political process.[78] Additionally, polling by the American National Election Service found in 2008 that 60 percent of the those surveyed do not believe that public officials care what they think,[79] 49 percent believe that the public does not have in say in what the government does,[80] 51 percent believe government officials are crooked,[81] and 69 percent believe that government is run for the benefit of a few big interests.[82] Even though the Supreme Court rejected in *Buckley* as constitutionally compelling the need to deter the skyrocketing cost of campaigns and to equalize voices, it is clear that neither of these objectives has been secured without regulation. As witnessed by the 2012 presidential campaigns, costs continue to rise for campaigns and wealthy individuals and donors expend significant amounts of money to affect the outcome of elections.[83] Moreover, there is good evidence that *Citizens United* has

---

78 Dan Eggen, *Poll: Large majority opposes Supreme Court's decision on campaign financing,* WASHINGTON POST (February 16, 2010), at A1, noting an ABC poll finding 80 percent of those surveyed disagree with the Supreme Court's *Citizens United* decision. Interestingly, while in 2000-2001 national polls routinely asked about public support for campaign finance reform and legislation and revealed significant majorities in support of contribution and other limits, few surveys now seem to ask about this topic and instead frame the question in regards to support or opposition to *Citizens United.*

79 American National Election Service, *The ANES Guide to Public Opinion and Electoral Behavior* (n.d.), located at http://electionstudies.org/nesguide/toptable/tab5b_3.htm (site last viewed on March 26, 2013).

80 American National Election Service, *The ANES Guide to Public Opinion and Electoral Behavior* (n.d.), located at http://electionstudies.org/nesguide/toptable/tab5b_2.htm (site last viewed on March 26, 2013).

81 American National Election Service, *The ANES Guide to Public Opinion and Electoral Behavior* (n.d.), located at http://electionstudies.org/nesguide/toptable/tab5a_4.htm (site last viewed on March 26, 2013).

82 American National Election Service, *The ANES Guide to Public Opinion and Electoral Behavior* (n.d.), located at http://electionstudies.org/nesguide/toptable/tab5a_2.htm (site last viewed on March 26, 2013).

83 Campaign Finance Institute, Independent Spending Roughly Equaled the Candidates' in Close House and Senate Races; Winning Candidates Raised More than any Previous Election (November 16, 2012), located at http://www.cfinst.org/Press/PReleases/12-11-09/Early_Post-Election_Look_at_Money_in_the_House_and_Senate_Elections_of_2012.aspx (site last viewed on March 26, 2013); Michael Beckel and Russ Choma, Impact of the Citizens United decision on the 2012 election (November 1, 2012), located at http://thepresidency.us/2012/11/impact-of-the-citizens-united-decision-on-the-2012-election/ (site last viewed on March 26, 2013). *See also:* Marian Currinder, *Campaign Finance*, in MICHAEL NELSON, ED., THE ELECTIONS OF 2012 (2013).

facilitated the entry of more corporate money into elections, giving these entities more of a financial voice in elections than they have had in the past.

Money and Politics: Asking a Different Question

So all of the discussion above leads to a really fundamental question: What role should private money have in the financing of elections in the United States? No one is going to deny that elections are expensive. Media time is costly as are get out to vote campaigns, voter registrations, and a host of other activities that demand significant resources. Some will argue that we expend too little on elections already, especially when compared to how much as a society we spend on our pets for example.[84] Others might assert that money needs to be raised and spent, especially by challengers, to offset incumbent advantages.[85] These and other points are well taken, but they fundamentally miss the mark. The question is not necessarily how much we spend on elections but rather whether the current system of financing elections is incompatible with the values of American democracy. Should money influence political choices and outcomes? Can we reconcile American democracy with free market capitalism in a way that allows the conversion of economic resources into political influence? This is really the basic cluster of questions that neither Congress, state legislatures, nor the Supreme Court have addressed. Nor is this a question that most election law scholars seem to be asking. They have failed to get to the deeper question of looking at whether the theories or democratic values that give meaning to the Constitution, and which should give definition to election law, are supported or undermined by the economic values that seem to be at the basis of how the United States currently finances its political process.

Now, asking this question is no different than raising other more fundamental questions about values and institutions in American society. For example, some would assert that the way health care is allocated in the United States is fundamentally at odds with the way it should be allocated. By that, health care should be allocated on the basis of medical need or illness, not the ability to pay.[86] Yet the United States has a pay-for-access and a profit-based system denying millions access to the health care system. It is a system more costly, with lower access, and less equitable outcomes overall than many other health care delivery

---

84 *See, e.g.*, BRADLEY A. SMITH, UNFREE SPEECH: THE FOLLY OF CAMPAIGN FINANCE REFORM (2003).

85 *See, e.g.*, Gary C. Jacobson, *The Effects of Campaign Spending on Congressional Campaigns*, 72 AM. POL. SCI. REV. 469 (1978); and THE POLITICS OF CONGRESSIONAL ELECTIONS (2004).

86 KIP SULLIVAN, THE HEALTH CARE MESS: HOW WE GOT INTO IT AND HOW WE'LL GET OUT OF IT (2006); and MICHAEL WALZER, SPHERES OF JUSTICE: A DEFENSE OF PLURALISM AND EQUALITY (1984).

systems found elsewhere in the world.[87] Even with reforms found in the Affordable Care Act, many of these problems may not be solved because the market system for delivery of health care in the United States is incompatible with the basic values of what a health care system is supposed to secure—affordable, quality health care available for all who need it. The debate that does not take place in the United States is to ask if the economic marketplace is the correct or appropriate institution to allocate health care. This is the question that needs to be asked about political influence in the United States.

Is the economic market the correct way to allocate political power or influence in the United States? Should dollars convert over into political influence? And if so, how does such a conversion affect American democratic values? There are really two basic answers to this question. The first assents to the legitimacy of money's role in allocating political influence in American politics. For the most part, this perspective would urge some form of deregulation of money, arguing for a dismantling of all contribution limits to go along with the current lack of expenditure limits. That position, at least until recently, has been one of asserting no limits and full disclosure. Yet as we shall see, that position, once held by former FEC commissioner Brad Smith and others, has now evolved and he, along with James Bopp, and Justice Clarence Thomas, now even contests the legitimacy of disclosure rules. These individuals seem ready to embrace the idea that money is constitutionally protected speech. They seem to believe that there is no problem in letting economic wealth and resources be converted into a factor driving political power or influence in American politics, even if done in a clandestine fashion.

A competing perspective, held partially by former Justice Stevens, argues that money is not speech but property and that contribution and expenditure limits are constitutional.[88] While Stevens may not have gone so far as to assert that money should not be converted into political influence, there is a broader argument that can build upon the money-is-not-speech argument to assert that American democratic theory needs to significantly confine the ability to convert economic resources into political influence.

---

87 Organization for Economic Cooperation and Development, *OECD Health Data 2012: How Does the United States Compare* (2012), located at http://www.oecd.org/health/health-systems/BriefingNoteUSA2012.pdf (site last visited on March 26, 2013); Atule Gawande, *The Cost Conundrum: What a Texas Town Can Teach Us about Health Care*, THE NEW YORKER (June 1, 2009), located at http://www.newyorker.com/reporting/2009/06/01/090601fa_fact_gawande (site last viewed on March 26, 2013).

88 Nixon v. Shrink Missouri Government PAC, 528 U.S. 377, 398 (2000).

Deregulate but Disclose

For the most part, *Buckley* established disclosure as part of what Bruce Ackerman and Ian Ayres call the old paradigm for campaign finance reform.[89] By that, they argue that the prevailing paradigm supporting disclosure saw money in the political process as similar to pollution—it is best to limit both and also restrict where either of them can be dumped.[90] However, they argue that the full disclosure or publicity route has proved to be unsuccessful or otherwise plagued by constitutional infirmities,[91] thereby leading Ackerman and Ayres to reject disclosure and opt instead for what they describe as a new paradigm for campaign finance reform that relies upon market analogies.[92] They called their proposal the "secret donation booth." Under this regime, contributions to candidates would be anonymous,[93] thereby eliminating the incentives to engage in *quid pro quo* activity. While Ackerman and Ayres appear to be unique in rejecting disclosure for anonymity, they are correct that the prevailing *Buckley* paradigm does support it.[94]

Why disclosure-only? The case for disclosure-only can be articulated on at least two grounds. First, by those who believe that such a regime is the best or most acceptable way to regulate the role of money. Second, it is advocated in lieu of other campaign finance mechanisms because other more extensive regimes are unconstitutional or because disclosure is offered as a Trojan Horse in lieu of real regulation.

Generally, disclosure-only is advocated by its proponents because they do not believe that other forms of regulation are constitutional. For example, Martin Redish believes that money given in a political context is protected speech and that the use of money for this purpose is a speech-act deserving of constitutional protection.[95] While Redish's *Money Talks* is silent on the issue of disclosure, presumably he would advocate it in some circumstances, yet his solution to the corruption and unequal flow of money in the political system would be to address the root problem of economic inequalities that exist. Redistributive policies that alter economic power in society are thus a preferred solution.[96]

Bradley Smith seemed at one time to be the most forceful advocate of the disclosure-only regime. Three reasons undergird Smith's support for the disclosure-only position. First, money used for political purposes is protected speech.[97]

---

89 BRUCE ACKERMAN AND IAN AYRES, VOTING WITH DOLLARS, 3 (2002).
90 *Id.* at 3.
91 *Id.* at 4-5.
92 *Id.* at 18, 21 (praising reforms that embrace "market signals").
93 *Id.* at 6.
94 *Id.* at 4, fn. 1 and 2 (discussing supporters of disclosure-only proposals).
95 *Id.* at 126.
96 *Id.* at 234.
97 BRADLEY A. SMITH, UNFREE SPEECH: THE FOLLY OF CAMPAIGN FINANCE REFORM, 193 (2001).

Second, most campaign finance reform regulations are difficult to administer.[98] Third, disclosure works.[99]

For Smith, he appears to accept the *Buckley* argument that the only acceptable justification for the regulation of money in politics is to address the problem of corruption or its appearance.[100] Yet unlike the Court which endorsed contribution limits in *Buckley*, Smith sides with Chief Justice Burger's concurrence[101] in that case that the least restrictive means to address *quid pro quo* corruption disclosure,[102] thereby rendering any other form of regulation unconstitutional because it is not narrowly-tailored to secure this compelling interest.[103] Moreover, disclosure does work according to Smith. He cites the 1971 FECA laws as an example of how disclosure brought to light the Watergate abuses and the eventual resignation of Richard Nixon as evidence that disclosure can root out corruption.[104] Elsewhere, he argues that disclosure can bring corruption and conflicts of interest to light.[105] Overall, a disclosure-only regime seems capable of serving the compelling government interests that the *Buckley* Court identified.

However, Smith's endorsement of disclosure-only seems half-hearted at best. For example, he appears to view it as a form of regulation that could be too cumbersome and interfere with First Amendment rights.[106] Second, he cites *McIntyre v. Ohio*[107] to argue that there are limits on what can be disclosed, suggesting that this case places some outer limits on publicity in the name of protecting privacy.[108] Third, he even suggests that there may not be strong enough

---

98 *Id.* at 91.

99 *Id.* at 32.

100 *Id.* at 203-4.

101 *See:* Buckley v. Valeo, 424 U.S. 1, 235-56 (1976) (Burger, J., concurring in part and dissenting in part).

102 Smith, Unfree Speech at 133.

103 *Id.* at 135.

104 *Id.* at 32.

105 *Id.* at 175.

106 *Id.* at 91.

107 514 U.S. 334 (1995) (holding that an Ohio law that prohibited individuals from distributing anonymous political literature violated the First Amendment).

108 Smith, Unfree Speech at 222. *See also:* Richard L. Hasen, "*The Surprisingly Easy Case for Disclosure of Contributions and Expenditures Funding Sham Advocacy*," 3 ELEC. L. J. 251 (2004), for a discussion of the status of McIntyre v. Ohio in the face of the recent McConnell v. Federal Election Commission ruling upholding, with limit comment, various disclosure provisions in BCRA.

In addition to McIntyre, the Court in both Watchtower Bible and Tract Society of New York v. Village of Stratton, 536 U.S. 150 (2002) (local law requiring a displayed permit to go door to door for political purposes struck down) and NAACP v. Alabama, 357 U.S. 449 (1958) (First Amendment freedom of association bars compelled disclosure of membership lists) has ruled that the First Amendment protects anonymous political activity, adding some confusion to how to reconcile the political campaign finance disclosure cases with these precedents.

of a governmental justification to compel disclosure and that it may in fact burden grassroots political activity.[109] Fourth, Smith contends that bribery laws are already in place to address corruption, thereby questioning the need for disclosure. Finally, Smith even concedes that disclosure might not be able to address certain problems such as issue advocacy.[110] Overall, by the time one finishes reading *Unfree Speech* it is unclear whether Smith really supports disclosure as the ideal form of regulation; whether he supports it because it works; whether he thinks it is actually unconstitutional; or that he thinks it is the only form of regulation that passes constitutional muster. Instead, disclosure appears to be a bone thrown to advocates for more forceful reform, hoping that endorsing it will be sufficient to deflect demands for other changes.

In addition to Smith, Kathleen Sullivan,[111] Larry Sabato and Glenn Simpson,[112] and Todd Lochner and Bruce Cain[113] also endorse disclosure-only as their preferred campaign finance reform solutions. For example, in their *Dirty Little Secrets: The Persistence of Corruption in American Politics*, Larry Sabato and Glenn Simpson document the history of campaign finance reforms in the United States, indicating that disclosure has been a preferred solution dating back to 1907[114] and that it was the central principle of FECA and the post-Watergate reforms.[115] After an exhaustive analysis of then recent money abuses in American politics, Sabato and Simpson conclude that new reforms are needed. The regime they call for is described by them as "deregulation plus."[116] Deregulation plus is essentially a disclosure-only regime where all contribution limits would be abolished[117] and where the fear of public backlash following disclosure[118] would serve as a deterrent to groups that do not disclose.

In support of their deregulation plus regime, Sabato and Simpson draw an analogy between spending on campaigns and elections to that of trading in stocks on Wall Street:

---

109   Smith, Unfree Speech at 224-25.

110   *Id.* at 221.

111   Kathleen M. Sullivan, "*Political Money and Freedom of Speech*," 30 U. C. DAVIS L. REV. 663 (1997).

112   LARRY J. SABATO AND GLENN R. SIMPSON, DIRTY LITTLE SECRETS: THE PERSISTENCE OF CORRUPTION IN AMERICAN POLITICS (1996).

113   Todd Lochner and Bruce E. Cain, "*The Enforcement Blues: Formal and Information Sanctions for Campaign Finance Violations*," 52 ADMIN. L. REV. 629 (2000); and "*Equity and Efficacy in the Enforcement of Campaign Finance Laws*," 77 TEX. L. REV. 1891 (1999).

114   Sabato and Simpson at 11-12.

115   *Id.* at 32, 54.

116   *Id.* at 330.

117   *Id.* at 334.

118   *Id.* at 320.

> Consider the American stock markets. Most government oversight of them simply makes sure that publicly traded companies accurately disclose vital information about their finances. The philosophy here is that buyers, given, the information they need, are intelligent enough to look out for themselves. There will be winners and losers, of course ... but it is not the government's role to guarantee anyone's success ... The notion that people are smart enough, and indeed have the duty, to think and choose for themselves, also underlies our basic democratic government. There is no reason why the same principle cannot be successfully applied to a free market for campaign finance. In this scenario, disclosure laws would be broadened and strengthened, and penalties for failure to disclose would be ratcheted up, while rules on other aspects—such as sources of funds and sizes of contributions—could be greatly loosened or even abandoned altogether.[119]

For Sabato and Simpson, a broadened disclosure regime is preferred for several reasons. First, restrictions on spending implicate First Amendment values.[120] Second, public financing will not be able to address the problems associated with spending by third-party groups.[121] Third, all the current loopholes in the system have effectively created a system without any spending or contribution limits.[122] Fourth, broadened disclosure would bring to light the activities of many groups presently hidden.[123] Fifth, as noted above, well-informed citizens can make their own judgments regarding what they think the contributions and spending patterns mean to them and therefore judge accordingly.[124]

Sabato and Simpson acknowledge two possible objections to their deregulation plus regime. First, what if groups opt not to disclose? This is where the fear of backlash comes in. That is, the remedy for groups seeking to remain clandestine is that there would be a public backlash against them or the candidates they support if they are caught.[125] Second, Sabato and Simpson worry that a broadened disclosure regime would bring too many "politically active but politically inconsequential players into the federal regulatory framework."[126] Their solution is to set a high disclosure requirement of between $25,000 to $50,000 in total expenditures per election cycle.[127] Below this threshold, there would not be a requirement to disclose.

---

119 *Id.* at 330.
120 *Id.* at 332.
121 *Id.* at 332.
122 *Id.* at 332.
123 *Id.* at 330.
124 *Id.* at 330.
125 *Id.* at 330.
126 *Id.* at 332.
127 *Id.* at 332.

Kathleen Sullivan has also pressed the case for a disclosure-only regime in a pair of articles. Sullivan contends that there are three types of campaign finance reforms currently being advocated: (1) New limits on political contributions; (2) public financing; and (3) restrictions on expenditures.[128] In part, her argument is that all three of these proposals would run into a variety of constitution problems, but more importantly, Sullivan attacks what she calls the political theory of campaign finance reform, examining the "supposed seven deadly sins of political money."[129] Sullivan argues that efforts to regulate these seven sins—political inequality in voting; distortion; political inequality in representation; carpetbagging; diversion of legislative and executive energies; quality of debate; and lack of debate[130]— generally face constitutional problems or that the sins alleged are "empirical problems"[131] that have not yet been adequately demonstrated or clarified to support the restrictions imposed.

In lieu of the three reform strategies noted above, Sullivan endorses Chief Justice Burger's opinion[132] in *Buckley*[133] and Justice Thomas's views[134] in *Colorado Republican Federal Campaign Committee v. Federal Election Commission*[135] that contributions and expenditures should be treated the same and left unregulated. In its place, she asserts that political money will not proliferate indefinitely, so long as "the identity of contributors is required to be vigorously and frequently disclosed."[136] Instead, deregulating contributions accompanied by increased disclosure will have three salutatory effects. First, with more money in the system, the value of any one contribution would decrease because politicians would have more potential donors to seek out and therefore feel less indebted to any one contributor. To paraphrase Sullivan's language, with more *quids* in the

---

128 Sullivan 1997 at 667.

129 *Id.* at 671.

130 One can, however, also argue that Sullivan's choice of the sins to be remedied by campaign finance reform misses the real targets of reform. By that, ensuring that races are more competitive, or that the challengers have adequate resources to mount effective races against incumbents, are perhaps more crucial issues and concerns than the seven sins that Sullivan directs her arguments against.

131 Sullivan 1997 at 687.

132 Kathleen M. Sullivan, *Against Campaign Finance Reform*, 1998 UTAH L. REV. 311, 313 (1998).

133 *See:* Buckley v. Valeo, 424 U.S. 1, 235-56 (1976) (Burger, J., concurring in part and dissenting in part).

134 Sullivan 1997 at 666; and Sullivan 1998 at 313.

135 518 U.S. 604, 638 (1996) (stating that "Whether an individual donates money to a candidate or group who will use it to promote the candidate or whether the individual spends the money to promote the candidate himself, the individual seeks to engage in political expression and to associate with likeminded persons. A contribution is simply an indirect expenditure.").

136 Sullivan 1997 at 688.

system, politicians have "less reason to commit to any particular *quo.*"[137] Second, deregulating contributions would decrease the value of subterfuge whereby groups presently resort to independent expenditures and soft money contributions to parties.[138] Finally, disclosure would subject candidates to voter retaliation if exposed as taking too large contributions from some individuals or groups.[139] Proof, for Sullivan, that voter retaliation works can be found in the 1996 presidential race where disclosure of Democratic fundraising scandals had a temporary impact on President Clinton's poll numbers.[140] Overall, Sullivan describes an enforced disclosure regime as the preferred alternative to either a purely *laissez-faire* or more extensively regulated system with contribution and expenditure limits and public financing.

Todd Lochner and Bruce Cain also press the case for disclosure-only, but do so as a result of their claims that other systems of campaign finance regulation—such as contribution limits—face numerous enforcement problems. They base their claims both upon empirical studies of the Federal Election Commission (FEC) and the California Fair Political Practices Commission (FPPC).[141] In examining the enforcement practices of both, significant time delays in enforcement question whether the use of formal sanctions by either deters illegal campaign practices.[142] Similarly, they also question whether informal sanctions—the fear of public exposure—will be a sufficient deterrent.[143] This deterrence would work only if voters take the time to research violations and if the press sufficiently and adequately covers the violations.[144] While there is some evidence that press coverage of illegal activity does have an impact upon candidates, they overall conclude that the deterrent value is weak.[145]

Instead of contribution or other limits, Lochner and Cain argue that a disclosure-only regime might be easier to enforce. These types of regimes do not confront many of the difficult legal questions that other regulations face.[146] Thus, for Lochner and Cain, disclosure-only is opted for, even though the authors do not endorse it as necessarily the best system for regulating money in the political process.[147] Like Sabato and Simpson, they draw upon the market analogy and view politics as a free market.[148] According to Lochner and Cain:

---

137 *Id.* at 689.
138 *Id.* at 689.
139 *Id.* at 689.
140 *Id.* at 689.
141 Lochner and Cain 2000 at 630; Lochner and Cain 1999 at 1892.
142 Lochner and Cain 2000 at 649.
143 *Id.* 2000 at 653-54.
144 *Id.* 2000 at 653-54.
145 *Id.* at 654 (noting how press coverage of the 1992 banking scandal led to a greater number of defeats of congressional incumbents).
146 Lochner and Cain 2000 at 649.
147 *Id.*
148 Lochner and Cain 1999 at 1935.

If politics is indeed a market, then let the market solve the problem. Consider abolishing expenditure and contribution limits and instead emphasize transparency based on immediate internet disclosure. If voters actually care about where a candidate's money comes from, or how much money is spent, let them vote based upon their distaste.[149]

Thus, despite their admonitions that voters do not spend much time gathering information on candidates, and despite their criticism of the deterrence model, in the end Lochner and Cain resort to both in defense of their disclosure-only regime.

But the chorus for deregulate but disclose does not stop here. John Samples argues against campaign finance limits, contending that there is little evidence that money corrupts the political process or that it affects decisions on who runs or does not run for office.[150] James Bopp, a frequent litigator and critic of campaign finance reform laws that limit donations, argued at one point in favor of donate but disclose[151] before taking his current position against even disclosure.[152] Even those who erstwhile normally support disclosure seem to give it only a "qualified defense."[153]

Overall, in defending disclosure-only, several claims from its advocates can be gleaned. First, disclosure-only regimes will more readily discourage the proliferation of money than will other regimes. Second, disclosure-only regimes will deter large contributions or contributors because of fear of voter backlash. Third, disclosure-only regimes are better able to address the problems associated with spending by third parties than other types of regimes. Fourth, disclosure-only regimes will produce more money in the political system, resulting in fewer *quid pro quos*. Fifth, disclosure-only regimes will discourage subterfuge. Sixth, disclosure-only regimes will equalize spending and competition. Seventh, disclosure-only regimes are easier to enforce and implement.

---

149 *Id.* at 1935.

150 JOHN SAMPLES, THE FALLACY OF CAMPAIGN FINANCE REFORM (2006); John Samples, *Against Deference*, 12 NEXUS 21, 23 (2007).

151 James Bopp, Jr., and Kaylan Lytle Phillips, *The Limits of Citizens United V. Federal Election Commission: Analytical and Practical Reasons Why the Sky Is Not Falling*, 46 U.S.F. L. Rev. 281 (2012); James Bopp, Jr., and Joseph E. LaRue, *The Game Changer: Citizens United's Impact on Campaign Finance Law in General and Corporate Political Speech in Particular*, 9 FIRST AMEND. L. REV. 251 (2010).

152 James Bopp Jr., and Jared Haynie, *The Tyranny of "reform and Transparency": a Plea to the Supreme Court to Revisit and Overturn Citizens United's "disclaimer and Disclosure" Holding*, 16 NEXUS: CHAP. J. L. & POL'Y 3 (2010-11).

153 Richard L. Hasen, *Chill Out: A Qualified Defense of Campaign Finance Disclosure Laws in the Internet Age*, 27 J. L & POL. 557 (2012).

Disclosure Is Not Enough

There are three major problems with the disclosure-only arguments: One is conceptual, the second empirical, the third is a structural democratic one. Conceptually, the case for disclosure-only lacks development or rests upon numerous faulty assumptions.

First, in arguing for disclosure-only, what is left unclear in many of its advocates' arguments is what it means to have disclosure and what it means to say that it works.[154] For example, what would have to be disclosed to qualify as a disclosure-only regime? Would it be disclosure of all contributions (and expenditures)? But what does it mean to say all contributions? Is it contributions made down to one cent? Is it contributions from individuals, corporations, unions, PACS, conduit funds?[155] Does it also include contributions to PACS? If so, what do we wish to know? Is it simply dollar amounts or do we also wish to know names, addresses, and employers? In the case of Sabato and Simpson, at least they are clear in terms of exempting some groups and individuals from disclosure if they fall below a certain threshold. However, while such a threshold might minimize excessive regulatory entanglement and perhaps comply with the constitutional requirements of *NAACP v. Alabama*,[156] *Watchtower Bible and Tract Society of New York v. Village of Stratton*,[157] and *McIntyre v. Ohio*, Sabato and Simpson ignore an unintended effect of their threshold—many small groups have huge impacts in local federal races and there would be an incentive to proliferate lots of small groups to avoid disclosure. Why would groups still wish to avoid disclosure? If the identity of groups or contributors is a signal regarding where a candidate stands on issues—such as in the case of candidates who receive money from the National Rifle Association or from Emily's List—then many candidates or groups might wish to obscure the source of their money.[158]

---

154 *See:* Richard Briffault, *Updating Disclosure for the New Era of Independent Spending*, 27 J. L. & POL. 683 (2012); Richard Briffault, *Campaign Finance Disclosure 2.0*, 9 ELECT. L. J. 273, 275 (2010); and Richard L. Hasen, *Chill Out: a Qualified Defense of Campaign Finance Disclosure Laws in the Internet Age*, 27 J. L. & POL. 557 (2012), for thoughtful discussions on what disclosure actually means in the age of the Internet.

155 Wisc. Stat. § 11.01(5m) (2003) ("'Conduit' means an individual who or an organization which receives a contribution of money and transfers the contribution to another individual or organization without exercising discretion as to the amount which is transferred and the individual to whom or organization to which the transfer is made"). Wisc. Stat. 11.06(11) mandates the public disclosure and reporting of conduit funds.

156 357 U.S. 449 (1958) (holding that a state law requiring a private association to publicize the names of its members violated the First Amendment right to freedom of association).

157 536 U.S. 150 (2002).

158 *See:* Buckley at 67 (stating that knowledge of a candidate's contributions "allows voters to place each candidate in the political spectrum more precisely than is often possible solely on the basis of party labels and campaign speeches" and that the "sources of a

Moreover, both Sabato and Simpson and Sullivan rely upon disclosure as a deterrent effect, although the nature of the deterrence for them is very different. For the former, deterrence comes into play as a way to encourage groups and individuals to disclose for fear of public backlash if they do not but are nonetheless caught. For Sullivan, deterrence comes into play as a way to discourage candidates from taking too large contributions from big donors, less voter backlash. Now assuming in the first case that groups can be detected if they try to hide from disclosing, there are several problems with the voter backlash thesis. First, while both Sabato and Simpson and Sullivan contend that deregulating contributions will remove the disincentive for groups to give independently or seek subterfuge, they—and especially Sullivan—also stipulate that fear of voter backlash will discourage contributions. Does not this fear of backlash create an incentive for subterfuge?

Yet even if fear of backlash does not discourage clandestine activity, there are real questions regarding the efficacy of deterrence. Within the field of criminal justice, while deterrence is often articulated as a goal of punishment, proof of its efficacy is questionable.[159] A deterrence theory in criminal justice assumes, among other things, that: (1) potential offenders are aware of the punishment; (2) offenders weigh the punishment against the benefit of committing the crime; (3) offenders believe that they will be caught; and (4) the society-defined punishment is actually perceived as punishment to the offenders.[160] The same logic applies to the backlash thesis advocated by both Sabato and Simpson and Sullivan in that one needs to assume that voters are rational, paying attention to campaign contributions, that they weigh contributions when making electoral choices, and that they will punish candidates because they are taking contributions from donors whom they do not approve. It is not clear that this model works in the real world.

Even Kathleen Sullivan seems to acknowledge that the backlash is of limited value, noting that revelations of Democratic Party fundraising only had a temporary impact on Clinton's polling numbers and that he did win the election. Clinton and the Democrats did the crime but did not have to the do time because the backlash was muted. So much for deterrence.

---

candidate's financial support also alert the voter to the interests to which a candidate is most likely to be responsive and thus facilitate predictions of future performance in office").

See also: MICHAEL X. DELLI CARPINI AND SCOTT KEETER, WHAT AMERICANS KNOW ABOUT POLITICS AND WHY IT MATTERS, 44-45 (1996) (noting how individuals use a variety of cues, presumably including the source of a candidate's contributions, in making voting decisions.

159 *See:* SAMUEL WALKER, SENSE AND NONSENSE ABOUT CRIME AND DRUGS, 100 (2001); David Garland, THE CULTURE OF CONTROL: CRIME AND SOCIAL ORDER IN CONTEMPORARY SOCIETY, 59-60 (2001); and FRANKLIN E. ZIMRING, GORDON HAWKINS, AND SAM KAMIN, PUNISHMENT AND DEMOCRACY: THREE STRIKES AND YOUR'RE OUT IN CALIFORNIA, 94-95, 103-5 (2001) (indicating that the California three strikes and you're out policy rested upon the concept of deterrence and that the evidence indicates that the three strikes laws did not deter).

160 Walker, Sense and Nonsense at 100.

There are other problems in defining what disclosure means among its advocates. In terms of expenditures, does disclosure include real-time disclosure, a statement indicating the source of the contributions? Moreover, if one is to have disclosure-only, how should it occur? Should it be on-line or in paper form? Should it be updated daily, weekly, or monthly? All of these are issues left unresolved or explained in terms of constructing a disclosure-only policy.

Dennis Thompson also points out that a disclosure-only regime would never be satisfactory because it would fail to reveal the tacit promises, agreements, or understandings made when contributions are made.[161] Disclosure-only, more importantly, would fail to address many of the critical problems that money creates in campaign and elections. It would be, in many ways, an after the fact remedy at best. As Bradley Smith's Watergate example demonstrates, disclosure did not prevent the Nixon fundraising abuses, it only caught them several years later after the election had occurred. Disclosure-only is not prophylactic, it is a post abuse remedy, and it often does little to punish the wrongdoer.

Disclosure-only also presupposes that citizens are informed, aware, and capable of digesting and understanding campaign finance reform information. This is certainly true in the Sabato and Simpson model where they draw parallels between political campaigns and Wall Street, or Lochner and Cain in describing elections to be like a marketplace. None of these assumptions are likely to take place on a sufficient scale. Specifically, the disclosure-only policy seems to assume rational, informed voters who will seek out campaign finance information, weigh it in comparison to other knowledge they have about candidates, and then express an informed preference based upon all this. However, even Lochner and Cain acknowledge this depiction of voters is unrealistic,[162] and such a model of behavior is unlikely to occur except among a few, with many instead perhaps voting more out of concern regarding the economy, war and peace, or other issues more salient.

As Elizabeth Garrett points out,[163] disclosure has its limits. Voters have limited time, knowledge, and expertise.[164] They face many complex choices. They do not act as the fully informed market participants that Smith, Sullivan, and Sabato and Simpson envision. Instead, voters use a variety of cues when making voting choices—such as who gives the candidate money or the party of the candidate—and they also need information packaged in a way that is digestible and useable to them if disclosure-only is to work.[165] Yet none of the advocates of the disclosure-

---

161 DENNIS F. THOMPSON, JUST ELECTIONS: CREATING A FAIR ELECTORAL PROCESS IN THE UNITED STATES, 110 (2002).

162 Lochner and Cain 2000 at 648.

163 Elizabeth Garrett, *"Voting with Cues,"* 37 U. RICH. L. REV. 1011 (2003).

164 Delli Carpini and Keeter, What Americans Know About Politics at 271 (generally noting the lack of knowledge Americans have about politics and specifically discussing how this lack of knowledge and expertise affects political engagement and motivation).

165 Delli Carpini and Keeter at 44-45 (discussing the use of cues among voters as surrogates for more substantive political knowledge).

only regime has paid any attention to these issues. None of this is to say that the source of political money is unimportant to voters. Instead, how campaigns are financed is a process issue different from the content of issues that people consider when making voting choices. Conflating the two is a mistake, demonstrating a misunderstanding regarding the difference between how elections are run and the factors that influence electoral choice.

The analogy of comparing elections and voters to the stock market and investors is inapt on several grounds. First, presumably investors are more informed about financial matters than would be general voters simply by the fact that investors might tend to be better educated than many voters. Second, however, the recent Wall Street scandals involving Enron, Worldcom, and a host of other companies demonstrate that even investors are not well informed and that there are many abuses in the financial markets, some of which could be attributed to a lack of disclosure (but also many of them sourced in illegal behavior that included lying and possible abuse of market positions). If Sabato and Simpson's call to make the Federal Election Commission act more like the Securities and Exchange Commission in policing disclosure, the passage of Sarbanes-Oxley[166] and other Wall Street reforms demonstrate a demand for strengthened regulatory behavior on the part of the SEC beyond simply mandating more disclosure.

Third, Wall Street regulation has never been simply a disclosure-only regime. The existence of antitrust laws and the enforcement activity by the Federal Trade Commission, among other agencies, is proof that simple disclosure of business practices is not enough to protect either investors or consumers.[167]

Finally, unlike playing the stock market which produces private goods, voting has an external effect such that one person's choice of whom to vote for will have an impact on others in terms of what candidates are elected. Put simply, there are numerous individual and collective benefits attached to voting choices and the

---

166 Public Company Accounting Reform and Investor Protection Act, 18 U.S.C. §1350 *et seq.*

167 Drawing analogies of the political to the economic marketplace seem to be at odds with several arguments to segment or bracket the two. *See:* Federal Election Commission v. Massachusetts Citizens for Life, Inc. 479 U.S. 238, 257 (1986) (stating that "Direct corporate spending on political activity raises the prospect that resources amassed in the economic marketplace may be used to provide an unfair advantage in the political marketplace") and Federal Election Com'n v. Massachusetts Citizens for Life, Inc. 479 U.S. 238, 268 (1986) (Rehnquist, C.J. concurring and dissenting in part) (stating that "I do not dispute that the threat from corporate political activity will vary depending on the particular characteristics of a given corporation; it is obvious that large and successful corporations with resources to fund a political war chest constitute a more potent threat to the political process than less successful business corporations or nonprofit corporations").

See also: Michael Walzer, *Liberalism and the Art of Separation*, 12 POLITICAL THEORY 315 (1984) (arguing for the need to draw lines or separate the forces of the economy from impacting upon other aspects of society).

regulation of campaigns that may distinguish the regulation of elections and voters from that of the stock market and investors.

In making the case that disclosure-only is the best possible solution, Sabato and Simpson state that it has been used since 1907 and especially since Watergate as a guiding principle to regulate money in politics. Instead of viewing history as vindication of disclosure-only, the failure of it to clean up campaigns and elections over the last 100 years should be proof that more than disclosure-only is needed.

Thus, disclosure-only fails for lack of conceptual clarity, exaggerated conceptions of voter rationality, and misplaced use of both the marketplace and deterrence analogies. Moreover, as some have argued, from an empirical point of view, disclosure-only regimes fail to demonstrate any superiority in terms of discouraging the proliferation of money, deterring large contributions or contributors because of fear of voter backlash, addressing third-party money, or discouraging subterfuge. If in fact the goal of donate but discourage is to address the goals of preventing corruption or its appearance or producing elections less dependent upon money, then these types of regimes fail miserably to live up to their promise.[168]

Yet the deregulate yet disclose position once held by many is either no longer their position or their original argument was merely a Trojan Horse to contend against contribution limits until such time as they could then dismantle them and then go after disclosure. Bradley Smith now contends that many disclosure laws violate a right to privacy and hurt public discourse.[169] William McGeveran similarly worries about disclosure and privacy rights.[170] John Samples also opposes disclosure and too finds that it hurts deliberation.[171] Bopp sees in disclosure the handiwork of tyranny and tyrants.[172] Bopp even argues that disclosure chills speech and seems bent on offering evidence of this on the election law listserv and elsewhere, although he does seem to support disclosure for candidate contributions, for now.[173]

---

168 David Schultz, *Disclosure Is Not Enough: Empirical Lessons from State Experiences*, 4 ELECTION L. J. 349 (2005).

169 Bradley A. Smith, *In Defense of Political Anonymity*, CITY JOURNAL (Winter 2010), at 74, 75, 78.

170 William McGeveran, *Mrs. McIntyre's Persona: Bringing Privacy Theory to Election Law*, 19 WM. & MARY BILL RTS. J. 859 (2011).

171 John Samples, The DISCLOSE Act, Deliberation, and the First Amendment, CATO INST. (June 28, 2010), http:// www.cato.org/pubs/pas/pa664.pdf.

172 James Bopp, Jr. and Jared Haynie, *The Tyranny of "Reform and Transparency": A Plea to the Supreme Court to Revisit and Overturn Citizens United's "Disclaimer and Disclosure" Holding*, 16 NEXUS CHAP. J. L. & POL'Y 3 (2011).

173 However, there is evidence that disclosure does not discourage contributions. *See:* Jill Nicholson-Crotty, *Does Reported Policy Activity Reduce Contributions to Nonprofit Service Providers*, 39 POLICY STUDIES JOURNAL, 591 (2011).

> Because public disclosure of a person's political activity and/or political viewpoints can lead to harassment and that, as a result, lack of anonymity chills speech, the government needs a compelling justification to require disclosure. I agree that one of those instances where disclosure is justified is contributions to candidates.[174]

Cleta Mitchell goes so far as to argue that disclosure is incompatible with the First Amendment.[175] Even Clarence Thomas, in *Doe v. Reed* seems skeptical of disclosure laws because of concerns about harassment,[176] and privacy.[177] Hasen notes many other groups, often affiliated with Republican, conservative, pro-business, and anti-gay causes, oppose disclosure.[178] Jim Bopp states his stance well: "Blacks, gays and leftist[s] were harassed yesterday; conservatives and Christians are harassed today. And no one is safe from the thugs and bullies tomorrow."[179] Bopp, Samples, and the others who first argued against contribution limits and now disclosure do so frankly because such policy positions seemingly hurt the interests and parties they espouse.

Of course, in some cases privacy and anonymity may be in order. In the case of *NAACP v. Alabama*,[180] there was clear evidence of harassment and intimidation that included "economic reprisal, loss of employment, threat of physical coercion, and other manifestations of public hostility.[181] This case also took place at a time when the civil rights movement was growing and lynching, cross burnings, and other acts of intimidation were taking place across the South. There were also documented instances of persecution cited by the Court in *Brown v. Socialist Workers '74 Campaign Committee*.[182] The evidence in both cases was enough for the Court to reject attempts to force disclosure of membership and contributor lists. Yet as Hasen points out, there is scant evidence of donor intimidation or harassment, despite the best efforts by some to find it or trump on instances.[183] Even Kathleen Sullivan, a supporter of disclosure-only laws, concedes that disclosure of donors does little to impede their activity. Part of the problem is in defining harassment, intimidation, or chilling of speech. As Smith and his coauthors ask

---

174 Bopp and Haynie. *See also:* James Bopp, Jr., Election Law Listserv (January 19, 2013), https://mail.google.com/mail/u/1/?shva=1#inbox/13c4aaf04af1be52 (site last viewed on January 21, 2013).

175 Cleta Mitchell, *Donor Disclosure: Undermining the First Amendment*, 96 MINN. L. REV. 1755 (2012).

176 130 S.Ct. 2811, 2845 (2010).

177 *Id.* at 2839.

178 Richard L. Hasen, *Chill Out: a Qualified Defense of Campaign Finance Disclosure Laws in the Internet Age*, 27 J. L. & POL. 557 (2012).

179 *Id.* at 565.

180 357 U.S. 449 (1958).

181 *Id.* at 462.

182 459 U.S. 87 (1982).

183 Hasen 2012 at 559.

in their election law book, are instances of leaflets being torn, swearing, pushing over a table, and perhaps even some pushing and shoving demonstrators or others atypical and evidence of intimidation?[184] Is being mooned a form of intimidation or chilling?[185] It is not so clear that these are such instances of intimidation and chilling or that this type of behavior is not what should be expected in the world of politics. Politics is about passion and advocacy and to some extent people should expect that articulating positions will elicit responses. This, after all, is the purpose of advocating positions and communicating in general—getting a response.

Moreover, there may be legitimate cases where disclosure does compromise or hurt deliberations. Jury deliberations are private. But a general across-the-board argument for privacy or non-disclosure of donations seems overly broad and contrary to the general democratic values of transparency and public decision-making. Yes, in many cases tyrants seek disclosure, but the essence of oppression is secrecy and operating in the shadow. There may be cases where donations up to a certain dollar amount should be shielded from disclosure to protect people from job retaliation. But to argue that corporations, PACs, and large donors should be protected from disclosure and prevent them from being chilled in their speech is incorrect. Moreover, to assert that these entities are weak and powerless or discrete and insular and needing protection in the political marketplace is disingenuous at best. Furthermore, to argue for secrecy in government and politics goes against the very notion of what a democracy is—something of concern to the people—or a republic—a public thing. In both cases exposure or disclosure is necessary to promote accountability.[186] The argument for disclosure here is a structural democratic claim in favor of building up a wall that shields the polity from being influenced by money and economic market factors.

First, Anthony Johnstone makes the case for disclosure in terms of Madisonian democracy.[187] He places the argument for disclosure in terms of the Republican concern to address corruption, as manifest in James Madison's arguments in *Federalist* 10 regarding the need to combat and check factions.[188] This is a conception of corruption that transcends the simple notion of *quid pro quo* that dominates current justifications for contribution limits and disclosure.[189] The concern with factions is to root out groups who wish to oppose the public interest or the rights of others—it is an anti-democratic or anti-popular government motive. To a large extent the difference between a faction and any other group is

---

184 MICHAEL DIMINO, BRADLEY SMITH, AND MICHAEL SOLIMINE, VOTING RIGHTS AND ELECTION LAW, 667 (2010).

185 Doe v. Reed, 823 F.Supp. 2ND 1195 (W.D. Wash. 2011).

186 SISSELA BOK, LYING: MORAL CHOICE IN PUBLIC AND PRIVATE LIFE (1999); and SECRETS: ON THE ETHICS OF CONCEALMENT AND REVELATION (1989).

187 Anthony Johnstone, *A Madisonian Case for Disclosure*, 19 GEO. MASON L. REV. 413 (2012).

188 *Id.* at 415, 438, 442.

189 *Id.* at 438.

one of purpose and intent—there are licit and illicit intents. Disclosure furthers what Johnstone calls an anti-factional interest.[190] This is an interest in ascertaining information about factions so that we know their purposes. Exposing their purposes is critical to promoting a democratic government because it is part of controlling the effects of factions.

But disclosure does more. It may discourage illicit actions. Is there anything unconstitutional in seeking to deter factions or groups from engaging in activities that are impermissible? No. In general, the law seeks to deter individuals and groups from engaging in antisocial and illegal behavior. To say someone is chilled from committing a crime is nonsensical. Similarly, to say that one is chilled from expending large sums of money to buy or leverage political influence also is nonsensical and it seems to presuppose that it is perfectly legitimate to leverage economic resources to achieve this purpose.

This is the real nub of the issue. Smith, Samples, and Bopp all seem to think it is legitimate to convert economic resources over into political resources and therefore want to argue that money is speech, that limits on donations and expenditures are unconstitutional, and that efforts to regulate money in politics and to promote disclosure is chilling protected freedoms. As Deborah Stone would describe it, they believe that market transactions or marketplace logic is the default way decisions should be made in the United States.[191] In essence, their First Amendment enshrines capitalism. For the most part, the Supreme Court seems to be willing to accept this assumption that economic resources should convert over into political influence. This is the core problem that the Supreme Court has failed to address.

Democracy and Capitalism

The real question in the money and politics or money is speech controversy is over the legitimate or permissible relationship between democracy and capitalism. Historically many argue that there is an interconnection between the rise of capitalism, religion, and democracy.[192] All three emerged roughly at the same time in Europe during the sixteenth and seventeenth centuries. Scholars asserted that the concept of economic liberty and being free to act as the pejorative economic man in the marketplace reinforced and gave impetus to the individual liberty

---

190   *Id.* at 442.

191   DEBORAH STONE, POLICY PARADOX: THE ART OF POLITICAL DECISION MAKING (2001).

192   *See, e g.*, MAX WEBER, THE PROTESTANT ETHIC AND THE SPIRIT OF CAPITALISM (2010); ROGER H. TAWNEY, RELIGION AND THE RISE OF CAPITALISM (2013); Göran Therborn, *The Rule of Capital and the Rise of Democracy*, 103 NEW LEFT REV. 3 (May-June 1977); GEOFF ELEY, FORGING DEMOCRACY, THE HISTORY OF THE LEFT IN EUROPE, 1850-2000 (2002). *Contra:* HANS BLUMENBERG, THE LEGITIMACY OF THE MODERN AGE (1985), challenging the Weberian thesis.

and the right to make choices in the political marketplace. Limited government protected both economic and political liberty.

Milton Friedman, in his classic *Capitalism and Freedom*,[193] emphasized this connection, seeing not only historical connections between free markets and individual freedom, but that such an interrelationship between the two systems remains critical to the present. When the gates of communism came crashing down in the 1990s many argued that a prerequisite to building democracy in these former totalitarian states was first privatization of state enterprises and the establishment of market economies.[194] To a large extent, the evolution of Western capitalism and democracy have been inextricably connected. To many, it is no coincidence that the American Declaration of Independence and Adam Smith's *Wealth of Nations* were both penned in the same year. For Milton Friedman, F.A. Hayek,[195] and others, economic liberty and political liberty are reinforcing and mutually necessary in creating democracy. In other cases, the argument is that democracy requires a certain level of economic affluence and development, although strictly speaking this does not mean capitalism.[196]

But there is a contrary perspective that challenges the connection between markets, political freedom, and democracy. Capitalism and democracy or free markets and limited government are not always reinforcing but can be in tension

---

193 MILTON FRIEDMAN, CAPITALISM AND FREEDOM (2002).

194 *See generally:* DANIEL YERGIN AND DANIEL STANISLAW. THE COMMANDING HEIGHTS: THE BATTLE FOR THE WORLD ECONOMY (2002); MANFRED STEGER, GLOBALISM: THE NEW MARKET IDEOLOGY (2002); RAYMOND PLANT, THE NEO-LIBERAL STATE (2009); ANDERS ÅSLUND, HOW CAPITALISM WAS BUILT: THE TRANSFORMATION OF CENTRAL AND EASTERN EUROPE, RUSSIA, AND CENTRAL ASIA (2007); ANDERS ÅSLUND, HOW UKRAINE BECAME A MARKET ECONOMY AND DEMOCRACY (2009); David Schultz, *The Crisis of Public Administration Theory in a Postglobal World*, in DON MENZEL AND HARVEY WHITE, EDS., THE STATE OF PUBLIC ADMINISTRATION: ISSUES, CHALLENGES, OPPORTUNITIES, 453 (2011).

195 F.A. HAYEK, THE ROAD TO SERFDOM (2007).

196 *See generally:* GIOVANNI SARTORI, THE THEORY OF DEMOCRACY REVISITED, part II, 405-17 (1987); J. ROLAND PENNOCK, DEMOCRATIC POLITICAL THEORY, 218-36 (1979); ROBERT A DAHL, POLYARCHY: PARTICIPATION AND OPPOSITION (1971); ROBERT A. DAHL, WHO GOVERNS? DEMOCRACY AND POWER IN AN AMERICAN CITY (1971); ROBERT A. DAHL, DEMOCRACY AND ITS CRITICS (1989); Samuel P. Huntington, *Will More Countries become Democratic?* 99 AM. POL. SCI. REV. 193 (1984); Seymour M. Lipset, *Some Social Requisites of Democracy: Economic Development and Political Legitimacy*, 53 AM. POL. SCI. REV. 69 (1959); Martin C. Needler, *Political Development and Socioeconomic Development: The Case of Latin America*, 62 AM. POL. SCI. REV. 62: 889 (1968); W.W. ROSTOW, THE STAGES OF ECONOMIC GROWTH (1971); Dankwart A. Rustow, *Modernization and Comparative Politics: Prospects in Research and Theory*, 1 COMPARATIVE POLITICS 37 (1968); PIPPA NORRIS, MAKING DEMOCRATIC GOVERNANCE WORK: HOW REGIMES SHAPE PROSPERITY, WELFARE, AND PEACE, 65 (2012), for a review of the literature on the connection between levels of economic development and democracy.

if not in outright conflict.[197] Chile under General Pinochet was the epitome of free market capitalism and totalitarianism. Similarly China has perhaps one of the most successful capitalist systems in the world right now under the direction of an oppressive state with limited political freedom that gives lip service to communism. But in the United States, we supposedly have blended the right combination of capitalism and democracy.

Additionally, there are a host of democratic theorists who contend that capitalism and democracy are in conflict. Robert Dahl describes this opposition as one where the political process is not autonomous and instead is controlled or limited in its autonomy by economic enterprises, market choices, and private investment decisions.[198] C.B. MacPherson asserts that capitalism's extractive capabilities undermine the developmental capacities of some by transferring them from one to another. In effect, capitalism undermines the ethical capacities of individuals necessary to engage in democratic decision-making by taking away from some the economic means to act as an equal participant in the polity.[199] Carol Gould pushes this argument further by asserting that economic inequalities and hierarchies undermine social cooperation and the political balance between freedom and equality.[200] Charles Lindblom describes the market as a prison and corporate economic power as incompatible with democratic self-governance.[201] Others also see the failure to address corporate power in America as a threat to democracy.[202] The fundamental problem here is that market or economic logic has penetrated democratic theory and practice.[203] How so?

Culture is a totality, as the philosopher Georg Hegel once stated. There is the marketplace or the economy, the government, and then civil society. Daniel Bell, a famous sociologist, once wrote in the *Cultural Contradictions of Capitalism* that these three components make up a culture. Bell contended that the three also have their own logic and values. The hallmark of Modernity is their separation. The political theorist Michael Walzer argued that the emergence of contemporary free

---

197 SAMUEL BOWLES AND HERBERT GINTIS, DEMOCRACY AND CAPITALISM: PROPERTY, COMMUNITY, AND THE CONTRADICTIONS OF MODERN SOCIAL THOUGHT (1986); NORBERTO BOBBIO, DEMOCRACY AND DICTATORSHIP (1989); C.B. MACPHERSON, THE LIFE AND TIMES OF LIBERAL DEMOCRACY (2011); C.B. MACPHERSON, DEMOCRATIC THEORY: ESSAYS IN RETRIEVAL (1973); CHARLES LINDBLOM, POLITICS AND MARKETS: THE WORLD'S POLITICAL ECONOMIC SYSTEMS (1980).

198 Dahl, Democracy and Its Critics at 324-32.

199 MacPherson, Democratic Theory.

200 CAROL C. GOULD, RETHINKING DEMOCRACY: FREEDOM AND SOCIAL COOPERATION IN POLITICS, ECONOMY, AND SOCIETY (1988).

201 Charles E. Lindblom, *The Market as a Prison*, 44 JOURNAL OF POLITICS 324 (1982).

202 Jane Mansbridge, *On the Importance of Getting Things Done*, PS, 1 (January, 2012); Robert A. Dahl, *On Removing Certain Impediments to Democracy in the United States*, 92 POL. SCI. Q. 1 (1977); and Dahl, Democracy and Its Critics.

203 C.B. MACPHERSON, THE RISE AND FALL OF ECONOMIC JUSTICE AND OTHER ESSAYS, 101-20 (1987).

societies resided in how the unity of totalitarianism is broken up by the walls of pluralism. We maintain freedom in our society by walling off issues—we separate the public from the private and the secular from the parochial, for example—in order to promote freedom. We define limits to how far the government can go by creating constitutions and a bill of rights. We limit the abuses of the marketplace with government regulation, and the power of society to intrude upon privacy is maintained by marking distinctions between private morality and public neutrality and by declaring that the government should not promulgate personal ethics or religious values. Freedom in modern society is maintained by maintaining walls.

But the danger is when boundaries are crossed, such as when the market intrudes upon how we value human life, when government invades personal rights, or when private morality dictates how others should live. A society without walls of separation runs the danger of turning oppressive. Think about how governments and markets interact in at least four ways. First, they represent the two dominant ways to distribute goods and services.[204] Except in the case of face-to-face barter economies, free market and government distribution of goods and services provide rival ways to coordinate their production and distribution. They do that either by decentralizing and privatizing these decisions (in the case of market mechanisms) or centralizing them (as with planned economies). Often these decisions are not dichotomized; in most societies there is a continuum or hybrid of market-government and decentralized-centralized mechanisms that operate.

Second, public power is necessary to create free markets. Polanyi argued that free markets are not architectonic. They did not just arise and develop on their own.[205] Their establishment, especially during the nineteenth century in Europe, was the product of significant uses of governmental authority and power in order to enforce the rules of free markets. Even Milton Friedman, a conservative free-market economist from the United States who was best noted for his arguments in favor of privatization and minimal governmental intervention into the economy, conceded that public authority is needed to enforce the basic rules of the marketplace.[206] Max Weber's writings on bureaucratic behavior are often read as lessons for organizational theory.[207] But it should be remembered that he discussed bureaucracy and authority within the context of capitalism and the role of the former in helping to sustain it. Modern bureaucracies and economic orders, specifically capitalism, are interconnected.

Third, governmental authority is required to address and regulate market failures, such as free rider problems, (negative) externalities, information asymmetries, and

---

204 Charles Lindblom, Politics and Markets: The World's Economic Systems (1980).
205 KARL POLANYI, THE GREAT TRANSFORMATION (2001).
206 Milton, Friedman, Capitalism and Freedom (1962).
207 Max Weber, *Bureaucracy*, in HAN GERTH AND C. WRIGHT MILLS, EDS., FROM MAX WEBER: ESSAYS IN SOCIOLOGY, 196 (1979).

monopolies.[208] For many economists, unregulated free markets produce problems that only government regulation can correct. These may be problems surrounding maintenance of demand,[209] distributional issues, or other pathologies that impede efficiency or the ability of markets to react to disequilibrium.[210]

Fourth, government intervention may be necessary to provide public infrastructure investment or insure profitability of private businesses.[211] While Adam Smith's *The Wealth of Nations* is best remembered as the first statement defending free markets and capitalism, the book also offers an important defense for government investment in basic infrastructure (roads and canals in Smith's day and perhaps schools and telecommunications today) in order to sustain and support private investment.[212] Moreover, James O'Connor has argued that modern capitalist states serve two basic functions—to promote legitimization or support for the regime and to undertake activities that make it possible for private businesses to maintain profitability or maintain capital accumulation.[213]

The general point here is that markets may be great mechanisms to allocate sail boats and luxury items, but not political influence and democratic values. Allocation of political power and influence should be distributed according to non-market criteria. As Daniel Bell pointed out, market logic and concepts were increasingly (even during the time he wrote) coming to encroach or infringe upon other parts of American culture including, for our purposes here, the polity or political process. Others such as Michael Sandel have argued that the danger now is that the United States is turning from a market economy to a market society where increasingly all types of social intercourse are being reduced to a cash nexus.[214] Robert Kuttner makes a similar point.[215] To a large extent American political power is being subjected to a marketization of its operations.

The issue here is not one of efficacy or money. By that, the primary issue is not whether money makes a difference in terms of who is elected or who has political influence.[216] One could debate forever whether money buys influence, but there

---

208 JOHN CASSIDY, HOW MARKETS FAIL: THE LOGIC OF ECONOMIC CALAMITIES (2009).

209 JOHN MAYNARD KEYNES, THE GENERAL THEORY OF EMPLOYMENT, INTEREST AND MONEY (1964).

210 ARTHUR M. OKUN, EQUALITY AND EFFICIENCY: THE BIG TRADEOFF (1975).

211 JAMES O'CONNOR, THE FISCAL CRISIS OF THE STATE (1973).

212 ADAM SMITH, AN INQUIRY INTO THE NATURE AND CAUSES OF THE WEALTH OF NATIONS (1937).

213 O'Connor, pp. 3-5.

214 MICHAEL SANDEL, WHAT MONEY CAN'T BUY: THE MORAL LIMITS OF MARKETS (2012).

215 ROBERT KUTTNER, EVERYTHING FOR SALE: THE VIRTUES AND LIMITS OF MARKETS (1999).

216 The issue is not necessarily whether money corrupts but the legitimacy of the use of money and economic resources to allocate or determine political influence. Despite that argument, one can still contend that money does corrupt. *See, e.g.*, LAWRENCE LESSIG, REPUBLIC LOST: HOW MONEY CORRUPTS POLITICS—AND A PLAN TO STOP IT (2011).

is significant evidence that economic inequalities have political consequences.[217] Additionally, most of the debate about money in politics treats the latter as a variable and not a structural determinant. By that, if money is a variable then one should be able to look to causal connections between it and political influence or outcomes. This is the wrong way to look at it. Economic resources may be more a structural condition built into the very logic of how the American politics process operates. Specifically, political influence is associated with affluence and the American policy process seems skewed to favor class preferences, especially when one examines the relationship between class and political engagement.[218] Schattschneider contends that the mobilization of bias in the American political process has produced a political system favoring the more affluent.[219] Stated otherwise, when the policy preferences of the more affluent are different from the lower and middle classes, the former generally have their preferences reflected in policy outcomes.[220] The issue instead is one about justice and fairness. It is about whether money is the appropriate criterion to use to determine who has political influence or authority. It is about setting boundaries, as Michael Walzer would argue, demarcating distinctions between the market economy and the political system. While the field of political economy may be a legitimate academic discipline, the American political system is not a market democracy—the economic marketplace and the political forum or agora should be distinct. The allocative criterion for a political democracy is not the same as that for market capitalism. This is what the Bradley Smiths, John Samples, and James Bopps fail to appreciate.

Even though American democracy has grown along with capitalism, the two should not be conflated. For one, classical republican theory which tremendously influenced the American political founding and founders, is characterized by fear of corruption that comes from, in part, a concern about unequal distributions of property and wealth.[221] Classical republican theorists such as James Harrington drew a connection between political power and wealth or property, seeking in such divisions threats to a republican form of government.[222] James Madison too, in

---

217 LAWRENCE JACOBS AND DESMOND KING, THE UNSUSTAINABLE AMERICAN STATES (2009); DESMOND KING ET AL., DEMOCRATIZATION IN AMERICA: A COMPARATIVE-HISTORICAL ANALYSIS (2009); AMERICAN POLITICAL SCIENCE ASSOCIATION, AMERICAN DEMOCRACY IN AN AGE OF RISING INEQUALITY (2004).

218 WARREN E. MILLER AND J. MERRILL SHANKS, THE NEW AMERICAN VOTER (1996); MICHAEL S. LEWIS-BECK, ET AL., THE AMERICAN VOTER REVISITED (2008), LARRY M. BARTELS, UNEQUAL DEMOCRACY: THE POLITICAL ECONOMY OF THE NEW GILDED AGE (2008).

219 E.E. SCHATTSCHNEIDER, THE SEMI-SOVEREIGN PEOPLE, 20-47 (1960).

220 MARTIN GILENS, AFFLUENCE AND INFLUENCE: ECONOMIC INEQUALITY AND POLITICAL POWER IN AMERICA (2012).

221 J.G.A. POCOCK, THE MACHIAVELLIAN MOMENT: FLORENTINE POLITICAL THOUGHT AND THE ATLANTIC REPUBLICAN TRADITION (2003).

222 PHILLIP PETTIT, REPUBLICANISM: A THEORY OF FREEDOM AND GOVERNMENT (1999); J.G.A. POCOCK, VIRTUE, COMMERCE, AND HISTORY: ESSAYS ON POLITICAL THOUGHT AND HISTORY, CHIEFLY IN THE EIGHTEENTH CENTURY (1985).

Federalist 10 stated the "most common and durable source of factions has been the various and unequal distribution of property."[223] Harrington, republican theorists in general, and James Madison would have endorsed the idea that somehow a wall must be fashioned that prevents the effects of wealth (as a faction) from adversely affecting the political process. Thus, for those originalists looking to a theory of democracy to support a jurisprudence that sustains limits on the use of money for political purposes, there is good evidence that a founding set of American values would sustain that attempt.[224]

Additionally, one can occasionally point to some dicta in Supreme Court decisions suggesting a broader understanding regarding a democratic theory of election law that would wall off impermissible uses of money in the political process. For example, Justice White, dissenting in *First National Bank of Boston v. Bellotti*, declared that it was reasonable to be concerned about the use of concentrated wealth in politics:

> States have provided corporations with such attributes in order to increase their economic viability and thus strengthen the economy generally. It has long been recognized however, that the special status of corporations has placed them in a position to control vast amounts of economic power which may, if not regulated, dominate not only the economy but also the very heart of our democracy, the electoral process. Although *Buckley v. Valeo*, 424 U.S. 1, 96 S.Ct. 612, 46 L.Ed.2d 659 (1976), provides support for the position that the desire to equalize the financial resources available to candidates does not justify the limitation upon the expression of support which a restriction upon individual contributions entails, the interest of Massachusetts and the many other States which have restricted corporate political activity is quite different ... It is not one of equalizing the resources of opposing candidates or opposing positions, but rather of preventing institutions which have been permitted to amass wealth as a result of special advantages extended by the State for certain economic purposes from using that wealth to acquire an unfair advantage in the political process, especially where, as here, the issue involved has no material connection with the business of the corporation.[225]

In addition to Justice White acknowledging as legitimate the need to draw boundaries between the economic and political spheres, Justice Rehnquist in the same case hits a similar theme in stating "It might reasonably be concluded that

---

223   ALEXANDER HAMILTON, JAMES MADISON, AND JOHN JAY, THE FEDERALIST, 56 (1937).
224   Conversely, for advocates of pluralist democracy, they seemed largely inatentative to the role that unequal resources played in terms of group strength, mobilization, and political bias. This is largely the critique of the pluralist project. *See, e.g.*, Schattschneider, The Semi-Sovereign People, 20-47; THEODORE J. LOWI, THE END OF LIBERALISM (1969); GRANT MCCONNELL, PRIVATE POWER AND AMERICAN DEMOCRACY (1966).
225   435 U.S. 765, 809 (1978).

those properties, so beneficial in the economic sphere, pose special dangers in the political sphere."[226] Finally, the majority opinion in *Federal Election Commission v. National Right to Work Committee* perhaps articulated it the best when it quoted the government defending a federal campaign finance law that its purpose was "to ensure that substantial aggregations of wealth amassed by the special advantages which go with the corporate form of organization should not be converted into political 'war chests' which could be used to incur political debts from legislators who are aided by the contributions."[227]

What these comments from the Supreme Court suggest is a recognition that money used for political purposes needs to be limited. Politics in general, and campaigns and elections in particular, may be expensive, but, as noted earlier, that is a different assertion from the one being made here. Money may be necessary to run campaigns and elections, but their costs or funding sources should not undermine democratic values. The problem of *Buckley v. Valeo* according to Dahl is that the Justices failed to understand how a democratic system derives its legitimacy from political equality.[228] Allowing the allocative criteria of the economy to substitute for equality in the political arena gives money and wealth a role that it just should not have in American democracy.

The American Constitution, as Justice Holmes is repeatedly quoted from *Lochner v. New York*, does not embody a specific economic theory. The same can be said about American democracy. The democratic theory at the foundation of American election law and which should guide the jurisprudence in this area should treat seriously the notion that a wall of separation needs to be erected between the economy and the polity that is no less high than the one between church and state. Neutrality, at least in the political realm, demands distinct values and criteria separating it from the economy. This then implies that the use of money to affect political decisions is an illicit or illegitimate purpose that ought to be chilled, and seeking to prevent that conversion from occurring is a compelling governmental interest that should be enough to substantiate the conclusion that money is not speech.

---

226 *Id.* at 826.
227 459 U.S. 197, 207 (1982).
228 ROBERT A. DAHL, HOW DEMOCRATIC IS THE CONSTITUTION?, 152 (2003).

Conclusion
Toward a Democratic Theory of Election Law

Election law in the United States faces a multifaceted crisis that challenges the political legitimacy of the American electoral and political process.

On one level the crisis is partisan. There is a significant and serious disagreement between Republicans and Democrats (and with minor parties too) or conservatives and liberals regarding a host of election law types of issues. Debates over voter fraud and identification, campaign financing and *Citizens United*, ballot access, and disclosure among perhaps numerous other issues are viewed differently depending on one's partisan or political affiliation.

On a second level the crisis is about performance. One of the lessons learned from the Florida 2000 controversy is how poorly-run American elections can be. There are problems with registering voters, setting up polling places, counting ballots, and administering elections. These problems did not end with Florida 2000 but persist to this day with ongoing controversies and accusations regarding voter suppression, partisan gerrymandering, and assertions that money is buying elections. One can also look to the generally low voter turnout in elections (and a systemic pattern or bias in terms of who votes) as evidence that there is something wrong with election performance. Additionally, the partisan gridlock at the national level may also speak to something being wrong in terms of how elections are failing to produce outcomes that make it possible for federal government to do its work.

On a third level, though, the crisis is fundamentally doctrinal. No one can honestly make the claim that the Supreme Court has developed clear rules across the range of topics that come within the gambit of election law. Court doctrine continues to declare that partisan gerrymandering is justiciable but one is left with no definition of what it is and how to remedy it. Race is a factor that may be considered in drawing district lines, but only up to a point. Money disbursed for political purposes implicates First Amendment concerns, yet money is and is not speech. Expenditures are different from contributions but, for many Justices, there is no satisfactory basis for that distinction. Disclosure serves many important governmental interests, but fears of chilling speech for some mean that privacy rights trump. Voting is a fundamental right, but states may impose many limitations on franchise.

Principled decision-making has long been held to be the core of what the judiciary is supposed to do. There is an argument that engaging in ad hoc jurisprudence is something that the courts should avoid. Law should aspire to generality, to crafting rules that have broader applicability and appeal to a richer sense of theory.[1] Yet some, such as Cass Sunstein, plea for judicial minimalism and that is what we seem to have in the field of election law. Decisions in election law seem less principled, more case specific, and simply jumbled. Perhaps the best example of this minimalism is *Bush v. Gore*, where the Court sought to confine the precedential value of its opinion by declaring: "Our consideration is limited to the present circumstances."[2] If ever a statement revealed ad hocism and a failure to ground a decision in a broader theory about democracy, it was surely this one.

But why a lack of theory? The root of the problem could be shifting Supreme Court personnel, contrasting ideologies, or even something as simple as bad jurisprudence. But the core contention of this book has been that election law has turned into a narrow field captured mainly if not solely by lawyers and law professors who have divorced the topic from a broader linkage to democratic theory. The field of election law has become formalistic and it is rudderless because of a lack of theory, specifically a lack of a democratic theory to provide the principles and generality that the decisions and debates about voting, elections, and representation among other topics require.

Theory can exist on many levels or orders.[3] Some of those orders ask about the specific roles of actors within a political process, or seek to justify particular policies. These are lesser-order concepts of theory. Theory can also be second order, inquiring into questions about what governments should do. But the type of theory absent from election law is first order, asking more fundamental questions about the nature of political order and what it means to be an American democratic system. It is a theory that asks what it means to be a democracy, at least in the American context. It asks about what the fundamental values of an American democracy are and then seeks to match specific institutions and their performance to achieve and maximize these values. A democratic theory provides the framework that guides constitutional interpretation of election law issues. The democratic theory offers what Owen Fiss once called the mediating principles that guide interpretation of the Constitution.[4]

The point that is being made here can be seen by way of a reference to mixing bowls.[5] Think about how mixing bowls are purchased—usually four to a

---

1   *See, e.g.*, Frederick Schauer, Thinking Like a Lawyer, 24-29 (2009), for a general discussion of the role of generality in the law.

2   531 U.S. 98, 109 (2000).

3   David Schultz, *The Crisis of Public Administration Theory in a Post-global World*, in Don Menzel and Harvey White, eds., The State of Public Administration: Issues, Challenges, Opportunities, 453 (2011).

4   Owen M. Fiss, *Groups and the Equal Protection Clause*, 5 Phil. & Pub. Aff. 107 (1976).

5   I use the example of mixing bowls when teaching non-profit law to dramatize the relationship among a non-profit's mission, vision, values, and goals. All of these should line up together much like the way mixing bowls set inside one another line up.

package with them stacked, from the smallest to the largest, one inside of another. Conceptualize democratic theory and election law the same way. American democratic theory is the largest bowl. Sitting inside it is the Constitution and inside that is election law. There should be an alignment that begins with democratic theory that structures or guides interpretation of the Constitution, which then provides meaning to election law, with the last element here dictating specific institutions and practices necessary to fulfill or sustain democratic values.

Election law jurisprudence fails to offer or be guided by a broader vision regarding how to think about the relationship between it, democracy, and the Constitution. While in some cases, as this book has demonstrated, the Supreme Court engages in some rudimentary discussion of democracy, such as references to the *Federalist Papers*, John Stuart Mill, or perhaps even some acknowledgment here and there to political science or political theory literature, there is no systemic vision being offered that explains its decisions. The failure to rise to a level of generality or principle means that many of the major debates in election law are left unresolved, or if resolved, it is not really clear that the decision provides a clear rationale regarding who is the party and when, why some actors have more rights than others, or what really qualifies as a burden on associational rights. Were the Court to develop a more coherent and principled theory of election law tied to democratic theory, arguably many of the problems and controversies that exist could be resolved.

But perhaps this is not the job of the Court. Supreme Court Justices are not political theorists and they should not be expected to wax on the fundamentals of democratic theory. The same is true of most lawyers and law professors who dominate the field of election law. They are practitioners, advocates, or individuals trained in the law and not in thinking about democracy. Yet they all seem to be the ones defining what the field of election law is and driving the jurisprudence and "theory." The result is a narrow conception of theory, captured by a narrow often partisan field of interests. The field of election law needs reinvention and a broadening now that it is maturing. It needs to form a theoretical basis or be guided by theory. This book has begun the steps toward establishing a foundational democratic theory for election law. It did that in several ways. First, it enunciated more general articulations of democratic theory, seeking to uncover some of the more common themes and values. Second, it did that by describing American conceptions of democratic theory, with one indebted to the constitutional Framers and referred to as Madisonian democracy, the other to the pluralist rethinking of American democracy at the midpoint of the twentieth century.

While sharing many commonalities, the two conceptions of democracy differ over critical issues such as the role of groups and the nature of the public interest. But in the process of describing them, common values did emerge regarding issues about elections, voting, representation, accountability, and other points. The description of these two theories of democracy then set the context for several chapters that tried both to clarify how appeal (or lack thereof) to a broader theory explains the jurisprudence and controversies within its decisions. The discussions in those various chapters were also meant to further clarify and develop important values and themes about what democratic theory is supposed to represent in the United States. But in the course of discussing these subjects, this book also pointed out that both Madisonian and pluralist theories of democracy may be deficient in terms of how they address issues such as voting, representation, the rights of entities, and the role of money in politics. Both theories seem wedded to notions of democracy that may well be antiquated and ill-suited for the twenty-first century. Thus, not only is election law a rootless or theoretically-thin field, but when it does appeal to theory it does so to conceptions that may be out of date.

The sources of American democratic theory are many and can be located in case law, explicit theory, history, practice, and the ideals of the country as found in the preamble to the Constitution. But a democratic theory must also take notice of changing technologies that have transformed the nature of the agora and how people interact. It must also understand historical changes in the nature of the connection between politics and economics, and it must be a theory that thinks to the future and does not just reside in the past. To paraphrase Robert Dahl, democracy and election law are awaiting or are poised for another great transformation.

Will consideration of all of these factors add up to a coherent democratic theory? Probably not. Kenneth Dolbeare, an American political scientist, edited a widely used collection of writings on American political thought.[6] In his introduction to the book he asserted that there was probably no overarching American political theory—at best it is an ideology. Similarly, Richard Hofstadter's chapter on the Founding Fathers in his *American Political Tradition* asserted that these individuals, often seen as wise sages, were really more pragmatic and realistic politicians than normally assumed.[7] Alexis de Tocqueville additionally notes in his *Democracy in America* that Americans are less interested in theory and more in being practical.[8] The point is that there is perhaps no definitive, coherent theory of American democracy in the same way that there is no definitive version of what democracy is. Democracy is an open concept, with fuzzy or blurred boundaries. Its exact meaning, as Ludwig Wittgenstein might assert (the Wittgenstein of *Philosophical Investigations*) is found in its use.

All of this is not to say that democracy has no meaning. This book is an argument or an appeal to theory. It is not the final word on what democracy should be or mean in the American context, it is part prolegomena, part theory in itself. It tried to make some arguments for what democracy should represent in the American context, and it also tried simply to identify some controversies in election law and suggest how appeals to specific values might make resolution

---

6   Kenneth M. Dolbeare, ed., American Political Thought (1998).

7   Richard Hofstadter, The American Political Tradition and the Men who Made It, 3 (1989).

8   Alexis de Tocqueville, Democracy in America, ed. J.P. Mayer, trans. George Lawrence, 459-64 (1969).

of the debates possible. In doing that, a premium was placed on openness and transparency, accountability, competitiveness and stability, and perhaps most importantly, drawing a wall of separation between the decision-making process of the economic market and the values that ought to structure how a democracy should decide. To assert this is not to argue that the political system is divorced from the economy or from a sociology, but instead to contend that the values that determine how economic transactions are made are different from those which should affect the political process.

Not everyone will agree with the arguments made in this book. It challenges much of the current debate in election law. Many of the leading election law scholars really seem to embrace the idea that individuals and entities should be able to convert whatever economic resources they have into political influence, even in a clandestine fashion. Their free market democracy might even enjoy favor under the current Supreme Court. Additionally, some simply argue for specific ideological positions. In one case they perhaps have an economic theory of democracy, in the other they may have no theory at all and are simply arguing partisan or ideological positions that benefit the particular interests they are supporting. All that is fine, but none of this is a democratic theory or a reasonable basis for providing coherence to the field of election law and the functioning of American politics.

This book does not conclude with an assertion that Supreme Court Justices should be either democratic theorists or philosopher kings. Nor is it an argument that political theorists should be Supreme Court Justices. Instead it is simply to say that the field of election law has matured sufficiently in the last 20 or 25 years since it was defined as a field of inquiry and practice such that it now needs to forge a more theoretical basis grounded in a set of democratic values that give real meaning to what Constitution is supposed to be sustaining. To paraphrase Chief Justice Marshall, we must never forget that it is an American democracy we are expounding. Election law as a field of inquiry and means of putting democracy into practice must be more reflective in forging decisions and outcomes that create laws that link institutions and practices to the furtherance of democratic values.

Index

absentee voting 96-7, 99-100
accountability under direct democracy 131-6
Ackerman, Bruce 247
adjudication on election law as theoretically rudderless 13-14
administration/politics dichotomy, and neutrality 169-77
advocacy, express/issue 236
American Political Tradition, The (Hofstadter) 121, 272
American Revolution and disputed political terms 59-61, 139
Anderson, David 116
apportionment of legislative seats 19-20
  see also reapportionment
Aristotle 47, 60
Arrow, Kenneth 139
Articles of Confederation 62
associational rights of political parties 28-30
associations 75-80
Ayres, Ian 247

Bailyn, Bernard 59
ballot access for third parties 223-7
Bell, Daniel 263, 265
Bell, Derrick 126-7
bicameralism 69
Bickel, Alexander 15
Bill of Rights 72-3
Bipartisan Campaign Reform Act 2002 (McCain-Feingold Act) 4, 8, 242
Bodin, Jean 60
Bopp, James 253, 258-9
Bork, Robert 16
Brennan Center 104-5, 116
Briffault, Richard 161
Bryce, James 15

Building Confidence in US Elections: Report of the Commission on Federal Election Reform (Carter-Baker Commission) 104-5
burden of proof 190
Burke, Edmund 139

Cain, Bruce 42, 252-3, 256
capitalism and democracy 229, 261-8
  see also money and politics
Capitalism and Freedom (Friedman) 262
Carter-Baker Commission 104-5
caucus system 98-9
Charles, Guy-Uriel 41, 165
checks and balances 69
citizenship
  and right to speak and vote 54-6
  and voting rights 88-9
civic engagement
  and democracy 51
  educative benefits from 51, 137-8
civil rights eras 189, 190
civil service, reform of 170-77
collective action and democracy 51
Committee for the Reelection of the President (CREEP) 21
competition
  between interest groups 79
  in elections, importance of 150-51
Considerations on Representative Government (Mill) 53
Constitution of 1787
  as check on majority tyranny 70
  as exclusionary 189
  Federalist/Anti-Federalist camps on 72
  First Amendment and partisan gerrymandering 157-62
  liberty at the core of 122
  political cultures influencing 61-2

voting rights 88-90
  and voting rights 85-8
constitutionalism as disputed term during
    American Revolution 60-61
contributions
  defined 23n61
  and democratic functions 26
  disclosure-only regime
    arguments against 254-61
    arguments for 247-53
  disclosure under FECA 26-7
  limits on 231-43
  as protected speech 25
  regulation of 21-7
control of the agenda and democracy 51-2,
    53
corporations
  eligibility to vote 54-6
  impact on national elections 4
  independent campaign expenditures 237
  McCain-Feingold Act 2002 8
  political parties, comparison with 204
corruption
  governmental interest in preventing 26
  see also money and politics
county unit system 147
Cox, Archibald 46-7
critical elections 222-3
Cronin, Thomas 127, 129
Cultural Contradictions of Capitalism
    (Bell) 263

Dahl, Robert 47-56, 57-8, 70, 96, 200, 263
Davidson, Chandler 190
democracy
  apportionment of legislative seats
    19-20
  and capitalism 229, 261-8
  and contributions and expenditure 26
  defining 47-58
  democratic political culture as needed
    for 56
  direct 53
  institutions, need for in 57-8
  link with values and institutions 58
  Madisonian 59, 62-73, 80-81, 122-3,
    260-61
  neutrality, lack of in rules of 120-21

pluralism 59, 73-80
political parties, importance of to 198-9
and the Supreme Court
  money and politics 21-7
  partisan gerrymandering 30-38
  political parties, rights of 28-30
  voting rights 17-21
see also representation
Democracy and Distrust (Ely) 8, 46
Democracy in America (Tocqueville) 13,
    51, 78, 272
democratic revisionism 79
democratic theory
  in action, election law as 45
  American 59-62, 80-82
    no definitive American 272
  and changing technologies 272
  and contributions and expenditure 26
  control of the agenda 51-2, 53
  diversity of opinion and thought 51, 56
  effective participation 49-50
  election law as rules of 46-7
  enlightened understanding 50-51
  and equality 48-9
  and federalism 56
  inclusion 54-6
  individual moral autonomy 48-9
  lack of in election law 269-71
  lack of in Supreme Court decisions 7-9
  and majority rule 52
  not the Court's job 271
  representative government 52-3
  rule of law, adherence to 56
  in scholarship on election law 37-43
  tradeoffs, need for 57
  values for 47-56
Dewey, John 137
Dimino, Michael 40-41
direct democracy
  accountability and disclosure 131-6
  appeal of 137
  control of the agenda 53
  courts lack of deference to 131
  educative benefit of participation 137-8
  hostility towards minority rights 127-8,
    138
  initiative and referendum 125
  legislative deliberation compared to 130

losses of minority rights in 126-7
media exposure, importance of 129-30
money, influence on outcomes of initiatives 129
practical problems with 138
Progressive politics 125
special interests, little impact on 130-31
unlimited money for initiatives 128-9
Direct Democracy (Cronin) 127, 129
Dirty Little Secrets: The Persistence of Corruption in American Politics (Sabato and Simpson) 249-60
disclosure
  defining, problems in 256
  as deterrence 255
  direct democracy 131-6
  disclosure-only regime
    arguments against 254-61
    arguments for 247-53
  informed citizens, assumption of 256-7
  stock market and investors analogy 257-8
  under FECA 26-7
discourse, political, and disputed terms during American Revolution 59-61
disenfranchisement
  felons 101
  fraud, voter, paucity of evidence for 102-7
  in history 100
district lines
  drawing of as controversial 141
  see also redistricting
diversity of opinion and thought 51, 56
Dolbeare, Kenneth 272
Downs, Anthony 79
Dworkin, Ronald 168-9

early voting 97
Easton, David 6
economic power
  and democracy 229
  see also money and politics
education and effective participation 51, 137-8
effective participation
  and democracy 49-50
  and education 51, 137-8

Election Crimes: An Initial Review and Recommendations for Future Study (EAC) 105
election law
  allocation of power and values by 6
  and American democratic theory 81-2
  crisis in, levels of 269
  decisions as controversial 5-7
  as democracy in action 45
  impact on election results 3-4
  importance of as subject 7
  increased news coverage of 4-6
  lack of democratic theory 7-9, 269-71
  as linking values and theory to institutions 58
  as rules of democracy 46-7
  as the rules of the game 45-6
  as young field of study 1
Election Law: Cases and Materials (Lowenstein, Hasen and Tokaji) 38-40
Election Law in the American Political System (Gardner and Charles) 41
Election Law Journal (ELJ) 41-2
elections
  analogy with stock market 257-8
  competition in, importance of 150-51
  critical 222-3
  Florida 2000 1-3
Elections Assistance Commission (EAC) 105
eligibility to vote 54-6
elite theory of politics 79
Ely, John Hart 8, 46
enlightened understanding and democracy 50-51
equality
  and democracy 48-9
  depth of 49
  and individual moral autonomy 48-9
expenditure
  defined 23n61
  and democratic functions 26
  disclosure-only regime
    arguments against 254-61
    arguments for 247-53
  disclosure under FECA 26-7
  limits on 231-43

as protected speech 25
regulation of 21-7
express advocacy 236

factions and public opinion 64-73
Federal Corrupt Practices Act 1925 231
Federal Election Campaign Act 1974 21-4, 26-7, 231, 236
federalism
    as check on political power 69-70
    and democracy 56
Federalist Papers 63-4
    9 64
    10 15, 39, 64, 66-7, 69
    47 50, 64
    49 50, 64
    51 39, 64, 65, 69
    78 14
    84 72
    interest groups 77-8
    problem of politics 62-70
felon disenfranchisement 101
finance *see* money and politics
First Amendment
    harm in partisan gerrymandering 177-82
    and partisan gerrymandering 157-62
    political neutrality, commitment to 173-6
Florida 2000 1-3
franchise rights *see* voting rights
fraud
    by election officials 102
    voter
        as about election law 4-5
        activities included 102
        analogy with speeding/littering 114-15
        empirical proof of, issues with 108-14
        paucity of evidence for 102-7
        photo identification 5, 93, 113-17
free market and democracy 229, 261-8
    see also money and politics
free speech and money in politics 21, 25-6
freedom of association 28-30, 212
Friedman, Milton 262, 264
Frohling, Richard G. 106

Fund, John 102-3, 108, 112
fundraising, regulation of 21-7
    see also money and politics

Gamble, Barbara 127
Gardner, James 41, 142
Garrett, Elizabeth 256
gay rights, initiatives concerning 128
geography
    rejection of in reapportionment 149
    sorting of population by party preference 150-51
Gerber, Elisabeth 129
gerrymandering
    failure to reflect population changes 142-4, 145-6
    one person, one vote standard, establishment of 147-50
    origin of term 141, 142
    partisan
        allowance of, occasions for 181-2
        entrenchment of incumbents as motive 151-2
        and the First Amendment 157-62
        harm in 177-82
        lack of standard to judge by 156, 160
        lack of theorizing on 30-38
        law/language parallel 167-8
        Liberalism and neutrality 162-9
        as non-justiciable 158
        rights/structure argument 165-9
        as structural problem 160-61
        Supreme Court decisions 152-6
    racial 143, 182-8
    responses to prevent 142
    Supreme Court responses to 143-51
Goodnow, Frank J. 172-3
Gould, Carol 263
governance, comparison with government 95-6
government
    blurring of public/private lines 94-6
    central problem of 15
    governance, comparison with 95-6
    and interest groups 78
    see also representative government and democracy

Governmental Process, The (Truman) 77-8
Grofman, Bernard 190

Habermas, Jürgen 163
Haider-Markel, Donald P. 128
Hamilton, Alexander 14
hard and soft money 236, 242
Harrington, James 266
Hasen, Richard 38-40, 42, 159, 160, 169, 259
Hatch Act 174-5
Hegel, G.W.F. 168
Hershey, Marjorie 116-17
Hofstadter, Richard 63, 121, 272

identification of voters 5, 93, 113-17
Ideological Origins of the American Revolution, The (Bailyn) 59
Impact of the National Voter Registration Act, The (EAC) 107
inclusion
    and democracy 54-6
    and voting rights 83-4
individual moral autonomy and democracy 48-9
informed choice and democracy 50-51
initiative and referendum
    accountability and disclosure 131-6
    courts lack of deference to 131
    in direct democracy 125
    hostility towards minority rights 127-8
    influence of money on outcomes 129
    legislative deliberation compared to 130
    media exposure, importance of 129-30
    minority rights, losses in 126-7
    special interests, little impact on 130-31
    unlimited money for 128-9
institutions
    democracy, need for in 57-8
    eligibility to vote 54-6
    link with values and democracy 58
interest groups, role of 75-80
internet voting 97
Issacharoff, Samuel 40, 159-60
issue advocacy 236

Jenkins, Iredell 169
Jim Crow era 189-90
Johnstone, Anthony 260-61
judicial review
    problem of 14-17
    Supreme Court 16-17
justice, rules of, lack of neutrality in 119-20

Kamuf, Joann 161
Kant, Immanuel 48, 163, 168
Karlan, Pamela 40, 159-60
Keyssar, Alexander 100
Kuttner, Robert 265

language
    disputed terms during American Revolution 59-61
    and law parallel 167-8
Laswell, Harold 6
law
    connection with politics 13
    language parallel 167-8
    see also election law
Law of Democracy, The (Issacharoff, Karlan and Pildes) 40
Liberalism
    harm in partisan gerrymandering 177
    neutrality and partisan gerrymandering 162-9
liberty
    at the core of the Constitution 122
    economic and political 262
    and majority rule/minority rights 122-3
Lindblom, Charles 263
Lipset, Seymour Martin 75-7
Lochner, Todd 252-3, 256
Locke, John 48, 52, 60, 66, 163
Lowenstein, Daniel 1, 38-40

McCain-Feingold Act 2002 4, 8, 242
McGeveran, William 258
MacPherson, C.B. 263
Madison, James 15, 50, 64-5, 66-7, 266-7
Madisonian democracy 59, 80-81, 122-3, 260-61
    and the problem of politics 62-73
Magleby, David B. 127

majority rule
  balance with minority rights 15-16
  and democracy 52
  and liberty 122-3
  and minority rights 52, 62-73, 122-3
malapportionment *see* gerrymandering
Meier, Kenneth J. 128
Mill, John Stuart 50, 51, 53, 214
Minnite, Lori 102, 106, 108, 111, 113
minority factions 71
minority-majority seats 185-8
minority rights
  initiative and referendum, hostility towards 127-8, 138
  and majority rule 15-16, 52, 62-73, 122-3
  Progressive politics as threat to 126-36
Mitchell, Cleta 259
money and politics
  boundaries between, need for 264-8
  capitalism and democracy 229, 261-8
  confusion over rules 243-4
  contributions and expenditure, limits on 231-43
  corruption 230
  court decisions 4
  disclosure-only regime
    arguments against 254-61
    arguments for 247
  fear concerning 230
  hard and soft money 236, 242
  hostility toward regulation efforts 241-2
  influence of money on initiative outcomes 129
  McCain-Feingold Act 2002 4, 8
  political parties, expenditures of 205-9
  public opinion on corruption 244
  role private money plays, debate over 245-6
  speech, money as 229, 231-2, 241
  spoils system 230-31
  structural determinant, money as 266
  Supreme Court and democratic theory 21-7
  unlimited funds for initiatives 128-9
Motor Voter Law 106-7
multimember districts 192, 193-4
Munro, William 124-5

Nader effect 221
neutrality
  emergence of neutral competence ideology 173
  harm in partisan gerrymandering 177
  lack of in rules and procedures 119-21
  in Liberalism 162-3
  Liberalism and partisan gerrymandering 162-9
  and politics/administration dichotomy 169-77
Nixon, Richard 21-2
non-justiciable political questions 146-7

O'Connor, James 265
On Liberty (Mill) 51, 214
one person, one vote standard
  balanced against other criteria 150
  establishment of 147-50
online voting 97
organizations, eligibility of to vote 54-6

participation, effective
  and democracy 49-50
  educative benefit of 51, 137-8
partisan gerrymandering
  allowance of, occasions for 181-2
  entrenchment of incumbents as motive 151-2
  and the First Amendment 157-62
  harm in 177-82
  lack of standard to judge by 156, 160
  lack of theorizing on 30-38
  law/language parallel 167-8
  Liberalism and neutrality 162-9
  as non-justiciable 158
  rights/structure argument 165-9
  as structural problem 160-61
  Supreme Court decisions 152-6
patronage system, reform of 170-77
Pendleton Act 1883 170-71
photo identification of voters 5, 93, 113-17
Pildes, Richard 40, 160
place, concept of in districting 149
Plato 47
pluralism 59, 73-80
Polanyi, Karl 264

political cultures, influences on
  Constitution of 1787 61-2
political discourse, disputed terms during
  American Revolution 59-61
political gerrymandering *see* partisan
  gerrymandering
Political Liberalism (Rawls) 49, 163
Political Man: The Social Bases of Politics
  (Lipset) 75-7
political parties
  autonomy of 216-17
  ballot access for third parties 223-7
  competition between, importance of
    198-9
  corporation and unions, comparison
    with 204
  critical elections 222-3
  declining membership of 221
  defining who the party is 28, 219-21
  evolution and change in 221-3
  expenditures of 205-9
  functions of 200-202
  implementation of policies by 200-201
  importance to democracy 198-9
  internal/external affairs of 213-18
  lack of clarity on status of 199
  love/hate attitudes towards 197-9
  other groups, comparison with 202-4
  as private or public entities 209-13, 220
  rights of 28-30
  role of government in society, different
    views on 202
  stability promotion by channeling
    opposition 201-2
  uniqueness of 205-9
politics, connection with the law 13
politics/administration dichotomy, and
  neutrality 169-77
Politics of Voter Fraud, The (Minnite) 106
polyarchies *see* democracy
Popper, Karl 110
population changes, gerrymandering in
  failure to reflect 142-4, 145-6
power, political
  bicameralism 69
  checks and balances 69, 72
  federalism as check on 69-70
  separation of power 69

pre-clearance of changes in voting
  procedures 190-92
Preface to Democratic Theory, A (Dahl) 70
presumption 190
primaries 98
privacy for ballot sponsors in direct
  democracy 131-6
problem of politics and Madisonian
  democracy 62-73
processes and procedures, lack of
  neutrality in 119-21
Progressive politics
  accountability and disclosure 131-6
  courts lack of deference to 131
  direct democracy 125
  era of in American politics 81
  legislative deliberation compared to
    130
  media exposure, importance of 129-30
  minority rights, losses in initiatives
    126-7
  and minority rights, threat to 126-36
  money, influence on outcomes of
    initiatives 129
  origin of 123-4
  special interests, little impact on
    130-31
  unlimited money for initiatives 128-9
proportional representation 192, 193
public opinion and factions 64-73
punch card voting mechanisms 2
Putting an End to Voter Fraud (Senate
  Republican Policy Committee)
  103-4

Quiet Revolution in the South (Davidson
  and Grofman) 190

race
  gerrymandering based on 143, 144-5,
    182-8
  and representation 188-95
Rawls, John 49, 162, 163, 164-5
reapportionment 145-6
  1960s revolution in 188-9
  competitive elections, importance of
    150-51
  as controversial 141

geography, rejection of 149
one person, one vote standard
   balanced against other criteria 150
   establishment of 147-50
and race 182-95
Supreme Court responses to 143-51
timing of 149-50
see also gerrymandering
Reconstruction Congress 189
Redish, Martin 247
redistricting 145-6
   1960s revolution in 188-9
   competitive elections, importance of 150-51
   as controversial 141
   geography, rejection of 149
   one person, one vote standard
      balanced against other criteria 150
      establishment of 147-50
   and race 182-8, 188-95
   Supreme Court responses to 143-51
   timing of 149-50
   see also gerrymandering
referendum
   accountability and disclosure 131-6
   courts lack of deference to 131
   in direct democracy 125
   hostility towards minority rights 127-8
   influence of money on outcomes 129
   legislative deliberation compared to 130
   media exposure, importance of 129-30
   minority rights, losses in 126-7
   special interests, little impact on 130-31
   unlimited money for 128-9
representation 145-6
   1960s revolution in 188-9
   Americanization of term 139
   centrality of 140
   competitive elections, importance of 150-51
   as disputed term during American Revolution 59
   district lines, drawing of 141
      timing of 141
   effectiveness of 140, 150
   factions, control of by 67-8

   flaws of current system 194-5
   geographical sorting of population 150-51
   geography, rejection of 149
   meaning of 139-40
   multimember districts 192, 193-4
   one person, one vote standard
      balanced against other criteria 150
      establishment of 147-50
   proportional representation 192, 193
   and race 182-8, 188-95
   reapportionment 141
      as controversial 141
      geography, rejection of 149
      Supreme Court responses to 143-51
   see also gerrymandering
representative government and democracy 52-3
rights
   rights/structure argument 165-9
   voting, and the Supreme Court 17-21
   see also minority rights; voting rights
Roosevelt, Teddy 125
Rousseau, Jean-Jacques 48
rule of law, adherence to, and democracy 56
rules and processes, lack of neutrality in 119-21
rules of the game, election law as 45-6

Sabato, Larry 249-60, 254-5, 256, 258
Samples, John 253, 258
Sandel, Michael 265
Schattschneider, E.E. 198, 200, 266
scholarship on election law
   benefit of democratic theory grounding 17
   democratic theory in 37-43
   narrow focus on cases and doctrine 42-3
   as theoretically rudderless 13-14
Schultz, David A. 47, 108, 112, 113
Schumpeter, Joseph 53, 79
Second Treatise (Locke) 66
secret donation booth 247
self-interest 51, 66
separation of power 69

Shuck, Peter 158, 160
Simpson, Glenn 249-60, 254-5, 256, 258
Smith, Bradley 40-41, 109, 247-9, 258
soft and hard money 236, 242
Solimine, Daniel 40-41
sovereignty as disputed term during American Revolution 60
special interest groups 71
    initiative and referendum, little impact on 130-31
    role of 75-80
speech, money as 229, 231-2, 241
spoils system, reform of 170-77, 230-31
stability, democratic, maintenance of 73-5
stare decisis 239
Stealing Elections: How Voter Fraud Threatens Our Democracy (Fund) 102-3, 112
stock market and investors analogy 257-8
Sullivan, Kathleen 251-2, 255
Supreme Court
    ballot access for third parties 223-7
    civil service reform and neutral competence 173-7
    and democratic theory
        money and politics 21-7
        partisan gerrymandering 30-38
        political parties, rights of 28-30
        voting rights 17-21
    Florida 2000 2-3
    internal/external affairs of political parties 214-16
    judicial review 16-17
    lack of theory in decisions 7-9
    non-justiciable political questions 146-7
    racial gerrymandering decisions 183-8
    redistricting problems, responses to 143-51
    voting rights 89-91
symmetry standard 179-80

Taft-Hartley Act 1947 204, 230-31
Tarr, Alan 142
Theory of Justice, A (Rawls) 164-5
third parties, ballot access for 223-7
Thomas, Clarence 259
Thompson, Dennis 256
Tilman Act 1907 230
Tocqueville, Alexis de 13, 15, 51, 76-7, 78, 137, 272
Tokaji, Daniel 38-40
tradeoffs, need for in democracy 57
Truman, David 77-8

unions, political parties comparison with 204

values
    American 59-62
    for democracy 47-56
    and effectiveness of institutions 58
    link with institutions and democracy 58
    shaping the political system 121-2
Vargas, Sylvia 127
Vercellotti, Timothy 116
Von Spakovsky, Hans 108
voters, analogy with investors 257-8
voting rights
    absentee voting 96-7, 99-100
    administrative regulation 91-3
    alternative methods of voting 96-8
    beyond general elections 98
    blurring of public/private lines 94-6
    caucus system 98-9
    citizenship 54-6, 88-9
    complexity of defining the demos 83-4
    and the Constitution 85-8
    counter-tradition of suppression 101
    creation of 88-100
    denial of in history 100
    early voting 97
    election officials, fraud by 102
    eligibility to vote 54-6
    exclusionary impact of present system 99-100
    felon disenfranchisement 101
    fraud, voter
        activities included 102
        analogy with speeding/littering 114-15
        empirical proof of, issues with 108-14

paucity of evidence for 102-7
   photo ID 113-17
and inclusion 83-4
internet voting 97
low voter turnout 100
meaning of 55
and participation in voting 87-8
photo identification of voters 93, 113-17
primaries 98
procreation rights, parallel to 89, 90
redefinition of needed 85
states as decision-makers in 101
Supreme Court 89-91
and the Supreme Court 17-21
women 88-9

Voting Rights Act 190-93
Voting Rights and Election Law (Dimino, Smith and Solimine) 40-41

Walzer, Michael 263-4, 266
Washington, George 197-8
Watergate 21-2
Wattenburg, Martin 200
Weber, Max 264
Wechsler, Herbert 16
White, Horace 121
White primary cases 50, 98, 209-10
Wilson, Woodrow 125, 171-2
Wittgenstein, Ludwig 46
women, voting rights of 88-9
Wyckoff, Paul 112

Table of Cases

Anderson v. Celebrezze 226
Arkansas Educational Television Commission v. Forbes 226
Austin v. Michigan of Commerce 237

Baker v. Carr 31-2, 33, 145-6, 152-3
Boy Scouts v. Dale 213
Brown v. Allen 14
Buckley v. American Constitutional Law Foundation 133, 205
Buckley v. Valeo 21, 23, 25-7, 132-3, 231-6, 238-43, 247, 248, 251
Bullock v. Carter 223
Burdick v. Takushi 91, 93, 226
Burson v. Freeman 8-9, 57
Bush v. Gore 3, 6, 13, 17

California Democratic Party v. Jones 30, 98, 200, 216
Citizens United v. Federal Election Commission 4, 8, 55, 242, 244-5
City of Mobile, Alabama v. Bolden 184
Clingman v. Beaver 212, 217-18
Cohn v. California 135
Colegrove v. Green 13, 143-4, 145
Coleman v. Franken 96
Colorado Republican Federal Campaign Committee v. Federal Election Commission (Colorado Republican I) 205-7, 208-9, 251
Colorado Republican Federal Campaign Committee v. Federal Election Commission (Colorado Republican II) 207-9
Crawford v. Marion County Election Board 93, 108-9

Davis v. Bandemer 31-2, 33, 152-3
Davis v. Federal Election Commission 242
Doe v. Reed 133-4, 259

Easley v. Cromartie 181-2, 187-8
Elrod v. Burns 175-6
Eu v. San Francisco County Democratic Central Committee 29, 215-16
Ex Parte Curtis 173

Federal Election Commission v. National Right to Work Committee 268
Federal Election Commission v. Wisconsin Right to Life Committee 242
First National Bank of Boston v. Bellotti 27, 267
First National Bank v. Bellotti 128-9
Fisher v. University of Texas, Austin 191

Gomillion v. Lightfoot 144-5, 183
Gray v. Sanders 147

Harper v. Virginia State Board of Elections 18, 90

Indiana Democratic Party v. Rokita 116-17

League of United Latin American Citizens v. Perry (LULAC) 36-8, 150, 155-6, 157-8, 180
Lucas v. Forty-Fourth General Assembly of Colorado 148-9

McConnell v. FEC 242
McIntyre v. Ohio 248
Marbury v. Madison 14-15
Marsh v. State of Alabama 94-5
Miller v. Johnson 187
Minor v. Happersett 54, 88-9
Munro v. Socialist Workers Party 225

NAACP v. Alabama 132-3
New York State Board of Elections v. Lopez Torres 218

Nixon v. Shrink Missouri Government PAC 237-8

Oregon v. Mitchell 54

Randall v. Sorrell 238-41
Reitman v. Mulkey 128
Reynolds v. Sims 18, 19-20, 89, 147-8
Reynolds v. United States 213
Richardson v. Ramirez 101

Salyer Land Company v. Tulare Lake Basin Water Storage District 95-6
Shaw v. Hunt 187
Shaw v. Reno 185-6
Shelby County v. Holder 187, 189, 191
Skinner v. Oklahoma 18, 19, 89, 90
Smith v. Allwright 29, 50, 98, 99, 209-13, 219
Speechnow.org v. Federal Election Commission 4, 243
Storer v. Brown 225

Tashjian v. Republican Party of Connecticut 28-9, 98, 212, 214-15

Tennant v. Jefferson County 149
Timmons v. Twin Cities Area New Party 226

United Jewish Organizations of Williamsburg, Inc. v. Carey 183-4
United Public Workers v. Mitchell 174
United States Civil Service Commission v. National Association of Letter Carriers 174-5
United States v. Carolene Products 7-8
United States v. Classic 17-18, 19, 89, 210
United States v. O'Brien 24
United States v. Wurzbach 173-4

Vieth v. Jubelirer 32-6, 153-4, 157

Washington State Grange v. Washington State Republican Party 30, 218
Wesbury v. Sanders 147
West Virginia v. Barnette 73
Williams v. Rhodes 224-5

Yick Wo v. Hopkins 90

Made in the USA
Lexington, KY
18 January 2019